INTRODUCTION TO
STOCK EXCHANGE INVESTMENT

INTRODUCTION TO
STOCK EXCHANGE INVESTMENT

Janette Rutterford

MACMILLAN

First published 1983
Reprinted 1985 (with corrections)

Published by
Higher and Further Education Division
MACMILLAN PUBLISHERS LTD
Houndmills, Basingstoke, Hampshire RG21 2XS
and London
Companies and representatives
throughout the world

Printed in Hong Kong

ISBN 0–333–34229–1 (hard cover)
ISBN 0–333–34230–5 (paper cover)

To my father and mother, without whom
I would never have finished this book

Contents

Preface

Aim of the book

The desire to write this book arose from the lack of a good textbook
suitable for my third-year undergraduate course on Stock Exchange
investment. The books available fell into two main categories. The first
category consisted of US texts which described the US stock markets
and were thus of only indirect interest to UK-based students. The
second category was aimed at the UK market but the books were either
simple, factual texts which described rather than attempted to value
securities, or 'how to make a million' books which were strong on
recommendations but weak on theory.

This book therefore aims not only to provide an introduction to the
world of investment, describing how the Stock Exchange works, the
types of security quoted on it and the main types of investor, but also to
explain the *principles* underlying Stock Exchange investment. The book
concentrates on the two main characteristics of any security, risk and
return, and, using these characteristics, shows how securities such as
equities, gilts and options and overseas investments can be compared
and valued. The book also explains how to approach the design of an
investment portfolio and discusses alternative investment strategies,
both those advocated in theory and those used in practice in the stock
market.

Structure of the book

The book is divided into three main parts, with an introductory chapter
which explains the role of the Stock Exchange and how it works, and a
concluding chapter. Part I begins with Chapter 2, which shows how any

quoted security can be evaluated according to its risk and return and how risk and return can be measured. Chapters 3–6 show how these measures can be derived for the different types of security quoted on the Stock Exchange – fixed interest securities, shares and options on shares.

Part II concentrates not on how to value and compare individual securities but on how to *combine* securities into portfolios. Portfolio theory and the capital asset pricing model, described in Chapters 7 and 8, show how substantial diversification can lead to portfolios with better risk and return characteristics than portfolios consisting of only a few securities. Chapter 9 contrasts an investment strategy based on these models, where the emphasis is on diversification and on the expectation of a 'fair return' for the risk level of the portfolio, with the more common investment strategy where only a few securities are held in the expectation that these securities will produce 'abnormal' returns for the risk involved.

Part III is devoted to two somewhat peripheral subjects which are nevertheless of increasing importance to UK investors. The first subject, covered in Chapter 10, is that of international investment, which has traditionally been of greater importance to UK investors than, say, to their US counterparts, and which has become of even greater significance with the relaxation of exchange controls. The second subject, discussed in Chapter 11, is that of the investing institutions, which is again perhaps of greater significance in the UK stock market than in other major stock markets. The impact of the investing institutions on the UK Stock Exchange has been major, both as a result of their dominance as security-holders and their importance as traders in securities.

Chapter 12, the concluding chapter, considers the general objectives of the investor and the factors which should be taken into account when determining those objectives. The chapter also describes the alternative investment strategies available to the investor. By the time Chapter 12 has been reached, the reader should be clear as to which type of policy he or she prefers. The chapter finishes by describing performance measures which investors can use to evaluate their or other investors' investment performance.

Readership

The book thus attempts to put a theoretical framework, based on the quantifying of risk and return, on the subject of Stock Exchange investment. This should be of interest both to students of Stock Exchange investment and to individuals who come into contact with

Stock Exchange investment, such as bankers, accountants, analysts, actuaries and, of course, investors. Because the book is not confined to a student readership, the aim has been to keep the maths to a minimum, concentrating on explaining concepts by the use of examples rather than equations. Most of the calculations shown in this book can be carried out on a simple, hand-held calculator. The exceptions are valuing options and finding optimal portfolios; these require small computer programs which can be run on a micro-computer.

One point which I must make. Throughout the book I have referred to the investor as 'he'. I obviously expect a female as well as male readership, especially since the author is female, but I felt that to change constantly from 'he' to 'she' throughout the book would disturb the reader's concentration more than would be gained by striking a blow for equality of the sexes.

Acknowledgements

My thanks to the *Financial Times*, the Stock Exchange and the London Business School for permission to reproduce extracts from their publications. These extracts are crucial to the book, since one of its aims was to show how published financial data, in particular that provided in the *Financial Times*, can be used in investment decision-making.

Finally, I would like to thank all those who helped me to start *and* to finish this book. In particular, my thanks go to my father, who was the only person who had the courage to comment on the whole book. My thanks also go to colleagues who commented on various sections of the book and encouraged me, including Professor Harold Edey, Swee Ung, Steve Lumby, Nandan Choudhury, Martin Walker, Christopher Napier and Professors Susan Dev and Bryan Carsberg, and to Vivien Hope, who, with the help and hindrance of the word processor and my handwriting, converted the text into something worth looking at. My editor, John Winckler, must also be mentioned as the person who really convinced me to finish the book by the promise of a 'free' lunch. Finally, the person who suffered the most was my husband, Sebastian Wakefield, who bore with me during the eighteen months I took to write this book.

July 1983   JANETTE RUTTERFORD

Glossary of terms used

ACT	Advance corporation tax
AM	Arithmetic mean
β	Beta risk of a security (derived from the capital asset pricing model)
$\beta_i^2 S_m^2$	Market risk of a security
C	Value of call option
$CORR_{AB}$	Correlation coefficient of returns of securities A and B
COV_{AB}	Covariance of returns of securities A and B
$CULS$	Convertible unsecured loan stock
CT	Corporation tax
D	Duration (measure of volatility of gilt to changes in interest rates)
D_i	Dividend or income to be paid on a security in period i
dps	Dividend per share
e	Exponential function
$E(infl)$	Expected annual rate of inflation
$\epsilon_{j,t+1}$	Excess return on security j in period $t+1$
eps	Earnings per share
$E(R)$	Expected return on a security
$E(R_m)$	Expected return on the market (all risky, marketable assets)
$E(R_m) - R_F$	Market premium for taking on risk
$E(R_p)$	Expected return on a portfolio
$e^{-R_F t}$	The present value of £1 invested risk-free for a period t where the interest payments are continuously compounded
$E(U(W))$	Expected utility of wealth
$_i f_j$	Forward interest rate for loans from year i to year j
ϕ_t	Information on a security known in period t
g	Constant growth rate of dividends
GM	Geometric mean

HPR	Holding period return
k_i	Proportion of earnings paid out as dividends for security i
n	General term for the number of years, securities, etc.
$N(d_i)$	The value of the cumulative normal probability distribution (with a mean of 0 and an area under the curve of 1) evaluated at d_i
P	Value of put option
P_0	Current market price or value of a security (sometimes abbreviated to P)
P_1	Value of a security at the end of period 1
PE	Price–earnings ratio
p_i	Probability of state i occurring
$PV(X)$	Present value of a future cash flow X
R or r	Holding period return or annual return on a security
$R_\$$	Return expressed in dollar terms
R_F	Return on a risk-free security
r_i	Spot rate in year i, i.e. the annual rate of interest required for lending for n years starting now
$R_{j,t+1}$	Return on security j in period $t + 1$
ROI	Return on investment
$R_£$	Return expressed in sterling terms
S or S_1	Current share price used for option valuation
S_A	Standard deviation of returns of security A (sometimes the subscript is omitted)
S_p	Standard deviation of returns of portfolio
$S^2(e_i)$	Specific or diversifiable risk of security i
Σ	Summation sign
t	Time period
TWROR	Time-weighted rate of return
$U(W)$	Utility of wealth
V_A	Variance of returns of security A (square of standard deviation)
V_p	Variance of returns of portfolio
X	Exercise price of option
x	General term used for an unknown variable
X_0	Spot exchange rate
X_1	Spot exchange rate at the end of period 1
X_f	Forward exchange rate

The stock exchange

Introduction

This book is about investment in securities quoted on the UK Stock Exchange. This is not as limiting as it appears. As can be seen from Table 1.1, the market value of all securities listed on the Stock Exchange on 31 March 1982 was almost £460b. There are over 7,200 different securities to choose from and turnover in these securities averaged £757m. for each day of trading during 1981.

Such opportunities for Stock Exchange investment do not exist in many countries. The UK stock market is the third largest in the world in

1

terms of value after the US and Japan. It is the second largest after the US in terms of turnover. This means that a substantial proportion of the funds required for investment in this country are channelled via the

Table 1.1   *Market values of all UK Stock Exchange listed securities*
(31 March 1982)

	Number of securities	Market value (£m.)
UK public sector		
Short	29	24,219
Medium	38	30,812
Others	34	26,056
	101	81,087
Irish public sector		
Short	27	1,134
Medium	24	677
Others	28	646
	79	2,457
Corporation and county stocks		
Great Britain and Northern Ireland	401	2,178
Public board, etc.	98	247
Public sector: overseas	171	885
Eurobonds		
UK and Irish companies	82	1,400
Overseas companies	675	17,786
	757	19,186
Company securities		
UK and Irish		
Loan capital	1,721	4,501
Preference capital	1,265	1,535
Ordinary and deferred	2,132	104,300
	5,118	110,336
Overseas		
Loan capital	26	404
Preference capital	57	325
Ordinary and deferred	396	238,890
	479	239,619
TOTAL	7,204	455,995

Source: *Stock Exchange Fact Book*, March 1982.

Stock Exchange. Whether investing directly, by holding Stock Exchange securities, or indirectly, by saving through a pension fund or insurance company, the individual investor is providing funds for investment in industry and commerce.

Financial investment

For example, an entrepreneur setting up a business making Wellington boots will have to provide the money needed to pay for machinery, equipment and other start-up costs. He will invest this money at the outset in the hope that he will earn more money in the future, thereby making an overall gain on the venture. This type of investment is known as 'physical' investment because the entrepreneur is directly involved in the physical activity of making Wellington boots. The stock market investor, on the other hand, makes a 'financial' investment. He has no direct interest in the size or colour of the Wellington boots nor of the number produced; he is only concerned with the amount of money he has invested in, say, the shares[1] of the company making boots and how much money he will receive in the future. This type of investment is 'pure' in the sense that the investor has no interest in his investment other than the future income it will generate.

By restricting ourselves to pure financial investments, we also exclude investments in works of art. These can be acquired in the expectation of financial gain but are usually purchased for display and appreciation of their beauty. The British Rail pension fund has acquired paintings and sculptures as financial investments in the hope that when sold they will provide a good return for the beneficiaries of the pension fund. The problem with such investments is that other investors will be buying them for consumption, in the form of enjoyment of their beauty as well as for investment purposes, and this makes it difficult to value them as pure investments. Attitudes towards the beauty of an ICI share certificate will not change as rapidly as towards a Picasso. Also, works of art may not store as well as money. An entry in a Swiss bank ledger will not deteriorate in the way a fine carpet may do in a damp cellar![2]

---

[1] A share is a specific type of security. 'Security' is a general term for any type of financial investment traded on the Stock Exchange.

[2] Similarly, gambling and other forms of speculation are excluded from our definition of 'pure' investment. The thrill of gambling will be included in the price in the form of a lower return than that on an equally risky financial investment. This is not to say that the topic of this book, Stock Exchange investment, is not enjoyable.

Quoted investments

Financial investments are therefore easier to value than more subjective types of investment. They always consist of the exchange of a known amount of money in return for the expectation of future receipts of money. The distinguishing feature of those financial investments which are quoted on the Stock Exchange is that, at least in theory, these securities can be bought and sold at any time. In other words, another investor can always be found who is willing to acquire the security and hence the entitlement to the future payments due on that investment. Of course, the price he is prepared to pay may not be the one the seller expected to receive. This can be due either to changes in expectations concerning the amount of money the investment will pay in the future (for example a company is doing badly and likely to cut its dividend) or to more general market factors such as a change in interest rates. Uncertainty about the future characterises all financial investments and this inherent risk will be discussed in detail in Chapter 2.

The concentration of this book on securities which are quoted on the Stock Exchange means that we exclude such financial investments as bank deposit accounts and National Savings certificates. In these cases, money is invested for a certain period from a day to several years, which is sometimes specified and sometimes flexible. However, the transaction is entirely between the borrower and provider of funds. No third party can buy the entitlement to the proceeds of your National Savings certificates from you and the value of your investment in National Savings is not quoted daily in the *Financial Times*. The concentration on the Stock Exchange also excludes investments in commodities such as gold and cocoa (although the securities of mining or commodity trading companies do come within the scope of this book).

Quoted or marketable securities are those which have a market price. The investor can consult his newspaper or telephone his stockbroker to find out the current quoted price. However, a stock market quotation is not to be confused with a *listing*. Although most quoted securities are listed, which means that the issuers of the securities have to comply with rules laid down by the Stock Exchange, some are unlisted, for example on the new unlisted securities market (USM),[3] and yet can be bought and sold at a market price.

---

[3] Companies dealt in on the USM (run by the Stock Exchange) or on the over the counter (OTC) market (run by the investment bankers Granville & Co. Limited and other dealers in securities) are usually either too small or too new to have the track record required for a full listing.

Comparing investments

Although securities represent funds provided to finance a wide range of physical investment, from North Sea oil exploration to ball-bearing production lines,[4] they are all basically about receiving future cash flows in return for an initial investment. So, how do we compare quoted securities?

Market price and return

Each security has a market price and an expected pattern of future cash flows. Market prices can be compared easily enough. If one security costs £20 and another £100, the effects of purchasing either the £100 security or five of the £20 securities can be considered. Another way of comparing two securities which have different prices is to examine not the absolute cash flows they yield but the returns relative to their cost. For example, suppose the £100 security pays £5 per year in perpetuity and the £20 security £1.10 per year in perpetuity. From this we can deduce that their annual returns are respectively 5% and 5½% of the initial cost.

Irregular future cash flows are more difficult to compare since both the amounts *and* timing of these future payments will differ between investments. For example, suppose Mr Hope can buy either security *A* or security *B* for £100. Security *A* will pay £5 per year for two years and at the end of that time the £100 will be returned to the investor. Security *B* will make one payment of £110.25 in two years' time. Table 1.2 illustrates the cash flows of the two investment possibilities. By conven-

Table 1.2   Comparing securities with different cash flows (£)

	Year		
Security	0	1	2
A	−100	+5	+105
B	−100	—	+110.25

---

[4] Some funds lent to the government may not be used for physical investment but, say, for expenditure on social services.

tion it is assumed that year 0 represents the point in time when the investment is made; the cash flows at time 0 are negative because they represent purchase payments by the investor. It is also common practice to assume that all cash flows occur at the end of each year, to simplify calculations. This implies a gap of twelve months between each payment related to securities A and B.

Suppose both securities are issued by the same company and all future payments are certain to be made. Mr Hope must compare two securities which have the same price (£100), the same life of two years and no risk (since all the payments are certain).

Mr Hope will first consider the *return* on securities A and B – how profitable they are relative to his investment cost of £100. Consider security A. Mr Hope gets 5% interest each year and his money back. This must represent an annual return of 5%. Now consider security B and compare it with an investment of £100 at 5%. At the end of one year such an investment would be worth

$$£100 (1 + 0.05) = £105$$

If Mr Hope then reinvested the original sum plus the accrued interest for a further year at 5%, it would be worth

$$£105 (1 + 0.05) = £110.25$$

So, an investment of £100 for two years earning 5% interest (with no withdrawals) would be worth £110.25. Since Mr Hope is due to receive £110.25 in two years' time on security B, he must be getting an annual return of 5% on his investment of £100 in B.

Timing of cash flows

Thus, both security A and security B yield 5% annual return. Mr Hope cannot distinguish between them by choosing the security which offers the highest return as he would like to do. He must compare the different timings of cash flows by considering his consumption preference, that is, when he would prefer to receive the cash payments, bearing in mind how much he wishes to spend or consume at each point in time. For example, Mr Hope may need a regular income and so prefer A, or have no need of money for the next two years and so choose B.

In practice, Mr Hope will hold several different securities with a variety of cash flow patterns and so, even if he needs a regular income, he will be able to buy security B since his other investments will provide the income he needs before year 2. He can also either sell security *B* via the stock market whenever he decides he needs some money or borrow from the bank on the strength of owning security *B*. Thus, the requirement for a particular pattern of cash flows to match consumption preferences does not limit Mr Hope in his choice of investments. In fact, in a market where Mr Hope is able to borrow and lend freely at the same rate of interest, he can alter the cash flows from any security to match his consumption preferences exactly.

Uncertainty of cash flows

The pattern of future cash flows attached to each security will usually differ not only in amount and timing but also in the uncertainty attached to them. A British government security, for example 2½% Consols, quoted at £15 (for £100 nominal)[5] will promise to pay the owner £2.50 per annum in perpetuity and the investor can be certain of receiving that income for as long as he holds the security (since the government will always pay the interest on its debt even if it has to borrow money to do so). On the other hand, an investor holding shares in a company may *expect* to receive regular dividend payments but there is no certainty attached to either the amount of the future dividends or even to the payment of any dividend at all. The company concerned may in a bad year cut the dividend, as many large companies did in 1981, or even go into liquidation and cease dividend payments altogether.

Suppose Mr Faith is comparing the purchase of £15 worth of 2½% Consols with £15 of shares in Colimited whose shares cost £1 each and are expected to pay a dividend of 20p per share in the next year. Mr Faith has to compare two different income streams, one of which is fixed indefinitely and one of which is unknown after the first year. Table 1.3 emphasises Mr Faith's problem.

He will have to estimate what income he expects Colimited shares to generate from year 2 onwards and how certain he is of his estimates. He will then have to decide whether he is prepared to take on the risk of receiving more or less income than he expects or whether he prefers the more certain return of the government bond. Chapter 2 discusses in more detail the different types of risk inherent in financial investment and the relationship between the risk and return of securities.

---

[5] £100 nominal means that the holder will receive interest on £100 (e.g. 2½% Consols will pay £2.50 for each £100 nominal held, whatever the market price) and eventual repayment on maturity of £100 if the stock is dated.

Table 1.3   Comparison of two securities of different risk (cash flows, £)

Security	Year					
	0	1	2	...	n	...
2½% Consols	−15	+2.5	+2.5	...	+2.5	...
Colimited shares	−15	+3.0	?	...	?	...

Role of the stock market

The financial securities we have been considering are all traded on the UK Stock Exchange. This body provides the market for stocks and shares in the UK. Centred on London, the Stock Exchange also has closely linked provincial trading floors in Birmingham, Dublin, Glasgow, Liverpool and Manchester but can be considered as a single market. The Stock Exchange, with over 4,000 individual members who work in firms of stockbrokers and jobbers, provides the intermediary mechanism whereby buyers and sellers of securities are brought together.

The Stock Exchange offers the advantages of any regulated market. Investors know where to go, they do not have to worry about finding the other party to the transaction they wish to make and they are to some extent protected from negligence or fraud by the rules the Stock Exchange requires its members to follow and by its compensation fund.

However, the stock market also performs two unique functions within the economy.

Transfer of risk

Firstly, physical investment is a risky business. Uncertainty clouds future demand for a manufacturer's products and other factors which will affect the future profits of the venture. Suppose Mr Wheeler wishes to set up a factory making tandems. If he is prepared to take on the risk[6]

---

[6] Risk can be viewed as quantifiable uncertainty, that is where more than one outcome is likely but where the likelihood of each possible outcome can be assessed. See Chapter 2 for a discussion of risk.

of the business himself, he can provide the necessary finance from his own resources, so that whatever profits or losses he makes belong to him alone. Mr Wheeler may decide, though, to share or transfer some of the risk of making and selling tandems by issuing securities to investors. He could issue fixed interest securities called stocks where he would promise to pay a fixed amount of interest on the money loaned to him by the investors. In this case, investors would not take on as much risk as Mr Wheeler. They would receive the same payment on their investment every year whereas Mr Wheeler would collect the fluctuating balance of profits. They would, however, bear the risk of the venture failing, in which case they could lose some or all of their initial investment.

Mr Wheeler might decide to transfer more risk to investors by issuing shares in his company, Twosome Tandems plc. Instead of receiving fixed interest payments, these shareholders would take payment in the form of dividends, high in good years, low or non-existent in bad years. They would also rank last in the queue of creditors should the company fail.

Whichever securities Mr Wheeler decides to issue, investors will take on the risk of Twosome Tandems via the medium of the Stock Exchange, which will arrange the issue of securities for Mr Wheeler's company. In this way, the Stock Exchange in its role of *primary* market (for the issue of *new* shares) enables the risk of physical investment to be transferred to financial investors.

Two major factors have stimulated the growth since the nineteenth century of new issues of securities for companies via the Stock Exchange. New issues for UK public companies exceeded £2,600m. in 1981 although, in real terms, this is about the same as the £245m.[7] issued in the boom post-war year of 1920. Firstly, the creation of the limited liability company in 1855 meant that any losses incurred by a share-holder were limited to the capital he had invested in the company. Previously, liabilities incurred by the owners of a business (and still today by members of partnerships) were not limited to their investment in the failed concern but could extend to the whole of their personal wealth. The risk of loss for shareholders in Twosome Tandems, a limited liability company, is therefore restricted to the amounts they invest in Twosome whereas their possible gains are unbounded.

Secondly, the new businesses spawned by the Industrial Revolution – railways, steel, mass manufacture – were capital-intensive and required more investment than the entrepreneurs running them or wealthy individuals could provide. Banks were unwilling to furnish more than a proportion of the funds needed since they required relatively safe investments for their depositors. The issue of shares via the Stock

---

[7] Both figures are from the Midland Bank series of new issue statistics published in the *Midland Bank Review*.

Exchange offered a means of allowing a large number of small investors to supply the risk capital required by these industries. It also implied, with suppliers of investment capital being able to choose between alternative ventures, an efficient allocation of resources. Investors would use the stock market to allocate their funds to the companies which provided the best return, given the risk involved, and which would bring the most financial benefit to the economy.[8]

Transfer of waiting

The Stock Exchange, as well as providing a primary market for new securities, also acts as a secondary market, where securities can be traded throughout their lives. This can be for an indefinite period, as in the case of shares. For example, Marks and Spencer shares have been traded on the stock market since 1927 and are expected to be traded as long as Marks and Spencer continues in existence. An investor buying a Marks and Spencer share now would not expect to see his investment repaid by the company. He could, however, realise his investment at any time by selling his shares via the Stock Exchange to another investor. Similarly, investors in fixed interest stocks which usually have a finite life of between ten and twenty-five years, can trade in these stocks at any time. Whoever holds a particular stock at maturity will be entitled to the repayment of the original amount lent to the issuer of the stock but this does not have to be, and most likely will not be, the person who originally invested in the stock ten or twenty years before.

This marketability of stocks and shares strongly affects the willingness of investors to hold long-term securities (by which we usually mean securities with an original life of at least ten years).

Each investor will have different consumption preferences and these may not match the maturity of the securities the investor holds, or the investor's consumption preferences may change over time. Suppose Mrs Field invested £1,000 five years ago in a fixed interest stock which had a ten-year life and envisaged holding that stock until maturity. She suddenly decides that she wishes to buy a larger house and needs the

---

[8] The efficient allocation of resources depends on there being a perfect capital market, discussed in more detail in Chapters 8 and 9. One factor which could prevent efficient allocation of resources is imperfect knowledge. Stock Exchange and accounting rules governing the quality of information in share prospectuses left much to be desired in the first decades of this century. See, for example, the case of the Royal Mail (1931), described in Hastings (1977).

money invested in the stock now. In the meantime, Mr Wake has inherited a lump sum on the death of his mother and wishes to invest it. Through the medium of the Stock Exchange, Mr Wake could purchase all or some of Mrs Field's stock. Both Mrs Field and Mr Wake are willing to hold a long-term security because they know they can sell at any time if they so wish. Even though Mrs Field expected to hold the stock to maturity, she would have been unwilling to buy it if she had known that she would be unable to realise it before the ten years were up.

The nature of most physical investment is such that it can take many years before the business has generated enough cash for the original investors to be able to withdraw their funds. As a result, securities based on physical investment are naturally long term. The primary market for new issues of these securities would not be successful were it not for the existence of the secondary market, which transforms these long-term securities into short-term ones by offering permanent marketability. If these stocks and shares could not be traded throughout their life, investors would require a 'liquidity premium', in the form of a higher return, for holding an asset which could not be sold before the end of its life.[9] The existence of a stock market prevents investors from having to wait before realising their investments and, by removing the need for a liquidity premium, reduces the cost of issuing long-term securities.

Buying and selling securities

The UK Stock Exchange operates what is known as a 'single capacity' system of trading which means that stockbrokers and jobbers each act in a separate capacity, the former earning commission as agents for the buyer or seller, the latter acting as principals by dealing in securities for their own profit or loss. Each jobber makes a market by quoting prices at which he is prepared to buy and sell the securities in which he trades and, since at least two jobbers should trade in each security, competition should prevent them from making excess profits as principals. The market is also closed in the sense that jobbers will deal only with brokers and brokers agree to put their business through the jobbers. Very few securities are traded outside this system.[10]

---

[9] For example, building societies offer extra interest for deposits which cannot be withdrawn on demand.
[10] An example is transactions in eurobonds (described in Chapter 10) which do not have to be passed through jobbers.

Role of jobber

The role of the jobber on the UK Stock Exchange is unique amongst Stock Exchanges. The jobber is, in essence, a trader in securities. He buys and sells securities from and to brokers on his own account. Suppose he is dealing in ICI shares. Throughout the day the jobber will buy and sell ICI shares, not necessarily in matching amounts or 'bundles', so that at any point in time he may have a stock of ICI shares (be long in ICI), or have sold ICI shares he does not have (be short in ICI). If more brokers wish to buy ICI shares than sell, the jobber will adjust his price upwards. If more brokers wish to sell than buy, the jobber will lower his prices. In this way the jobber alters prices until he matches demand and supply for ICI shares. However, in the case of all securities except those issued by the British government, he does not have to balance his books at the end of the day. Trading on the Stock Exchange is divided into periods called accounts. An account lasts two weeks (three weeks if it includes a holiday such as Christmas) and ends on a Friday. Settlement of all transactions carried out during an account is made on the second Monday after the end of the account. This means that the jobber does not have to deliver securities he has sold until up to three or even four weeks after he agreed to sell and all the bargains he has struck during the account will not be matched until 'account' or 'settlement' day. The jobber therefore does not have to balance his purchases and sales exactly. However, the jobber will never wish to be excessively short or long in any securities. If he is long, he will have expensive financing costs for holding the shares. If he is short, he may be caught out by a sudden increase in price when replacing the securities he has sold.

Other Stock Exchanges, for example New York, Tokyo and Paris, use a continuous or regular auction system instead of jobbers. Brokers wishing to buy or sell a particular share will go to the trading post where this share is auctioned and an intermediary will call out prices until the market is cleared, which is when buyers and sellers have agreed on prices at which they are prepared to trade. The other major difference between the UK and other Stock Exchanges is that, elsewhere, the roles of principal and agent are often combined. For example, in Germany the banks and in Japan the securities firms may act as both agent and principal provided they declare in which capacity they are trading.

Both the jobbing and auction systems were developed before the invention of modern communications. All traders had to gather in one place to buy and sell securities. On the over the counter (OTC) market[11] in the US, dealing is done on the telephone, and on ARIEL, a computer

---

[11] This deals in securities of US companies which are smaller than those whose securities are quoted on the New York Stock Exchange but are still large by UK standards.

system set up by some UK financial institutions, purchases and sales by institutions are matched, with the computer as intermediary.[12] Since 1979, securities registered on the UK Stock Exchange have also been bought and sold through a computerised central system which matches buyers and sellers on a jobber-by-jobber basis. This system, known as Talisman, is run by the Stock Exchange.

Description of a transaction

Let us now examine exactly how a transaction is processed through the Stock Exchange. Mr Wake wishes to buy some shares with the proceeds of his legacy. He will do this via his stockbroker who will act on his behalf. All Mr Wake has to do is notify the broker which shares he wants to buy and, if he wishes, specify limits on the price he is prepared to pay for these shares. Suppose he decides on 500 RTZ shares. As Mr Wake's agent, the broker will try to buy at the lowest price for RTZ shares prevailing in the market at the time he is instructed to purchase.

Jobbers operate from pitches on the trading floor of the Stock Exchange and the broker will go to those jobbers who trade in the specific share Mr Wake wants to buy. The number of jobbers on the London Exchange has declined dramatically in the last twenty years from 104 in 1959 to seventeen in 1981. It is now unlikely that more than two jobbers will trade in a particular share and, for the less actively traded securities, the jobbers now have agreements to operate jointly.[13] This decline in numbers is due to the increased financing costs of holding stock, as interest rates have risen, and to the larger average size of transactions or bargains (£36,054 in 1981 compared with £3,673 in 1964).

The broker will ask each jobber who trades in RTZ for a quote and the jobber will reply with two prices, for example 538p–545p. This means that he is prepared to buy any number of RTZ shares at 538p and sell any number at 545p. The difference in price is the jobber's turn and is how he makes a profit. Competition between jobbers should reduce this spread to a minimum but, here again, for certain shares jobbers now agree minimum spreads.

Suppose jobber *A* quotes 540p–547p and jobber *B* 538p–545p. Note that neither jobber is aware of whether the broker wishes to buy or sell

---

[12] ARIEL has not been a great success, perhaps because the Stock Exchange has responded to the threat presented by ARIEL by reducing its commission charges for large transactions (since these are the ones made by the financial institutions).

[13] See the back page of the *Financial Times*, 15 June 1981.

RTZ. Since the broker wishes to buy RTZ, he will agree a deal with jobber *B*. Each will make a quick note of the transaction and the broker, on returning to his office, will arrange for a contract note to be made out for his client, Mr Wake.

As mentioned earlier, dealings in shares are for credit and are settled on settlement day, usually between ten and twenty-five days after the transaction is agreed between broker and jobber. This means that Mr Wake could carry out several transactions in RTZ shares during the account and would only have to settle the *net* amount (plus transaction costs) on settlement day.

Fixed interest securities issued by the British government (known as gilts), newly issued securities and bearer securities are the only securities traded for cash settlement the next day. There is no credit period within which a gilt bargain can be 'closed' (reversed) as for shares bought and sold during an account.

Transaction costs

Transaction costs on securities dealing consist of the broker's commission, VAT on the commission, government taxes in the form of stamp duties and a levy of 60p on transactions worth over £5,000 to support the supervisory Council for the Securities Industry (CSI),[14] set up in 1978. The Stock Exchange has operated a minimum commission system since 1912 and most brokers charge this minimum. The charges are on a sliding scale according to the value of the transaction.

Shares

For example, on share bargains worth between £300 and £7,000 commission of 1.65% of the value of the transaction is charged, with a minimum of £7 for a sale and £10 for a purchase. For bargains under £300, the commission is discretionary. For bargains over £7,000 and up to £15,000, additional commission of 0.55% is charged on the value exceeding £7,000, and so on. Thus, the bigger the share deal, the lower the average percentage commission. Commission on a £500 purchase would be the minimum of £10, equivalent to 2% of the purchase price,

---

[14] The Council for the Securities Industry was set up by the Bank of England to act as a self-regulatory body for the institutions involved in the securities industry.

Table 1.4   Comparison of transaction costs in the world's major Stock Exchanges

Centre (All rates apply to transactions by residents)		Commission on considerations of			Commissions plus transaction taxes (including VAT)		
		£500 £	£50,000 £	£500,000 £	£500 £	£50,000 £	£500,000 £
London*	Buyers	10.00	335	2,015	21.60	1386	12,318
	Sellers	8.25	335	2,015	9.59	386	2,318
Paris £1 = FFr 8.50	Buyers	3.50	350	1,075	5.62	562	2,764
	Sellers	3.50	350	1,075	5.62	562	2,764
Frankfurt £1 = DM 3.85	Buyers	5.50	525	5,200	6.12	588	5,825
	Sellers	5.50	525	5,200	6.12	588	5,825
Tokyo £1 = Y400	Buyers	6.25	425	3,063	6.25	425	3,063
	Sellers	6.25	425	3,063	7.75	575	4,563
New York† £1 = $1.85	Buyers	14.30	243	1,698	14.30	243	1,698
	Sellers	14.30	243	1,698	15.80	347	2,470

* Allowing for increases in commissions implemented in 1982 and for VAT at 15%.
† Including usual discounts since there are no minimum commissions.
Source: Stock Exchange evidence to the Wilson Committee (1980).

whereas commission on a £50,000 bargain would be £334.50 or 0.67% of the value of the transaction. VAT, currently 15%, is payable on the brokerage commission. However, if some shares are bought and sold within the same account, no transfer stamp duty is payable and brokerage commission is normally waived on the closing transaction.

Contract stamp duty is a tax payable on the drawing up of the 'contract' representing a purchase or sale of shares. It varies between 10p and 60p according to the value of the transaction. Transfer stamp duty is a tax on the purchase of shares (not the sale) and is payable at the rate of 1% of the value of the shares by UK residents.

Appendix 1 at the end of this book gives details of all the relevant costs in the buying and selling of shares and other securities. Table 1.4 shows figures produced by the Stock Exchange comparing costs of different size share bargains in the major Stock Exchanges of the world. Although London compares reasonably favourably on brokerage commission costs, the *total* cost of buying and selling shares, including government taxes, is the highest of all the centres for all sizes of transactions shown. We examine the £500 transaction in more detail and break down the costs in Table 1.5.

Thus if an investor wishes to buy and sell say £500 of ICI shares, he can expect to pay over £31 in transaction costs or around 6% of the value of the shares. For it to be worth his while to buy the shares, they must rise in value to at least £532 before he even recoups his transaction costs.

Table 1.5   *Transaction costs on £500 share transaction*

Cost of purchase	
Shares	£500.00
Brokerage commission (minimum)	10.00
VAT on brokerage	1.50
Contract stamp duty	0.10
Transfer stamp duty	5.00
TOTAL COST	516.60
Cost of sale	
Shares	£500.00
Brokerage commission (1.65%)	8.25
VAT on brokerage	1.24
Contract stamp duty	0.10
TOTAL COST	509.59

Fixed interest securities

The brokerage commission on fixed interest bargains is lower than for shares because average fixed interest transactions (mostly gilts which are by far the most actively traded stocks) are larger. The average fixed interest security bargain during 1981 was worth £118,000 compared with £8,200 for shares. Brokerage commission (at the current rates) on those bargains would have been £184 on £118,000 of gilts with at least ten years to maturity[15] and £122 on an £8,200 share bargain.

Commission on gilts is 0.8% on the first £2,500, with a minimum charge of £7, and in declining percentages on larger amounts. Commission is negotiable on gilts with less than five years to maturity. Charges for transactions in other fixed interest securities, such as company debentures and loan stocks, are between those for gilts and shares. Appendix 1 gives details of the scales of minimum commission charges. Other transaction costs are also lower for gilts than for shares since no transfer stamp duty is payable.

An additional complication with the calculation of dealing costs for gilts is the question of accrued interest. Shorts (gilts with less than five years to maturity) are dealt in exclusive of interest. This means that gross interest is added to or subtracted from the price depending on whether or not the stock is entitled to the next interest payment when it is bought or sold. Gilts other than shorts have interest included in the price. This is discussed in greater detail in Chapter 3.

Table 1.6 gives an example of the transaction costs of buying long gilts. (Selling costs in the case of gilts are identical to purchase costs.) An investor buys £8,000 nominal of Treasury 13% 2000. The price quoted is £88 per £100 nominal. Accrued interest is included in the

Table 1.6   Transaction costs of buying long gilts

Cost of purchase	
£8,000 of Treasury 13% 2000 at £88	£7040.00
Brokerage commission at 0.8% on the first £2,500 and 0.25% on the remainder	31.35
VAT on brokerage	4.70
Contract stamp duty	0.60
CSI levy	0.60
TOTAL COST	£7077.25

---

[15] That is, at least ten years before they will be repaid by the government.

price. Transaction costs for the gilt are low relative to the share dealing costs, being £37.25 or 0.53% of the value of the gilt.

At the sacrifice of a little flexibility on exactly when the transaction is carried out, gilts can be bought and sold more cheaply via the Post Office. A stockbroker will carry out a buy or sell transaction within minutes whereas the National Savings Stock Register can take one or two days to execute the order, during which time the price may have changed – in either direction. This cheap method of buying and selling gilts, and the non-liability to 1% transfer stamp duty on purchase, are two of the ways in which the British government attempts to stimulate the secondary market (and hence the primary market) in gilts. Other incentives will be discussed in the chapter describing gilts, Chapter 3.

Minimum commission

We have seen that brokerage commission is relatively cheaper the larger the transaction. However, it must be remembered that the effort on the part of the broker is the same, whether the transaction is large or small. Complaints by institutional investors, who felt that brokers were being paid substantial commissions for executing their transactions which were in fact no more difficult to carry out than small ones, led to a reduction in the charges on various *large* transactions in 1972, 1976 and 1982.

The argument for maintaining minimum charges upheld by the Stock Exchange is that the brokers compete by providing free services to their clients in the form of securities research and investment advice. Brokers claim the removal of minimum charges would lead to a reduction in the quality of the non-dealing services they provide and to mergers between brokers, thereby implying a long-term lessening of competition. On the New York Stock Exchange, minimum commissions were abolished in 1975. This has led to the separation of dealing and advisory services, the former becoming cheaper and the latter no longer free, as well as to the closure of some broking firms.

It can be argued by institutional investors that, since they usually have their own research staffs, they should not pay for duplicate brokers' research by way of high brokerage commissions. Minimum commission charges, which force the institutions to subsidise brokers' non-dealing activities, should, therefore, benefit the small investor whose commission payments are too small to pay for these advisory services. However, small investors are usually low on a broker's list of priorities and they may not receive research reports or recommendations until after the institutions have been circulated.

It must be noted that minimum commissions have already been abolished on dealings in international securities. Also, the Stock Exchange, in an agreement with the government, has agreed to phase out minimum commissions on all transactions by the end of 1986.

The changing face of the stock market

Type of security

The face of the stock market has changed over the years in two main ways. Firstly, the type of security dealt in has altered. Fifty years ago, the emphasis was on overseas securities and utilities[16] as well as British government securities and UK company shares. Now, although many overseas securities are still listed on the UK Stock Exchange, as can be seen in Table 1.1, their number has dwindled. Similarly, with the nationalisation of the gas, coal and electricity industries, the number of utilities' securities still quoted is minimal. The two major types of security now dealt in are British government securities and ordinary shares. As can be seen in Table 1.7, out of an annual average turnover for the period 1978–81 of £174b., nearly £133b. (or 76%) of turnover was in British government securities, with a further £26b. (or 15%) in ordinary shares. Gilts, as British government securities are known, form the subject of Chapters 3 and 4 and ordinary shares the subject of Chapter 5.

The figures in Table 1.7 for ordinary shares refer both to UK and non-UK ordinary shares. Chapter 10, which is devoted to the topic of international investment, discusses the special characteristics of investment in overseas securities, whether they are quoted on the UK Stock Exchange or on overseas stock markets such as New York or Tokyo.

Table 1.7 also reveals an increase in the level of Stock Exchange activity during the period 1964–81. This is partly due to the increased number and size of transactions in both ordinary shares and gilts over the period. It is also partly due to the introduction of new types of security. For example, options on ordinary shares can now be traded on the Stock Exchange. Options are described in Chapter 6.

Also, the Stock Exchange set up in 1980 an unlisted securities market (known as the USM) to allow small companies, which find the condi-

---

[16] A utility usually refers to a company providing a service such as gas, electricity or coal.

Table 1.7   Transactions in securities on the Stock Exchange, 1964–81

		Annual average			
	British government securities	Company securities			Total
		Fixed interest	Ordinary shares	Other	
Number of bargains ('000)					
September 1964–67	381	456	3,693	143	4,673
1968–72	458	670	5,187	132	6,447
1973–77	689	441	4,332	136	5,598
1978–81	894	342	4,104	145	5,485
Value of turnover (£b.)					
September 1964–67	18.7	0.5	4.2	0.9	24.3
1968–72	29.6	1.4	12.0	1.4	44.0
1973–77	71.7	1.7	16.3	7.6	97.3
1978–81	132.6	1.7	26.3	13.1	173.7
Average value per bargain (£'000)					
September 1964–67	49.1	1.1	1.1	6.3	5.2
1968–72	64.6	2.1	2.3	10.6	6.8
1973–77	104.1	3.8	3.8	55.9	17.4
1978–81	148.3	5.0	5.8	90.3	31.7

Sources: Wilson Report (1980) and Stock Exchange Fact Book. By permission of the Controller of Her Majesty's Stationery Office and of the Stock Exchange.

tions attached to a full Stock Exchange listing too burdensome, to gain access to the capital markets. There are about 150 securities currently quoted on the USM and the number is growing rapidly. The USM is not to be confused with the UK over the counter (OTC) market, run by the investment bankers, Granville & Co. Limited, since 1971. OTC shares are traded under Rule 163 of the Stock Exchange which allows an essentially unregulated market to be made in shares with an intermediary, in this case Granville's, able to act as both principal and agent. It was as a result of the success of this OTC market that the Stock Exchange set up the USM, to attract the same type of companies but to operate within the regulatory framework of the Stock Exchange. Table 1.8 gives an extract from the *Financial Times*, showing the prices of shares traded by Granville's. USM ordinary share prices are not quoted separately in the *Financial Times* but are included amongst the prices of the listed ordinary shares on the next-to-back pages of the *Financial Times*.

Table 1.8   OTC share prices as given in the Financial Times

Granville & Co. Ltd (formerly M. J. H. Nightingale & Co. Ltd)

27/28 Lovat Lane London EC3R 8EB   **Telephone 01-621 1212**

1982–83 High	Low	Company	Price	Change	Gross Div.(p)	Yield %	P/E Actual	Fully taxed
142	120	Ass. Brit. Ind. Ord.	141	—	6.4	4.5	8.2	—
158	117	Ass. Brit. Ind. CULS	157	—	10.0	6.4	—	13.1
74	57	Airsprung Group	67	—	6.1	9.1	7.6	6.7
46	34	Armitage & Rhodes	34	—	4.3	12.6	3.8	16.1
305	197	Bardon Hill	305	—	11.4	3.7	12.8	—
134	100	CCL 11pc Conv. Pref.	133	—	15.7	11.8	—	10.9
270	240	Cindico Group	240	—	17.6	7.3	9.7	9.6
86	54	Deborah Services	54	—	6.0	11.1	3.6	7.6
84	77	Frank Horsell	84	—	—	—	7.1	7.5
83	75	Frank Horsell Pr Ord 87	83	—	8.7	10.5	7.0	6.8
83	61	Frederick Parker	68	—	7.1	10.4	4.3	12.7
55	35	George Blair	35	—	—	—	6.1	12.7
100	74	Ind. Precision Castings	79	—	7.3	9.2	10.1	—
152	100	Isis Conv. Pref.	152	—	15.7	10.3	—	8.7
137	94	Jackson Group	137	—	7.5	5.5	4.2	15.2
187	111	James Burrough	187	—	9.6	5.1	13.6	25.7
260	162	Robert Jenkins	162	—	20.0	12.3	1.8	11.4
83	54	Scruttons "A"	73	—	5.7	7.8	9.5	8.6
167	112	Torday & Carlisle	112	—	11.4	10.2	5.0	—
29	21	Unilock Holdings	26	—	0.46	1.8	—	6.8
85	66	Walter Alexander	66	—	6.4	9.7	4.7	8.3
260	214	W. S. Yeates	260	—	17.1	6.6	4.0	

Prices now available on Prestel page 48146.

Source: *Financial Times*, 4th March 1983.

Type of investor

As well as the types of security traded on the Stock Exchange having changed over time, the major types of investor have also altered, with the main change being the decline of individual investors and the rise of institutional investors. Individuals, especially the younger generations, now invest *indirectly* in the stock market through the institutional investors. Their savings are channeled into pension funds and insurance companies and, to a lesser extent, into unit trusts and investment trusts. Individual investors, who held nearly two-thirds of the market value of UK ordinary shares in 1957, now hold only one-third. On the other hand, the investing institutions (comprising pension funds, insurance companies, unit trusts and investment trusts), who held only 19% in value of UK company ordinary shares in 1957, now hold over 50% in value. They also hold over 40% in value of British government securities and over two-thirds in value of UK company fixed interest securities. The implications of this trend, which is continuing apace, and the roles of these investing institutions are considered in Chapter 11. The formulation of investment objectives, investment policy and the measurement of investment performance for both individual and institutional investors are described in the final chapter, Chapter 12.

Summary

This chapter has described what is meant by financial investment in a quoted security which can be bought and sold through the Stock Exchange and which promises the holder a series of future payments, the amount, timing and certainty of which vary according to the type of security.

The vital role of the stock market as a centre of trading in securities and, more importantly, as a means of transferring risk and the postponement of consumption was discussed. The primary market allows companies to spread the risk of physical investment among shareholders and between holders of different securities. The secondary market in effect converts long-term securities into short-term ones by allowing them to be bought and sold throughout their life. No investor need postpone consumption by having to wait for the maturity of his investment.

The Stock Exchange dealing systems were then described, in particular the roles of the stockbroker and of the jobber. The technicalities of buying securities were explained and the transaction costs of buying and selling shares and fixed interest securities outlined. The chapter concluded with a brief look at the major changes which have taken place in the stock market in recent years, especially the changes in the types of security traded and the change from direct investment in the stock market by individual investors to indirect investment via the investing institutions.

Problems

1. Mary Contrary has just joined a pension fund as a securities clerk. She has asked her departmental manager to describe how the buying and selling of securities are carried out on the London Stock Exchange – she has vaguely heard of such terms as 'jobbing' and 'account day'. She also asks what are the transaction costs of buying government bonds and shares.

   Assume you are the departmental manager and provide Mary with the information she requires.

2. You are a private investor wishing to buy 500 ICI shares and instruct your stockbroker accordingly. Explain the process which will take place between the jobber, broker and purchaser of the 500 shares and show how much the transaction will cost the investor in total. What would be the transaction costs associated with the purchase of the same amount of long-term, fixed interest government stock? Would the transaction costs on ICI shares be any different if the shares were bought and then sold within the same account?

3. Describe the main changes in type of security and type of investor which have taken place on the UK Stock Exchange over the past few decades. Why do you think these changes have occurred?

4. (i)   What is the difference between quoted and unquoted securities and between physical and financial investment?
   (ii)   What is meant when the Stock Exchange is described as a primary and secondary market for securities?
   (iii)   Describe the main functions of a stock market within the economy.
   (iv)   Explain the roles of stockbrokers and jobbers in the UK stock market. What changes have taken place in recent years?

PART I

EVALUATION OF SECURITIES

Risk and return

Introduction

This chapter discusses the two most important attributes of the 7,200 securities quoted on the Stock Exchange – risk and return. When considering any security, the investor is always concerned with the return expected on the investment and the risk of the investment, that is, how likely it is that the return expected will be achieved. In a certain world, the return would always be exactly as expected and there would be no risk. The investor would merely have to compare the returns available on different investments and choose those which offered the highest returns.

Unfortunately, the existence of uncertainty means that returns on investments are not always as expected. The hoped-for dividends on the shares in the speculative Australian mining company may never materialise or the company whose unsecured loan stock you hold may go into

27

liquidation. All securities quoted on the Stock Exchange are subject to risk. Different types of security will have different kinds of risk attached to them (for example, UK government securities do not suffer the risk of default but are vulnerable to changes in interest rates). However, the effect of all these different kinds of risk is the same – the *actual* returns achieved will be different from those *expected* by the investor. The riskier the security the more likely it is that the hoped-for return will not be reached or the greater the shortfall from the expected return.

So, the investor needs to be able to quantify both the uncertain return and the level of that uncertainty for each security before he can make investment decisions. Depending on his attitude towards risk and return, he will then be able to choose the securities which offer him the combination of risk and return which best suits him.

The chapter starts by introducing the standard measure of return, known as the holding period return, which is all the investor would need to be able to make investment decisions under certainty. We then go on to consider investment decisions made under uncertainty and different types of risk to which securities are subject, namely, uncertainty of income, default risk, interest rate risk and inflation risk.

Given uncertainty, it is not possible to determine the future holding period return on any security, since a range of returns is likely. The concept of a probability distribution of returns is then introduced. This enables the investor to quantify both the return he *expects* to get and the risk of not achieving that return. The investor can then decide, according to the level of return he wishes to achieve and the amount of risk he is willing to bear, which securities he prefers. If he is averse to taking on risk, he will prefer the securities which offer the least risk for any given return or the most return for any given level of risk. We will assume that the average investor on the Stock Exchange is what is known as 'risk averse'.

The concept of utility, which combines the attitudes of each investor to both risk and return into one measure, is then discussed. Utility also takes into account the wealth of the investor and so each security must be analysed to see how its returns will affect the investor's wealth. Utility enables the investor, if he knows his utility function (which he can estimate by evaluating his attitude to certain risk–return alternatives) to calculate the expected utility of each investment opportunity. All he then has to do is to choose the one which offers him the highest expected utility.

The chapter concludes with a section on two ways of reducing risk without reducing expected return. These are 'pooling' and 'hedging' and the Stock Exchange investor can apply these methods of reducing risk by diversifying his securities portfolio (discussed in detail in Chapter 7) and by making use of the various futures markets referred to in the text.

Holding period return

Any investor, when deciding on which securities he wishes to hold in his portfolio, has to be able to compare them directly. Each security is characterised by a market price, the cost of the security, and a pattern of cash flows. Suppose share A cost 486p and, at the end of six months, paid a dividend of 20p before it was sold for 500p. How can it be compared with share B, bought at 30p, held for one year and then sold for 35p with no dividend payment? Obviously the different costs of the shares must be taken into account, as well as the different time periods involved.

Return

Calculating the percentage holding period return for each security avoids the problem of comparing different size investments. This return is simply the gain during the period held (money received less cost) divded by the cost. So,

$$R = \frac{D_1 + P_1 - P_0}{P_0} \tag{2.1}$$

where P_0 is the cost, P_1 the value of the investment at the end of the holding period and D_1 any interest or dividend payments made during the period. Using equation (2.1), the holding period returns of shares A and B can be calculated and compared as in Table 2.1.

Table 2.1   Holding period returns of A and B

Share	Holding period return	Holding period (months)
A	$R_A = \dfrac{(20 + 500) - 486}{486}$	
	$= 0.070$	
	$\boldsymbol{R_A = 7.0\%}$	6
B	$R_B = \dfrac{(0 + 35) - 30}{30}$	
	$= 0.167$	
	$\boldsymbol{R_B = 16.7\%}$	12

The holding period returns of *A* and *B* are not yet directly comparable since *B* was invested for twice as long as *A*. When *A* was sold, the proceeds could have been reinvested for another six months but we do not know what return would have been available to the investor at that time. An alternative solution would be to calculate the equivalent six-monthly return on *B*. This is done in Table 2.2 by equating the return on money invested for two six-month periods, at a return r_B per period, to money invested for an equivalent one-year period at return R_B, the one-year holding period return.

We can now compare *A*, which offered a return of 7% over six months, with *B* which offered a higher return over the same period of 8%.

Most investors would no doubt choose the investment which offered the highest return over any particular period. If we look at Table 2.3 to see which investments have typically yielded the highest returns in the past, we note that ordinary shares have, on average, out-performed long-term gilts on annual return over the past sixty years.

Table 2.2   Six-month holding period return

Suppose £100 is invested for 6 months at 5%

At the end of 6 months, it will be worth

   £100 (1 + 0.05) = £105

If reinvested for another 6 months at 5% it will be worth

   £105 (1 + 0.05) = £110.25

or

   $£100 (1 + 0.05)^2$

If we define r_B to be the six-monthly return equivalent to an annual holding period return on *B* of R_B, we can write

   $(1 + r_B)^2 = 1 + R_B$

We know $R_B = 16.7\%$ or 0.167, giving

   $(1 + r_B)^2 = 1.167$

Solving,

   $r_B = 0.080$

   $\mathbf{r_B = 8.0\%}$

Table 2.3   *Returns and risk of different types of security*

1923–80	Annual average return (%)	Range of returns (%)
Long-term gilts	4.9	−16 to +52
Ordinary shares	13.0	−47 to +157

Source: London Business School, *Risk Measurement Service,* July–September 1981.

With this evidence before him, the investor would surely always buy shares. And yet, many investors choose gilts or hold at least some gilts in their investment portfolio. The reason why people invest in gilts can be seen from the third column in Table 2.3, which shows the *variation* in annual return achieved on shares and gilts. Although gilts have offered a lower return on average, they have also offered less chance of a large negative return or loss. This means that the investor cannot just look at return alone when making investment decisions, he must also consider *risk*.

Types of risk

There are several different types of risk which can lead to variability in return on a security. Some securities, such as gilts, will have few risks attached to them, whereas company shares will be subject to many possible reasons for fluctuations in return. One of the risks to which only ordinary shares are subject is uncertainty of income.

Uncertainty of income

The risk of uncertainty of income is a risk to which all ordinary shareholders are subject. This can be seen by looking at the holding period return on an ordinary share, which can be written as

$$R = \frac{D_1 + P_1 - P_0}{P_0}$$

where D_1 is the dividend expected to be paid during the holding period, P_0 the share purchase price and P_1 the price at the end of the period.

When we considered shares A and B, we knew the values of D_1, P_0 and P_1 because in that case we were looking at *past* returns achieved on the investments. Unfortunately, an investor is always making investment decisions concerning the future. All he knows is P_0, the current market price of the share. He has no idea what the share price will be when he sells it, nor what dividend payments he will receive. In contrast with its fixed interest securities, such as debentures or loan stocks, a company does *not* contract to pay its ordinary shareholders any fixed or even minimum level of dividend.

Ordinary shareholders own the assets of the company after all other claims on it have been satisfied but the company is under no obligation to pay out these shareholders' funds as dividends. Probably only part of the total profit attributable to ordinary shareholders in any one year will be paid out as dividends, the remainder being retained within the company. If a company is doing well, the ordinary shareholder will expect both to receive a dividend D_1 and for the share price P_1 to exceed P_0, reflecting the retention of earnings by the company.[1]

However, if the company does badly, it does not have to make any payments to ordinary shareholders as it does to its debt-holders. The profitability of any company is subject to certain risks. For example, an economic recession could lead to a reduction in sales, or a political decision could mean higher tax payments. Technical change could render the company's products obsolescent or, on a simpler level, an event such as a fire could wipe out some of the assets of the company. These factors render the profits of the company uncertain and, since ordinary shareholders are entitled only to the balance of income and capital after all other security holders have been paid, ordinary shares are the most risky of all securities. On the other hand, ordinary shareholders stand to gain more than fixed interest security-holders, whose return is more limited.

Corporate fixed interest debt-holders suffer, as we have mentioned above, less uncertainty of income since they are promised specific interest payments by the company. However, they are subject to another type of risk, the risk of default.

Default risk

If a company does badly, it may be unable to pay the interest on a fixed interest security or to repay the principal on maturity. Only gilts, fixed interest securities issued or guaranteed by the UK government, are not subject to default risk; the government is the only borrower which can

---

[1] Some fast-growing companies have a policy of paying no dividends at all over a period of years. In these cases the holding period return is purely the capital gain or loss, $P_1 - P_0$.

always avoid default in the last resort by printing more money.

All types of fixed interest corporate debt are subject to default risk, from debenture stocks secured on the assets of the company to unsecured loan stocks,[2] but each will be subject to a different *level* of risk of losing on their investment. On default, debenture holders can appoint a receiver whose job it is to realise the security they hold and, if it is worth at least the sum they are owed,[3] will suffer no loss. Unsecured loan stock holders have no security and rank equal with the other unsecured creditors of the company.

Corporate fixed interest securities do not represent a major part of the Stock Exchange in this country (less than 1% of 1980 turnover and 1.3% of 1980 market value), but in the US they are an important form of investment. Each major US company will have several corporate bonds, each with carefully defined rights to the assets of the company in the event of default. For example, a 'subordinated' debenture means that it comes lower down in the queue than an 'unsubordinated' debenture, and will only be entitled to payment, in the event of default, after the unsubordinated debenture holders have been fully repaid. Table 2.4 shows an extract from the *Wall Street Journal* giving market information on just a few US corporate bonds. Opinions on the credit-worthiness and hence the default risk of these bonds, from AAA for, say, a highly rated bond to C or D for bonds which are probably already in default, are provided by Moody's and by Standard & Poors.

Ordinary shareholders do not suffer default risk since they are not entitled to any particular level of income or to any prespecified repayment which might run the risk of not being paid. Preference shareholders[4] lie somewhere between fixed interest debt-holders and ordinary shareholders; although they are entitled to fixed interest payments, if these are not made, the company is not legally in default, since preference shareholders are part-owners and not creditors of the company.

Other risks

It is easy to see why securities issued by companies, even if they promise a fixed income, have an element of risk. In an uncertain and competitive world some companies may well fail and, given that companies have

---

[2] Debenture stocks, unsecured loan stocks and preference shares are described at the end of Chapter 4, pp. 116–20.
[3] Net of the costs of using the receiver to realise the security.
[4] Preference shares are described at the end of Chapter 4, pp. 119–20.

Table 2.4 US Corporate Bonds

New York Exchange Bonds

Friday, October 15, 1982

Total Volume $41,430,000

	Domestic Fri.	Domestic Thu.	All Issues Fri.	All Issues Thu.
Issues traded	1120	1177	1132	1189
Advances	397	567	403	574
Declines	544	398	548	400
Unchanged	179	212	181	214
New highs	229	395	233	401
New lows	1	1	1	1

SALES SINCE JANUARY 1

1982	1981	1980
$5,214,504,000	$4,176,414,000	$3,807,373,000

Dow Jones Bond Averages

–1980– High	–1980– Low	–1981– High	–1981– Low	–1982– High	–1982– Low		FRIDAY –1982–	FRIDAY –1981–	FRIDAY –1980–
76.61	60.96	65.78	54.99	69.06	55.67	20 Bonds	69.04 – .02	56.75 – .15	67.37 – .09
78.63	59.40	66.18	53.61	70.72	53.80	10 Utilities	70.18 – .54	56.11 – .17	66.47 – .04
74.92	61.55	66.15	56.32	67.91	57.36	10 Industrial	67.91 + .51	57.40 – .12	68.27 – .15

Bonds	Cur Yld	Vol	High	Low	Close	Net Chg.
ConEd 5s87	6.7	12	75¾	74½	74½	–1¼
ConEd 4⅜s92V	7.6	18	57¾	55⅛	57¾	+1⅝
ConEd 4⅜s92W	7.5	9	58	56½	58	– ½
ConEd 4⅝s93	8.4	5	55	55	55	–3
ConEd 9⅝s00	12.	20	79	77	77	–2½
ConEd 7.9s01	12.	49	68½	68	68½	–1⅜
ConEd 7.9s02	12.	3	67¾	67¾	67¾	–1¾
ConEd 7¾s03	12.	12	66½	66	66	–1½
ConEd 8.4s03	12.	2	71	69⅝	69⅝	–1⅞
ConEd 9⅛s04	12.	4	75¾	75½	75¾	–2¼
ConGs 2¾s86	3.6	1	75½	75½	75½	– ⅝
CnNG 5s85	5.8	1	86	86	86	.....
CnNG 4¾s86	6.0	1	79½	79½	79½	.....
CnNG 8¼s94	11.	1	72½	72½	72½	+ ⅝
CnNG 9s95	12.	1	78¼	78¼	78¼	+ ¾
CnNG M 8⅜s96	12.	5	71⅛	71⅛	71⅛	–1⅞
CnNG 7¾s96	12.	15	65⅝	65⅝	65⅝	+1⅝
CnPw 4⅝s91	7.9	8	58⅞	58⅞	58⅞	+ ⅞
CnPw 6⅞s98	12.	15	56½	56½	56½	– ¼
CnPw 6⅝s98	12.	10	54	54	54	– ⅛
CnPw 7⅜s99	12.	29	62	60⅝	62	– ½
CnPw 8⅝s00	13.	2	65	65	65	+2⅜
CnPw 8⅛s01	13.	15	63⅜	63	63⅜	+ ¼
CnPw 7½s02J	13.	27	59	58¼	59	–1
CnPw 7½s02O	13.	25	58	58	58	–1⅜
CnPw 8⅜s03	13.	49	65⅞	65	65½	+ ½
CnPw 11½s00	14.	15	83⅞	83⅜	83⅞	–1⅛
CnPw 9¾s06	13.	84	74	72⅛	73⅜	+1
CnPw 9s06	13.	5	68½	68½	68½	.....
CnPw 8⅞s07	13.	27	67⅜	66	67	– ⅝
CnPw 8⅜s07	13.	70	66⅛	65	65⅛	–1¼
CnPw 9s08	13.	10	69¼	69¼	69¼	.....
CtlAir 3½s92	cv	5	32	32	32	–1
CtlCan 5¾s85	6.8	5	84⅞	84⅞	84⅞	+4⅞
Ct IC 8½s85	9.7	50	88	88	88	+1
CtlOil 8⅞s01	12.	25	77	77	77	+1¼
CtlTl 10½s83	11.	2	99 1-32	99 1-32	99 1-32	..
CoopL 4½s92	cv	11	116	116	116	–1
CornG 7¾s98	11.	1	73	73	73	+5
Crane 6½s92	11.	10	59½	59½	59½	.....
Crane 7s94	13.	30	55⅞	54⅛	55⅞	–1⅛
Crane 10½s94	13.	3	82	82	82	+1
CrdF 8s92	12.	3	69	69	69	–4⅞
CrocN 5¾s96	cv	1	70	70	70	+1⅞
CrwnZ 8⅞s00	13.	5	70	70	70	.....
Culb 11½s05	14.	1	80	80	80	–7
CumE 8⅞s95	12.	11	73½	73½	73½	+5¾
Dana d5⅞s06	cv	25	55	54½	54⅞	– ⅛
DatGen 13s05	13.	15	98	98	98	–1
Datpnt 8⅞s06	cv	155	66½	65½	66	– ½
Dayc 5¾s94	cv	5	49½	49½	49½	+ ⅜
Dayc 6s94	cv	15	52	52	52	.....
DaytH 9¾s95	12.	2	82	82	82	+1½
DaytP 8⅛s01	12.	20	65⅝	65½	65½	.....
DaytP 8s03	13.	3	64	64	64	–2⅞
DaytP 8¾s06	13.	15	66	66	66	+7⅞
DaytP 17s91	15.	50	113	113	113	+1
Deere 4½s83	4.8	1	94¼	94¼	94¼	+7-32
Deere 7.9s87	9.1	30	87½	87	87	– ¼
Deere 10½s85	11.	47	98	96¾	98	+1½
DetEd 6s96	12.	10	51	51	51	–3
DetEd 9.15s00	13.	54	69	68½	69	+ ¼
DetEd 8⅛s01	13.	6	62½	62	62	– ½
DetEd 7⅞s01	13.	23	57¾	57½	57¾	– ¼
DetEd 7½s03	13.	20	58	58	58	–2
DetEd 9⅞s04	13.	31	75	73¼	74	–1⅛
DetEd 11⅞s00	13.	20	89½	88	89½	– ½
DiaSTel 7s08	12.	10	58⅜	58⅜	58⅜	+3⅜
Divers 10½s91	17.	2	60½	60½	60½	.....
DmBk 7¾s96	13.	2	62	62	62	.....
Dow 6.70s98	11.	4	60	60	60	+1¼
Dow 8⅞s2000	12.	19	76	74½	74½	+1⅞
Dow 8.9s2000	12.	12	73½	72⅞	72⅞	–1
Dow 8½s05	12.	20	73½	72½	72½	–1¾
Dow 7⅞s07	12.	14	67⅛	67	67	–1
Dow 8⅝s08	12.	10	73½	72½	72½	–1⅜
duPnt 8.45s04	11.	10	76	76	76	–1
duPnt 8s86	8.7	20	93⅛	91⅞	91⅞	–1⅛
GTCal 8⅞s96	12.	12	72	72	72	.....
GWat 8¾s96	13.	12	70	70	70	–1
GaPac 5¼s96	cv	29	82½	82	82½	+ ½
GaPw 8⅞s00	13.	5	70	70	70	–2
GaPw 7⅞s01	12.	29	60½	59⅝	60½	.....
GaPw 8⅛s01	13.	10	62	62	62	–3
GaPw 7⅝s01	13.	17	61	61	61	–3¾
GaPw 7½s02J	13.	20	58⅜	58⅜	58⅜	–1⅞
GaPw 8⅝s04	13.	3	67¼	67¼	67¼	–2⅜
GaPw 11¾s05	13.	39	91	88	88	–2½
GaPw 14½s10	14.	10	103¾	103	103	.....
GaPw 16⅛s11	15.	16	109¾	109½	109½	– ½
GaPw 16¼s11	15.	24	108¾	107¾	108⅜	+ ⅛
GaPw 16¼s12	15.	10	109	109	109	.....
Getty 10s87	10.	5	98⅞	98⅞	98⅞	.....
GloMar 12⅞s98	17.	60	74½	74½	74½	.....
GloMr d16s01	18.	176	87½	86⅜	87¼	+ ½
GloMar 16⅛s02	18.	444	87¼	86¾	87¼	+ ½
GdNgt 12¼s94	14.	13	85	85	85	.....
Gdrch 8¼s94	13.	7	63½	63½	63½	.....
Gdrch 7s97	13.	3	53½	53½	53½	–1½
Gdrch 9¾s82	9.8	40	99⅛	99⅛	99⅛	–1-32
Grace 4¼s90	cv	2	75⅛	75⅛	75⅛	+ ⅛
Grace 12⅝s90	13.	5	100½	100½	100½	+ ½
GtNoR 2⅝s10	9.7	6	27	27	27	–1
Greyh 6½s90	cv	60	87½	87	87½	– ½
Greyh 9⅝s01	13.	13	74	72	72	+1
GreyF 9.7s84	10.	4	96	96	96	.....
GreyF 16⅛s92	15.	10	104⅜	104⅜	104⅜	+ ⅜
Grum 4¼s92	cv	8	130	130	130	+3¾
GlfWn 6s88	8.6	1	70⅛	70⅛	70⅛	.....
GlfWn 7s03A	13.	37	53¼	53	53¼	+ ¼
GlfWn 7s03B	13.	16	53	53	53	.....
GlfMG 4s44	9.3	2	43	43	43	–2
GlfOil 8½s95	10.	65	84	82½	82½	–1½
GlfOil 13½s09	15.	56	93¼	92	92½	– ⅜
GlfStU 3⅜s83	3.7	10	91	91	91	+7½
GlfUtd 9¼s05	cv	21	107	106	107	+1
GlfUtd 9¼s06	cv	12	106	106	106	.....
Hallb 16s88	14.	80	112¼	112¼	112¼	.....
HamP 5s94	cv	25	68¼	68¼	68¼	.....
Hellr 9½s89	12.	61	81	80	80	– ⅛
Hellr 9⅛s91	12.	33	78½	76⅜	76⅜	–2⅜
Hercul 6½s99	cv	18	84	82½	82½	– ½
Honey 14⅛s11	14.	1	102⅜	102⅜	102⅜	+ ⅛
HookC 4⅞s91	9.2	10	53	53	53	–1½
HoCp 10¾s90	13.	4	84⅞	84⅞	84⅞	+2⅞
HoCp 8¾s06	cv	37	126	125¼	126	.....
HousL 5½s85	cv	5	91	91	91	–1
HugheT 9½s06	cv	129	91	88½	90	+1
Humn 11.7s98	13.	113	88⅜	87⅝	87⅝	–1⅛
Hutton 12s05	13.	24	90⅝	87¾	90⅝	+1½
Hutton 9½s05	cv	41	120	118	119½	+ ½
IBM Cr 14⅜s86	14.	60	107	106	106	–1¼
ICI 8⅞s03	13.	10	67	67	67	+1¼
ITTF 11¼s85	12.	25	97	97	97	.....
ITTF 8½s02	14.	2	61⅞	61⅞	61⅞	+ ⅛
ITTF 11s88	12.	4	95	95	95	–3
IllBel 7⅝s06	11.	21	69½	68½	68½	– ¼
IllBel 8s04	11.	5	71	71	71	– ¼
IllBel 8¼s16	12.	7	71¼	71¼	71¼	– ⅜
IllPw 12⅝s10	13.	6	99	99	99	+2⅞
Inco 6.85s93	13.	150	53¼	52½	53	+ ½
Inco 12⅞s10	15.	23	83⅞	82	83⅞	+1⅞
InMic 11s83	11.	4	99½	99½	99½	+1¼
InMic 10¼s87	11.	10	90⅛	90⅛	90⅛	+1½
InMP 10⅞s84	11.	19	98	97⅛	97⅛	– ⅞
IndBel 10s14	12.	10	84⅛	83	83	–3
IndBel 8s14	11.	25	69⅝	69⅝	69⅝	+ ⅛
Inexc 8½s00	cv	38	75	74	74½	+1½
IngR 8¾s85	9.4	7	93	93	93	– ½
InldStl 4½s89	7.8	5	57⅝	57⅝	57⅝	–2⅜
InldStl 7.9s07	14.	25	57½	57	57	.....
InldStl 11¼s90	13.	15	85	85	85	–2
Intrfst 7¾s05	cv	18	101	101	101	.....
IBM 9½s86	9.9	133	95½	94	95½	– ¼
IBM 9⅜s04	11.	1014	88½	86	87¼	–1⅜
IntHrv 4⅝s88	12.	4	40	40	40	.....

Source: *The Wall Street Journal*, 18 October 1982. Reprinted by permission of *Wall Street Journal*, © Dow Jones & Company, Inc. (1982).

limited liability, investors in these companies will, in the last resort, only have recourse to the assets remaining within the company which may not be sufficient to repay their investments in full. It is less easy, though, to understand why fixed interest securities issued by the British government offer uncertain returns.

The British government first borrowed from the City of London in the sixteenth century although the secondary market in government securities only became fully developed in the nineteenth century when London was the financial centre of the world. These securities came to be known as gilts because there was absolutely no risk of default. There was never any doubt that the government would pay the interest or repay on maturity, since the government could create the money when needed. In fact, in the nineteenth century, a group of people called the 'three percenters' lived on unearned income from investment in gilt-edged stocks which provided an annual return on capital of around 3%. With a £5,000 investment in gilts, the annual income of £150 was sufficient to maintain a family in middle-class ease.

However, inflation and rapidly changing interest rates have dealt a blow to the stability of gilt prices. For example, Treasury 3% are currently quoted at around £30 for £100 nominal.

Yield on gilts

Before we can fully analyse the risks inherent in investing in gilts, we must understand more about the return, or yield as it is known, of gilts.

Let us again consider 2½% Consols,[5] one of the undated gilts. The term 'undated' means that the government promises to pay £2.50 per annum (for every £100 held) indefinitely. The quoted price of 2½% Consols always refers to £100 nominal of the stock. However, each year the £2.50 received by the investor will appear less valuable to him. £2.50 received now is worth more than £2.50 received next year because it can be invested to yield more than £2.50 in one year's time. Suppose the current one-year interest rate is 10%. £2.50 could be invested to become £2.50 × (1.10) or £2.75 in twelve months' time and so £2.50 received in one year's time is only worth £2.50/(1.1) or £2.27 today. This £2.27 is known as the present value of £2.50. The present value of receiving £x in

---

[5] Gilts, such as 2½% Consols, 3% Treasury, etc. are described in detail in Chapter 3. 2½% Consols is just one of the UK government securities issued to the public to finance government borrowing. Holders of 2½% Consols are entitled to receive interest of £2.50 every year until such time as the government chooses to redeem them. Other gilts may have a specified date on which they will be redeemed. For simplicity, it is assumed that interest on 2½% Consols is paid annually.

the future is always less than £x because of the opportunity cost of not being able to invest the money in the interim. In other words, the investor has forgone the opportunity of investing £x for one year.

The investor can now calculate the present value of receiving a string of future £2.50s if he knows the prevailing interest rate, R, on equivalent investments.[6]

The present value of £100 nominal of 2½% Consols is P_0, and P_0 can be written as

$$P_0 = \frac{D}{(1 + R)} + \frac{D}{(1 + R)^2} + \dots \frac{D}{(1 + R)^n} + \dots \qquad (2.2)$$

where D represents the yearly interest payment of £2.50. Of course, the present value, P_0, of the gilt must be its market price if the market is efficient.[7] So, knowing P_0, the investor can determine R, called the discount rate because it is used to discount future cash flows, and which represents the actual rate of return he will get on his gilt-edged investment.[8]

Equation (2.2) is exactly equivalent to equation (2.1) on p. 37 for the holding period return:

$$R = \frac{D_1 + P_1 - P_0}{P_0} \qquad (2.1)$$

This can be seen in Table 2.5 where equation (2.1) is first rearranged to be an expression for the initial price P_0 and then the holding period is extended by one year at a time until the investment is assumed to be held indefinitely.

Equation (2.5) states that the price of an undated fixed interest stock is equal to its coupon (the nominal interest rate) divided by the required yield. The lower the coupon, relative to the required yield, the lower the price. If we substitute, say, a current market price of £20 for 2½% Consols we can find its required yield.

$$£20 = \frac{£2.50}{R}$$

$$R = 12.5\%$$

---

[6] In fact, there will be a string of different interest rates, $R_1, R_2, R_3 \dots$ for each future time period which will not necessarily all be the same. See Chapter 4 for a description of this yield curve.

[7] See Chapter 9 for the meaning of an 'efficient' stock market.

[8] Assuming the gilt is held indefinitely.

Table 2.5   Value of a fixed interest security   37

The holding period return is

$$R = \frac{D_1 + P_1 - P_0}{P_0} \tag{2.1}$$

Multiplying by P_0

$$RP_0 = D_1 + P_1 - P_0$$

$$P_0(1 + R)) = D_1 + P_1$$

$$P_0 = \frac{D_1}{(1 + R)} + \frac{P_1}{(1 + R)}$$

where P_1 is the price of the security at the end of the holding period, say one year. Now suppose the security is held for two years. We can write

$$P_0 = \frac{D_1}{(1 + R)} + \frac{D_2}{(1 + R)^2} + \frac{P_2}{(1 + R)^2}$$

where D_2 is the income received in year 2 and P_2 the price of the security at the end of the two years. If the security is held for n years we can write

$$P_0 = \frac{D_1}{(1 + R)} + \frac{D_2}{(1 + R)^2} + \dots \frac{D_n}{(1 + R)^n} + \frac{P_n}{(1 + R)^n}$$

In the special case of an undated gilt, such as 2½% Consols, this becomes

$$P_0 = \frac{D}{1 + R} + \frac{D}{(1 + R)^2} + \dots + \frac{D}{(1 + R)^n} + \dots \tag{2.2}$$

where D is the fixed annual interest payment received indefinitely.

Equation (2.2), for an undated gilt which will pay interest in perpetuity, can be simplified.

$$P = \frac{D}{(1 + R)} + \frac{D}{(1 + R)^2} + \dots + \frac{D}{(1 + R)^n} + \dots \tag{2.3}$$

If we multiply through by $(1 + R)$

$$(1 + R)P = D + \frac{D}{(1 + R)} + \dots + \frac{D}{(1 + R)^{n-1}} + \frac{D}{(1 + R)^n} + \dots \tag{2.4}$$

and subtract (2.3) from (2.4), most of the terms on the right-hand side cancel out because we have the same infinite series.

We are left with

$$(1 + R)P - P = D$$

$$P = \frac{D}{R} \tag{2.5}$$

Currently, investors require an annual return of 12½% on this undated gilt-edged stock. Because the coupon is so far below this, the price of £100 nominal is very low at £20. When Consols were issued, the required yield would have been around 2½–3% and the market price approximately equal to the nominal price of £100. Interest rates are now much higher and so the present value, or market price, of a stream of £2.50 interest payments is worth substantially less than its value 100 years or more ago.

This introduction to the yield on gilts now allows us to analyse the two main types of risk affecting all fixed interest securities including gilts, interest rate risk and inflation risk.

(i) INTEREST RATE RISK

Let us consider the case of an investor who purchases £100 nominal of 2½% Consols when the prevailing yield on the gilt is 10%. His purchase price, P_0, will be

$$P_0 = \frac{£2.50}{0.10} = £25$$

(A) Suppose, after one year, interest rates and hence required yields on gilts increase. The required yield on 2½% Consols rises to 15%. The market price of his gilt will be

$$P_1 = \frac{£2.50}{0.15} = £16.70$$

(B) Alternatively, suppose in that time the required yield on 2½% Consols falls to 5%. The market price in this case will be

$$P_1 = \frac{£2.50}{0.05} = £50$$

If the investor then sells the gilt, his return, if scenario (A) takes place, will be

$$\text{Return } R_A = \frac{D_1 + P_1 - P_0}{P_0} = \frac{2.50 + 16.70 - 25}{25}$$

$$R_A = -23\%$$

If scenario (B) takes place, his return will be

$$\text{Return } R_B = \frac{D_1 + P_1 - P_0}{P_0}$$

$$= \frac{2.50 + 50 - 25}{25}$$

$$R_B = 110\%$$

A change in interest rates has had a dramatic impact on the investor's return on his supposedly risk-free gilt. Only when interest rates, and hence prices of gilts, are stable can a gilt be truly considered risk-free.

So, an investor in an undated stock runs the risk that, when he wishes to dispose of the stock, interest rates will have risen and the value of his gilt fallen. How does interest rate risk operate on gilts which are not undated and have a finite life with explicit redemption dates?

Suppose the investor knows that he has a need for funds at a specified date in the future. For example, he has to repay a £10,000 loan in exactly five years' time. If he puts his money into gilts with longer than five years to run or, indeed, undated stocks, he runs the risk that interest rates will rise during the five years he will hold the stock and that, when he comes to sell the gilts to pay off his loan, their value will be less than the £10,000 he needs. On the other hand, if he invests in short-term gilts, with less than five years to run, he runs the opposite risk of a possible fall in interest rates. If the gilts mature before he needs the £10,000, he will have to reinvest them. This leaves the investor open to the risk that interest rates will fall before the gilts are repaid, so that he will only be able to reinvest the proceeds at a lower yield than if he had chosen gilts with the full five-year life. This example illustrates the fact that, unless an investor matches the maturity of his gilt-edged investments exactly with the maturity of his liabilities, in this case chooses gilts with a five-year life, he will expose himself to risks due to changes in interest rates. In fact, even if the investor matches maturities, the gilt will pay interest before maturity which he may not wish to spend. The interest may therefore have to be reinvested, perhaps at a lower rate than that yielded by the gilt.

Pension funds and insurance companies have commitments at specified dates in the future which they can quantify more or less exactly, for example maturing insurance policies and pension payments. These institutions can thus choose gilts which match their commitments and avoid to a great extent interest rate risk. Other investors are unlikely to be able to specify exactly *when* they will need money in the future and are probably unable to state the future value of these commitments. Life assurance payments or pensions may be expressed in nominal[9] terms which can be matched by the maturity of nominal amounts of gilts. In contrast, an investor wishing to buy a house in five years' time which costs £40,000 today does not know how much money he will then need to be able to afford an equivalent house. The *real* value of the house may remain constant, but inflation will increase the nominal cost of the house. For example, £60,000 may be needed in five years to be able to buy what £40,000 would buy today.

(ii) INFLATION RISK

This brings us to the second type of risk attached to gilts and in fact all other fixed interest securities. Suppose Mr Stone, wishing to buy a house which currently costs £40,000, invests a sufficient amount in gilts maturing in five years' time to repay him £40,000. He will probably find that this will not be enough to buy the house of his dreams. Even if he *expects* inflation to be such that he will need £60,000 in five years' time and he invests in gilts which will repay £60,000, Mr Stone still runs the risk that inflation will not be as he anticipated and he will need more (or less) than £60,000 to buy that house.

Let us look at a simple numerical example which brings out the impact of inflation.

Suppose Mrs Silver buys a gilt for £95 which only has one year to maturity, at which time she will receive the principal of £100 plus an interest payment of £5.

Mrs Silver's return on that gilt held for one year will be

$$R = \frac{D_1 + P_1 - P_0}{P_0}$$

$$R = \frac{(5 + 100) - 95}{95}$$

R = 10.5%

Now suppose she expects inflation to be 5% during the next year so that £105 in one year's time will have the same purchasing power as £100 now. Mrs Silver can calculate her expected real return by expressing all cash flows in current purchasing power terms.

---

[9] A future liability of £100 in nominal or money terms means that £100 will actually have to be paid out in the future. A future liability of £100 in *real* terms means that an unknown amount, £x, will have to be paid out, where £x then has the same purchasing power as £100 today.

$$\text{Expected real return } R_{Real} = \frac{100 - 95}{95} \times 100$$

$$R_{Real} = \mathbf{5.3\%}$$

There is no risk as yet in this investment decision. If the market as a whole requires a real rate of return of 5.3% on a one-year gilt, Fisher[10] has postulated that nominal interest rates (actual market interest rates) will fully reflect expected inflation. Thus, if inflation is expected to be 5%, the nominal interest rate can be calculated as follows:

$$(1 + \text{nominal}) = (1 + \text{real}) (1 + \text{expected inflation rate})^{11} \quad (2.6)$$

$$= (1.053) (1.05)$$

$$= 1.106$$

Nominal interest rate = **10.6%**

The market prices the gilt at £95 to take into account the expected 5% inflation. If no inflation were expected, the market price would be higher at £99.72.

$$P_0 = \frac{D_1 + P_1}{1 + R}$$

$$= \frac{105}{1.053}$$

$$= \mathbf{£99.72}$$

According to Fisher's theory, nominal interest rates rise to take account fully of expected inflation and this pushes down the prices of gilts. We now have an explanation of why gilt prices have fallen so dramatically over the past twenty years. The current purchasing power of £100 is one-fifth of what it was in 1960.

---

[10] See Irving Fisher (1930).

[11] This formula is often approximated to

Nominal IR = real IR + expected inflation rate

In this example, we would get

Nominal IR = 5.3% + 5%

= **10.3%**

So far, inflation risk is not a problem to Mrs Silver, provided she is aware of expected inflation and provided expected inflation is included in nominal interest rates as Fisher suggests. She will be able to compare investments and make investment decisions with equanimity. However, there are two factors which can make inflation risk a real risk.

Firstly, interest rates may not exactly adjust to expected inflation as Fisher predicts. However, it is difficult to test Fisher's theory since, although tests can be carried out to see whether interest rates have taken account of *actual* inflation, it is more difficult to determine whether interest rates have taken account of *expected* inflation, because of the difficulty of measuring expected inflation. (If interest rates do adjust in this way, one would expect investors to require the same *real* rate of interest on, say, gilts, over time, with the nominal, required return actually varying from this constant because of expected inflation.)

Secondly, even if expected inflation is fully catered for in market prices, *un*expected inflation can affect the real returns of investors and prevent Mr Stone from realising enough in real terms to buy his house.

Suppose Mrs Silver buys the gilt described above for £95 and that inflation during that year turns out to be 10%. The purchasing power of £105 received at the end of that year will only be £105/(1.1) or £95.45. So Mrs Silver's *actual* real return will be

$$R_{actual} = \frac{95.45 - 95}{95}$$

$$R_{actual} = 0.5\%$$

Inflation risk, in the sense that the actual real returns achieved on investments could be less than the expected real returns, is a risk for all types of fixed interest securities. So, Mrs Silver cannot avoid inflation risk by investing in particular fixed interest securities. However, if next year's inflation can be estimated more accurately than inflation in several years' time (and if nominal interest rates do fully take account of expected inflation), then Mrs Silver will suffer less inflation risk if she invests in short-term rather than long-term or undated securities – simply because current estimates of inflation are less likely to be wrong in the short rather than the long term. In that sense, Mrs Silver will suffer less inflation risk, the shorter-term the gilt she buys.[12]

However, although inflation risk is present to a greater or lesser extent when investing in any fixed interest security, it need not be attached to ordinary share investment. The dividends paid on shares are

---

[12] The impact of different amounts of inflation risk on different maturity gilts is discussed further in Chapter 4.

not fixed. If inflation is high, the company should be able to achieve high nominal profits and to pay out high nominal dividends. In fact, if the company has issued a substantial number of fixed interest securities, the value of the ordinary shares may increase by more than inflation to balance the loss incurred by the fixed interest security-holders whose investments are worth less because of inflation.

Measurement of risk and return

The previous section discussed the different types of risk attached to investment in securities – uncertainty of income, default risk, interest rate risk and inflation risk. As well as being subject to various types of risk, different securities suffer these risks to greater or lesser extents. However, whatever the risk, it is always reflected in the variability of returns achieved on any security and derives from the fact that we live in an uncertain world.

When looking into the future, we can predict different possible states of the world, for example the company whose loan stock we are considering buying may or may not default; the actual inflation rate, which we expected to be 5%, may turn out to be 10 or 8 or 3%. If only one possible state could occur, we would live in a certain world with certain returns on investment and zero risk.

Having identified the different types of risk which exist and realising that they are the result of the possibility of different states of the world occurring in the future, how can we quantify the risk and likely return of any investment?

We use probabilities to attach numbers to the likelihood of each possible state of the world occurring. For example, suppose we look at what happened to £100 invested in company X shares at the beginning of each year for the past fifty years. What were the end-of-year values of

Table 2.6   *Frequency distribution of the value of one-year investments of £100 in company X in each of the last fifty years*

End-of-year value £	Frequency with which value occurred
104	10
106	15
108	15
110	10
	50

the investment in each of those fifty years? Suppose we find that the end-of-year value was £104 in ten of those years, £106 in fifteen years and so on as in Table 2.6.

What can we say about the end-of-year value of £100 invested now in company X? If the factors underlying company X's share performance are fundamentally unchanged, we can convert these long-run frequencies of past returns into probabilities concerning the future. We can say that there is a probability of 10 in 50 or a 0.2 chance that the value will be £104 giving a 4% return and so on, as in Table 2.7.

These probabilities (p_i) add up to one because we have taken into account all eventualities and no more than one of these could occur. (The states of the world considered are, in other words, exhaustive and mutually exclusive.) All we have done here is apply the way we think about, say, cards to investments in shares. Since there are four aces in a pack we deduce that there is a probability of 4 in 52 or 1 in 13 that an ace will be picked at random from the full pack. What we mean by this is that if we pick cards at random often enough from the full pack we will expect one out of every thirteen picked to be an ace. We are using long-run average frequencies to estimate the likelihood of future events.

Probabilities derived from inspecting past frequencies are known as 'objective' probabilities. They have been calculated by looking at actual past events. With investments in securities, objective probabilities can be calculated by looking at the frequency distribution of returns the security has achieved in the past. If a particular share has provided variable returns in the past and if it has not fundamentally changed its business, it is likely to be equally volatile in the future. Frequency distributions will therefore provide a good picture of what may happen in the future. Alternatively, data on past performance may not be available or factors affecting the security's return may have altered. In this case, 'subjective' probabilities based on the best estimates of the investor or his advisors will have to be used to provide the probability distribution of future returns.

Table 2.7   Probability distribution of end-of-year values of £100 invested now in company X

Value at end of year £	Holding period return on investment (%)	Probability P_i
104	4	0.2
106	6	0.3
108	8	0.3
110	10	0.2
		1.0

Expected return

Armed with our probability distribution, we still need to measure risk and return to be able to compare investments. We have an idea of the different returns which are likely, but is there one figure which will give us the best estimate of the return we will actually achieve? The most likely outcome, known as the mode (the one with the highest probability), is either 6% or 8% in this example – both have a probability of 0.3. This measure of return is inconvenient if there is, as in this case, more than one mode in the probability distribution. The median, defined to be that return where there is a 50% chance that the actual return will be less than or more than this figure, must, in our example, lie somewhere between 6 and 8%. The median, as with the mode, does not take into account all the possible returns in the distribution.

The third possible estimate of the future return is the mean or expected return. This is the average of all the possible returns weighted by their probabilities. It is equivalent to the *average* return one would expect to get if one kept on investing each year in company X. The expected return gives a single figure which takes into account all possible returns and which is useful statistically as we shall see later. For these reasons, and because it is intuitively easy to understand, the expected return is the measure normally used for estimating future, uncertain returns.

$$\text{Expected return} = p_1 R_1 + p_2 R_2 + p_3 R_3 + \dots + p_n R_n$$

where each R_i $(i = 1,\dots,n)$ is a possible return and p_i the probability that this return will occur

In this case, the expected return $E(R)$ is

$$E(R) = p_1 R_1 + p_2 R_2 + p_3 R_3 + p_4 R_4$$

$$E(R) = (0.2 \times 4) + (0.3 \times 6) + (0.3 \times 8) + (0.2 \times 10)$$

$$= 7\%$$

More generally we can write $E(R)$ as

$$E(R) = \sum_{i=1}^{i=n} p_i R_i \tag{2.7}$$

where Σ is a summation sign indicating that we should add together as many $p_i R_i$ terms as there are.

At the beginning of the chapter, we compared securities by looking at their actual returns. Because we were looking at historic returns, we knew the P_0, P_1 and D_1 for each security and hence its return, R. When comparing future investments to be made in an uncertain world, the values of P_1 and even D_1 may not be known in advance. Estimates of the possible returns which could be achieved and the probabilities of these returns must be made and, from these estimates, the *expected* return can be calculated. Securities can therefore be compared by looking not at their actual but at their expected returns.

Definition of risk

However, we know that in a risky world, we would not necessarily always buy the security which offered the highest expected return because each security will have a different level of risk attached to it. For example, suppose an investor is comparing the two investment opportunities, each costing £100, described in Table 2.8.

In this example, both A and B offer the same expected return. The investor cannot choose between them on the basis of expected return alone. He needs to consider the risks of A and B, firstly to see whether they are worth purchasing at all and secondly to see which of A and B he prefers.

Intuitively we can see that security B is riskier than A but how do we

Table 2.8   *Comparison of risk and return of securities A and B*

	Value at end of year £	Return (%)	Probability
Security A	110	+10	0.3
	120	+20	0.4
	130	+30	0.3
			1.0

Expected return of A: $0.3 \times 10 + 0.4 \times 20 + 0.3 \times 30 = $ **20%**

	Value at end of year £	Return (%)	Probability
Security B	60	−40	0.3
	120	+20	0.4
	180	+80	0.3
			1.0

Expected return of B: $0.3 \times -40 + 0.4 \times 20 + 0.3 \times 80 = $ **20%**

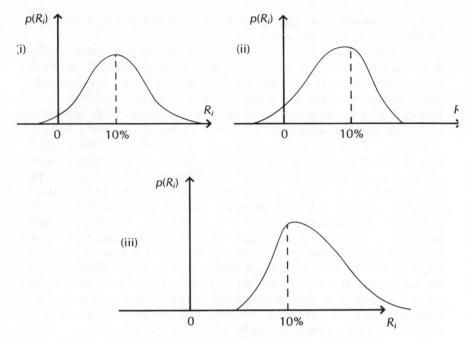

Figure 2.1   Normal and skewed probability distributions

measure that risk? Is it the risk relative to the initial investment of £100 or relative to the expected value of £120? If security *B* becomes worth £60, the investor will actually lose £40 in cash but he will lose £60 relative to the *expected* value of *B*. The £60 will be the more relevant figure, since not only will the investor have lost £40, if *B* turns out to be worth £60, but he will also have lost the opportunity of investing his £100 in something else of equivalent risk which could have yielded him £20. His concern will therefore be with how different the return could be from £120.

Another problem in deciding on how to measure risk is whether the investor is concerned only with downside risk (risk that the return will be *less* than he expects) or the risk that the return will be more *or* less than he expects. Consider the probability distributions in Figure 2.1. They all have the same expected return of 10%.

Figure 2.1(i) shows a normal distribution. This is the well-known probability distribution which occurs when a number of random and separate possibilities are envisaged. It is symmetric, which means that the distribution below the expected value is the mirror image of the distribution above the expected value. Thus, in this case of a normal probability distribution, any measure of downside risk (the risk that the return will be *less* than expected) will give the same result as a measure of total dispersion about the expected value (the risk that the return will be less *or* more than expected).

On the other hand, if the distributions are skewed (not symmetrical), as in Figures 2.1(ii) and 2.1(iii), measures of downside risk and total dispersion do not give the same result. In Figure 2.1(ii), the downside risk is greater than the risk of doing better than expected, whereas in Figure 2.1(iii) the opposite is the case. A measure of total dispersion would not be able to distinguish between Figures 2.1(ii) and 2.1(iii).

However, a measure of total dispersion, the standard deviation, is the most common measure of risk used in the theory of investment. There are three major reasons for this. Firstly, if security return distributions are normal, as in Figure 2.1(i), the expected return and standard deviation are the only two measures needed to describe fully the probability distribution. It is also true, in this case, that the standard deviation is equivalent to a measure of downside risk. Secondly, most frequency distributions of past security returns do appear to conform more to normal than to skewed distributions. Even if they are not exactly normal, it is a statistical fact that the returns of a portfolio made up of a collection of such securities will be normal and most people do hold portfolios of securities. Thirdly, the standard deviation is a particularly easy measure to handle as we shall see below.

The remainder of this book will assume that the standard deviation adequately quantifies the total risk of investing in a security – the uncertainty surrounding the actual returns which will be achieved. The greater the uncertainty, the greater the standard deviation and vice versa. If there is no uncertainty, that is the return is known for certain, the dispersion, and hence the standard deviation, will be zero. However, we cannot be sure that investors do regard the standard deviation as an adequate measure. They may prefer another measure of risk altogether (such as the maximum possible cash loss from an investment, which does not require knowledge of the full probability distribution of returns) or they may require more than one measure of risk, perhaps needing a measure for skewness as well as dispersion. Nevertheless, the above-mentioned attractions of the standard deviation have led to its supremacy as a measure of risk, and until more is known about how investors do quantify risk, the standard deviation is an adequate and simple measure.

Measurement of risk

The formula for the standard deviation of a probability distribution is rather complicated to look at but simple to understand. The square of the standard deviation, known as the variance, is usually calculated first.

Table 2.9   Calculation of variance

End-of-year return R_i	Dispersion $E(R)-R_i$	Square of dispersion $(E(R) - R_i)^2$	Probability p_i	$(E(R)-R_i)^2 p_i$
4	3	9	0.2	1.8
6	1	1	0.3	0.3
8	−1	1	0.3	0.3
10	−3	9	0.2	1.8
$E(R) = 7\%$	0	20	1.0	$V = 4.2$

$V = 4.2$

$S = \sqrt{V}$

$S = \sqrt{4.2} = \textbf{2.1\%}$

The standard deviation, S, is 2.1%

The variance is the sum of the *squares* of the dispersions around the expected return, $E(R)$, weighted by their probabilities (as for the expected return). Squares are used because if actual dispersions were added they cancel each other out and sum to zero. So we can calculate the variance, V, as

$$V = \sum_{i = 1}^{i = n} \left((E(R) - R_i)^2 \, p_i(R_i) \right) \tag{2.8}$$

The standard deviation S is then the square root of V. In Table 2.9 we use the investment in shares of company X, described in Table 2.7, as an example.

As an exercise, check that the standard deviations of securities A and B, described in Table 2.8, are 8% and 46% respectively. The standard deviation is always expressed in the same units as the expected return and is intuitively easier to use than the variance, especially with a normal distribution. With a normal distribution, we can say that there is approximately a 2 in 3 (more accurately, 68.3%) chance that the return will actually be within + or − 1 standard deviation of the expected value. For example, if the expected return on a security is 10% and its standard deviation (on a normal distribution) is 2%, there is a 2 in 3 chance that the return will actually be between 8 and 12%. Similarly, there is only 1 chance in 100 that the return will lie outside the range 5–15%. These generalisations cannot be applied to securities A and B of Table 2.8 since their probability distributions are only very simple approximations to a normal distribution.

Knowing only the expected returns of *A* and *B* did not allow the investor to make any investment decisions under uncertainty. Knowing both their expected returns and their risks now enables the investor to do two things:

(i) decide whether *A* and *B* offer sufficient reward in the form of expected return for their risks;

(ii) assuming both *A* and *B* are attractive investments, decide which of *A* and *B* to choose.

The theories discussed in this book assume the investor is averse to taking on risk – in other words, he requires more expected return before he will take on more risk. Since *A* has a lower standard deviation, for the same expected return, the investor will prefer *A*.

Expected utility

Although all investors are presumed risk averse, each investor will make different trade-off decisions between risk and expected return. This trade-off will be affected by such factors as unwillingness to bear risk which will be reflected in how much additional expected return the investor requires for taking on an additional unit of risk. Similarly, another factor will be how much the investment could affect the investor's total wealth. A potential loss of £1,000 would probably worry a millionaire less than someone with earnings of £100 per week.

The concept of utility allows the investor to combine his attitudes to risk and return at different levels of wealth into one measure – utility of wealth. Utility in this case can be thought of as the satisfaction the individual gets from different amounts of wealth. The different probable outcomes of any investment will lead to different probable levels of wealth. If an investor knows how much utility he will get from each level of wealth, he can calculate his *expected* utility from each investment – just as he can determine the expected return of any investment. He will then choose any investment which increases his expected utility and, in particular, those which increase it most.[13] Each investor will have a different utility function which will lead to his preferring different investments.

As an example, let us consider Mr Black who is evaluating the investments described in Table 2.10.

[13] In order for an investor to wish to maximise expected utility, we assume he is rational, i.e. prefers more wealth to less wealth, etc. See Francis and Archer (1979), ch. XI for a more detailed discussion of utility functions. We need to calculate *expected* utility because we are dealing with uncertain returns.

7

Table 2.10 Comparison of securities I and J with different expected returns and different risks

Security	Cost of investment £	Value at end of year £	Return R_i (%)	Probability P_i	Expected return $E(R)$	Standard deviation S (%)
I	100	105	5	0.5	10	5
		115	15	0.5		
J	100	102	2	0.5	12	10
		122	22	0.5		

Unlike the example in Table 2.8, the investments do not offer the same expected return nor do they have the same standard deviation. The choice is no longer as simple – it depends on whether Mr Black requires more or less than the additional 2% expected return offered by *B* in exchange for an additional 5% standard deviation. With a simple expected return/standard deviation analysis, Mr Black can choose only if he lays down rules such as 'no more than 7% standard deviation' (in which case he prefers *A*) or 'at least 12% return' (in which case he prefers *B*). However, knowledge of his utility function allows him to choose the one which maximises his expected utility. Suppose Mr Black has the following utility of wealth function where *W* is his wealth:

$$U(W) = 0.1W - 0.000025W^2 \qquad (2.9)$$

Equation (2.9) is a quadratic equation in *W*.[14] This means that, when plotted on a graph (as in Figure 2.2 on p. 53), Mr Black's utility function is a curve with a decreasing slope, the larger *W*. We shall see later that this type of curve implies that Mr Black is risk averse. In other words, he requires a higher expected return, the higher the risk of the investment.

---

[14] A quadratic equation of the type $Y = f(x)$ is one which has a squared term in x

$$Y = a + bx + cx^2$$

where a, b and c are constants. The equation of a straight line does not have a squared term in x:

$$Y = a + bx$$

Utility functions for risk averse investors do not have to be quadratic, for example, we can have $U = a + bW + cW^2 + dW^3$ (cubic), etc. See Francis and Archer (1979) for further details. However, if a probability distribution of returns is *not* normal, the investor's utility function has to be quadratic for expected return and standard deviation to be the only characteristics which concern him (that is, he is unconcerned about skewness).

In this example, we are concerned with whether Mr Black, given his particular utility function, prefers I or J. To ascertain this, we must know his current actual wealth – suppose it is £500. We now calculate the expected utility he would derive from each investment. We do this in the same way as we calculated expected return in equation (2.7). Thus, expected utility is simply the sum of the utilities attached to the possible wealth after investment, weighted by their probabilities. Expected utility of wealth, written $EU(W)$, is:

$$EU(W) = \sum_{i=1}^{i=n} p_i \, U(W_i) \tag{2.10}$$

The expected utilities of wealth after investing in I or J are shown in Table 2.11. Mr Black's *current* utility of wealth is $U(W)$ where $W =$ £500.

$$U(W) = 0.1(500) - 0.000025(500)^2$$

$$= 50 - 6.25$$

$$U(W) = 43.75 \text{ U}$$

The actual values we calculate for utility do not matter. What counts is the relative ranking of utilities.[15]

Table 2.11   Mr Black's expected utility of wealth from investments I and J

	(1)	(2)	(3)	(4)	(5)= (2) × (4)
	Value of security at year end £	Probability of outcome, p_i	Wealth at year end, W_i (net of cost of investment) £	Utility of wealth, $U(W_i)=$ $0.1W_i-0.000025W_i^2$ (U)	$p_iU(W_i)$ (U)
Initial wealth £500, cost of investment £100					
I	105	0.5	505	44.12	22.06
	115	0.5	515	44.87	22.44
				$EU(W_I) =$	44.50 U
J	102	0.5	502	43.90	21.95
	122	0.5	522	45.39	22.69
				$EU(W_J) =$	44.64 U

[15] Units of utility are usually termed 'utiles' (U). They can be of any size, like temperature. What counts is whether A is hotter than B, not the absolute heat values of A or B.

In both cases, expected utilities are greater than Mr Black's existing utility and so both investments are worthwhile. However, investment *J* offers the highest expected utility to Mr Black and would be preferred by him.

So, expected utility enables Mr Black to make investment decisions under uncertainty using one simple measure rather than separately evaluating the expected return of each investment, its risk and its effect on his wealth.

If we plot Mr Black's utility function on a graph, we get a curve as in Figure 2.2. This is the curve of a risk averse investor. Mr Black is averse to risk in the sense that he requires additional expected return for taking on additional risk. We saw that this was true when we looked at the expected utilities he derived for securities *I* and *J*. He preferred *J* because, in his view, the additional 2% it offered in expected return more than compensated for the additional 5% in standard deviation.

Another way of showing that this is the graph of a risk averse investor is to consider Mr Black's attitude to a 'fair gamble', that is, a gamble with an expected value of zero. For example, suppose Mr Black were offered a 50% chance of winning £50 and a 50% chance of losing £50. If his current wealth is £500, we can see from the graph that he loses more utility (−3.8 U) if his wealth is reduced to £450 than if he gains from increasing his wealth to £550 (+3.7 U). A risk averse investor, like Mr Black, will always refuse a fair gamble.

Most gambles in real life, such as on horse races or the football pools, have a negative expected value because of the government tax on

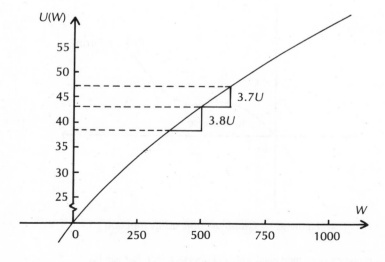

Figure 2.2   Mr Black's utility function

gambling and the profits of the companies organising the betting. The question then arises as to how we can assume investors have risk averse utility functions when the incidence of gambling is so high. Various solutions to this paradox have been proposed, for example that the shape of the utility function changes according to the level of wealth and incorporates both a risk averse and risk preferring section,[16] as in Figure 2.3.

Alternatively, gamblers might ascribe better odds (probabilities) to the possible outcomes of the gamble than actually hold because they believe they are 'lucky'.

The underlying topic of this chapter has been: how do investors compare different securities? We have suggested that they should determine the probability distribution of returns for each security, although only the expected return and standard deviation need in practice be calculated.

Each individual then has to decide whether the expected return offered on each security is sufficient to reward him for its risk, assuming he is risk averse, and then has to compare the risk–return trade-offs offered by those securities. Knowledge of his utility of wealth function enables the investor to choose between securities, taking into account in a single measure his attitudes to risk and return at each level of his wealth. If the risk averse investor does not know his utility function, he will choose securities which offer the highest expected return for a given level of risk or the lowest risk for a given expected return. However, it will be difficult without knowledge of the utility function to make

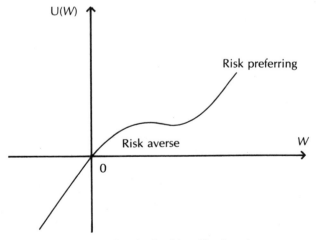

Figure 2.3   Graph of cubic utility function

---

[16] A risk preferrer is an individual who will always *accept* 'fair gambles'.

decisions between securities, such as between *I* and *J* in Table 2.10, which have different expected returns and different risks. We shall return, in Chapter 7, to the topic of how investors' utility functions can be derived and how they can be used in investment decision-making.

Reduction of risk

Since we assume throughout this book that investors are risk averse, it would be interesting to finish this chapter by investigating whether there are any simple mechanisms whereby risk can be reduced, without sacrificing return. If there are, any sensible investor will follow them.

There are, in fact, two principal ways in which risk can be reduced. The first, pooling, is the reason for the existence of such bodies as insurance companies and investment trusts, and the second, hedging, requires the participation of speculators in the market.

In Chapter 1 we considered the role of the Stock Exchange as a means of *transferring* risk from entrepreneurs to investors and between investors. Pooling and hedging offer means whereby the overall level of risk can not only be transferred but actually *reduced*.

Pooling

Consider the risk of your house being totally destroyed. Each house owner bears this risk which can be well quantified by probabilities using past frequencies of houses being destroyed.[17] Although this risk is small, the house may well represent the most valuable asset in the investor's portfolio and he may therefore wish to insure against an occurrence which has a high expected cost to him. In other words he will pay a fixed premium to an insurance company in return for the insurance company guaranteeing to pay him should his house be damaged or destroyed. If many house owners pool their risks in this way, the insurance company will actually bear less risk than if each house owner had separately borne the risk. This is because the risk of each house being destroyed is *independent* of the risk of another house being destroyed (events which might affect all houses such as nuclear war are specifically excluded in insurance policies) and, when these independent risks are considered,

---

[17] The underlying factors affecting events such as houses being destroyed or the expected life span of individuals (for life assurance) do not change so rapidly over time that they cannot easily be adjusted.

the standard deviation of the pooled risk is less than the sum of the individual risks.

Why this is so will be shown when we discuss portfolio theory in Chapter 7. We will merely state the result here. If each house is insured for the same amount and the risk of each house being destroyed is equal and has standard deviation S_H, then the risk borne by the company insuring n such houses is S where

$$S = \frac{S_H}{\sqrt{n}}$$

For example, if the company insures 10,000 houses, its standard deviation or risk will be

$$\frac{1}{100\text{th}}$$

of the risk of the individual house owner. The overall risk of these n houses being destroyed has been reduced by pooling. An important proviso must be attached to this statement. The overall risk will be reduced by the presence of the insurance company only if the probability of the event occurring is not increased as a result of the insurance being taken out. If people, knowing that they are insured, are more careless, the overall risk borne by the insurance company may not be less than the sum of the individual risks.

Of course, insurance has nothing to do with the stock market. Insurance policies are arranged via Lloyds, a completely separate market, or with insurance companies (who may then use Lloyds). Also, the returns on securities are not independent; they are affected by common economic factors. However, it will be seen, again in Chapter 7, that the combination by an investor of securities into a portfolio will always be worthwhile in the sense that his overall risk will be reduced to less than the weighted average of the risks of the component securities. This method of reducing the risk of investing in securities is called diversification and forms the basis of portfolio theory.

Hedging

As with pooling, the possibility of reducing risk by hedging applies only to a specific kind of risk. This is one where two parties are subject to exactly opposite risks, say one person bears the risk of event A happening and the other of event A not happening. If these two people can get together and agree on a transaction before the outcome of A is known they will both have hedged their risk. For example, a producer of cocoa wishes to know how much cocoa to grow next year. He will be influenced by the price of cocoa prevailing next year which he would like to know now. Similarly, a manufacturer of chocolates wishes to plan his production of sweets and would like to be assured of future supplies at fixed prices. If the producer and manufacturer get together to agree today on a price for cocoa to be delivered next year, they will both have hedged their risks. The producer's uncertainty of the future price he can get for his cocoa and hence how much he should grow has been resolved. The manufacturer's uncertainty concerning future prices and supplies of raw materials is removed. Both parties have hedged the risk of a change in the price of cocoa – on the manufacturer's side the risk of cocoa prices going *up* and on the producer's side the risk of cocoa prices going *down*. They have used what is known as the *forward* market for their transaction. Forward markets exist in major commodities such as sugar, cocoa, metals and in foreign exchange. They are markets in which future transactions are agreed now but not paid for or delivered until a specified date in the future. These markets provide hedges in exactly the same way as we described in the cocoa market. For example, in the foreign exchange forward market, UK buyers of US goods bear the risk of the cost of the dollars they need for their purchase going up in sterling terms, whereas British sellers of goods priced in dollars bear the risk of the value of dollars falling in sterling terms. Forward transactions in dollars will enable them both to hedge their risks.

These forward markets (or futures markets as the more regulated ones are known[18]) have evolved in response to the need for certain risks, such as fluctuations in commodity prices or exchange rates, to be hedged. Such markets require the existence of speculators since there may not be an even balance of opposite risks to be hedged. More traders may wish to hedge against the price of cocoa rising in value than against its falling and so speculators will have to step in to take the risk of the cocoa price falling. In fact, if speculators accurately forecast which way prices are going to move, they will improve the market in cocoa, for they will buy when prices are low, hold stocks and sell when prices are high. In this way, they will remove excess quantities of cocoa from a depressed market and provide needed cocoa in a buoyant market. However, inexpert speculators will have the opposite and damaging effect. The existence of speculators willing to take on risk means that risk can not only be reduced by hedging but also transferred to investors willing to accept risk as on the Stock Exchange.

We may ask ourselves: of what use is hedging in the stock market?

---

[18] Futures markets are more regulated in the sense that, as for the Stock Exchange, there is a physical market place. Also, all transactions are recorded, prices are published, transactions are standardised and there is an intermediary who requires security (in the form of deposits of money) from parties to all transactions to prevent default.

Commodities and foreign exchange markets operate outside the Stock Exchange orbit and do not involve transactions in quoted securities. There are two main reasons why the Stock Exchange investor should be interested in hedging.

Firstly, he now has the opportunity to undertake hedging transactions in quoted securities. As far as shares are concerned, he can trade in options (described in Chapter 6) which are in some ways equivalent to forward transactions in shares[19] and, by combining different kinds of options with the shares themselves, he can hedge against the risk of share prices rising or falling within a specified period. Another recent development (the traded option market opened in London in 1978[20]) is a futures market in fixed interest securities which opened in London in 1982. This allows the risk of changes in interest rates (which we have called interest rate risk) to be hedged. Also, since 1982, the other type of risk attached to fixed interest securities, inflation risk, can to some extent be hedged with respect to gilts. This is as a result of the availability to all investors of index-linked gilts which guarantee a coupon fixed in real instead of nominal terms.[21] Both the financial futures market and index-linking will be discussed in more detail in Chapters 3 and 4, which are devoted to fixed interest securities.

The second reason why the stock market investor should be interested in hedging is because the foreign exchange markets, both spot[22] and forward, must be understood before international investment can be undertaken. Most overseas investments require the purchase of foreign currency and so involve two considerations, that of the risk and return of the investment itself *and* that of the risk of holding the foreign currency in which they are denominated. The subject of international investment is discussed in Chapter 10.

---

[19] For a discussion of the difference between options and forward or futures hedging, see Gemmill (1981).

[20] Options to buy or sell shares have existed for many years. However, only since 1978 has there been an official secondary market in options, run by the Stock Exchange.

[21] We shall see in Chapter 3 that the coupon and redemption payments of an index-linked gilt are, in fact, only fully hedged against the retail prices index for a period which is not exactly the same as the holding period.

[22] A spot transaction is one where a commodity is paid for and delivered on the spot (now) rather than at some future date.

Summary

This chapter has described the two major characteristics of any investment, its expected return and risk. The different types of risk underlying various types of investment were discussed, from supposedly risk-free gilts to company shares. The major types of risk described were uncertainty of income, default risk, interest rate risk and inflation risk.

The next section considered how uncertain return and risk could be measured so that different investments could be compared. Probability distributions, either derived objectively from observation of past returns or subjectively by estimating future possible returns, were used to quantify expected return. The standard deviation of the probability distribution of returns is a suitable measure of risk provided the distribution is normal or investors ignore skewness.

The investor's attitude to the risk and expected return of investment can be neatly described in his utility function. Each investor may have a different attitude to risk and return and hence a different utility function. Such a utility function is expressed in terms of the investor's wealth and not the rates of return of the investment. Obviously different returns will imply different changes in the investor's wealth. In the special case where the investor only compares the expected returns and standard deviations of investments, his utility function can be shown to be quadratic and such an investor will be risk averse.

This book assumes that, when considering Stock Exchange investments, investors can be viewed as risk averse. If this is the case they will be interested in any means whereby risk can be reduced, and the last section of the chapter considered two possible methods of reducing risk, pooling and hedging.

Problems

1. Mr Woolly is choosing between two possible investment opportunities:
   (a) A gilt-edged stock which will mature in exactly one year and on that date the nominal amount (£100) and a 3% interest payment will be made. The price of £100 nominal of this stock is £98 today.
   (b) 100 shares costing 98p each in a company specialising in software for microcomputer systems. The return on the shares is uncertain but the investor has read a report on the company which estimates the one-year return to be as follows, subject to how the economy behaves and how the company's products are received by the market.

Economic

	Growth	Recession
Well received	30%	15%
	p = 0.2	p = 0.3
Poorly received	10%	−10%
	p = 0.3	p = 0.2

New products

where p = probability.

    (i) Using expected value and standard deviations, calculate the expected return and risk of the two investments.

   (ii) Bearing in mind that inflation is expected to be 5% in the next twelve months, which investment would you advise Mr Woolly to make?

  (iii) What other factors would you take into consideration?

2. Mr Gray has derived his utility function (by comparing his preference for various gambles and certain outcomes) as

$$U(W) = 1 - \frac{10000}{W}$$

He is now considering investing his entire wealth of £10,000 (he has no earned income) in fixed interest securities for a period of one year. His stockbroker recommends one of the following gilts both priced at £90.

Gilt	Coupon (annual)	Possible price in one year's time	Probability
A	10	90	0.3
		95	0.4
		100	0.3
			1.0
B	7	80	0.3
		100	0.4
		120	0.3
			1.0

Their interest payments (to be paid in twelve months' time) are certain, but their end-of-year prices are uncertain due to interest rate risk. Mr Gray wishes to invest all £10,000 in either gilt *A* or gilt *B*.

   (i)   Calculate the expected return and risk of each gilt. Does this knowledge help Mr Gray to decide? Why/why not?

   (ii) Which gilt will Mr Gray choose?

3. Mrs de Salvera is fifty-five and self-employed. She wishes, on retirement, to use her investments to buy a house in the country and believes that house prices will remain constant in real terms. She is unwilling to buy shares and intends to invest her savings for the next five years in fixed interest securities.

   (i)   Which types of risk will Mrs de Salvera incur if she buys fixed interest securities?

   (ii) How can she choose particular fixed interest securities to minimise those risks?

4. To what kinds of risk are the different types of financial investments subject? Explain how such risks can be reduced in the various financial markets without sacrificing return.

Gilt-edged securities

Introduction

Chapters 3 and 4 are devoted to a type of security often ignored in investment text books – fixed interest securities.[1] Such a lack of emphasis on this type of investment can partly be explained by the preference for the more glamorous company share sector and partly by the poor performance of fixed interest securities in this century. (For example, £100 spent on 2½% Consols at the beginning of 1919 would have been quoted at £33 on the first day of 1980 and worth in real terms only 4% of its 1919 value.)

This view of fixed interest securities is changing. Interest rates are

---

[1] That is, securities which entitle the holders to a fixed rate of interest throughout the life of the loan. *NB*: in the UK, fixed interest securities are often called 'stocks', whereas in the US this term refers to the ordinary shares of companies.

now fluctuating both up and down thereby allowing the value of fixed interest securities to rise as well as fall. Also, the sheer size of the fixed interest securities market, in particular gilts,[2] has brought these securities back into prominence.

The National Debt of the British government has dramatically increased during the twentieth century, fuelled by two World Wars, the nationalisation of the major public utilities and growing budget deficits. By March 1981, the UK's National Debt was £110b., of which the majority, over £86b., was financed by gilt-edged securities. The British government's aim has been to lengthen the maturity of its debt and this has led to the UK Stock Exchange offering one of the best markets in the world for long-term government fixed interest securities.

Turnover in fixed interest securities represented 84% of all turnover on the Stock Exchange in 1980, with gilts alone contributing to over 77% of total turnover. Corporate fixed interest securities, such as debentures, loan stocks and preference shares, have declined in importance in the UK over the years, with companies turning to their banks for short-term variable rate debt finance rather than incur long-term high fixed interest debt commitments in periods of uncertainty and high inflation. On the other hand, the UK government has chosen to turn to the stock market for the financing of its ever-increasing need for funds and, in order to maintain the primary market for its securities, has encouraged, by various incentives, turnover in the secondary market. Given this dominance of gilts in terms of turnover and market value

Table 3.1   Holders of gilt-edged securities (31 March 1981)

	Gilts held (%)		
	0–5 year	*5–15 year*	*Over 15 year*
Official holders	18	18	4
Banks	12	4	1
Trustee Savings banks	6	2	—
Discount houses	5	—	—
Insurance companies	7	22	44
Pension funds	1	10	28
Building societies	17	4	—
Others	34	40	23
	100	100	100
TOTAL (£b.)	25.5	27.6	33.4

Source: *Bank of England Quarterly Bulletin,* December 1981.

[2] See Chapter 2, p. 35 for an explanation of why UK government fixed interest securities are called 'gilt-edged' or 'gilts'.

over other fixed interest securities in the stock market, this chapter, although relevant to *all* fixed interest securities, will concentrate predominantly on gilts.

Table 3.1 shows who holds these government securities. It can be seen that all the major financial institutions hold substantial portfolios of gilts of differing maturities. The attractions of holding gilts to these investors are various. For example, insurance companies have long-term commitments. If they buy gilts with the same maturities as these commitments they can be certain of being able to meet their liabilities in nominal terms. Also, banks and building societies keep a certain proportion of their investments in what are known as liquid assets[3] (easily realisable short-term investments of minimal risk) in order to be able to pay depositors wishing to withdraw funds from their accounts. Short-term gilts are considered to be suitable liquid assets.

Another reason why both institutions *and* individual investors include gilt-edged securities in their portfolios will become clear on reading Chapters 7 and 8. Since gilts are less risky than company shares, both portfolio theory and the capital asset pricing model (discussed in those chapters) show that any investor wishing to hold a portfolio which is less risky than one consisting entirely of company shares should include some gilt-edged securities in his portfolio.[4]

However, these reasons why investors hold gilts do not explain the higher turnover of gilts relative to company shares experienced on the Stock Exchange. For example, twice the market value of all gilt-edged securities was turned over during 1980 compared with only 25% of the value of all UK company shares. How can we explain this high turnover in gilts?

The price and hence returns of gilts are affected above all by present and future interest rates, although different gilts are affected to different extents by changes in these rates. In recent years, interest rates and expectations concerning future interest rates have changed frequently. This has provided scope to any investor who feels he or she can accurately predict interest rate changes either by switching between gilts or by switching between gilts and other securities such as shares. The high turnover in gilts is partly due to the transactions of such investors. Even the financial institutions which have long-term commitments actively deal in part of their gilt portfolio. Unless gilts are held to match a specific nominal liability, they can no longer be considered invest-

---

[3] Liquid assets include Treasury Bills (ninety-one-day securities), certificates of deposit (securities relating to large bank deposits), short-term gilts and deposits with the Bank of England.

[4] An investor could, of course, reduce risk by investing in company fixed interest securities (which have default risk) or non-quoted investments such as National Savings accounts. However, gilts represent the least risky quoted investments available.

ments which can be bought and then ignored – as we saw with the 2½% Consols acquired in 1919. Investors who wish to do this may be better advised to put their money on deposit with a bank or building society where interest rates will not be fixed but will vary according to prevailing market rates. The volatility of interest rates and hence prices of gilts implies that investors must carefully choose when to buy and when to sell gilts to maximise their returns.

Most investment advice to the small investor concentrates on share investment for two reasons. Firstly, share investment has been the traditional first love of the small investor and, secondly, the gilt-edged market is dominated to a much greater extent than the share market by large institutions dealing in large amounts. (See Table 3.1.) The average size of a gilt-edged bargain in 1980 was £152,000 and institutions expect to deal in amounts of £1m. Also, the type of analysis needed to understand gilt price movements is different from that required for shares and the small investor unversed in these techniques is at a considerable disadvantage.

However, the principles underlying these techniques are relatively straightforward, and, as we shall see, the traditional valuation methods used by investors in the market, such as redemption yields, are now being superseded by more sophisticated and accurate analyses of interest rates. Any investor who understands both techniques need have no fears of investing in fixed interest securities.

This chapter will first describe the gilts available and how they can be distinguished from one another, in terms of coupon, maturity and accrued interest. The method of issue of gilts is then outlined as well as recent innovations in the gilts market (such as index-linked gilts) which have been introduced by successive governments to cope with the increased inflation and interest rate risk associated with investment in fixed interest securities. The chapter concludes with a section on how to calculate returns on investments in gilts, describing the two most common measures, the interest yield and the redemption yield. Chapter 4 continues the discussion on gilts with a more sophisticated approach to determining returns and to measuring the impact of interest rate changes on gilt prices.

Description of gilts

The description 'gilt-edged' is sometimes applied to fixed interest securities issued by borrowers other than the British government such as UK corporations and local authorities, Commonwealth governments and quasi-official UK bodies. Technically, only those securities issued or

Table 3.2 Details of British funds as given in the Financial Times

BRITISH FUNDS

1982 High	Low	Stock	Price £	+ or −	Yield Int.	Yield Red.
		"Shorts" (Lives up to Five Years)				
98⅝	91	Exch. 3pc 1983	98 9/16	.....	3.05	10.24
101¾	95¾	Treasury 12pc 1983‡‡	100¼	−¼	11.97	10.92
100⅝	92⅞	Treasury 9¼pc '83	98⅞	−⅜	9.36	11.13
104⅝	96⅞	Exch. 13½pc '83	102 9/16	−½	13.13	10.85
101¾	91⅞	Exch. 10pc 1983	99¼xd	−⅜	10.08	10.82
98¼	87⅜	Funding 5½pc '82-84‡‡	96½	−¼	5.70	8.86
103¾	91⅞	Exch. 11¼pc 1984	99⅞	−¾	11.26	11.25
107¼	96¾	Exchequer 14pc. 1984	103⅝	−¾	13.51	11.24
94½	81⅛	Exch. 3pc 1984	93xd	−½	3.23	7.97
105¼	91½	Treasury 12pc 1984	101⅝	−¾	11.81	10.93
112	96¾	Treasury 15pc 1985	106⅜	−⅞	14.37	11.57
112¼	89½	Exch. 12pc Cnv. '85	103¾	−1	11.57	10.11
91¾	73½	Treasury 3pc 1985	88¾	−¾	3.38	8.16
105½	87½	Treasury 11½pc 1985	100⅛	−½	11.49	11.42
26¾	22¾	Treas 8¾pcCv85 (£25pd)	22¾	−1 1/16	8.93	9.17
107⅝	88⅝	Exch. 12¼pc 1985	101½	−¾	12.07	11.64
106⅝	86⅛	Exch. 11¾pc '86	100½	−¾	11.69	11.52
89½	69	Treasury 3pc 1986	86¾	−1⅛	3.46	7.34
107¾	86¾	Treasury 12pc '86	101½xd	−⅝	11.82	11.48
100	80⅜	Treasury 8½pc '84-86‡‡	96⅞xd	−⅞	8.77	9.59
116¾	96⅜	Treas. 12¼pc '86 Cnv.	105½xd	−2¼	11.61	10.40
114	91⅞	Exch. 14pc 1986	107½	−1¼	13.02	11.39
112	90	Exch. 13¼pc 1987	105	−1⅛	12.62	11.64
103½	97	Exch. 10½pc 1987	97	−1¼	10.82	11.35
92¾	73⅞	Funding 6½pc '85-87‡‡	92¼	−½	7.05	8.95
85¼	64½	Treasury 3pc 1987	83¼xd	−½	3.60	3.37
109	85⅞	Treas. 12pc 1987	101⅞	−1	11.78	11.46
		Five to Fifteen Years				
98	72½	Treasury 7¾pc '85-88‡‡	94	−1	8.51	9.99
102¾	95¾	Exch 10½pc '88	95¾	−1⅝	11.08	11.54
81	60⅛	Transport 3pc '78-88	75⅛xd	−1	3.98	8.70
62¾	55¾	Treas 9½pc '88 (£60pd)	55¾	−1⅝	10.38	11.47
107⅞	79⅞	Treasury 11½pc 1989	100	−1⅞	11.91	12.04
85⅝	62½	Treasury 5pc '86-89	80	−1¼	6.31	9.13
117¼	85⅞	Treasury 13pc 1990‡‡	109	−1⅞	12.53	12.16
112	85⅝	Exch. 12½pc 1990	103½	−2⅛	12.40	12.27
98⅛	70⅛	Treasury 8¼pc '87-90‡‡	87xd	−1½	9.47	10.84
110¾	77⅞	Treasury 11¾pc 1991	97xd	−1⅞	11.99	12.14
84⅞	59¾	Funding 5¾pc '87-91‡‡	79½	−1¼	7.33	9.60
104⅛	76⅜	Exch. 11pc 1991	96⅛	−1¾	11.61	11.95
116⅞	81⅞	Treasury 12¾pc '92‡‡	108⅝	−1¾	12.29	12.04
102¼	70	Treasury 10pc 1992	93⅞	−1¾	11.01	11.61
112¾	80⅞	Exch. 12¼pc '92	104¼	−1¾	12.37	12.10
118¾	88⅝	Exchequer 13½pc '92	110½	−2	12.54	12.12
116½	80⅜	Treasury 12½pc '93‡‡	101⅞xd	−2	12.12	11.99
81½	56¼	Funding 6pc 1993‡‡	76¼	−1¼	8.02	9.83
124¾	88	Treasury 13¾pc 1993‡‡	111	−1¾	12.46	12.01
128¼	91⅝	Treasury 14½pc '94‡‡	119⅛	−1¾	12.59	11.99
119¼	86¾	Exchequer 13½pc 1994	110	−1⅝	12.45	12.11
115½	80⅛	Exch. 12½pc 1994	106½	−1¾	12.46	12.03
96⅛	66¾	Treasury 9pc '94‡‡	87½	−1¾	10.35	10.97
113¾	76½	Treasury 12pc '95	104¼	−1¾	12.03	12.01
66¾	42⅝	Gas 3pc '90/95	62¼	−¾	4.84	7.86
103¼	68½	Exch. 10¼pc 1995	94	−1¾	11.38	11.77
116⅜	83¼	Treasury 12¾pc '95‡‡	106⅞	−1¾	12.02	11.79
127¾	86¼	Treas. 14pc '96	117¾	−1¾	12.46	12.07
97	66⅝	Treasury 9pc '92/96‡‡	88	−1¾	10.48	11.05
133	96	Treasury 15¼pc '96‡‡	122¾	−1¾	12.58	12.02
120	86	Exchequer 13¼pc '96‡‡	110	−1¾	12.36	11.87
63¾	43⅝	Redemption 3pc 1986-96	59¼	−¾	5.11	7.99
124	83½	Treasury 13¼pc '97‡‡	114⅛	−1¾	12.15	11.89
105⅛	69⅝	Exchequer 10½pc 1997	95⅝	−1¾	11.36	11.43
94⅛	64	Treasury 8¾pc 1997‡‡	85½	−1¾	10.53	11.08
132¼	94¼	Exch. 15pc 1997	121¾	−1⅞	12.50	12.06
		Over Fifteen Years				
79⅛	54½	Treasury 6¾pc '95-98‡‡	70¾	−1⅞	9.64	10.77
138¾	99½	Treas. 15½pc '98‡‡	127¾	−1⅞	12.42	11.95
116⅝	78¼	Exch. 12pc 1998	102	−2	11.84	11.80
100⅝	66	Treasury 9½pc 1999‡‡	91¾	−1¾	10.80	[illegible]
116	81¼	Exch. 12¼pc 1999	105¾	−1⅞	11.86	11.75
107	71⅛	Treasury 10½pc 1999	93½	−1¾	11.30	11.46
124¼	82¼	Treas. 13pc 2000	108xd	−2⅛	11.50	11.75
131	89	Treas. 14pc '98-01	115⅛	−1¾	12.23	11.93
116½	76½	Exch. 12pc '99-02	106⅜	−1¾	11.79	11.74
129½	85⅞	Treas. 13¾pc 2000-03	119	−1¾	12.08	11.85
113¼	78¼	Treasury 11½pc '01-04	102⅝	−1⅞	11.49	11.48
50¾	33¼	Funding 3½pc '99-04	44½xd	−¾	7.80	9.66
123⅜	81⅝	Treasury 12½pc '03-05	0107⅞	−1⅞	11.59	11.37
87¼	59¾	Treasury 8pc '02-06‡‡	78½	−1¾	10.38	10.65
116⅜	75⅞	Treasury 11¾pc 03-07	106	−1⅞	11.58	11.53
128½	90	Treas. 13½pc '04-08	117⅞	−1⅞	11.73	11.57
64	44¼	Treasury 5½pc '08-12‡‡	56½	−1¾	9.97	10.39
85½	55⅝	Treasury 7¾pc '12-15‡‡	76¾	−1¾	10.49	10.61
124	81⅛	Exch. 12pc '13-'17	108xd	−1¾	11.10	11.07
		Undated				
42¾	27⅜	Consols 4pc	37½	−¾	11.09	—
37¼	26⅜	War Loan 3½pc‡‡	32xd	−¾	10.96	—
42	31½	Conv. 3½pc '61 Aft.	37¾	−½	9.44	—
32¾	21	Treasury 3pc 66 Aft.	29	−½	10.54	—
27	17¾	Consols 2½pc	22¾xd	−½	10.90	—
26⅞	17⅝	Treasury 2½pc	23	−½	11.10	—
		Index-Linked & Variable Rate				
100⅜	99⅜	Treas. Variable '83	99⅞	−⅛	10.15	10.42
					(1)	(2)
104¼	95	Treas. 2pc I.L. '88	104¼	+¼	1.77	2.30
108¼	93	Do. 2pc I.L. '96	106¼	.....	2.62	2.75
100¼	93¾	Do. 2½pc I.L. 2001	97¾	−¼	2.62	2.74
98⅝	95½	Do. 2½pc I.L. 2003	96¼	−¼	2.64	2.75
104½	86⅜	Do. 2pc I.L. 2006	101¾	−¼	2.53	2.63
99½	96	Do. 2½pc I.L. 2009	96¾	−¼	2.59	2.69
106½	90	Do. 2½pc I.L. 2011	104	.....	2.58	2.67

Prospective real redemption rate on projected inflation of (1) 10% and (2) 7%.

Source: *Financial Times*, 9 December 1982.

guaranteed by the British government, known as British funds, should be considered as free of default risk and therefore 'gilt-edged' in that sense. Other bodies may, in exceptional circumstances, default.[5]

We will concentrate on the securities known as British funds, whose prices are quoted daily in the *Financial Times*. Table 3.2 gives an extract from the *Financial Times* where details of ninety-six different British funds (or gilts) are given.

Most gilts are registered securities, which means that the name of each holder is noted in a register. A few gilts, such as 3½%[6] War Loan, can be issued in bearer form. Bearer securities are not registered

[5] For example, the fixed interest debt of the Mersey Docks and Harbour Board had its quote suspended from 1970 to 1974 with only reduced interest payments being made during that period.

[6] The *Financial Times* notation is 3½ pc.

anywhere, the only proof of ownership being the physical possession of the relevant certificate. Some investors consider that the disadvantage of bearer securities, their risk of being lost or stolen, is outweighed by their anonymity. However, it is not common for gilts to be issued in bearer form nowadays. Investors wishing to acquire bearer fixed interest securities can acquire eurobonds, discussed in Chapter 10.

The gilts in Table 3.2 have different names, the three most common being Exchequer, Treasury and Funding, all of which simply denote the British government as borrower. Only two gilts issued on the nationalisation of certain industries can now be easily identified: Gas 3%and Transport 3%; the remainder were not specifically named after the industry concerned. A few longstanding gilts with different names remain, for example, 2½% Consols, which consolidated several different gilts into one, and 3½% War Loan, issued in 1932 to replace a First World War issue.

Obviously, this handful of different names is not sufficient to be able to distinguish one gilt from another. Two other distinguishing features are usually included in the full name of each gilt: its coupon and its maturity date.

Coupon

For example, Treasury 10% 1992 will pay the holder £10 per annum for every £100 of the gilt held until 1992. The amount of the gilt held, the 'nominal' value of the investment, is the amount to be repaid (in 1992, in this case). As interest rates change, the value of the gilt, and hence its market price, will vary and may be very different from the nominal amount.

Although gilts can be bought in any amount, they are usually quoted in amounts of £100 nominal. In the case of Treasury 10% 1992, the price for £100 nominal quoted in Table 3.2 is £93⅞ – the gilt-edged market has not yet converted to decimals! For an outlay of £93.88, an investor will be entitled to receive £10 each year until the government repays the nominal amount of £100 in 1992.

The interest rate on the nominal amount, in this case 10%, is known as the 'coupon' of the gilt. This refers to the coupon which is attached to bearer securities and which has to be physically surrendered to the borrower when interest is due to show entitlement to receive that interest. Since gilts are mostly registered securities, this term is a misnomer. Interest on gilts is automatically paid to the registered holders. Such interest payments are usually made in two equal six-monthly instalments on two prespecified dates. (Only 2½% Consols pay interest quarterly.) With Treasury 10% 1992, £5 (net of personal income tax at the basic rate[7]) will be paid on 21 February and 21 August each year until 21 February 1992 when the last interest payment and the £100 repayment will be made.[8]

As can be seen from Table 3.2, the coupons currently payable on gilts vary from 2½ to 15½%. The very low coupon gilts were issued when prevailing interest rates were low, for example 2½% Consols in 1905, whereas the 14 and 15% coupons were issued in more recent high-interest days. However, some low-coupon gilts are still issued today because they are preferred by certain types of investor for tax reasons. The taxation of income from gilts affects different investors in different ways as can be seen below.

The return actually achieved on a gilt, as with any security, is made up of income received during the period held and a capital gain or loss. So the holding period return, R, can be written

$$R = \frac{D + (P_1 - P_0)}{P_0}$$

where D represents, for a gilt, the interest payments received, and $P_1 - P_0$ the capital gain or loss either on disposal or on redemption of the gilt. Now, the interest payments on gilts, D, are taxable at the personal or corporate tax rate of the investor depending on who the investor is. The capital gain, $P_1 - P_0$ (if this is positive), suffers capital gains tax or is not taxed at all if the gilt is held for twelve months or more before disposal or redemption. High rate taxpayers will generally prefer to receive their return in the form of capital gain rather than interest payments whereas low rate or non-taxpayers will be less concerned as to how they receive their return. So, high rate taxpayers will tend to go for low coupon gilts which have a high capital gain potential; see, for example, in the five to fifteen years section in Table 3.2, Gas 3% 1990–5 whose market price of £62¼ is less than two-thirds of its nominal value on redemption. Higher coupon gilts, for example in the same section Exchequer 10¼% 1995 priced at £94, have a higher income and price and so a smaller potential capital gain. In fact, if the coupon of a gilt exceeds prevailing interest rates, the price will be greater than £100, giving the holder income and a capital *loss* on redemption. For instance, Treasury 12% 1995 is priced in Table 3.2 at £104¼, £4.25 more than will be received on maturity.

Most interest payments on gilts have standard rate personal tax deducted from them before being paid out. If the taxpayer pays tax at a

---

[7] This book does not aim to give a detailed explanation of the tax implications of various investments. For such a text, see Cummings (1981), ch. 22.

[8] For details of coupon payment dates, see Monday issues of the *Financial Times*, when they replace the high/low figures in Table 3.2.

different rate, he either claims tax back or pays the balance to the Inland Revenue. Interest can be paid gross (before deduction of tax) to *overseas* investors on certain gilts (those marked # in the *Financial Times*) and to UK resident[9] investors who have bought their gilts via the Post Office and are thus registered on the National Savings Stock Register. This latter facility is helpful to small investors who do not pay tax and do not want the bother of claiming it back.

Maturity

The other distinguishing feature of gilts is their maturity – the date at which the nominal amount borrowed by the government will be repaid. In fact, gilts are listed by maturity and divided up into groups by maturity in Table 3.2.[10] Gilts which will be redeemed at the latest within five years are known as 'shorts'; 'mediums' are those which are redeemable within five to fifteen years and 'longs' those which will be repaid at a date more than fifteen years away from now. Treasury Bills, which are the short-term marketable government debt, are not traded on the Stock Exchange but sold via the discount houses to the institutions.[11]

Of course, 'longs' will eventually become 'mediums' and then 'shorts' before being redeemed. Only the fourth category of gilts, 'undated' gilts, will probably never be redeemed and so never change category. This group of six gilts consists of those stocks which the government has no obligation to repay by a specific date. The government may have stated that it would not repay *before* a certain date, for example, 3½% War Loan 1952 or after, but no final redemption date has been specified. The government would only redeem these undated stocks if it could replace the debt more cheaply – issue gilts with a lower coupon on the same nominal value. So, the undated stocks will only be repaid if interest rates fall below, say, 4 or 3%. It may seem incredible now that this should ever be the case, but in 1948, 3½% War Loan was viewed as a 'short' because it was considered likely that it would be redeemed in 1952.

Some gilts have a spread of maturity dates, for example, Funding 5%

---

[9] Investors who are liable to UK tax.

[10] Except for a section, discussed below, devoted to variable rate and index-linked gilts.

[11] A bill is a promise to pay the bearer a fixed sum of money on maturity (usually no more than one year away). Treasury Bills are bills of ninety-one days' maturity issued by the UK government. A discount house is a financial institution which discounts bills – both commercial and Treasury – that is, pays the issuer a sum less than the face value, this discount being equivalent to a rate of interest in return for providing funds.

1986–9. In this case the government can repay on any 15 October between 1986 and 1989. How can investors estimate the maturity of a gilt on which the government has the option of when to repay? As with the undated stocks, the government will only repay if it can replace with a lower coupon stock. So unless interest rates fall below 5%, the government will not replace Funding 5% 1986–9 until the last possible moment in 1989. If the coupon of a gilt is above or at the same level as prevailing interest rates, redemption may be before the last possible date (since the government may choose to refinance at a lower coupon) and is therefore more difficult to estimate.

Another factor which could alter the effective maturity of any fixed interest security would be the existence of a sinking fund. This means that a sum of money is set aside by the issuer to buy back securities each year, either by repurchasing through the market or by repaying certain securities selected at random (by drawings) at a predetermined price. If a stock has a sinking fund, its *expected* life will be less than the period to maturity. However, only two small issues of gilts, 3% Redemption 1986–96 and 3½% Conversion 1961 or after, have sinking funds although sinking funds are more popular with company fixed interest securities. The reason why a sinking fund is used is to prevent the borrower having to refund the whole amount at maturity with another issue when interest rates may be high. The government now has such a wide spread of maturities that this is no longer a problem.

Accrued interest

When comparing prices of gilts with different maturities, it must be borne in mind that shorts are treated differently from other gilts in that they do *not* have accrued interest included in their price. Instead, this is added on or subtracted when the transaction is agreed. For example, suppose Exchequer 13¼% 1987, a short, is to be purchased four months or 119 days after the last coupon payment date. The quoted price for this stock is, say, £105 but the amount payable by the purchaser for each £100 nominal, is

Quoted price   £105.00

plus

Accrued interest $\frac{120}{365} \times £13.25$ £4.36

Total price *excluding* transaction costs[12]   **£109.36**

Accrued interest is based on 120 days, and not 119 days, because the gilt
will only be paid for on the day after the purchase.

Sometimes accrued interest has to be *deducted* from the price. This
will occur when a short is purchased 'ex div'. Some gilts in Table 3.2
have 'xd' after their price, standing for 'ex dividend'. If a gilt is
purchased 'ex div', the purchaser will not be entitled to the imminent
interest payment whereas if he purchases the gilt 'cum div' he will be
buying the gilt plus the entitlement to that interest payment. Gilts are
usually quoted 'ex div' five weeks and two days before the interest
payment. So, with a short purchased 'ex div' say fifteen days before the
interest payment, the price would be adjusted to take account of the two
weeks' interest forgone. For example, again with Exchequer 13¼%
1987 quoted at £105, the price paid would be

  Quoted price   £105.00xd

minus

  Interest forgone $\frac{14}{365} \times$ £13.25   £(0.51)

Total price *excluding* transaction costs   **£104.49**

Gilts other than shorts include accrued interest in their quoted prices
until they go 'ex div'. In both cases, that is for shorts and other gilts,
accrued interest is considered part of the price for tax purposes.

Special ex div

Normally, a security is quoted 'cum div' one day and 'ex div' the next so
that holders registered on the last day before the security goes 'ex div'
receive the dividend or interest payment. However, gilts other than
shorts and War Loan 3½% can be traded both 'cum div' *and* 'special ex
div' at the same time for the three weeks prior to going officially 'ex div'.
This enables jobbers to balance their books.

Investors with different tax rates can therefore choose whether they
wish to buy or sell a gilt 'cum' or 'ex' dividend without having to wait
until the gilt goes officially 'ex div'. Suppose a high marginal rate

---

[12] For details of transaction costs, see Chapter 1, pp. 14–18, and Appendix 1.

Table 3.3   Effects of tax on buying gilts 'cum' or 'ex' dividend

Gas 3% 1990–5	Net cost to pension fund (0% tax rate) £	Net cost to individual on, say, 55% tax rate £
Ex div price £44	**44**	**44**
Cum div price £45.25	45.25	45.25
Less interest	(−1.50)	(−0.68)
Net cost cum div	**43.75**	**44.57**
Prefers to buy:	**Cum div**	**Ex div**

taxpayer wishes to buy a gilt during these three weeks. If he buys a gilt full of accrued interest ('cum div'), he will have to pay tax, say at 55%, on the interest payment. If he buys the gilt 'special ex div', the price will be lower to reflect the loss of the interest payment (remember, gilts other than shorts have accrued interest included in the price). The price will not in fact fall by as much as the whole gross interest amount, but by, say, 75–90% of it, depending on the relative demand and supply from high and low rate taxpayers.

For example, suppose Gas 3% 1990–5 is quoted at £45.25 'cum div' and £44 'special ex div', a difference of £1.25. If the high rate taxpayer buys 'cum div', he will pay £45.25, be entitled to £1.50 interest, 68p after tax on a 55% tax rate. His net cost will be £44.57 compared with £44 if he buys 'special ex div'. On the other hand, a pension fund will prefer to buy 'cum div' since it pays no income tax. By paying £45.25 it will be entitled to receive the full £1.50 interest (after reclaiming tax) to give a net cost of £43.75. Table 3.3 outlines the situation.

The difference in amount between the fall in the gilt price due to the interest payment and the interest payment itself will depend on prevailing tax rates and the tax positions of buyers and sellers of the gilt.[13]

Tap stock

Another symbol sometimes seen in the *Financial Times* against certain gilts is ●, which signifies that these are tap stocks. This term has to do with the manner in which gilts are issued. These offers are not

---

[13] These changes in price around interest payment dates could lead to tax being always avoided on interest payments. Taxpayers could sell 'cum div' to non-taxpayers and repurchase 'ex div'. However, the Inland Revenue has stamped on these practices, known as 'bond-washing', by treating any such profits as income rather than capital gain.

underwritten[14] in the same way as company securities and it is often the case that a new gilt issue is not fully subscribed. Any stock not taken up by the public is bought by government departments, such as the Bank of England, and released to the market as demand requires. In other words, the government underwrites its own gilt issues. Whilst the gilt is thus available for sale by the government, it is said to be 'on tap'. It trickles out to the market at a speed which depends on the attractiveness of its price to investors. Government departments also buy in stock from the market when it is near to redemption and these official holdings both of tap stock and shorts close to maturity can be seen in Table 3.1 on p. 63 under the heading 'official holders'.

The Bank of England issues and redeems gilts on behalf of the Treasury. However the Bank does not deal directly with the stock market. The Government broker, traditionally a senior partner of the stockbroking firm Mullens & Co., acts as an intermediary. He will convey the feelings of the market to the government, advise on pricing of new issues and feed in demand for tap stocks from jobbers who specialise in gilts. So, new issues of gilts are sold both in the primary market through the public offer and in the secondary market through sales of tap stock.

Innovations

Companies, faced with periods of high uncertainty, inflation and volatile interest rates during the 1970s, preferred to abandon the fixed interest securities market as a major source of borrowing rather than introduce changes to maintain its attractiveness to lenders. The UK government, on the other hand, continued to use gilt-edged securities as a major source of funds for its public sector borrowing requirement. To this end, several innovations have been introduced to make the gilt-edged market attractive both to the lenders and to the borrowers.

Methods of issue

For example, before March 1979, the price of all new issues was always fixed in advance. This left the government vulnerable to sudden

[14] When a new issue of securities is underwritten, financial institutions agree to buy any securities not taken up when the offer expires at the offer price. The issuer is thus assured of receiving the amount of the issue less a commission to the underwriters.

improvements in the market during the few days between the fixing of the price and the closing of the offer. This happened in 1979 with Exchequer 13¼% 1987 and Treasury 13¾% 2000 – 3 both of which were heavily oversubscribed. To protect itself, the government now puts out new stock to tender[15] setting a minimum price at the current market level. (By not having to issue the gilts at their nominal value of £100, the government can issue gilts whose coupons are different from prevailing interest rates.) If the market improves before the closing date the tender offers will be higher than the minimum price. If the market does not improve, the government is protected by the minimum price and by the fact that any unsubscribed stock goes to official departments for sale 'on tap'.

The government has also increased its flexibility with regard to new issues. Instead of having to issue a new gilt by means of a public offer, it can now issue new tranches (amounts) of existing gilts of a type which are in short supply, or it can arrange to sell existing gilts held by government departments (and not just the new tap stocks) by swapping them for non-negotiable government securities.

Dealing with uncertainty

An increase in uncertainty about future inflation and interest rates has made the holding of fixed interest long-term securities relatively less attractive than under more stable conditions. The government has introduced variations on the traditional type of gilt to attract lenders into continuing to fund the ever-growing National Debt.

(i) CONVERTIBLE AND PARTLY PAID GILTS

For example, a short, 12% Exchequer Convertible 1985 was issued in early 1981 which offered holders the option to convert this gilt (at terms already known) on specified dates between late 1981 and 1983 into a medium-term stock, 13½% Exchequer 1992. Investors who felt unwilling to invest for the full eleven years had the option not to convert and thus to hold a gilt with only a few years to maturity.

Another 'sweetener' has been the introduction of part payment on subscription. New issues of stock can sometimes be paid for in instal-

---

[15] A tender offer for securities is one where all would-be purchasers state the price at which they are willing to buy the securities. The price at which they are sold is the maximum one at which all the securities can be sold.

ments (the payments are timed to coincide with government financing needs) thus allowing investors a period of credit and effectively reducing the cost of the gilt. These gilts can be bought and sold in their partly paid form and are denoted in Table 3.2 by (£xpd) after the name where £x is the amount already paid for £100 nominal. See, for example, in the 'Shorts' section of Table 3.2, Treasury 8¾% Convertible 1985 which is quoted '£25pd'.

(ii) VARIABLE RATE GILTS

Conditions of economic uncertainty and other factors, such as the central role of interest rates in government policy, mean that interest rates now fluctuate considerably even within a short period of time. As discussed in Chapter 2, investors in gilts and other fixed interest securities bear the risk that interest rates will rise and so reduce the value of their investments. This leads to an unwillingness to subscribe to new issues of gilts if interest rates are expected to rise in the near future. To get round this problem, in 1977 the government issued a variable rate Treasury Stock 1981 (and has since issued other gilts of this type) where each interest payment was set at ½% above the average rates of interest[16] on Treasury Bills prevailing in the six months prior to the ex dividend date. The coupon on this type of gilt therefore varies, reflecting current short-term interest rates. Whether interest rates go up or down, the value of variable rate Treasury Stock should remain close to its nominal value. See, for example, in Table 3.2 under the Index-Linked and Variable Rate section, Treasury Variable 1983, which is priced at £99⅞. Investors in this type of gilt are protected against interest rate risk although not against inflation risk if interest rates do not adjust fully for expected inflation. The appeal of this gilt, though, is usually limited to low rate or non-taxpaying investors since the coupon (and hence income) will most probably be high. Variable rate gilts are also limited to short maturities and so do not offer any long-term protection against interest rate risk.

---

[16] The rate of interest on Treasury Bills is described by a discount rate. For example if bills are sold at a discount of 2%, that is, sold for £98 to have £100 repaid by the government in three months' time, this implies a three-month interest rate of

$$\frac{2}{98} \times 100 = 2.04\%.$$

(iii) INDEX-LINKED GILTS

A long-term index-linked stock which offered a fixed *real*[17] interest rate rather than a fluctuating *nominal* rate would protect investors against both inflation and interest rate risk for a longer period. Insurance companies and pension funds are by far the most important purchasers of long-dated gilts (their purchases net of sales of longs amounted to £4.6b. in 1979) and have future liabilities such as pension payments which are mostly based on earnings in the few years prior to retirement and so will increase in line with inflation. These institutions would like to be able to match such liabilities with an income from investment which similarly keeps up with inflation.[18]

The demand for index-linked stock grew throughout the 1970s, culminating in a recommendation for the encouragement of such issues in the Wilson Committee Report of 1980.[19] The government responded in 1981 by issuing a gilt offering a 2% *real* interest rate and maturing in 1996.[20] This issue was designed to help the pension funds meet their real liabilities and was, in fact, initially restricted to institutions engaged in pension fund business. However, the 1982 budget allowed all investors to acquire index-linked gilts and several more such issues were made. As can be seen in Table 3.2, by December 1982 there were seven index-linked gilts in issue worth in nominal terms around £5b. This relatively small amount (under 6% in nominal terms of all gilts in issue) obviously allows pension funds and other investors to hedge only a proportion of the inflation risk inherent in their fixed interest investments.

What exactly does the term 'index-linked' mean, and how does this link reduce inflation risk? Index-linked stocks have their interest payments and redemption payments linked to the retail prices index, an index made up of the prices of various goods and services assumed to represent the typical expenditure of the average consumer. Thus, the retail prices index (RPI) will include the cost of petrol, mortgage

---

[17] A real rate of interest is one where the nominal or money interest rate (the one usually quoted for securities) has been adjusted for the effects of inflation. So,

$$(1 + \text{nominal IR}) = (1 + \text{inflation rate})(1 + \text{real IR})$$

$$\text{e.g. } (1 + 10\%) = (1 + 7.8\%)(1 + x\%)$$

where $x\%$ is the *real* interest rate, which must in this instance be 2%.

[18] See Chapter 11 for a discussion of how the objectives of these institutions affect the securities they hold.

[19] See the Wilson Report (1980) ch. 17.

[20] Before this, several index-linked government National Savings Certificate issues offering a real return of around zero had already been made. Such issues can only be bought via the Post Office and are *not* marketable securities.

repayments, bread, tea and so on in proportions representative of actual consumption. This index is the most widely quoted measure of inflation in the UK and is, for example, an index against which earnings are measured. If earnings (and pensions) do keep up with inflation, gilts whose payments are linked to the RPI will indeed allow pension funds to meet their liabilities. If, on the other hand, an individual investor has liabilities which are not the same as those included in the RPI, he will not be able completely to hedge inflation risk by investing in index-linked stocks. In fact, the gilts' interest and redemption payments are based on the RPI eight months before each payment. So, an interest payment in November will be based on the RPI in March. This lagging allows the actual amount of the interest (or redemption payment) to be known several months in advance of the payment and certainly before the gilt goes ex div. However, it also means that index-linked gilts do not provide a perfect hedge against inflation throughout their lives. This will become evident when we discuss how to calculate returns on index-linked gilts at the end of the next section.

Of course, gilts do not have to be linked to the RPI. The French government, with its 7% fifteen-year government bond issued in 1973, chose to index it instead of the price of gold – the French have traditionally viewed gold as the most secure investment. The disadvantage of this is that a government has even less control over the price of gold than it does over the RPI. Between 1976 and 1981 the price of gold fluctuated between $104 and $667 an ounce. The 1981 interest payment alone was worth over 60% of the original amount issued.

Returns on investments in gilts

We now investigate the various methods used to calculate the return on gilt-edged securities which are, in fact, applicable to all fixed interest securities. We consider first of all the straightforward gilts which are not index-linked.

We have defined the holding period return of a security as

$$R = \frac{D + P_1 - P_0}{P_0}$$

where D represents any dividend or interest payments made during the period, P_0 the cost and P_1 the selling price of the security. In the case of a gilt, D is known with certainty (in money terms) and so the risk of holding the gilt comes from two sources. Firstly, from the change in its price, $P_1 - P_0$, during the holding period which, for a gilt with no default risk, will be due to changes in market interest rates and hence required yields on gilts – interest rate risk. Secondly, there is the risk that the values of P_1 and D when received will be less in *real* terms than expected – inflation risk.

Holding period return is useful for comparative purposes since it can be applied to all securities. It can also be used to calculate the deviation of the *actual* return from the *expected* return. Unfortunately, in order to calculate R, P_1 must be known. This is a simple matter if we are calculating the *historic* return achieved on disposal of a security. It is not so easy when trying to calculate the return we *expect* to get from the security. P_1 must be estimated and, to obtain a reasonable estimate, we need an understanding of how gilt prices are affected by interest rate changes as well as a forecast of how and why interest rates themselves will change. We leave a discussion of these topics until Chapter 4. For the moment, we concentrate on two measures of return commonly used for gilts and fixed interest securities, both of which get round the problem of having to estimate P_1.

Interest yield

If we go back to Table 3.2, we can see that the *Financial Times* provides two different types of yield (return) for each gilt, interest yield and redemption yield. Interest yield, the simpler measure of the two, avoids the problem of having to estimate P_1 to calculate the capital gain or loss on the gilt by simply ignoring it. It concentrates only on the first part of the holding period return – the return from income (or interest in this case), D/P_0, where P_0 is the current market price.

For example, in Table 3.2, Treasury 10½% 1987 has an interest yield (sometimes called running income or flat yield) of 10.82%. This is calculated as follows

$$\text{Interest yield} = \frac{D}{P_0} \times 100$$

In this case, the current market price, P_0, is £97, which gives

$$\text{Interest yield} = \frac{£10.5}{£97} \times 100$$

$$= £10.82\%$$

Similarly, the interest yield on Treasury 3% 1986 is

$$\text{Interest yield} = \frac{£3}{£86.75} \times 100$$

$$= 3.46\%$$

In order to be able to compare yields on gilts of different maturities and yields on gilts with returns on other securities, yields are usually calculated on the 'clean' price, that is, net of accrued interest. The calculations for shorts, as above, are straightforward, since their quoted prices do not contain accrued interest. However, the quoted prices of other gilts, which contain accrued interest, have to be adjusted before the interest yield (and, as we shall see, the redemption yield) can be calculated for comparative purposes. In order to be able to do so, the date of the most recent interest payment must be known. This can be found in each Monday's *Financial Times* where interest payment dates are substituted for the high/low prices for the year shown in Table 3.2.

For example, Treasury 5½% 2008–12 pays interest on 10 March and 10 September each year. The gilt prices shown in Table 3.2 were published on 9 December and refer to closing prices for 8 December. Settlement for Treasury 5½% 2008–12 bought on 8 December would be on 9 December, ninety days after the last interest payment on 10 September. So, ninety days' accrued interest would have been included in the quoted price of £56½.

The 'clean' price of Treasury 5½% 2008–12 is therefore

| Quoted price | = £56.50 |

less

$$\text{Accrued interest} = \frac{90}{365} \times £5.50 = (£1.36)$$

| 'Clean' price | = **£55.14** |

So the interest yield will be

$$\text{Interest yield} = \frac{£5.50}{£55.14} \times 100 = \mathbf{9.97\%}$$

as given in the *Financial Times*. Although the prices quoted in the

Financial Times of gilts other than shorts *include* accrued interest in the price, the yields shown for all gilts are based on 'clean' prices, that is, net of accrued interest.

The investor can also adjust the interest yield to reflect his particular tax position. So, if he pays tax at 40% on the income from Treasury 5½% 2008–12, his net interest yield will be

$$\text{Net interest yield} = \frac{£5.50}{£55.14} \times (1 - 0.4) \times 100$$

$$= \mathbf{5.99\%}$$

Of what use is the interest yield? It does not reflect the *total* return from holding a gilt since it ignores any capital gain or loss. What it does give is a simple indication to the investor of his return in terms of income by comparing the interest he receives with the actual price he paid for the gilt rather than its nominal value. For example, with Treasury 5½% 2008–12, although the coupon shows a return of 5½% on the nominal value of £100, interest rates are higher than when this gilt was issued; the price of the gilt has almost halved to give an income before tax of nearly 10% on the investment. In other words, if an investor bought Treasury 5% 2008–12 on 8 December 1982 and held it until redemption he would be certain of receiving an annual gross income of almost 10% on his original investment.

The interest yield has been widely used in one context – to compare the income from gilts with the income from ordinary shares (as measured by the dividend yield, again D/P_0, where D in this instance is the current dividend paid on the share). Traditionally, shares have had a higher dividend yield than the interest yield available on gilts, this difference in yield being known as the 'yield gap'. In 1959, the average interest yield on gilts for the first time exceeded the average dividend yield on shares, giving rise to the so-called 'reverse yield gap', reverse because it was considered to be in the wrong direction. There has been much discussion about the reverse yield gap, to no purpose since the relevant comparison should be between holding period returns on gilts and on shares, including the capital gain or loss for the period.[21] Since ordinary shares are expected to generate on average a higher capital gain than gilts, this is likely to reverse the effects of the reverse yield gap.

So, the interest yield as a measure ignores the possible impact of capital gain or loss on the overall return of a gilt. Most individual investors are unlikely to hold Treasury 5½% 2008–12 until maturity (probably in 2012), a period of almost thirty years, and so must come to

---

[21] Whether the gain or loss is actually realised by selling or the securities are retained for another period.

terms with the possibility of a gain or loss on disposal. However, pension funds with long-term commitments intending to hold the gilt to maturity may find the interest yield of some use.

Unfortunately, the interest yield has another disadvantage in that it ignores the time value of money. It assumes that the interest paid in any year up to 2012 is as valuable to the investor as this year's interest payment. The redemption yield, the second measure of return used in relation to gilts, overcomes this second disadvantage.

Redemption yield

In Chapter 2 we saw that the price P of an undated gilt could be written as

$$P_0 = \frac{D}{(1 + r)} + \frac{D}{(1 + r)^2} + \frac{D}{(1 + r)^3} + \dots \qquad (3.1)$$

where D was the annual interest payment and r the opportunity cost of the funds used to buy the gilt. For example, if the investor did not receive the first interest payment D for twelve months, he could not invest D in an equivalent risk-free investment paying r interest to give him $D(1 + r)$ at the end of the twelve months. So D received in one year's time would be worth only $D/(1 + r)$ to the investor now, and so on.

For a gilt with a maturity date, the price can be written as

$$P_0 = \frac{D}{(1 + r)} + \frac{D}{(1 + r)^2} + \dots \frac{D}{(1 + r)^n} + \frac{100}{(1 + r)^n} \qquad (3.2)$$

where £100 is due to be repaid at the end of n years. The price P_0 is simply the present value of a future income stream made up of regular interest payments D, and a redemption payment of £100 on maturity.

In other contexts, r may have been encountered as the 'internal' rate of return. In the case of gilts, r is known as the redemption yield (or yield to maturity), that is, the rate of return achieved on a gilt if it is purchased at the quoted price P_0 and held to maturity. The redemption yield is an improvement on the interest yield since it takes into account the time value of money. For example, the shorter the term of the gilt the more valuable the final redemption payment in present value terms. The redemption yield also avoids the problem of having to estimate the selling price P_1 by assuming that the gilt is not sold but held to maturity.

In other words, P_1 is always equal to £100.[22] Again, this assumption will only be realistic for the investor who intends to hold each gilt purchased to maturity.

The calculation of the redemption yield is actually somewhat more complex than appears from equation (3.2) because the 'clean' price has to be used and interest payments are in fact made six-monthly not yearly as was assumed in equation (3.2). Also, the first interest payment may not be in exactly six months' time. However, redemption yields can be calculated very quickly, despite these complexities, by using bond tables, a calculator or a computer. There follows a simple example to show how redemption yields are determined.

Take Treasury 12% 1986. Suppose that a purchase was made on 8 December 1982 at the price of £101½xd quoted in Table 3.2. Redemption will be on 12 June 1986 and interest payments will be on 12 June and 12 December each year. Since the gilt was purchased ex div, the first interest payment of £6 will be almost exactly six months from purchase on 12 June 1983. Because interest is paid at six-monthly intervals, we calculate the *six-months* redemption yield, r. The number of periods, n, is seven. We can therefore write

$$101\tfrac{1}{2} = \frac{6}{1 + r} + \frac{6}{(1 + r)^2} + \dots + \frac{6}{(1 + r)^7} + \frac{100}{(1 + r)^7} \qquad (3.3)$$

We have to calculate r by iteration, that is, by trying different values of r to see which will fit equation (3.3): $r = 6\%$ is tried first, using either a calculator or annuity and present value tables, to calculate the present value of a stream of payments discounted at 6%. These tables are provided in Appendix 2 on pp. 393–4. Present value tables will give the present value of a sum received in n periods' time, discounted at $r\%$ per period. Annuity tables will show the present value of an amount received *each period* for n periods with a discount rate of $r\%$ per period.

In the above case, we are due to receive £6 per period for seven periods discounted at 6%. From the annuity tables on p. 394, we find that the value of £1 received every period for seven periods discounted at 6% is £5.58. Since we will receive £6 per period, we must multiply by six to give a present value of the interest stream of £33.49. It remains for us to calculate the present value of £100 received in seven periods' time. The present value table on p. 393 shows that £1 received in seven periods' time discounted at 6% is worth £0.6651 today. So the present value of that £100 is £66.51. Adding together the present value of the interest payments and the present value of the redemption payment gives a price for the gilt of £100.00, quite close to the actual market price of £101½. Note that assuming a redemption yield equal to the coupon

---

[22] Unless we are discussing index-linked gilts. See below.

rate (in this case 6%) will always give a gilt price of £100. It was not necessary in this case to use tables!

Repeating this process with $r = 5\%$ (trying a lower yield to get a higher price than the market price) we find that P_0 comes out at £105.79. So we know that the redemption yield is between 5 and 6%.

To find the exact redemption yield the 'linear interpolation' formula[23] is used to find r:

$$r = r_1 + (r_2 - r_1) \frac{PV_1}{PV_1 + PV_2}$$

where r_1 is the lower redemption yield tried and r_2 the higher, with PV_1 the difference between P_0 and the price found using r_1 and PV_2 the difference between P_0 and the price found using r_2. To be able to use this formula, the price found using r_1 must always be *greater* than the actual price P_0 and the price found using r_2 must be *less* than P_0.

So,

$$PV_1 = £105.79 - £101.50 = £4.29$$

$$PV_2 = £101.50 - £100.00 = £1.50$$

This gives

$$r = 0.05 + (0.06 - 0.05) \times \frac{4.29}{(1.50 + 4.29)}$$

$$= 0.05 + (0.06 - 0.05) \times 0.74$$

$$= 0.0574$$

r = 5.74%

We have found, by using a fairly arduous method, that the six-months redemption yield is 5.74%. Calculator or computer programs can find r directly, without the need for iteration and linear interpolation.

In order to be able to compare fixed interest securities with different frequencies of interest payment, it is usual to quote the *annual* redemption yield, R. To calculate R, we know that £1 invested at $R\%$ for twelve months will yield the same amount as £1 invested compound for two periods at $r\%$. So, for the example above,

---

[23] Linear interpolation uses the principle of similar triangles to find the redemption yield given two trial redemption yields, one on *either* side of the true r. For further information, see Lumby (1981), pp. 43–4.

$$£1(1 + R) = £1(1.0574)^2$$

giving

R = 11.81%

The redemption yield given in Table 3.2 for Treasury 12% 1986 is slightly lower than our estimate, at 11.48%. This is because the annual redemption yields in the *Financial Times* are obtained simply by multiplying the semi-annual redemption yield, r, by two. If we use this simplified method to find the annual redemption yield, we get 5.74% $\times$ 2 = 11.48%, the same as the *Financial Times* figure. The compounded redemption yield of 11.81% is higher because it allows for reinvestment of the six-monthly interest payments.

Notice how the redemption yield for Treasury 12% 1986 (11.48%) is less than the interest yield (11.82%). This is because, with the market price at £101½, there will be a capital loss on redemption of £1.50, not taken into account in the interest yield. When the market price is less than £100, involving an eventual capital *gain* on redemption, the redemption yield will be *greater* than the interest yield.

Return on index-linked gilts

So far, we have seen how to calculate the interest yield and the redemption yield for gilts whose interest and redemption payments are fixed in nominal terms. The problem we now consider is how to estimate measures of return for index-linked gilts, whose interest and redemption payments are fixed in *real* terms and *not* fixed in nominal terms.

(i) REAL INTEREST YIELD

One solution would appear to be to calculate the interest yield in real terms since all the future cash flows are certain in real terms. Unfortunately, there are two factors which complicate the calculations.

Firstly, all the index-linked gilts listed in Table 3.2 under the heading 'Index-Linked and Variable Rate' have more than five years to redemption. Because of this, the price of each index-linked gilt will include accrued interest which must be deducted from the quoted price to obtain the 'clean' price normally used to determine the interest and redemption yields. This is a simple matter for ordinary gilts, since the next coupon payment (and hence the proportion of it included in the price) is always known. In the case of index-linked gilts, if these were truly inflation-proof, the nominal amount of each coupon to be paid would never be known in advance. This is because the rate of inflation right up to the date of the coupon payment would be used to determine how much the coupon would actually be. In fact, since the retail prices index (the index used as a measure of inflation) is usually published with a lag of around one month, it would be impossible to match exactly the RPI and the coupon payments. So, in order to be able to calculate the clean price of an index-linked gilt up to six months before a coupon payment,[24] and allowing for the lag of around one month in the publication of the RPI, the government has linked each coupon or redemption payment of an index-linked gilt to the change in the RPI from the base date (which is *eight* months before the gilt was issued) to *eight* months before the payment is made.

For instance, if we look at Treasury 2% I.L. 1988 as at 9 December 1982 (the date of Table 3.2), we know that the next coupon payment will be made on 30 March 1983 and that it will be based on the RPI level eight months earlier, that is, of July 1982, which is already published. Since the Treasury 2% I.L. 1988 was issued in March 1982, the base date for the index-linking of its coupon and redemption payments must be eight months before, July 1981, when the RPI stood at 297.1.[25] By July 1982, the RPI had risen to 323.0. Thus, by December 1982 it was known that the March 1983 coupon payment would be

$$£1 \times \frac{323.0}{297.1} = £1.0872$$

where £1 was the semi-annual coupon in 'real' terms.

Since the future coupon was then certain in nominal terms, the clean price could be calculated. Because the previous coupon payment had been on 30 September, by 9 December 70 days of accrued interest had been included in the price.

Quoted price   = £104.25

less

$$\text{Accrued interest} = \frac{70}{365/2} \times 1.0872^{26} = (£0.417)$$

Clean price   = **£103.833**

---

[24] The Bank of England announces the amount of each coupon payment no later than one business day before the previous coupon payment date.

[25] The retail prices index is published in the monthly government publication, *Employment Gazette*. Recent RPI figures are also available from Post Offices.

[26] We divide by 365/2 instead of 365 because we are using a semi-annual interest payment.

Unfortunately, although the lag of eight months between the RPI used and each actual coupon payment allows investors to know what the next coupon payment will be in nominal terms and allows them to calculate 'clean' prices, it does mean that index-linked gilts are not fully hedged against inflation risk.

For example, we can see that the 30 March 1983 coupon payment is hedged against the inflation which occurred between July 1981 (eight months before the gilt was issued) and July 1982 (eight months before the actual payment of the coupon). For the investor to be fully hedged against inflation risk, the March 1983 payment should be linked to the rate of inflation between the day when the gilt was issued and 30 March 1983. We consider this problem in more detail when we try to calculate a 'real' redemption yield in the next section.

Returning to the calculation of the real interest yield, we need to be able to express both the coupon and the clean price of the gilt in real terms, as of the same base date. We could then write

$$\text{Real interest yield} = \frac{\text{Real coupon}}{\text{Real price}}$$

Since there is a lag of eight months between the date of the RPI used to protect the payments against changes in prices and the actual dates of these payments, we are not sure of the true real value of the next coupon payment and so we are forced to express both the coupon and the price in 'real' terms with a lag of eight months.

We know that the annual coupon for Treasury 2% I.L. 1988 is £2 in real terms (with a lag of eight months) and so we determine the price in real terms using the same base date of July 1981 and applying the same lag of eight months. So, we deflate the price by

$$\frac{RPI_{April\ 1982}}{RPI_{July\ 1981}} = \frac{319.7}{297.1} = 1.0761$$

The 'real' clean price is thus $\frac{£103.833}{1.0761} = £96.49$

The 'real' interest yield is therefore

$$\frac{\text{'Real' coupon}}{\text{'Real' price}} = \frac{2}{96.49}$$

$$= \mathbf{2.07\%}$$

Despite having attained a result which approximates a 'real' interest yield, we now find that it is not of much use. As with nominal interest yields, it ignores both the time value of money and any capital gain or loss on redemption. In addition, it lacks the main attraction of the nominal interest yield, namely the speed and ease with which it can be calculated, and it is not a true 'real' yield. Finally, it is not of much use to the investor since it gives little idea of the level of income to be received from the gilt.[27] Because of these disadvantages, the *Financial Times* does not publish an interest yield for index-linked gilts, preferring to concentrate on the more complete redemption yield.

(ii) Real redemption yield

If all the cash flows relating to a particular index-linked gilt were fully index-linked, it would be a simple matter to express all the cash flows in real terms and to calculate a real redemption yield. For example, if all the interest and redemption payments were guaranteed to maintain their value in real terms relative to base date B, we could write

$$P_{0,B} = \frac{D}{(1 + r)} + \frac{D}{(1 + r)^2} + \dots + \frac{D}{(1 + r)^n} + \frac{100}{(1 + r)^n} \quad (3.4)$$

where $P_{0,B}$ is the market price of the index-linked gilt expressed in purchasing power terms as at date B and r the real redemption yield. Unfortunately, as we saw above, none of the future cash flows of an index-linked gilt are truly guaranteed in real terms right up to the date of payment but up to a date eight months earlier. This lag of eight months means that the investor (who holds the gilt to maturity) is protected against the increase in the RPI between eight months before the gilt was issued and eight months before final redemption.

The lag in inflation-proofing is emphasised in Figure 3.1 where I_1 is the inflation the investor is protected against and I_2 the actual inflation he experiences over the life of the gilt. Whether he is fully protected for

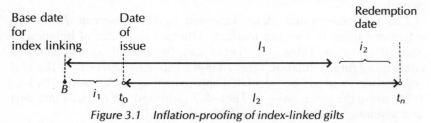

Figure 3.1   Inflation-proofing of index-linked gilts

---

[27] A nominal interest yield might give a better indication of this but is relevant only to the next coupon payment.

the holding period t_0 to t_n will depend on whether $I_1 = I_2$, or more particularly, $i_1 = i_2$, where i_1 is the inflation during the eight months before the gilt is issued and i_2 the inflation which occurs during the last eight months of the life of the gilt. If the historic inflation rate, i_1, is greater than the future inflation rate, i_2, the investor will be overprotected from inflation and if i_1 is less than i_2, he will be underprotected.

The problem, therefore, with determining a real redemption yield is that the period during which the cash flows are guaranteed in real terms is not the same as the period during which the cash flows occur. For example, when discounting a coupon payment to be made in six months' time in nominal terms the calculation would look like this:

$$\frac{D\ (1\ +\ infl_1)}{(1\ +\ r)\ (1\ +\ infl_2)}$$

where D was the latest coupon paid in nominal terms, $infl_1$ was the rate of inflation from eight months ago to two months ago, $infl_2$ the rate of inflation expected over the next six months and r the real redemption yield. Because $infl_1$ is not necessarily the same as $infl_2$, they cannot be cancelled out to give one of the terms in equation (3.4).

Since we cannot calculate a simple real redemption yield, we are forced to make an assumption about inflation – what I_2 will be. The City currently has two methods of doing this. One is to take the most recent level of inflation and to extrapolate this into the future. Basically, this is equivalent to taking i_2 as a forecast for I_1 (and hence i_1) and thereby assuming $i_1 = i_2$. By doing this, one is implicitly assuming that the investor will be more or less fully protected against inflation if he holds the index-linked gilt to maturity.

The second method is to make a 'sensible' estimate of future inflation. This is extremely difficult especially when looking at a time horizon of up to thirty years. However, it must be remembered that one of the assumptions of the redemption yield is that the required rate of return is constant over the life of the gilt, whatever the maturity of the gilt. It is no more unrealistic to assume a constant inflation rate for the same period.

The real redemption yields provided by the *Financial Times* are calculated using the second method, with two estimates of inflation, 7 and 10%, as in Table 3.2. These can be altered as expectations concerning future inflation rates change. Table 3.4 shows how the real redemption yield can be calculated approximately for Treasury 2% I.L. 1988, using the price given in Table 3.2 (adjusted for accrued interest) and assuming a future annual inflation rate of 7%.

Equation (3.8) looks like the equation for the nominal redemption yield, as given in equation (3.2), except that, since we are looking for a real yield, we will expect a much lower r. Using the same method as for

Table 3.4   Calculation of real redemption yield for index-linked gilt

Quoted price	£104.25 (9 December 1982)
Clean price	£103.833
Next coupon payment	£1.0872 on 30 March 1983 (index-linked from base date to July 1981)
Other payments	(to be based on 30 March coupon and inflated by the relevant factor $(1 + i)^n$ where i is the forecast semi-annual inflation rate)

Let R be the semi-annual *nominal* redemption yield

Let r be the semi-annual *real* redemption yield

We can write

$$P_0 = \sum_{i=1}^{i=n} \frac{D_i}{(1 + R)^i} + \frac{V}{(1 + R)^n}$$

where P_0 is today's price, D_i the interest payments in nominal terms, and V the amount paid on redemption, also in nominal terms. Substituting in known values, such as $D_1 = £1.0872$ and $P_0 = £103.833$, we get

$$103.833 = \frac{1.0872}{(1 + R)} + \frac{1.0872\,(1 + i)}{(1 + R)^2} + \dots + \frac{1.0872\,(1 + i)^{10}}{(1 + R)^{11}}$$
$$+ \frac{100(1.0872)\,(1 + i)^{10}}{(1 + R)^{11}} \qquad (3.5)$$

Taking out a factor $1/(1 + i)$ in the right-hand side of equation (3.5),

$$103.833 = \frac{1}{(1 + i)} \left\{ \frac{1.0872\,(1 + i)}{(1 + R)} + \frac{1.0872\,(1 + i)^2}{(1 + R)^2} + \dots + \frac{1.0872\,(1 + i)^{11}}{(1 + R)^{11}} \right.$$
$$\left. + \frac{100(1.0872)\,(1 + i)^{11}}{(1 + R)^{11}} \right\} \qquad (3.6)$$

If we substitute for R in equation (3.6) by using the relationship between the required real and the required nominal rate of return postulated by Fisher

$$(1 + R) = (1 + r)(1 + i) \qquad (3.7)$$

we get

$$103.833 = \frac{1.0872}{(1 + i)} \left\{ \frac{(1 + i)}{(1 + r)(1 + i)} + \frac{(1 + i)^2}{(i + r)^2\,(1 + i)^2} + \dots \right\}$$

Table 3.4 cont.

$$= \frac{1.0872}{(1 + i)} \left\{ \frac{1}{(1 + r)} + \frac{1}{(1 + r)^2} + \ldots + \frac{1}{(1 + r)^{11}} + \frac{100}{(1 + r)^{11}} \right\}$$

Multiplying both sides by $(1 + i)/(1.0872)$

$$\frac{103.833 \, (1 + i)}{(1.0872)} = \frac{1}{(1 + r)} + \frac{1}{(1 + r)^2} + \ldots + \frac{1}{(1 + r)^{11}} + \frac{100}{(1 + r)^{11}}$$

Since we have taken the forecast of 7% annual inflation rate, approximately equivalent to 3.5% for the six-months rate,[28] we can substitute for i.

The left-hand side of the equation becomes

$$\frac{(1.035) \, 103.833}{1.0872} = 98.85$$

We therefore have

$$98.85 = \frac{1}{(1 + r)} + \frac{1}{(1 + r)^2} + \ldots + \frac{1}{(1 + r)^{11}} + \frac{100}{(1 + r)^{11}} \tag{3.8}$$

---

the nominal redemption yield, we get a real redemption yield of just under $r = 1.15\%$. For the annual figure, we double 1.15%[29] to get an annual real redemption yield of 2.3%. This is the same as the figure given in Table 3.2.

Finally, let us see how we can use the real redemption yield for index-linked gilts. We are able to compare with nominal yields precisely because we have assumed an inflation rate. We can therefore gross up the real redemption yield to get a nominal figure:

$$(1.023) \, (1.07) = (1.0946)$$

giving a nominal yield of 9.5%. Alternatively, we can deflate the nominal yields of comparable ordinary gilts, such as Transport 3% 1978–88. This gilt's nominal redemption yield is given in Table 3.2 as 8.70%. Its real redemption yield, assuming an inflation rate of 7%, is r where

$$(1 + r) = \frac{(1.087)}{(1.07)} = 1.016$$

giving a real redemption yield of 1.6%.

---

[28] It is usual in the City simply to divide by two to get six-monthly interest or inflation rates from annual figures.

[29] See footnote 28.

However, the real redemption yield must be viewed with considerable caution as a useful measure of holding period return for index-linked gilts. Not only does it have all the faults of the redemption yield (which will be discussed in detail in the next chapter, Chapter 4), but it also includes an estimate of a future, constant rate of inflation for the period to redemption of the gilt. Some estimate of future inflation must be made before nominal returns can be compared with real returns but it would obviously be better if these were made on a year-by-year basis rather than assuming that a constant rate of inflation will prevail over the next ten, twenty or thirty years.

Summary

This chapter has looked at gilts, the most important type of fixed interest security quoted on the UK Stock Exchange. Gilts vary according to their coupon and maturity but all gilts have their interest and redemption payments guaranteed by the UK government. They are thus not subject to default risk.

Most gilts have interest and redemption payments fixed in nominal terms and are therefore subject to both interest rate risk and inflation risk. However, to encourage investors to continue to lend long-term to the government during the more uncertain 1970s, new types of gilts were developed (as well as new methods of issuing them), such as variable rate gilts and index-linked gilts, quoted in a separate section under British funds in the *Financial Times*. Variable rate gilts reduce interest rate risk and index-linked gilts reduce inflation risk.

The remaining section of the chapter was devoted to a description of how the two main types of return for gilts given in the *Financial Times*, interest yield and redemption yield, are calculated both for nominal and for index-linked gilts. The interest yield and, more importantly, the redemption yield are the two most common measures of return used for gilts. They are relatively easy to calculate and to understand. However, it remains to be seen whether these estimates of return on gilts help the investor to compare different gilts or to decide when to buy and sell gilts. A more detailed discussion on these questions is left to the next chapter.

Problems

1. The following gilt-edged securities were quoted in the *Financial Times* as follows on 2 February 1983.

Stock	Price £	Interest yield (%)	Redemption yield (%)
Treasury 3% 1987	84¾	3.54	7.06
Treasury 12% 1987	101⅛	11.87	11.66

   (i) Explain how the interest and redemption yields have been calculated and why you think Treasury 12% is quoted at a price which is greater than its nominal value.

  (ii) Suggest types of investor who might be interested in buying Treasury 12% 1987, explaining why they would prefer it to the Treasury 3% 1987.

2. The *Financial Times* of Monday 2 February 1983 gives you the following information on Treasury 9% 1992–6.

Interest due	Price	Last xd date
15 Sep. 15 Mar.	£87¾	9 August

   (i) How much accrued interest is included in the price?

  (ii) Using the clean price, calculate the interest yield on the gilt. Is it higher or lower than the gilt's coupon? When do you think the gilt will be redeemed?

 (iii) Estimate the redemption yield for the gilt.

3. (i) Calculate the gross redemption yield on an Exchequer 8¼% gilt assuming the interest and capital repayment will both occur in exactly twelve months' time from today. The price is £97⅞.

  (ii) Another gilt which will be redeemed at exactly the same time is Exchequer 3%, which is currently priced at £94½. Which gilt would you buy if you expect to hold it to redemption and
    (a) you are a charity paying no income or capital gains tax,
    b) you are an individual with a marginal tax rate on investment income of 65% and a marginal capital gains tax rate of 15%.

 (iii) At what marginal income tax rate would an investor be indifferent between the two gilts?

 (iv) Is it possible that you could receive a greater yield/lesser yield than you have calculated above if you sell the gilt before redemption? Why? Would the tax situation change?

4. Suppose it is March 1983. The quoted price of Treasury 2% index-linked 2006 is £103 and the next semi-annual interest payment is due on 19 July. The base date for index-linking of the gilt is November 1980 when the retail prices index was 274.1. The monthly retail price indices for January–November 1982 were:

January	310.6
February	310.7
March	313.4
April	319.7
May	322.0
June	322.9
July	323.0
August	323.1
September	322.9
October	324.5
November	326.1

  (i) What will the July 1983 coupon payment be in nominal terms?
 (ii) Calculate the 'real' interest yield on the gilt.
(iii) Suppose the *Financial Times* told you that the 'real' redemption yields on this gilt, assuming 7 and 10% p.a. inflation, were 2.38 and 2.30% respectively. How would you go about comparing this gilt with, say, Treasury 8% 2002–6 which, on the same day, had a quoted redemption yield of exactly 11%.
(iv) What factors would lead an investor to invest in the index-linked gilt, rather than an ordinary gilt of the same maturity?

5. Given the decline in UK *corporate* fixed interest new issues after 1973, how has the UK government managed to continue to issue successfully long-term fixed interest debt?

CHAPTER 4

Investing in fixed interest securities

Introduction

In Chapter 3, we looked at how gilts differ from one another, through their coupons and maturities, and examined how measures of return on gilts, notably the interest yield and the redemption yield, can be calculated. In this chapter, we concentrate on how to choose between fixed interest securities, in particular gilts, from the point of view of investment.

We saw in Chapter 2 that all fixed interest securities are subject to interest rate risk and inflation risk (as well as default risk for non-UK government securities). However, given its particular coupon and maturity, each fixed interest security will respond in a different way to changes in interest rates and unexpected inflation. So, in order to be able to choose between fixed interest securities, we need an understanding of how each one will be affected by such changes.

What we shall in fact find is that fixed interest security prices reflect what the market as a whole expects interest and inflation rates to be in the future. However, redemption yields do not give us this information. Forward interest rates, which are implicit in gilt prices, do. Armed with this knowledge of expected future interest rates, the investor can then follow one of two types of investment strategy. In the first instance, he can accept the market projections of future interest rates implicit in gilt prices. He can then attempt to minimise interest rate risk by matching the maturities of the gilts with the maturities of his liabilities or minimise inflation risk by either investing short term or by buying index-linked gilts. On the other hand, he can compare his own projections of future interest and inflation rates with those of the market and choose those gilts which will do best if his forecast proves a more accurate picture of the future than that of the market. If, for example, he believes that interest rates will fall over the next year by more than is predicted by the market and is reflected in gilt prices, he will invest in those gilts which are the most volatile to changes in interest rates and which will therefore experience the biggest price rises if his forecast is correct. We shall see that this volatility can be assessed by a measure called 'duration'.

Thus, the investor has a choice. He can either accept market forecasts of future inflation and interest rates and minimise the risk that actual rates will be different from those forecast by reducing his exposure to interest rate risk or inflation risk, or he can choose his level of exposure according to how he himself forecasts the future.

In fact, if an investor wishes to reduce interest rate risk, he now has another alternative besides matching. He can use the financial futures market. By buying or selling financial futures, the investor can fix his return on gilts without having to hold the gilts to redemption. For example, a gilt can be bought and immediately sold forward[1] to fix completely the return and avoid interest rate risk. In Chapter 3, we noted how an increase in inflation risk has led to the demand for and eventual supply of index-linked gilts. In the same way, an increase in interest rate risk during the 1970s has led to the establishment of financial futures markets as a means of hedging interest rate risk away.

The structure of Chapter 4 is as follows. We first of all examine the measures used to describe gilts in Chapter 3 to see how they can help in investment decision-making. We find that the only measure of any potential use is the redemption yield. However, the redemption yield does not help us to obtain market forecasts of future interest rates and, because of this, we turn to spot and forward interest rates for this information. We can then determine the term structure of interest rates, both now and in the future, which allows us to estimate the volatility of

---

[1] By selling forward, is meant the agreement *now* to sell at a fixed price and on a fixed date in the future.

different gilts to expected changes in interest rates and thus to choose in which gilts to invest. The remaining two sections of the chapter are devoted to the UK financial futures market (which is not strictly part of the Stock Exchange but which deals with fixed interest security futures) and to corporate fixed interest securities which can be valued exactly as are gilts but which are also subject to default risk.

Comparing gilts

In this section we look at the gilt measures discussed in Chapter 3 to see how they can help us compare gilts. For example, given the information on gilts provided in *Financial Times*, as shown in Table 3.2 on p. 66, the investor can compare the price, coupon, maturity, interest yield and redemption yield of every gilt.

Knowledge of the price alone will not help the investor since, on a cursory inspection, the longer-dated the gilt, the cheaper it looks. This is simply due to the fact that, the nearer the gilt is to maturity, the closer the price is to £100. No matter what happens to interest rates or inflation, the value of any gilt on its redemption date must be £100 and this value acts like a magnet to which the price of the gilt is drawn over its life. Only undated stocks, which have no prospect of redemption as long as prevailing interest rates are higher than their coupons, and index-linked gilts, whose redemption values are not fixed at £100, do not have this inexorable tendency.

The coupon of the gilt informs the investor whether he will receive a substantial amount of his return by way of income or capital gain. For example, in Table 3.2, Treasury 3% 1986 is priced at £86¾ and Treasury 12% 1986 at £101½. Treasury 3% will yield little in the way of interest over its life, the majority of its return being in the form of capital gain (£100–£86¾). On the other hand, Treasury 12% 1986 will yield all of its return via interest income with, in fact, a small prospective capital loss. The investor, from knowledge of his tax position, may be able to express a preference for high or low coupon stocks. Knowledge of the coupon and the price combine to give the interest yield and with this some understanding of the level of return the income from the gilt will generate. In the above example, the interest yield from Treasury 3% 1986 would only be 3.46% compared with 11.82% from Treasury 12% 1986.

However, the interest yield, as mentioned earlier, ignores the capital gain or loss element of return and the shorter the term of the gilt or the lower the coupon, the more misleading this will be as a measure. This can be clearly seen from Table 4.1.

Table 4.1   Comparison of interest yields and redemption yields

	Price £	Interest yield (%)	Redemption yield (%)	Difference (%)
Treasury 3% 1986	86.75	3.46	7.34	+3.88
Treasury 12% 1986	101.50xd	11.82	11.48	−0.34
Gas 3% 1990–5	62.25	4.84	7.86	+3.02
Exchequer 10¼% 1995	94.00	11.38	11.77	+0.39
Consols 4% undated	37.50	11.09	—	—

Source: Table 3.2.

For example, the difference between the interest yield and the redemption yield (the latter allows for the capital received on redemption) is almost 4% for the short, Treasury 3% 1986, and less than 0.4% for the long, Exchequer 10½% 1995. For long-term or high coupon gilts, therefore, the interest yield can be used as an estimate of the overall return to redemption whereas for short-term or low coupon gilts it gives only a partial measure of return. However, for undated stocks such as Consols 4%, the interest yield is the only measure of return available, since undated gilts have no expected redemption date.

Maturity is a useful comparative measure for gilts since investors can choose gilts according to their pattern of consumption preferences or their future liabilities. As was discussed in Chapter 2, one way of avoiding interest rate risk is to match exactly the maturities of assets and liabilities.[2] If a gilt with a longer maturity than the liability is chosen, the investor runs the risk that interest rates will have risen and the price fallen when the gilt has to be sold to meet the liability. If a gilt with too short a maturity is chosen, the investor runs the risk that interest rates will have fallen and the money received on redemption will have to be reinvested for the remaining term at a lower interest rate than the investor could have obtained on a gilt with the same maturity as the liability.

However, the investor may be unable or unwilling to match the maturity of his investments to that of his liabilities. Or he may wish to compare two gilts with the same maturity. In order to choose between gilts in these circumstances, he must be able to compare the interest rate risk and the return on each of the gilts he is considering and, to do this, he must turn to his only remaining measure, the redemption yield.

---

[2] In fact interest rate risk cannot be completely avoided since interest payments during the life of the gilt may not exactly match consumption needs and so have to be reinvested, perhaps at less advantageous rates. Only if an investor were to purchase a zero coupon fixed interest security (one which pays no interest during its life) could he avoid interest rate risk altogether.

Comparison of redemption yields

Suppose the Greenfields pension fund knows in 1983 that it has a liability to meet in two years' time but, since it pays no tax, it is indifferent between a high coupon or low coupon gilt of the same maturity, for example the two gilts described in Table 4.2.

From a comparison of redemption yields, it would appear that Treasury 12% 1985 offers the greater return since it has the higher redemption yield. Redemption yield is a measure of holding period return to redemption, and so, if Greenfields intends to hold the gilt until 1985, it would appear obvious that it should choose Treasury 12% 1985. A glance at Table 3.2 in Chapter 3 shows that all gilts have different yields to redemption and if redemption yields were the only measure of choice, this state could surely not persist since the gilts would have to provide the same redemption yield or their prices would fall until they did so. If Exchequer 8¾% 1985 were judged on redemption yield alone, no one would buy it and its price would fall until it too offered a redemption yield of 15%.

So, why cannot the redemption yield be used as a measure of comparison between two gilts of the same maturity? Table 4.2 highlights some of the problems of the redemption yield. Firstly, look at the cash flows in 1984. The £8¾ income from Exchequer 8¾% 1985 is discounted at 13.5% whereas the £12 income from an investment of equal risk. Treasury 12% 1985, is discounted at 15%. We know that the discount rate which should be used is the rate of interest Greenfields could get by investing in another investment of equivalent risk. The redemption yield does not tell us what that rate of interest-is. It is simply the single discount rate which, given the price, coupon and maturity of a gilt, discounts the future cash flows back to the price – the missing number in an equation. Also, if we look at Exchequer 8¾% 1985, we can see that the discount rate for cash flows in 1984 is the same as that for 1985 and yet we do not expect interest rates to remain constant

Table 4.2   Comparison of redemption yields of gilts with the same maturity

	Price £	Redemption yield (approx.) (%)	Now	1984	1985
Exchequer 8¾% 1985	92.125	13.5	£92.125	$= \dfrac{8.75}{1.135}$	$+\dfrac{108.75}{(1.135)^2}$
Treasury 12% 1985	95.125	15	£95.125	$=\dfrac{12}{1.15}$	$+\dfrac{112}{(1.15)^2}$

throughout the life of any gilt. This is the assumption underlying the use of a redemption yield, even if the gilt has a life of twenty years. So, the redemption yield does not help Greenfields in its understanding of the pricing of equivalent maturity gilts.

Now, consider Mr Gamble. He wishes to take on some interest rate risk since he believes that interest rates will fall within the next twelve months. He would like to know which gilt it would be best to choose to take advantage of this expected fall in interest rates and to maximise his gain from it. In other words, Mr Gamble wishes to estimate the sensitivity of each gilt to interest rate risk.

Does an analysis of redemption yields help Mr Gamble identify the sensitivity of different gilts to interest rate risk? One way of doing this would be to examine the effect of a given change in redemption yield on the prices of gilts with different maturities and coupons (the two major distinguishing factors). Table 4.3 quantifies the effect of a 2% rise or fall

Table 4.3   Effects of changes in redemption yield on prices of gilts with different maturities and coupons

(a)   *Different maturity gilts (assume 10% coupon)*

		Years to maturity				
		1	5	10	20	Undated
Redemption yield	10%	£100	£100	£100	£100	£100
	12%	£98	£93	£89	£85	£83
	14%	£96	£86	£79	£74	£71
Price range		£4	£14	£21	£26	£29
Price range as percentage of original price		4%	15%	24%	31%	35%

(b)   *Different coupon gilts (assume ten-year maturity)*

		Coupon		
		5%	10%	15%
Redemption yield	10%	£69	£100	£131
	12%	£60	£89	£117
	14%	£53	£79	£105
Price range		£16	£21	£26
Price range as percentage of original price		27%	24%	22%

in redemption yields from the assumed prevailing yield of 12%. Table 4.3(a) looks at the impact on the prices of gilts with a 10% coupon and different maturities. Table 4.3(b) looks at gilts with a ten-year life but different coupons. In both cases interest is assumed to be paid once a year at the year end.

From Table 4.3(a), Mr Gamble can see that the longer the maturity of the gilt, the more sensitive it is to changes in redemption yield. So, if he believes that redemption yields will fall, he would probably choose long-dated or undated gilts. Similarly, although the effect is less marked, Mr Gamble can see from Table 4.3(b) that the lower the coupon the more sensitive the gilt will be to changes in redemption yield. This is because investors in low coupon gilts purchased substantially below par receive proportionately more return from repayment on redemption and this effectively makes such stocks into longer-term gilts than high coupon gilts of the same maturity. Mr Gamble will therefore maximise his gain, in the event of a fall in redemption yields, by investing in low coupon long-dated gilts.

Duration

The effects of coupon and maturity on sensitivity to changes in redemption yield can be combined into one measure, called the duration of a gilt. Duration is defined to be

D = Weighted average of length of time before each payment × the relative present value of each payment

For example, the duration of a gilt with two years to redemption and a 10% coupon quoted at £96.60 would be calculated as follows:

$$D = \frac{1.PV_1}{£96.60} + \frac{2.PV_2}{£96.60}$$

where PV_1 is the present value of the payment one year from now discounted by the redemption yield, calculated to be 12%, and PV_2 the present value of the payment two years from now.

So,

$$D = \frac{1 \times \dfrac{10}{1.12} + 2 \times \dfrac{110}{(1.12)^2}}{96.60}$$

$$= \frac{1 \times 8.92 + 2 \times 87.69}{96.60}$$

$$= \textbf{1.9 years}$$

This measure will be discussed again later in the chapter but we can already see that low coupon gilts will have higher values of D than high coupon gilts and long-term gilts greater duration than shorts. In fact, gilts with the same value of D will have the same sensitivity to changes in redemption yields.

Mr Gamble can now, given an estimated change in redemption yield, calculate the effect of this change on different gilts and make purchase, sale or switching[3] decisions. This is all very well, but what does a change in redemption yield signify and how can Mr Gamble estimate how required redemption yields will change over any given period?

At any point in time, redemption yields of gilts of differing maturities follow a pattern (with exceptions in the case of low coupon gilts[4]). For example, in December 1982, the date of the gilt prices shown in Table 3.2, redemption yields increased slightly with maturity, reaching a peak of over 12% around 1990, and then declined slightly thereafter. This trend in redemption yields can be plotted on what is known as a yield curve which may be rising, humped, falling or flat. These four types of yield curve are drawn in Figure 4.1.

The yield curve is affected by present and expected future interest rates. For example, if short-term interest rates are low and considered likely to rise in the near future, the redemption yield on shorts will be lower than that on a five- or ten-year gilt, giving a rising yield curve. On the other hand, if inflation and hence interest rates were expected to decline in the longer term, long-term gilts would have lower redemption yields than medium-term gilts, giving a falling yield curve.

---

[3] Where the investor switches between gilts with different sensitivities to changes in redemption yields.

[4] Low coupon gilts are out of line in the yield curve or pattern for two reasons. Firstly, most of their value lies in the capital repayment at the end of their life and so they act as longer-term stocks than high coupon gilts of the same maturity. Secondly, tax effects may distort their redemption yields. If there is more demand for low coupon stocks than there is supply, because investors want return in the form of capital gain rather than income, this will push up the prices of low coupon gilts relative to other gilts and lower their redemption yields.

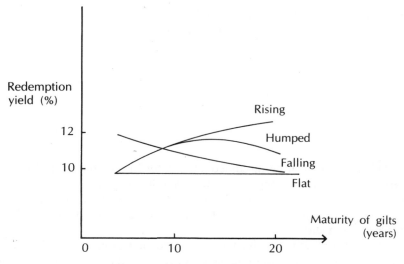

Figure 4.1   Possible redemption yield curves

If Mr Gamble could draw today's yield curve and his estimate of this curve in twelve month's time, he would be able to apply his knowledge of sensitivity to redemption yield changes to make investment decisions.

However, a redemption yield is a complex average of interest rates prevailing throughout the life of the gilt.[5] Each redemption yield is a different mixture of these interest rates. It would be far easier for Mr Gamble to concern himself with the relevant underlying interest rates and estimate sensitivities using these, rather than using misleading and complicated redemption yields. Interest rates are also economically significant figures. They are determined by the demand and supply for money and these in turn are determined by the number of productive investment opportunities, the consumption preferences of investors and the expected inflation rates. If inflation is expected to rise by 10% next year, Mr Gamble will be able to estimate the impact on interest rates but not necessarily on redemption yields.

---

[5] With a fixed interest security which paid no interest (zero coupon) and had an n-year life, the redemption yield would be the geometric mean of all the n spot rates. (See pp. 103–5 for an explanation of spot rates.) So, in the case of a zero coupon gilt, we could write r as

$$r = n \sqrt{(1 + r_1)(1 + r_2) \dots (1 + r_n)} - 1$$

For gilts with non-zero coupons, the relationship between a redemption yield and underlying interest rates is more complex.

Term structure of interest rates

Since redemption yields do not enable us to get an accurate picture of prevailing interest rates for different maturities of gilt (known as the 'term structure of interest rates'), we go back to the discounted cash flow valuation model for gilts and examine the underlying interest rates which determine their prices.

Spot rates

We know that we must be able to write

$$P = \frac{D}{(1 + r_1)} + \frac{D}{(1 + r_2)^2} + \cdots \frac{D + 100}{(1 + r_n)^n} \qquad (4.1)$$

where D is the annual interest payment,[6] r_1 the rate of interest required on one-year investments such as gilts, r_2 the *annual* rate of interest required for money invested now for two years, and so on; r_1 will not necessarily be equal to r_2 nor r_2 to r_3 (as was assumed in the case of the redemption yield) since interest rates will be expected to change over time. These interest rates, the r_i, are called spot interest rates because they are rates for investments made now or 'on the spot'. In other words, the investor contracts to lend money now for n years in return for which he receives an annual rate of interest of r_n throughout the n years of the loan.

Since the purchase of a gilt always involves a loan to the UK government, the investor will be guaranteed the interest and principal payments whichever gilt he invests in. Thus, he will require the same interest rate for lending for n years to the UK government for any gilt. This means that, at any point in time, the same set of spot rates can be used to value any gilt. So, different gilts will have cash flows paid in the same years discounted at the same rates. If we go back to Table 4.2 on p. 98, we can now write

$$\text{Exchequer } 8\sqrt[3]{4}\% \ 1985 \quad 92.125 = \frac{8.75}{(1 + r_1)} + \frac{108.75}{(1 + r_2)^2}$$

$$\text{Treasury } 12\% \ 1985 \quad 95.125 = \frac{12}{(1 + r_1)} + \frac{112}{(1 + r_2)^2}$$

---

[6] For simplicity, we assume annual rather than six-monthly cash flows.

This implies that money invested in either gilt for one year will provide the same interest rate, r_1, whether invested in Exchequer 8¾% 1985 or Treasury 12% 1985. Similarly, money invested for one year at r_1 will not necessarily provide the same annual interest rate as money invested for two years at r_2, because interest rates vary over time.

Our objective is to be able to draw a spot rate curve now and an expected spot rate curve in twelve months' time (or for whichever holding period is preferred) in order to be able to study changes in gilt

Table 4.4   Estimation of existing spot rates

Gilt	Coupon (%)	Maturity (years)	Price £
A	8.5	1	96.875
B	10	2	95

We assume all payments are at the year end and at exactly one-year intervals. From gilt A, we know that

$$P_0 = \frac{D_1 + 100}{1 + r_1}$$

or

$$96.875 = \frac{108.5}{(1 + r_1)}$$

which gives

$r_1 = 12\%$

From gilt B, we can write

$$P_0 = \frac{D_1}{(1 + r_1)} + \frac{D_2 + 100}{(1 + r_2)^2}$$

$$95 = \frac{10}{(1 + r_1)} + \frac{110}{(1 + r_2)^2}$$

We have already found r_1 to be 12%, so

$$95 = \frac{10}{1.12} + \frac{110}{(1 + r_2)^2}$$

Solving, we get

$r_2 = 13\%$

prices and calculate expected holding period returns and investment strategies for Mr Gamble. To draw the present curve, the spot rates, r_i, have to be determined. This can be done by looking at gilts of different maturities, as, for example, described in Table 4.4.

Provided there is a sufficient variety of maturities of gilts, the whole range of spot rates, from one to twenty-five years or more, can be determined and the present spot-rate curve drawn.[7]

Forward rates

The next step is to try to determine the future spot rates, that is, a future term structure of interest rates. This will enable Mr Gamble to see how interest rates are expected to change in the future. He can then decide which gilts to buy, given the market's and his own expectations. In fact, we can use the existing spot-rate curve to give an indication of future spot rates as follows.

Suppose Mr Gamble is considering the purchase of one of the gilts described in Table 4.4. If he buys A, he will get a one-year return of 12%. If he buys B, he will get an equivalent annual return of 13% for two years. But, if the going rate for lending money for one year is 12%, by buying B Mr Gamble is in effect agreeing to lend for one year at 12% and then for another year at a rate which gives an overall return of 13% per annum for two years. If we call this unknown rate for lending for one year from the end of year 1 to the end of year 2, $_1f_2$, we can write

$$(1 + r_1)\,(1 + {_1f_2}) = (1 + r_2)^2$$

$$(1.12)\,(1 + {_1f_2}) = (1.13)^2$$

$$_1f_2 = 14\%$$

$_1f_2$ is the *current* market rate for agreeing *now* to lend money for one year starting in twelve months' time. $_1f_2$ is called the forward rate for lending in year 2. It is implicit, since once r_1 and r_2 are known $_1f_2$ is fixed. Once we know all the spot rates r_i, we can isolate the implicit forward rates $_0f_1$, $_1f_2$, $_2f_3$, and so on ($_0f_1$ is obviously the same as r_1).

For example, to calculate $_2f_3$, we know that the following must hold:

$$(1 + r_1)\,(1 + {_1f_2})\,(1 + {_2f_3}) = (1 + r_3)^3$$

---

[7] Any gaps, from lack of suitable gilts, can be estimated.

where r_1 (or $_0f_1$), $_1f_2$, $_2f_3$ are the three implicit one-year forward interest rates for years 1, 2 and 3 which combine to give an equivalent annual interest rate of r_3 for three years. So, if we know that r_3 is 14% and $_1f_2$ is 14%, we can write:

$$(1.12)\,(1.14)\,(1 + {}_2f_3) = (1.14)^3 \qquad (4.2)$$

giving

$$_2f_3 = 16\%$$

An alternative way of finding $_2f_3$ would be to say

$$(1 + r_2)^2\,(1 + {}_2f_3) = (1 + r_3)^3 \qquad (4.3)$$

$$(1.13)^2\,(1 + {}_2f_3) = (1.14)^3$$

Since the investor is lending for three years at r_3, this must be equivalent to lending for two years at r_2 and for one year in year 3 at $_2f_3$. Equations (4.2) and (4.3) are exactly the same given that $(1 + r_2)^2 = (1 + r_1)\,(1 + {}_1f_2)$.

Of what use are these forward rates in estimating the future spot rates which will prevail, say, in one year's time? This depends on two factors: the efficiency of the market for gilts and the element of bias which may be included in forward rates as estimators of future spot rates.

If the market is active with many investors, low transaction costs and expectations on future interest rates are widely disseminated, these expectations will be incorporated into gilt prices and forward rates. Thus, such an efficient market will have forward rates which predict, as accurately as is possible at the time, future spot rates. In previous chapters, we have seen that transaction costs on gilts are relatively low (with no stamp duties and lower brokers' commissions than for equities) and turnover in gilts is high. Also, because interest rates form such a major element of government policy, any expectations or comments concerning future interest rates are widely publicised. We would therefore expect forward rates to be good predictors of future spot rates and such empirical evidence as there is, both for UK and US government fixed-term stock, on the whole supports this view.[8]

The implications of having efficient securities markets are very important and the whole of Chapter 9 is devoted to the concept of efficient markets. We simply point out here that an efficient gilts market leads to the conclusion that forward rates are the best estimates available for future spot rates. Although future spot rates will doubtless turn out not

---

[8] For a summary of the research in this area, see Van Horne (1978), ch. 4, pp. 95–112.

to be exactly as predicted by forward rates, it will not pay Mr Gamble to spend time and money on his own market forecasts. Since all that is publicly known about future interest rates is already incorporated into forward rates, it is unlikely that Mr Gamble's own views will add anything to the accuracy of the forward rates' forecasts. Despite this, much trading in gilts is based on the investors' own views of future interest rate movements which are different from those reflected in forward rates and gilt prices.

The second factor to be taken into account when using forward rates as estimates of future spot rates is whether they include any bias in their estimates. There are various hypotheses concerning this which are concerned with whether there is a bias or not and, if so, what is the cause of this bias. The four major hypotheses are outlined in Table 4.5.

The simplest hypothesis in Table 4.5 is the expectations hypothesis. This says that forward interest rates are unbiased predictors of future interest rates. So, for example, the forward rate, $_1f_2$, of 14% derived from Table 4.4 is the market's exact estimate of next year's r_1.

A major implication of the expectations hypothesis is that, if it holds, the investor need not worry about the maturity of the gilts he buys. For example, if Mr Gamble wishes to make a two-year investment in gilts, he can either buy a gilt maturing in two years' time, say, gilt B in Table 4.4, or a one-year gilt, say, gilt A, followed by a further one-year gilt (or, indeed, a three-year gilt which he will sell at the end of two years). The *expected* two-year holding period return from all these investment strategies is the same. If Mr Gamble buys gilt B, he will get an annual return of 13% for the two years. If he buys gilt A, he will get a return of 12% in the first year. Since $_1f_2$ is 14%, Mr Gamble expects to get a return of 14% on a one-year gilt if he buys it in one year's time (since 14% is the expected future one-year spot rate). Thus, his expected return from either strategy is 13% per annum.

The problem with this argument is that the risk inherent in each of the maturity strategies is not the same, even if the *expected* return is. If Mr Gamble wishes to invest for a period of two years, he will ensure a *certain* nominal return by buying B. If he buys A and then has to reinvest at the end of one year, he runs the risk that next year's r_1 will not be the 14% currently predicted and thus his return is not certain.

The liquidity premium hypothesis is based on the view that investors usually want to lend for a short time and borrowers (in the case of gilts, this is the UK government) wish to borrow long. So, for example, Mr Gamble would have to be paid a premium to invest in, say, a ten-year gilt when he only wishes to invest for two years. The inflation premium hypothesis is based on the idea that the risk of concern to the investor is not interest rate risk but inflation risk. If inflation can only be forecast accurately a short time ahead, investors (such as Mrs Silver in Chapter 2) will prefer to lend short term, as under the liquidity preference

Table 4.5   Hypotheses concerning relationship between forward rates and expected spot rates

Hypothesis	Argument	Effect
(1) *Expectations*	Every forward rate is the best market estimate of the relevant future spot rate	Forward rates can be used as estimates of expected spot rates
(2) *Liquidity premium*	Lenders prefer to lend short. Borrowers prefer to borrow long. So investors require a liquidity premium to compensate for the interest rate risk of holding longer-term securities than they wish to. The premium increases with maturity of investment	Forward rates are overestimates of future spot rates since they include a premium for agreeing to lend long
(3) *Inflation premium*	Risk is due mainly to inflation risk, that is, uncertainty about future *actual* inflation since only *expected* inflation is incorporated into interest rates. The shorter the term of lending, the better the lender can estimate inflation. So lenders prefer to lend for short periods and forward rates include an inflation premium to compensate lenders for uncertainty about future inflation	Forward rates are overestimates of future spot rates since they include a premium for inflation risk
(4) *Market segmentation*	In order to reduce interest rate risk, both borrowers and lenders match their assets and liabilities. For example, banks will prefer short-term gilts and pension funds long-term gilts	The premium or discount in the forward rate for a particular maturity will depend on the demand and supply for that maturity

argument. So, again, forward rates will include a premium to persuade investors to lend long. Finally, the market segmentation hypothesis presumes that the demand and supply for each maturity of gilt will be different, with the premium being positive or negative according to whether borrowers outnumber lenders or vice versa for that maturity.

If there is no premium incorporated into forward rates (for whatever reason) we would probably expect to see as many rising forward rate curves as falling ones. According to the expectations hypothesis, a rising forward rate curve would occur only when future spot rates were expected to exceed current spot rates. Similarly, a falling forward rate curve would imply that future spot rates were expected to fall below current levels. However, over the past fifty years, rising forward rate curves have predominated. This empirical evidence[9] supports the theory that forward rates are overestimates of expected spot rates and include a premium (depending on the theory, for liquidity or inflation) which increases as maturity increases. This is because, whether the expected spot rate curve is rising or flat, the forward rate curve will rise if it includes a liquidity or inflation premium. Only when the expected spot rate curve is falling may the forward rate curve also fall. Figure 4.2 shows the effects of a liquidity or inflation premium on the forward rate curve.

It would appear, therefore, that the forward rate curve will in general give an overestimate of future spot rates. However, the curve can be adjusted downwards by subtracting out the premiums; these can be calculated, for each maturity of gilt, by using historical data and assuming the same premiums will occur in the future.

Practical use of term structure

Obviously, in practice, computer models will be used to derive expected spot rates from data on forward rates and liquidity/inflation premiums (allowing for tax distortions). The future price of each gilt can then be estimated *without* making any assumptions on future interest rates. Only those which were implicit in the existing interest rate term structure will have been used. If a particular investor feels he has better estimates of future interest rates not available to the gilt market as a whole, he can calculate future prices of gilts and base investment decisions on his own data inputs.

At present, the use of term structure of interest rate models has not gained much popularity in the City, with most brokers and analysts still talking in terms of redemption yields. The computer models they use to estimate future gilt prices are based on changes in yields not interest rates. The implication behind a change in yield is unclear although it must imply a change in interest rates throughout the life of the gilt. In practice, interest rates may alter throughout the whole term structure but, more often, only short-term interest rates will change leaving

---

[9] For example, see Ibbotson and Sinquefield (1979).

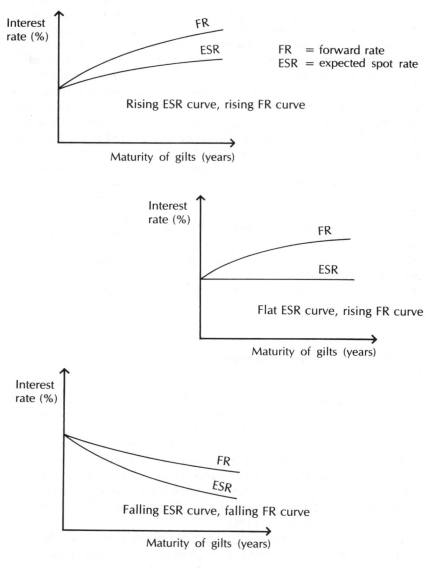

Figure 4.2   Effect of premium on forward-rate curve

expectations concerning long-term rates unaltered. Redemption yield changes cannot allow for such partial alterations in interest rates whereas the effect of a change only in r_1 can be analysed using the term structure of interest rates.

For example, suppose we are analysing the effect of changes in

Table 4.6   Effect of change in short-term interest rates on different maturity gilts

Before: $r_1 =$ 9%, $r_2 = 10\%$, $r_3 = 11\%$, $r_4 \ldots r_{10} = 11\%$

After: $r_1 = 11\%$, $r_2 = 12\%$, $r_3 = 13\%$, $r_4 \ldots r_{10} = 11\%$

Price	Before	After	Change
P_S	£97.90	£93.20	−£4.70
P_L	£94.40	£93.60	−£0.80

short-term spot interest rates on the two gilts described in Table 4.6. Both gilts have a 10% coupon; the short, S, has a three-year life, the long, L, a ten-year life. P_S is the price of gilt S, P_L the price of gilt L.

We assume a sudden change in one-year, two-year and three-year spot rates due, for example, to revised expectations concerning inflation. Table 4.6 shows that the short-term gilt is more severely affected than the long-term gilt and yet we saw earlier that long-term gilts were more sensitive to changes in redemption yields. These two results are not contradictory. L would have been more affected than S if *all* the spot rates r_1 through to r_{10} had been revised upwards, which is the implication underlying an increase in redemption yield. However, this may happen less often than changes only in short-term rates, and so measuring sensitivity to changes in redemption yields may be misleading.

A measure of sensitivity to changes in *spot* rates can be devised – a revised form of duration where, as before,

D = weighted average of length of time prior to each payment
× the relative present value of each payment

However, in this case the present values of the payments are calculated using spot rates and not redemption yields. For example, the duration of the short S in the 'before' situation of Table 4.6 is

$$D = \frac{1.PV_1}{£97.90} + \frac{2.PV_2}{£97.90} + \frac{3.PV_3}{£97.90}$$

where

$$PV_1 = \frac{10}{1.09} \qquad PV_2 = \frac{10}{(1.10)^2} \text{ and } PV_3 = \frac{110}{(1.11)^3}$$

$$D = \frac{1 \times 9.17}{97.90} + \frac{2 \times 8.26}{97.90} + \frac{3 \times 80.43}{97.90}$$

D = 2.7 years

Unfortunately, the use of duration as a sensitivity measure for interest rate risk is limited. Only when all $(1 + r_i)$ change by the same *percentage* amount throughout the term structure will gilts of the same duration be approximately equally sensitive. For example, if the one-year spot rate changed to 10%, $(1 + r_1)$ would rise to 1.10, an increase of 0.92%. $(1 + r_2)$ would thus have to increase by the same 0.92% to 1.11, $(1 + r_3)$, by 0.92% to 1.12, and so on. Since this is unlikely to happen in practice, more complex measures of sensitivity must be used.[10]

A further point on *any* estimates of changes in prices of dated gilts over any holding period: at the end of the period all the gilts under consideration will have become of shorter maturity and so will respond differently to interest rate changes. This factor must be taken into account in any model of gilt price sensitivity.

Financial futures

During 1982 a financial futures market, the London International Financial Futures Exchange (or LIFFE), opened in London. It is based on the successful Chicago financial futures market which started in 1976. We have already discussed in Chapter 2 the differences between a forward and futures market, the latter being centralised, regulated and dealing in standardised contracts. Thus, in, say, a foreign currency forward market, any amount of foreign currency (provided it is large enough) can in theory be bought or sold forward. In a futures market, multiples of a standard amount must be traded; for example, on the London and Chicago foreign currency futures markets, sterling is traded in futures contracts each for £25,000. In the UK financial futures market, the gilts contract is for £50,000 nominal.

As a particular risk has increased, and with it both scope for speculation and the need to hedge, so a futures market has developed. Foreign currency futures markets allow exchange risk to be hedged; commodity futures allow the risk of price changes in commodities to be hedged; index-linked gilts allow inflation risk to be hedged and now

---

[10] For example, each payment term would have to be weighted by a factor which measured the relative change in present value of the payment term for relative changes in each r_i. In this way, the impact of, say, changes in short- or long-term spot rates on the price and risk of particular gilts could be estimated.

financial futures allow interest rate risk to be hedged.

For example, if short-term interest rates are expected to rise, we saw in the example based on Table 4.6 that an investor could, by switching from shorts to longs, avoid most of the impact of that rise. However, if interest rates throughout the term structure are expected to rise, all gilts will fall in value although to differing extents. The investor faced with this situation can either switch to the least sensitive gilts to minimise his expected loss, hold on and hope his gilts will recover their value, or sell his gilt portfolio and buy other securities less vulnerable to interest rate risk. The existence of a financial futures market offers the investor another alternative. Instead of selling his gilts, he can sell futures contracts on gilts so that any fall in the value of his gilt portfolio will be balanced by a profit on the futures contracts. Instead of being vulnerable to interest rate changes which will affect the prices of his gilts, he can fix his return by using the financial futures market.

Suppose Colimited has £1m, which will be needed in six months' time for an investment project. The finance director of Colimited, Mr Shrub, decides to buy £1m.-worth of long-dated gilts although he is worried that they will fall in value if interest rates rise. To protect the company from a shortfall for the investment project when the gilts are sold in six months' time, the finance director decides to fix the sale proceeds of his gilts now. If a forward market in gilts existed, all he would have to do is to sell forward the gilts he holds, that is, to fix a price now for sale in six months' time. In a futures market, with standardised contracts, Mr Shrub will have to sell futures contracts in the security which most nearly resembles his gilts. The standard gilt contract in the UK financial futures market is for £50,000 of a *notional* twenty-year gilt with a 12% coupon. Mr Shrub will therefore have to sell approximately twenty futures contracts.[11]

The reason for having a notional futures contract for gilts is to widen the market as much as possible. If a particular existing gilt were designated, the amount in issue would be small relative to the amount of futures trading on it. This would allow speculators to engineer 'squeezes'[12] and distort the market. So, instead, a notional gilt is designated and a whole range of comparable gilts are allowed to represent the notional gilt on delivery. For example, in the London market, *any* gilt with a maturity of between fifteen to twenty-five years can represent the notional gilt. Of course, a deliverable gilt will have a

---

[11] The number will not, in fact, be exactly twenty, to allow for differences in volatility to interest rate changes between the actual gilt held by Colimited and the futures gilt contract.

[12] There are various types of squeeze, but a squeeze usually involves a speculator buying or threatening to take delivery of a contract he has already bought. A futures market squeeze would affect the deliverable gilt in the spot market.

different coupon and maturity from the notional gilt, but this is allowed for by using a conversion factor.[13]

Thus, Mr Shrub, if Colimited's gilts falls into the deliverable category, will be able to deliver them to the ultimate purchaser of his futures contracts. Alternatively, Mr Shrub can simply, at the end of the six months, buy back his futures contract just before delivery, making a gain or a loss, and at the same time sell the gilts on the stock market, making an offsetting gain or loss.

For example, if interest rates rise to the extent that Colimited's gilt-edged investment falls in value to £900,000, that loss will be offset by an equivalent gain on the futures contracts since it will now cost Colimited less to, say, buy back the six-months futures contract it had sold. Colimited will thus, in theory, make no loss *or* gain on the investment.[14] It has locked itself in to the return promised when the gilt was purchased. This hedge is outlined in Table 4.7.

Table 4.7   *Example of a financial futures hedge*

	Transaction	Cash flow £	Timing
Colimited	Buys gilt	−1,000,000	Now
	Sells gilt	+ 900,000	In 6 months
	Gilt loss	− 100,000	
	Sells futures contract	+1,000,000	In 6 months
	Buys back*	− 900,000	In 6 months
	Future contract gain	**+ 100,000**	
	NET GAIN/LOSS	**0**	

* Just before the futures contract matures

[13] The conversion factor takes into account the difference in coupon and maturity between the notional gilt and the deliverable gilt. The conversion factor is:

$$\frac{\text{Price deliverable gilt would have on redemption yield of 12\%}}{\text{Price of 12\% notional gilt on redemption yield of 12\% (=£100)}}$$

So, different amounts of different deliverable gilts will need to be delivered. Since the conversion factor assumes a 'flat' yield curve (of 12%), which is not often the case, there will usually be one particular gilt which is the 'cheapest' to deliver, in the sense that it will cost the least to buy in the spot market for delivery on the futures contract.

[14] In practice financial futures prices do not change in mirror-image fashion to the spot prices, even if the amounts held have been adjusted for differences in volatility to interest rate risk. (See footnote 11.) So, a 'perfect hedge, such as that described in Table 4.7, is unlikely to be achieved.

So, the existence of a financial futures market allows investors to reduce interest rate risk. Alternatively, the financial futures market allows speculators to *take on* interest rate risk, say by selling futures contracts for gilts they do not own. By doing this, a speculator is taking the view that interest rates will rise by more than expected by the market (as is incorporated in the term structure of interest rates) and that he will be able to buy back his contract at a lower cost.

Other fixed interest securities

The discussion on holding period returns of gilts and the importance of the term structure of interest rates applies to all fixed interest securities. In this section, therefore, we content ourselves with highlighting the major differences between gilts and other fixed interest securities.

'Other' fixed interest securities can be divided into four main groups: other 'public' fixed interest securities (including those issued by non-UK governments, local authorities and public boards) and three groups of 'private' fixed interest securities – debentures, loan stocks and preference shares. Convertible unsecured loan stocks, which entitle the holder to convert from a fixed interest security into ordinary shares, will be discussed in Chapter 6.

Table 4.8 shows the relative importance of these groups compared to British funds, both in terms of market value and turnover.

Table 4.8   *Market value and turnover of fixed interest securities*

	Market value (£m.) (at 31 March 1981)	Turnover (£m.) (1980)
Public		
UK gilts	76.079	151,698
Irish government	2,690	7,994
Overseas governments	231	225
Local authorities	2,333	3,820
Public boards	276	342
UK companies **(including utilities)**		
Debentures and loans*	3,910	1,241
Preference shares	828	168
Ordinary shares	91,943	22,079

* Including convertibles.
Source: *Stock Exchange Fact Book*, March 1981.

Other public fixed interest securities

Irish government securities are traded on the Dublin Stock Exchange and can be treated in the same way as gilts by Irish investors. Commonwealth governments have traditionally issued long-term debt securities in sterling and recently there have been a few sterling bonds issued by European governments.[15] Local authority stocks are considered almost as default-free as gilts since they are secured on the rates and no local authority has yet defaulted on its borrowings. They are usually shorter-term than gilts. Public boards are no longer an important sector of the stock market.

Private fixed interest securities

All three sub-categories, debentures, loan stocks and preference shares, are different from gilts in that they suffer from the additional risk of default – the risk that interest payments will not be made or capital not redeemed. Because of their additional risk, the returns available on company fixed interest securities are higher than those on gilts. This hierarchy of returns (expressed in the form of redemption yields) can be

Table 4.9   Financial Times–actuaries indices on fixed interest securities

FIXED INTEREST						AVERAGE GROSS REDEMPTION YIELDS		Thur Jan 13	Wed Jan 12	Year ago (approx.)
PRICE INDICES	Thur Jan 13	Day's change %	Wed Jan 12	xd adj. today	xd adj. 1983 to date	**British Government**				
						1 Low	5 years	9.24	9.36	13.16
						2 Coupons	15 years	10.64	10.73	14.22
						3	25 years	10.96	11.06	14.12
British Government						4 Medium	5 years	12.07	12.16	16.31
1 5 years	116.00	+0.33	115.61	—	0.00	5 Coupons	15 years	11.86	11.98	16.04
2 5-15 years	124.67	+0.68	123.82	—	0.00	6	25 years	11.39	11.46	15.41
3 Over 15 years	130.15	+0.74	129.19	—	0.00	7 High	5 years	12.14	12.29	16.18
4 Irredeemables	135.48	—	135.48	—	0.00	8 Coupons	15 years	12.04	12.14	16.21
5 All Stocks	123.53	+0.59	122.81	—	0.00	9	25 years	11.53	11.61	15.71
						10 Irredeemables	†	10.89	10.88	13.57
6 Debentures and Loans	99.27	-0.18	99.45	—	0.00	11 Debs & Loans	5 years	12.75	12.77	17.02
						12	15 years	12.71	12.68	16.81
						13	25 years	12.71	12.68	16.68
7 Preference	75.17	-0.00	75.18	—	0.00	14 Preference	†	13.21	13.21	16.10

‡Flat yield. Highs and lows record, base dates, values and constituent changes are published in Saturday issues. A list of constituents is available from the Publishers, The Financial Times, Bracken House, Cannon Street, London, EC4P 4BY

Source: *Financial Times*, 14 January 1983.

---

[15] For example, Sweden 13½% 1986.

seen in Table 4.9. Gilts are less risky than debentures and loan stocks which in turn are less subject to default risk than preference shares.

Table 4.8 clearly shows how company fixed interest securities are now dominated by ordinary shares, both in terms of market value and turnover. This has not always been the case. In the nineteenth century, companies could only borrow very short term from banks. Any long-term debt had to come from investors via the stock market, in the form of preference shares, debentures and unsecured loan stocks as the limited liability company structure became a more acceptable legal entity. The decline in the use of such debt capital, which has been replaced to a great extent by bank borrowing, is highlighted in the statistics for new issues of company securities in Table 4.10.

This decline can be attributed to many factors, of which two stand out. Firstly, the relative attractions of the three different categories (four if convertibles are included) have been affected by their respective tax treatments. For example, in 1965 the introduction of corporation tax rendered preference shares relatively unattractive to issue in comparison with debentures and loan stocks. Secondly, the high interest rates and inflation uncertainty of the 1970s made companies unwilling to incur long-term high fixed interest debt commitments and prefer to take out variable rate, shorter-term bank loans.

This second argument appears to be contradicted by the growing and thriving gilt-edged market. However, gilt-edged securities have attractions that company fixed interest securities cannot offer. For instance, the 1969 Finance Act removed the liability to capital gains tax of an investor in British funds who held his investment for twelve months or more. Also, brokerage commissions for gilts are lower than for com-

Table 4.10   Company security new issue statistics

Year	Debentures and loans (excluding convertibles)	Preference shares	Ordinary shares	Total
	£m	£m	£m	£m
1950	72	11	46	129
1955	65	19	155	239
1960	122	10	346	478
1965	427	3	46	476
1970	212	17	52	281
1975	96	45	1,321	1,462
1980	2	37	854	893

Source: *Midland Bank Review*, February issues.

pany fixed interest securities and transactions in gilts are free of 2% transfer stamp duty. This concession was extended to include debentures and loan stocks in 1976 but overall transaction costs are still higher for all forms of company fixed interest securities.

Gilt-edged securities are also more marketable since they have an active secondary market. The relatively poor secondary market in company fixed interest securities (which can be seen from Table 4.8) can be attributed to the fact that these stocks are much smaller in terms of the size of each issue and that they are mostly held by the institutions on a long-term investment basis. In 1980, insurance companies, pension funds and investment and unit trusts held over two-thirds in market value of all UK company fixed interest securities.

(i) DEBT CAPITAL

This consists of debentures and loan stocks. Debentures are secured forms of fixed interest debt. Should the borrower default, the debenture holders can appoint a receiver to sell those assets of the company which represent their security and to reimburse them with the proceeds, whether or not the company is still operating. This security is either a 'fixed' charge on a particular asset such as property or a 'floating' charge. A floating charge gives the debenture holders more powers and means that they are secured on all the assets of the company. The managers can buy and sell these assets until the company defaults at which time the floating charge 'crystallises' and the debenture holders can sell as many assets as they need to get the money they are owed. Debenture holders are usually protected by a trust deed which specifies exactly their rights in the event of default and also places restrictions on the company, for example limits on other debt it can issue.

Unsecured loan stock is less protected against default risk in that it has no security. In the event of default, it is only ranked with all the other unsecured creditors, for example suppliers to the company.

So, in addition to inflation and interest rate risk, to which gilts are subject, investors in company debentures and loan stocks are concerned with whether the income of the company will be sufficient to enable it to fund the interest and capital repayments on the securities – that is, with default risk. They are similarly interested in the company's ability to repay its debts in the event of its being wound up[16] before the due repayment date.

Interest paid on both these types of debt capital is deducted from the company's pre-tax profits and so the cost to the company of the interest payments is net of the associated corporation tax liability. From the

---

[16] This occurs when the company goes into voluntary or compulsory liquidation.

investor's point of view, the returns and yields on these securities are calculated exactly as for gilts, and income from these investments is taxed at the investor's personal tax rate.

(ii) PREFERENCE SHARES

These form part of the share capital of the company and so holders can be viewed as part-owners of the company. In return for accepting a fixed rather than a variable amount of dividend, preference shareholders rank before ordinary shareholders who are entitled to whatever is left after all creditors, debt-holders and preference shareholders have been paid. Preference shareholders suffer less uncertainty of income than ordinary shareholders since they know how much income they expect to get. However, the company does not *have* to pay the preference dividend as it does with debt interest. It is in the interests of the ordinary shareholder for the company to pay the preference dividend since no ordinary share dividends can be paid until it has. (With 'cumulative' preference shares, all previous years' unpaid preference share dividends have to be made up before any ordinary dividends can be paid.) Also, preference shares usually rank before ordinary shares, but after debt capital, on a winding up of the company.

It can be seen that preference shares occupy a middle position between debt capital and ordinary shares. Preference shareholders are not strictly subject to default risk, as are other fixed interest securities, since they are part-owners of the company and not creditors who can put the company into liquidation. However, they do run the risk of not receiving a fixed-dividend payment or being fully repaid on winding up. Their risk is greater than the debt-holders' default risk but less than the ordinary shareholders' uncertainty of income.

Another difference between preference shares and debt capital is their tax position. Since the introduction of corporation tax in 1965, preference and ordinary share dividends have been paid out of after-corporation-tax profits. This is in contrast to interest on debt capital which is paid out of the company's pre-tax profits and hence is allowable against the company's tax bill. This tax disadvantage has contributed to the decline of the preference share as a source of funds for companies. The main reason for the continued presence of preference shares on the stock market is the fact that the majority, although perhaps issued in the 1930s or before, are irredeemable.

When looked at from the investor's viewpoint, care must be taken when preference shares are compared with other fixed interest securities all of which are quoted gross (before) income tax. The net preference dividend can be grossed up as in the following example. If a company has 4.9% preference shares in issue quoted at £75 per £100 nominal, the interest yield on the preference shares will be:

$$\textit{Net} \text{ interest yield} = \frac{4.9}{75} \times 100$$

$$= 6.5\%$$

$$\textit{Gross} \text{ interest yield} = \frac{4.9}{75} \times \frac{100}{70} \times 100$$

$$= 7 \times \frac{100}{75}$$

$$= 9.3\%$$

Preference shares do have one advantage to *corporate* investors. In their case, the dividends count as 'franked' income, meaning income which can be offset against the holders' corporation tax bill. This is why well over 75% of all preference shares are held by corporate investors.

Summary

This chapter has discussed how to make investment decisions concerning fixed interest securities, a subject often neglected in investment texts. The chapter has concentrated on gilts, by far the most important type of fixed interest security traded on the UK Stock Exchange, since the valuation of other types of fixed interest security is very similar.

The measures used in Chapter 3 to describe gilts were examined to see how they could help the investor compare gilts. It was found that although the redemption yield was the most complete measure available, it did not have intuitive meaning and could be misleading. The chapter then described how, given the prices of different coupon and maturity gilts, the underlying term structure of interest rates could be derived. It was seen that the spot and forward rates implicit in the term structure could be used to derive market estimates of future interest rates and to examine the volatility of different gilts to changes in interest rates. Given this knowledge, investment decisions could then be made, according to investor beliefs (relative to market estimates) of future interest rates and the investor's willingness to take on interest rate risk.

The next section of the chapter briefly discussed how the London financial futures market can be used to increase (speculate on) or decrease (hedge) interest rate risk. The chapter concluded with a brief outline of the major differences between gilts and other types of fixed interest security traded on the UK Stock Exchange.

Problems

1. Mr Long is considering, in January 1985, investing low coupon 'shorts' for a period of one year. He has narrowed his selection down to

Gilt	Price £	Redemption yield (%)
Treasury 3% 1980–90	76⅞%	8.0
Treasury 3% 1987	89½%	7.0

   (i) If Mr Long believes that yields in general are going to fall by 1%, which gilt would he choose and why?
   (ii) Calculate the 'duration' for each of the above gilts. Does the duration measure help Mr Long's choice?
   (iii) Is Mr Long right in looking simply at redemption yields? Explain the problems in using redemption yields.

2. From prevailing gilt prices in January 1981, current spot interest rates have been calculated:

Year	Spot rate (%)
1981	11.50
1982	11.20
1983	11.00
1984	10.80
1985	10.50
1986 onwards	10.00

   (i) What shape is the current yield curve? Is this inconsistent with the inflation or liquidity premium hypothesis?
   (ii) What are the forward rates for 1981 onwards?
   (iii) Calculate, using the spot rates, the current market prices of the following gilts:
      (a)   5% Treasury 1983
      (b) 15% Exchequer 1983
      (c)   5% Treasury 1985
      assuming annual interest payments and redemption payments occur at the year end.

(iv) The redemption yields of gilts (a), (b) and (c) are 11, 11.2 and 10.6% respectively. Why is the redemption yield of gilt (b) higher than the redemption yields (a) and (c)?

(v) If all redemption yields were to fall by 2%, which of the three gilts would experience the greatest *percentage* price change? What factors could cause such a fall in redemption yields?

(vi) Suppose Miss Tery wishes to repay a loan of £10,000 in 1983, which gilt should she buy to minimise the risk that she will not be able to meet the loan?

3. The following information is from the *Financial Times* of 7 January 1982, which for the purpose of this question should be assumed to be today's date.

	Price (ex int) £	Interest yield (%)	Redemption yield (%)
Exchequer 8¾% 1983	94⅝	9.25	14.75
Exchequer 11¼% 1984	92⅛	12.21	15.68
Treasury 3% 1985	73⅞	4.06	12.78
Exchequer 12¼% 1985	88⅞	13.78	16.20

(i) Explain the meaning of the terms 'interest yield' and 'redemption yield' and discuss the shortcomings of their use for investment decision-making.

(ii) Explain the meaning of the term 'spot' interest rates and 'forward' interest rates. Estimate, from the above table, approximate spot and forward interest rates for the next three years. What do they tell us about the market's current expectations concerning future interest rates? Assume, for simplicity, that interest on these gilts is paid annually in arrears and that the gilts are all redeemable on 7 January in their respective years.

(iii) Suppose you believe that, in one year's time, one- and two-year spot interest rates will be 2% per annum less than predicted by current forward interest rates. Which of the above gilts would you buy? How much would you stand to make, per £100 nominal, if you buy today and sell, ex interest, in one year's time?

4. The following fixed interest securities are listed in ascending order of *gross* redemption yields.

	Gross redemption yield (%)
3% PRO Redeemable Debentures 1995	8
Treasury 13½% 1995	12
XZY 10½% Unsecured Loan Stock 1995	13
JLK 6% Redeemable Preference Shares 1995	16

(i) If all the corporate securities had been issued by the same company, in which order would you have expected them to be listed and why?

(ii) Suggest possible reasons why the securities are in the order listed in the above table.

(iii) Outline the main differences between unsecured loan stock and preference shares. Why are preference shares usually irredeemable?

(iv) Describe the main advantages of gilt-edged securities as fixed interest investments over similar corporate securities.

Ordinary shares

Introduction

We examine in this chapter the valuation of ordinary shares. Ordinary shares, or equities as they are also known, are by far the most important type of security issued by UK companies. On 31 March 1982, there were 1,708 loan capital securities and 1,194 preference shares of UK companies quoted on the Stock Exchange, compared to 2,058 ordinary shares,[1] and yet the ordinary shares represented 95% of the market value of all these UK corporate quoted securities. The ordinary shares were worth £103,620m., more than the market value of UK gilt-edged stock of £81,087m. Despite this, ordinary shares represented 23% of the total market value of the UK Stock Exchange on that date. This

---

[1] Including deferred ordinary shares, i.e. shares with one or more rights of the ordinary shareholders for example the right to dividends, deferred until some specified time in the future. Strictly, the rights attached to a share are determined by the terms of the issue and the company's constitution, rather than by its name, which can sometimes mislead. The rights of a listed share can be found by referring to the *Stock Exchange Official Year Book* (see footnote 3).

percentage figure is misleading, since 55% of the Stock Exchange's total market value consisted of the securities of overseas companies, that is, shares which are quoted primarily on overseas stock exchanges. If these shares are excluded, UK company ordinary shares represented 52% of the market value of the Stock Exchange with gilts contributing a further 41%. Ordinary shares are also quoted on the unlisted securities market, mentioned in Chapter 1, but the value of these shares is small in comparison to listed shares.

Turnover in equities during 1981 was £32,387m., 17% of the total Stock Exchange turnover. Thus, although ordinary shares have a greater market value than gilts, they have a lower turnover. As explained in Chapter 3, the high turnover in gilts is due to the volatility of interest rates and the large average size of each transaction, £154,000 compared to £8,200 for ordinary shares. The small average size of bargains in equities reflects the greater involvement of the small investor in ordinary shares as opposed to fixed interest securities.

In fact, this involvement is one of long standing. As industries grew, in the late nineteenth and early twentieth centuries, companies began to raise much-needed capital by issuing securities to the public. Initially, fixed interest securities were the most common form of security issued. Then, as the need for capital increased even further, company owners became unable to raise additional debt on acceptable terms and turned to issuing shares (both preference and ordinary), thereby encouraging investors to participate more fully in the risk and return of their companies. Ordinary shares, in particular, offered the prospect of unlimited returns with the proviso of coming last in the queue after debt-holders, creditors and preference shareholders in the event of a liquidation. Small investors, eager for high returns, were willing to accept this greater risk of ordinary shares because their liability on fully paid-up shares was limited to the amount they invested.[2] If a company went into liquidation with liabilities exceeding assets, shareholders, unlike partners in a partnership, would not have to provide additional funds with which to repay all the creditors.

As the stock market developed, both UK and overseas companies came to the UK investor for funds. A glance at a *Stock Exchange Official Year Book*[3] of fifty years ago reveals that UK and overseas corporate securities of many more different types were in issue than are quoted today. Securities such as redeemable preference shares, convertible debentures and deferred ordinary shares abounded, with a company possibly having well over a dozen different types of security in

---

[2] Shareholders who held partly paid shares (now no longer allowed by the Stock Exchange for listed shares) were liable for the unpaid element of their shares in the event of a liquidation.

[3] An annual publication by the Stock Exchange, giving details of all securities listed on the Stock Exchange.

issue, offering a wide variety of different levels of risk and return. Corporate securities are now much reduced in number and type, with fixed-coupon securities being mostly in the form of straight debentures, unsecured loan stocks and preference shares. The decline in number of these securities can be attributed to such factors as the nationalisation of the utilities (590 companies were merged when the gas companies were nationalised in 1948), takeovers and mergers, the decline in popularity of certain fixed interest securities discussed in Chapter 3, and the lower issue costs associated with larger issues of a single type of security. Convertible unsecured loan stock, a fixed interest security convertible into ordinary shares, is still relatively popular but pure equity is by far the most important type of corporate finance raised through the stock market. In 1981, new equity issues on the UK Stock Exchange totalled £2,111m., representing 80% of all corporate new issues of securities.

Table 5.1 Beneficial ownership of listed UK ordinary shares, 1957–75

Category of beneficial shareholder	Per cent of total shareholdings at market value			
	1957	1963	1969	1975
Persons	65.8	54.0	47.4	37.5
Investing institutions				
Insurance companies	8.8	10.0	12.2	15.9
Pension funds	3.4	6.4	9.0	16.8
Investment trusts	5.2	7.4	7.6	6.1
Unit trusts	0.5	1.3	2.9	4.1
	17.9	25.1	31.7	42.9
Other				
Charities, etc.	1.9	2.1	2.1	2.3
Stockbrokers and jobbers	0.9	1.4	1.4	0.4
Banks	0.9	1.3	1.7	0.7
Other financial companies	1.6	2.6	1.1	4.0
Industrial and commercial companies	2.7	5.1	5.4	3.0
Public sector	3.9	1.5	2.6	3.6
Overseas sector	4.4	7.0	6.6	5.6
	16.3	21.0	20.9	19.6
TOTAL	100.0	100.0	100.0	100.0
£b.	11.6	27.5	37.9	44.6

Source: Wilson Report (1980). By permission of the Controller of Her Majesty's Stationery Office.

Although the small investor still takes an active part in the market for ordinary shares, his role has diminished in the past few decades. Table 5.1 shows who held listed UK company ordinary shares in 1957, 1963, 1969 and 1975. The proportion, in market value terms, of ordinary shares held directly by the private investor declined from nearly 66% in 1957 to under 38% in 1975.

The private investor has not completely abandoned the stock market. He has changed his method of investment from direct holdings to indirect holdings via insurance companies, pension funds, unit and investment trusts. The primary reasons for this are the tax advantages of, say, investment coupled with life assurance, the often compulsory saving in the form of pension contributions, and the benefits of risk reduction through diversification[4] offered by such funds as unit trusts. As a result, the overall level of direct investment by the private investor has fallen. Older investors have been partly discouraged by sudden falls in share prices, such as occurred in 1974, and the younger generation has seldom invested directly, placing their savings instead in housing, life assurance and pensions. This has affected the average age of the private investor, as can be seen in a shareholder survey carried out by the pharmaceutical company, Fisons, in 1975. Of its individual investors, 85% were over 50, with a staggering 20% over 70.[5]

However, private investors still play an active part in the stock market, and recent developments may well stimulate an increase in direct investment. For example, the index-linking of capital gains tax on profits from Stock Exchange investment, introduced in April 1982, reduces the tax payable on gains from equity investment, a tax which has been particularly harsh on small investors who held shares for ten or twenty years. Similarly, the traded options market, which opened in 1978, offers investors the means for creating a wide variety of different risk–return combinations from investment in equities.

As can be seen from Table 5.1, institutions have become increasingly important investors on the Stock Exchange over the past twenty-five years, with pension funds, insurance companies, unit trusts and investment trusts increasing their percentage holding of UK equities from 18% in 1957 to 43% in 1975 and 53% in 1980. This change has been due to the massive increase in funds they have experienced as the private investor switched from direct to indirect investment. In fact, the effects of this change in type of investor have been substantial, and the whole of Chapter 11 is devoted to institutional investors and their impact on the stock market.

As a result, although the 'players' may have changed, the overall level of interest in the stock market, and in particular in ordinary shares, has

---

[4] Diversification, a form of reduction of risk through pooling, was mentioned in Chapter 2, p. 56, and is discussed in detail in Chapter 7.

[5] See Fison's fourth *Stockholder Survey* (1979).

been maintained, and this interest will no doubt continue as long as money can still be made and lost from this kind of investment. Investment in equities is to many people the most fascinating form of Stock Exchange investment.

The recent interest in investment in overseas securities (in particular in overseas equities), due to the relaxation of exchange controls in 1979, may to some extent have distracted the attention of UK investors from UK securities. The additional factors which need to be taken into consideration for investment in shares denominated in foreign currencies, for example the risk of changes in exchange rates, are discussed in Chapter 10, but the basic methods of valuing shares are the same, whatever the currency.

This chapter concentrates on the valuation of ordinary shares. The first section details their fundamental characteristics and is followed by a description of the major ways in which ordinary shares are issued to the public. The chapter then goes on to consider the advantages and disadvantages of the most commonly used measures of share performance as well as the more complex problem of how the expected holding period return on a share can be estimated. The chapter concludes with a description of the major share valuation models used in practice.

Description of ordinary shares

Ordinary shares are issued by limited liability companies as risk capital. As with fixed interest securities they have a nominal value (required by law), and this can be very different from the market value or price of the share. For example, a 25p nominal share can be quoted at, say, 437p. The actual nominal value of a share may reflect the original amount of money raised by issuing shares (since no share may be issued at a price below its nominal value) but, more likely, has more to do with the tradition in the UK of keeping nominal (or par) values below £1. Ordinary shares are usually described simply by the name of the company which issued them and by the nominal value, as can be seen in the extract from the *Financial Times* given in Table 5.2. Note that the nominal value is given there only if it differs from the most common value of 25p.

Most (but not all) the ordinary and deferred ordinary share prices are given in the *Financial Times*, which lists the share prices of those companies whose shares are traded on the Stock Exchange and who are willing to pay a £600 fee to the *Financial Times*. The shares are divided into twenty-eight sectors, for example Drapery and Stores; Food and

Table 5.2 Details of ordinary shares from the Financial Times

ELECTRICALS-

1982 High	Low	Stock	Price	+ or −	Div. Net	C'vr	Y'ld Gr's	P/E
148	92	A.B. Electronic.	117	......	4.0	—	4.9	—
87	78	+A. & G. Sec Elecs 5p	85	......	b1.75	2.3	2.9	21.3
290	143	+Air Call........	275	......	g4.2	3.0	2.2	(17.1)
250	118	Amstrad	235	......	†d3.95	5.1	2.4	11.6
52	18	Arlen Elect......	23	+1	d1.0	—	6.2	—
9	3	Audiotronic 10p	4	−1½	—	—	—	—
6	2	Do. 12pc Ptg. Pref.	5	......	B—	—	—	—
208	110	Auto'ted Sec. 10p	195	......	†h1.2	5.9	0.9	20.4
*350	157	BICC 50p........	335	−10	10.37	φ	4.5	φ
87	27	BSR 10p........	79	......	Z0.5	—	0.9	—
78	13	††Baker Elec. 10p	26	......	g1.0	—	5.5	—
224	146	Bowthorpe 10p.	224	+7	†2.96	3.9	1.9	17.5
34	20	Bulgin 'A' 5p	22	......	1.35	0.6	8.8	(33.8)
251	191	Cable and Wireless 50p	250	−1	b6.5	2.0	3.6	19.9
125	76	Cambridge Elec.	125	+1	b3.7	2.2	4.2	12.7
250	214	C.A.S.E. (20p).	235	+5	b3.15	3.8	1.9	(15.2)
*41	17	Chloride Grp.....	31	−1	—	—	—	—
58	15	Concord Rota. 10p	44	......	b2.0	2.2	6.5	10.1
59	34	CrayEl'tronic 10p	59xc	+3	†h1.13	2.8	2.7	18.0
*100	59	Crystalate 5p....	100	+1½	1.75	3.6	2.5	12.0
93	55	Dale Elect. 10p	67	......	d2.5	1.1	5.3	(24.8)
21	6	Derritron 10p...	9	−1	B—	—	—	—
16	8	Dewhurst 'A' 10p	12	......	0.15	—	1.8	—
32	22	Dowding & M. 10p	32	......	1.65	1.6	7.4	11.9
26	15	Dreamland 10p.	20	......	1.2	1.5	8.6	(9.6)
78	39	Dubilier 5p......	76	−1	1.55	2.6	2.9	(15.3)
205	80	ESI London	205	+3	H2.1	—	1.5	—
163	115	Elect'comps 10p.	147	−1	h1.95	3.9	1.9	18.9
56	32	Electronic Mach..	35	......	—	—	—	5.4
120	80	Elect. Rentals 25p	98	−1	4.31	1.4	6.3	(14.9)
149	108	Emess Lighting	122	......	6.75	2.4	7.9	(5.9)
37½	24	Energy Servs. 10p.	28½	−½	†0.75	3.1	3.8	10.5
400	230	Eurotherm Int. 10p.	400	......	d5.0	2.5	1.8	27.1
650	337	Farnell Elec. 20p	650	......	†5.2	1.1	1.2	26.6
109	95	+Feedback 10p	104	......	b2.0	3.0	2.0	21.0
698	425	Ferranti 50p....	655	+12	†6.5	5.4	1.4	13.9
55	25	Fidelity Rad. 10p.	43	+1	0.1	—	0.3	—
*99½	35½	First Castle 10p	57½	−1	b1.75	2.7	4.3	(9.8)
139	43	Forward Tech...	43	......	d5.27	1.1	17.5	(7.2)
185	146	Fujitsu Y50	153	+4	Q15½%	3.6	1.2	24.2
857	573	G.E.C...........	820	−8	†10.25	5.1	1.8	13.9
253	95	+Hadland (J.) ..	100	−5	d2.52	1.1	3.6	(35.0)
48	6	Hemokinetics 1c..	10	......	—	—	—	—
41	19	Highland El. 20p.	25	+2	0.5	—	2.9	—
21½	14	+Humberside El. 10p..	21	......	—	—	—	—
100	53	Jones Stroud ...	98	......	5.2	1.8	7.6	(8.7)
375	195	Kode Int.........	267	+2	7.0	φ	3.8	φ
245	86	Lec Refrig......	220	......	5.55	4.9	3.6	7.2
307	173	M.K. Electric ..	303	−2	12.0	1.9	5.7	11.5
5	1	††Mainline Elec. 10p.	2½	......	—	—	—	—
4	1	Do. 12pc Ptg. Pf. 10p.	2	......	—	—	—	—
288	178	Memec 10p......	280	......	3.0	φ	1.5	φ
£19	665	Mitel Corp.||....	£10⅞	......	—	—	—	—
28	10	Molynx 20p.....	18	. ...	—	—	—	—
£43¼	£27	Motorola $3......	£31⅞	......	Q$1.60	—	2.6	—
136	62	Muirhead	120	−4	3.0	2.1	3.6	16.1
107	75	Murray Tech. Invs.	87	......	—	—	—	—
29	9	Newman Inds ...	9	......	B—	—	—	—
373	197	Newmark Louis	230	+15	11.0	2.3	6.8	14.8
205	136	Nippon Elect. Y50	167	+2	Q13%	2.9	0.9	38.9
55	21	Normand El. 20p.	55	......	♦‡1.09	—	‡	—
£37	£22	Norsk Data A.S.	£31½	......	Q5%	φ	0.6	φ
£236	£133	Perkin-Elmer 4pc	£152	+2	Q4%	—	f2.6	—
74	39	Petbow Hldg 10p	62	......	—	—	—	—
51	16	Phicom 10p......	22	......	‡1.0	0.4	‡	—
£51	£42½	Philips Fin. 5¾%	£50	......	Q5¾%	—	f12.0	—
512	291	Philips Lp. F10.	482	−5	Q18%	φ	8.0	φ
151	60	Piezo El Prds. Ic.	80	−5	—	—	—	—
230	152	Pifco Hldgs. 20p.	205	−2	5.28	4.8	3.7	8.1
220	152	Do. 'A' 20p....	205	......	5.28	4.8	3.7	8.1
401	255	Plessey 50p.....	380	−3	†7.63	2.7	2.9	18.2
38	22	Pressac 10p	24	......	1.1	0.2	6.7	—
175	80	Quest Auto 10p.	80	......	g1.0	—	1.8	—
485	284	Racal Electncs..	385	......	†4.55	3.8	1.7	18.1
225	109	Rediffusion......	225	......	5.5	2.1	3.5	19.9
230	76	+Scan Data 10p.	95	+5	u2.0	4.4	3.0	8.1
315	165	Scholes (G.H.)..	310	......	†16.52	2.1	7.8	8.6
*151	66	Security Centres.	151	+3	‡1·5	2.4	1.4	39.1
85	42	††Sonic Tape ...	85	......	—	—	—	—
£13	630	Sony Co. Y50 ...	750	+40	†Q88%	φ	1.3	φ
93	31½	Sound Diffsn. 5p.	93	......	h0.6	1.5	0.9	(98.2)
545	365	Std. Tel. & Cables.	527	+4	13.5	q2.4	3.7	13.6
*79	38½	Suter Electrical 5p	57	+1	t1.74	4.7	4.4	10.3
53	29	Telefusion 5p...	51	......	†1.6	3.2	4.5	7.8
53	28	Do. 'A' N/V 5p.	50	......	†1.6	3.2	4.6	7.7
400	250	Tele. Rentals....	335	......	8.25	2.2	3.5	16.4
503	282	Thorn EMI.....	428	−4	14.63	2.0	4.9	12.2
135½	87½	Do. 7pc Cnv.Pf. 92-99.	119½	−½	7%	15.7	8.4	—
121	85	Thorpe F. W. 10p	121	......	†2.45	4.4	2.9	9.4
308	175	Unitech 10p.....	235	......	†7.0	1.9	4.3	14.3
82	19	+Utd. Electronic 20p..	37	−1	1.57	3.4	6.1	6.2
*335	128½	Utd. Scientific..	333xc	......	h3.0	3.2	1.3	29.5
215	35	Vitatron N.V. Fl 0.25..	70	......	—	—	—	—
125	69	Ward & Gold	112	−1	†5.4	2.4	6.9	(6.8)
137	80	+Webber El. 12½p..	98	......	d3.5	φ	5.1	φ
26½	13	Wellco Hlds. 5p	18½	−½	1.0	0.2	7.7	—
50	18¼	Wstn. Select 20p.	44	−1	2.3	1.3	7.5	13.6
121	53	Whitworth E1. 5p	114	......	1.51	8.0	1.9	7.2
265	162	Wh'lesale Ftg 10p.	220	+5	†4.13	3.2	2.7	16.3
190	120	Wigfall (H.)	135	......	6.0	1.4	6.4	(14.1)

Source: *Financial Times*, 25 March 1982.

Groceries; Chemicals and Plastics; and Electricals.[6] Table 5.2 shows details of the shares listed under the heading of 'Electricals'.

It will be seen from the table that some shares are mentioned twice, for example Pifco Holdings and Telefusion. This is because these companies retain a more complex capital structure, with two kinds of equity capital. As mentioned before, most companies now only have one kind of ordinary share, with perhaps an unsecured loan stock convertible into ordinary shares, but there are exceptions. The most common variation is the division of the ordinary share capital into two types, for example Telefusion 5p and Telefusion 5p 'A' non-voting shares. This type of capital structure was used by family-controlled companies as a means of raising new equity funds without sacrificing control. A small number of ordinary shares with voting rights controlled the company whilst the majority of shareholders held non-voting ordinary shares, identical in all respects save for the right to vote at General Meetings. For example, Marks and Spencer had this dual share structure until 1966 when the 'A' ordinary shares were enfranchised. The Stock Exchange now encourages companies to enfranchise their non-voting shares.

One of the features distinguishing ordinary shares from other types of security is the holders' right to vote, except in the special case of 'A' shares. Preference shareholders usually only have the right to vote in special circumstances, for example when the preference dividend has not been paid. However, participating preference shares, a type of share with a fixed interest dividend *plus* some right to a share in the profits, may well have voting rights. In Table 5.2, Mainline Electric has participating preference shares.

Fixed interest securities, whether company- or government-issued, have a specified maturity or spread of redemption dates. Ordinary share capital, however, like most preference share capital, is usually irredeemable.[7] Ordinary shares thus have an indefinite life, unless the company is wound up, voluntarily or involuntarily, or there is some scheme to reduce the share capital, or the company is taken over. So, except when the company is forced into liquidation, the voting shareholders have a say in whether their shares should be repaid or acquired.[8]

The attraction of ordinary shares is their limited liability and possible unlimited returns. An investor in fully paid ordinary shares can never

---

[6] For a full breakdown, see the back pages of the *Financial Times*. These share groupings are *not* the same as those of the FT–actuaries share indices discussed later in the chapter. For example, the groupings include three categories for non-UK shares – American, Canadian and South African – not represented in the FT–actuaries share indices.

[7] However, the Companies Act 1981 now allows companies to purchase their own shares and thus redeem them (if shareholders approve).

[8] Although, if 90% of a company's shares have been acquired or are held by another company, the remainder can be compulsorily purchased if 100% control is desired.

lose more than 100% of his investment but his return on the shares can be far greater than this.[9] Fixed interest securities have specified income, in the form of the periodic coupon and the repayment on maturity. Although the holding period rate of return can vary according to changes in price of the fixed interest security, the returns on fixed interest securities will on average be less volatile than those on ordinary shares, where both the income *and* the future share price are uncertain.

Because of this extra volatility of share price and income, and hence of holding period return, shares are in general riskier than fixed interest securities. As a result, ordinary shareholders require a risk premium for taking on this additional risk, that is, a return in excess of the return on less risky investments, such as gilts. We saw in Chapter 2 that risk could be measured by the standard deviation of the probability distribution of returns. In fact, in Chapter 7, we shall find that the relevant measure of risk for an ordinary share is its risk *relative* to other shares and to the stock market as a whole, since shares are not usually held in isolation but as part of a diversified portfolio.

Methods of issue

There are two types of issue of ordinary shares, which can be defined as primary and secondary. In a primary issue, new shares are issued and in a secondary issue existing shares are placed on the market.

Primary

Companies cannot issue new shares via the Stock Exchange unless they are listed and have thereby satisfied the listing requirements of the Stock Exchange (for example, as to size and profit record[10]) and paid their listing fee. Smaller companies may now be quoted on the unlisted securities market (discussed in Chapter 1) which has less stringent listing requirements.

Primary issues of ordinary shares are usually made in one of three instances: the raising of new funds by a company whose shares are

---

[9] This is why the probability distribution of returns on shares is not quite normal; returns can never be less than −100% but can exceed +100%.

[10] For full details of existing requirements, see the *Stock Exchange Yellow Book*, published by the Stock Exchange.

already listed; a takeover bid where the shares of company *B* are acquired in exchange for the newly issued shares of company *A*; and when scrip[11] issues are made to existing shareholders.

(i) NEW FUNDS

New funds for companies already listed are usually raised by means of rights issues, where existing shareholders are entitled to subscribe for new shares at a fixed price, usually below the existing share price, in proportion to their existing holdings. General offers for sale, by companies already listed, of new shares to the general public are no longer approved by the Stock Exchange, unless existing shareholders have priority.

For example, suppose the ordinary shares of Crumbly Cakes plc are quoted at 100p. A rights issue of one for four is announced, with the subscription price set at 80p per share. Mrs Tooth holds 1,000 shares and is therefore entitled to purchase 250 new shares at 80p each. She will then hold 1,250 shares and these shares should be worth, other things being equal, their previous market value plus the new funds invested:[12]

1,000 shares at 100p	= £1,000
New funds invested: 250 at 80p	= £200
	£1,200

$$\text{Ex rights price} = \frac{£1,200}{1,250}$$

$$= 96p$$

If Mrs Tooth does nothing, her shares would in this case fall in value from £1,000 to £960. So, in the case of a rights issue, action must be taken, either to take up the rights to buy new shares or to sell the rights

---

[11] A scrip issue is often referred to as a capitalisation or bonus issue.

[12] Of course, the funds raised may be needed for a profitable project, and the announcement of the rights issue may lead to an increase in the value of the company by greater than the amount raised through the rights issue.

to someone else.[13] These rights will be worth approximately the difference between the subscription price and the price of the share after the rights issue:

Ex rights price   = 96p

Subscription price   = (80p)

Value of one right   = **16p**

However, if Mrs Tooth sells her rights, she will have reduced her level of investment and percentage holding in Crumbly Cakes plc. A third alternative is for Mrs Tooth to sell just sufficient of her existing shares to be able to take up the rights without having to invest 'new' money. She would then maintain the level of her investment at £1,000.

Rights issues are usually underwritten by a merchant bank. In other words, if investors such as Mrs Tooth choose not to take up their rights (for example, if the share price falls below the subscription price on the new shares and the rights thus become worthless), the merchant bank, and other financial institutions to whom it sub-underwrites, contract to buy any new shares for which the rights have not been taken up. In this way, the company can be sure of receiving the new funds, whatever happens to its share price between the offer date and the closing date of the issue. An alternative to underwriting is a 'deep-discount' rights issue, where the subscription price is set so far below the current share price that there is no risk that the share price will fall below the subscription price during the three weeks or so of the issue period. In this way, the costs of underwriting, usually around 2½% of the funds raised, can be avoided. However, deep-discount issues are not as common as underwritten rights issues, since to raise the same amount of money as with a conventional rights issue, more new shares would have to be issued. If, as usual, dividends per share are maintained at pre-rights issue levels, a deep-discount rights issue would involve companies in substantially increased dividend payments.

(ii) Takeovers

Company *A* can choose how to offer to pay for its acquisition of company *B*. It can pay in cash or issue some new securities. The most

---

[13] The management of the company will arrange to sell any shareholders' rights not taken up and to distribute the proceeds of the sale to those shareholders. In such instances, the shareholders may take no action if they so wish without financial loss. However, in cases where the amount is small, the management may sell the rights not taken up for the benefit of the company.

common type of security used in such offers is ordinary shares, since one risky security is replaced by another. The shareholders of company *B* can then decide whether to sell any shares received and reinvest elsewhere or whether to retain the shares and hold an investment in company *A*. The possible advantage of shares over cash to the shareholders of company *B* is that, by holding on to the company *A* shares they receive, they can delay any crystallisation of capital gains tax.

(iii) SCRIP ISSUES

A scrip issue of shares is one where new shares are issued to existing shareholders, in proportion to their existing holdings (as for a rights issue) but where no payment is required. In the case of both takeovers and rights issues, the value of the company issuing the shares changes. In the case of scrip issues, there should be no fundamental change in the value of the company. An example of a scrip issue could be where Crumbly Cakes issued one new share free for each two existing shares held. No money would change hands. Mrs Tooth would then hold, instead of 1,000 shares, 1,500 shares. Since the value of the company would remain the same, other things remaining constant, each share would be worth

$$\frac{£1,000}{1,500} = 67p$$

and Mrs Tooth's total investment in Crumbly cakes would still be worth £1,000. An *accounting* change would take place in the sense that, in the balance sheet, the share capital would be increased and the reserves reduced, by the amount of the scrip or 'capitalisation' issue.

One may ask why companies make scrip issues. One reason is to reduce the share price, since it is believed that shares quoted at above, say, £5 per share are less marketable. It can be seen, for example in Table 5.2, that only three UK Electricals' shares are quoted at prices greater than £5. However, it can also be seen that this is a purely UK convention, since the US shares quoted in Table 5.2 have prices well in excess of £5 per share; Motorola shares are quoted at £31⅞.

Another reason for a scrip issue is that it provides a method of paying non-cash dividends. If Crumbly Cakes announces a 'scrip dividend' of 1/20 new share for each existing share held, what effect will this have on Mrs Tooth's investment?

Existing holding	1,000 shares
Scrip dividend $\frac{1}{20} \times 1,000$	50 shares
Ex dividend holding	1,050 shares

Again, no money has changed hands and the value of the company should therefore remain the same. Mrs Tooth's ex dividend holding must still be worth £1,000, and so the ex scrip share price will be £1,000/1,050 = 95.25p.

Mrs Tooth has not received any cash dividend. She can, however, sell her scrip entitlement of fifty shares at 95.25p if she wants income from the shares. She would thus realise approximately £47.50 and might be liable to capital gains tax on the proceeds. Mrs Tooth would then be left with 1,000 shares worth £952.50. (She could, of course, sell part of her existing holding if she wished, without a scrip issue, and achieve the same effect.)

If Crumbly Cakes had chosen to pay a cash dividend, say of 4.75p per share, instead of making a scrip issue, Mrs Tooth would have received £47.50 dividend (on which she would be liable for income tax[14]) and be left with shares worth, ex dividend, 100p − 4.75p or 95.25p per share, giving the same total of £952.50.

So, a scrip issue may affect the tax position of the investor differently from dividends, and alter the balance sheet of the company, but it does not change the fundamental value of the company or the value of Mrs Tooth's investment. Of course, if the company announces some other news at the same time as a scrip or rights issue, such as increased profits, or the issue is felt to be telling the market something about the company's future prospects, the ex scrip or ex rights price may be greater than the theoretical price calculated in the above examples.

Secondary

Secondary issues of shares are made when existing shareholders dispose of their shares in the market. These issues can occur in two ways – when the company is first listed and the original founders of the company sell shares both to realise some of their initial investment and to allow the

---

[14] The amount of capital gains tax and income tax to which Mrs Tooth is liable will depend on her individual tax position.

company to be able to raise new funds[15] in the future via the stock market, and when a large shareholder, such as the government or a financial institution, wishes to dispose of a major shareholding in the company.

In both cases, shares are usually sold via an offer for sale to the general public although some holdings are 'placed' via brokers with a few financial institutions. Offers for sale are preferred by the Stock Exchange since they should lead to a wider dispersion of ownership and increased marketability of the shares. In an offer for sale, the shares are usually sold by the company to a merchant bank at a fixed subscription price. The merchant bank then onsells the shares to the public, protecting itself (as with a rights issue) by having the shares underwritten. If an issue is oversubscribed, shares are allotted by the merchant bank according to some scheme such as the following:

Bids for up to 1,000 shares	Allotted in full
Bids between 1,000 and 5,000 shares	50% allotted
Bids over 5,000 shares	20% allotted

Offers for sale which are heavily oversubscribed will include multiple subscriptions by 'stags'. These are short-term investors who hope that the price the new shares reach on the stock market will quickly exceed the subscription price and that, by selling almost immediately, they will make a quick profit. Instead of issuing shares at a fixed price, the merchant bank can tender the shares to the public, as the government has done with gilts, avoiding the possibility of heavy 'stagging' of the issue.

Summary measures for ordinary shares

We saw in Chapter 2 that the two most important measures for any security were its expected return and its risk. Risk could be measured by standard deviation and expected return by the expected holding period return,

$$HPR = \frac{D_1 + (P_1 - P_0)}{P_0}$$

---

[15] In some cases, such issues may be a mixture of primary and secondary.

where P_0 was the cost of the security, D_1 the expected income to be received during the period, and P_1 the expected value of the security at the end of the period.

In Chapter 3, we looked at surrogate measures for the holding period return on gilts and other fixed interest securities, the interest yield and the redemption yield. The interest yield is given by

$$\text{Interest yield} = \frac{D_1}{P_0}$$

and is a measure of the income yield from the security, ignoring the capital gain or loss element, $(P_1 - P_0)/P_0$, because P_1 cannot be determined with certainty during the life of the gilt. However, P_1 is usually known with certainty at maturity, since it must then equal its redemption value. Thus, an estimate of total holding period return can be made, provided the gilt is assumed held to maturity, and this return, converted into an annual average, is termed the redemption yield.

In the case of ordinary shares, any estimate of expected holding period return is subject to much greater uncertainty. Since there is usually no fixed redemption date or redemption value for shares, P_1 is not known for *any* point in the future. Also, D_1 is not certain since the size of the future dividend D_1 is at the discretion of the company and depends on future profitability. Alternative summary measures have to be used for ordinary shares.

The extract from the *Financial Times* shown in Table 5.2 on p. 129 gives, as well as details of the previous day's closing share prices and the year's highest and lowest prices for the share, the four major summary measures for ordinary shares. These are the gross dividend yield, the net dividend per share, the dividend cover and the price–earnings ratio.

Dividend measures

The dividend yield is the equivalent for ordinary shares of the interest yield for gilts. It is merely the income element of the holding period reutrn, D/P_0, ignoring the capital gain or loss term, $(P_1 - P_0)/P_0$.

Dividends on UK company shares are usually paid twice yearly, in the form of an interim and a final dividend. The value of these dividends is determined by the Board of the company, subject to shareholder approval, and is usually announced only a few weeks before payment. So future dividend payments are unknown until shortly before they are paid. The dividend yield given in the *Financial Times* refers to *last* year's *known* interim plus final dividends and not the *unknown* dividends for *next* year. The dividend yield calculated is thus D_0/P_0 and not D_1/P_0 and represents part of the historic rather than the expected holding period return. In the case of gilts, D_1 is always equal to D_0 and so D_1/P_0 is known with certainty. With ordinary shares, there is no guarantee that D_1 will exceed D_0 or even equal D_0, although the company may drop hints about expected future dividends, for example 'The Directors expect, in the absence of unforeseen circumstances, to recommend a final dividend for 1980 of not less than that paid for 1979.'[16]

A tentative indicator of future dividends can be found in the symbols next to the net dividend figures in Table 5.2. These attempt to give an idea of trends in dividend payments – an indication of what D_1 will be relative to the D_0 given. For example, the symbol † shows that the most recent interim dividend (the first half of D_1) has been raised relative to last year's interim (or resumed), and the symbol ‡ shows that the interim dividend has been reduced or passed. Thus the investor might expect a raised total dividend next year for, say, GEC in Table 5.2 and a reduced dividend for Phicom.

The *gross* dividend yield is given in the *Financial Times*, although dividends on UK company shares are now declared and paid *net* of personal income tax at the basic rate. The calculation of gross as opposed to net dividend is to aid comparison with other types of security, since, for example, interest yields on gilts are also quoted before income tax.

The present system of tax on dividends has been in existence since 1973. Known as the imputation tax system, it was designed to render a company's liability to corporation tax the same, whether or not it paid dividends. Table 5.3 gives an example of two identical companies, one paying a dividend and one not, to show how the total amount of corporation tax paid is the same for both companies.

If a company pays a dividend to its shareholders, it remits to the Inland Revenue a tax payment equivalent to income tax on the gross dividend at the basic rate. This rate is currently 30% and so the tax payment will be 3/10 of the gross dividend and 3/7 of the net dividend.[17] The net dividend is received by the shareholder who is then only liable to additional tax if he pays tax at greater than the basic rate. If he is liable to tax at the basic rate, he simply retains the net dividend. If he is not liable to tax, he may claim a refund. The company offsets its dividend tax payment, known as advance corporation tax or ACT, against its total (or mainstream) corporation tax bill and so pays tax at 52% regardless of whether or not it pays a dividend.[18]

---

[16] From the Rio Tinto-Zinc Corporation rights issue document, dated 22 September 1980.
[17] If the basic rate of income tax were 33%, the ACT payable would be 33/100 of the gross dividend, equivalent to 33/67 of the net dividend.

Table 5.3   Impact of dividend policy on corporation tax liability

	Company A £000	Company B £000
Profit before tax	1,000	1,000
Corporation tax at 52%	(520)	(520)
Profit after tax	480	480
Net dividend paid	0	140
Advance corporation tax paid on dividend (ACT) (currently ³⁄₁₀ of gross, or ³⁄₇ of net, dividend)	0	60
Gross dividend paid	0	200
Tax paid		
ACT	0	60
Mainstream corporation tax	520	460
TOTAL tax paid	520	520

For example, in Table 5.2, Thorn EMI paid a total net dividend for its last financial year of 14.63p per share. This was equivalent to a gross dividend of

$$\frac{100}{70} \times 14.63p = 20.90p$$

and the shareholder was deemed to have paid the difference between 20.90p and 14.63p in income tax. The gross dividend yield, D_0/P_0, was

$$\text{Gross dividend yield} = \frac{20.9}{428}$$

$$= 4.9\%$$

and this is given in Table 5.2 in the next-to-last column.

---

[18] This simple exposition ignores the companies with no liability to mainstream corporation tax against which ACT can be offset, estimated in the 1982 Green paper on corporation tax (Cmnd 8456) to be about 60% of all companies. In these cases, a dividend payment will render the company liable to additional tax.

In Chapter 3, we saw that the interest yield on a gilt was a function of its coupon – a low coupon gave a low interest yield and a high coupon a high interest yield. The interest yield gave no indication of the total return to be expected on a gilt, that is, the return including a capital gain or loss on disposal. Similarly, with ordinary shares, dividend yield is no measure of the total expected return, which will consist of both income and any capital gain. The companies shown in Table 5.2 have gross dividend yields varying between 0 and 17.5%. These yields will be more a reflection of company dividend policy than company profitability. So, as with interest yield, we find gross dividend yield an incomplete measure of expected return.

The accounting profit reported after deduction of tax, interest on any corporate borrowings and preference share dividends is known as the earnings available to ordinary shareholders. These earnings, divided by the number of shares in the company, give the earnings per share (*eps*). It is up to the company directors to decide how much of these earnings will be paid out as dividends. For example, in recent years, companies making losses or reduced profits have often chosen to maintain the same level of dividend, out of past earnings, rather than reduce it in line with current earnings. Any earnings not paid out are termed retained earnings and can be reinvested by the company to yield future profits although, of course, a company with a high-dividend policy and low retained earnings can finance future investments with borrowings or a new equity issue instead.

Table 5.4 compares the holding period return of two companies with identical earnings, prospects and risk but with different dividend payout policies.

In this idealised example we can see that company X pays out all the period's earnings as dividends. Since it has no retained earnings, the value of the company would in theory remain unchanged, with $P_1 = P_0 = 100$p. Company Y pays a smaller dividend of 10p per share, retaining 40p per share within the company. Company Y should therefore be worth 40p per share more at the end of the period, so $P_1 = 140$p. Both companies yield the same holding period return, with company X's being provided in the form of dividend and company Y's partly from dividend and partly from capital gain on the share. Of course, in practice, company X and company Y could differ in their investment policies; for example, company Y might invest its 40p per share retained earnings profitably and company X might not borrow an equivalent amount to invest. In this case, company Y's share price would increase by more than 40p to reflect its increased future profits. However, if investment policy were the same for these two companies, dividend policy would be irrelevant. In this example, both companies have identical prospects and risk, and identical earnings of 50p per share, and so should yield the same total return to the investor. Thus earnings and

Table 5.4   *Impact of dividend policy on HPR*

	Company X	Company Y
No. of issued shares	100	100
Share price, P_0	100p	100p
Earnings for ordinary shareholders	£50	£50
per share	50p	50p
Net dividend	£50	£10
Per share	50p	10p
Retained earnings	0	£40
Per share	0	40p
Share price P_1	100p	140p
$HPR = \dfrac{D_1 + (P_1 - P_0)}{P_0}$	$\dfrac{50 + (100 - 100)}{100}$	$\dfrac{10 + (140 - 100)}{100}$
HPR	**50%**	**50%**

not dividend yields are indicators of total returns. Unfortunately, as we shall see below, earnings figures as reported in company accounts are not good indicators of future profitability.

Despite the difficulties surrounding the measure of dividend yield, it does, as with the interest yield, provide some indication of the *current* level of income from a share. This can be useful to investors who are liable to different tax rates on their dividend income and on their capital gains from shares. Pension funds, paying tax on neither, should be indifferent to the dividend yield on shares.[19] A private investor with a marginal income tax rate of, say, 75% on dividend income will probably prefer to receive his share return in the form of capital gains rather than dividends, and pay tax at a maximum rate of 30% on *real* gains. Such an investor, when comparing two shares between which he is otherwise indifferent, will choose the share offering the lower expected dividend yield and the higher expected capital gain.

As was mentioned earlier, an additional problem that the dividend yield has, compared with the interest yield, is that dividends are expected to grow whereas interest payments generally are not. However, in cases where companies try to maintain a stable dividend policy, some attempt can be made to estimate future dividends from past dividends. For example, a company could maintain a regular 5% growth in dividend or

---

[19] Although see Chapter 11, p. 335, for a discussion of why this is not so in practice.

always pay out a constant proportion of earnings. In this latter case, it would be said to have a constant dividend payout ratio, where this is equal to

$$\text{Dividend payout ratio} = \frac{dps_0}{eps_0}$$

We can see from Table 5.4 that company X has a dividend payout ratio of 50p/50p = 100%, whereas company Y's ratio is 10p/50p = 20%.

The reciprocal of the dividend payout ratio is termed the dividend cover:

$$\text{Dividend cover} = \frac{eps_0}{dps_0}$$

Dividend cover is one of the summary measures for ordinary shares provided in Table 5.2. What does dividend cover tell us? From our example, we see that company X has dividend cover of one and company Y dividend cover of five times. A dividend cover of one in the case of company X would seem to imply that a downturn in earnings might force company X to cut its dividend next year. On the other hand, a dividend cover of five in the case of company Y would appear to imply that company Y can afford to maintain the present level of dividend payments in the future even if it suffers a severe drop in earnings. The major problem with the use of dividend cover for such conclusions is that the level of a company's earnings may give a very misleading picture of its ability to pay dividends. Dividends are paid out of cash flow whereas the earnings figure is an accountant's calculation which includes non-cash items such as depreciation. A company may have high reported earnings and yet have insufficient cash to maintain its dividend payments. As we shall see in the next section, any measure which uses reported earnings is subject to difficulty of interpretation. See also the appendix to this chapter for further problems in calculating dividend cover.

Price–earnings ratio

Three of the four summary measures provided in Table 5.2 are concerned with dividends – the net dividend, dividend cover and the gross dividend yield. And yet, we have seen that dividend measures provide inadequate estimates for holding period return. The problem lies in the fact that, for any ordinary share, future earnings, dividends and share prices are unknown. The only information available concerns the current share price and past earnings and dividends.

The fourth summary measure given in Table 5.2 is the price–earnings or *PE* ratio, which uses two known figures, the current share price divided by the latest earnings per share. Thus,

$$PE_0 = \frac{P_0}{eps_0}$$

Because they are ratios, the dividend yield and dividend cover can be used for comparative purposes, unlike the net dividend per share. This use for comparison also holds true for the *PE* ratio and is its major attraction. For example, the *PE* ratios of the ordinary shares in the Electricals sector are given in the last column of Table 5.2. They range from 5.4 to 39.1 and, because they are ratios, questions such as 'Why is Cable and Wireless's *PE* ratio almost double that of Energy Services?' can be asked.

What does the *PE* ratio tell us? That investors are willing to pay 20 times last year's reported earnings for Cable and Wireless (C&W) compared to 10.5 times Energy Services' (ES) reported earnings. In some sense, C&W's earnings could be said to be more expensive and this could be because they are expected to grow faster than those of ES in the future. Table 5.5 gives a possible scenario for the two companies. Because, in this scenario, ES's earnings are expected to grow more slowly than those of C&W, the time taken to earn the share price is the same in both cases, nine years. C&W appears more 'expensive' because it has a higher expected growth rate.

So, the comparison of *PE* ratios is an attempt by the investor to use currently available information to find out something about the future expected growth in earnings.

Unfortunately, the expected growth rate in earnings is not the only factor affecting a company's price–earnings ratio. For example, the *PE* ratio will also be affected by the uncertainty surrounding future earnings. So, C&W and ES could have the same *expected* growth rate, but the variability (standard deviation) of the predicted earnings growth

Table 5.5 *Explanation of differences in* PE *ratios*

	Company	
	C&W	ES
PE_0	19.9	10.5
P_0	250p	28.5p
eps_0	12.6p	2.7p
Possible expected annual growth rate in *eps* (%)	20	4
Number of years for cumulative *eps* to equal share price	9	9

could be higher for ES than for C&W, either due to a riskier business activity or higher gearing, or both. Because of the greater certainty attached to C&W's predicted earnings growth, it would be more highly valued than ES with its riskier future earnings. So C&W could have a higher *PE* because its future earnings are less risky than those of ES. Similarly, as we shall see later, dividend payout policy also affects a company's *PE* ratio.

Before we go on to discuss how the *PE* ratio can be used to estimate expected holding period return, several problems which arise when using the *PE* ratio must be mentioned. Firstly, companies which are to be compared may well have different year ends. For example, the *PE* ratio for company *X* could be determined from 1982 earnings whereas the *PE* ratio for company *Y* could be calculated from earnings for the year ended 28 February 1982, almost twelve months earlier. The earnings for the most recent period could be higher due to inflation, reducing *X*'s *PE* ratio relative to *Y*'s. Alternatively 1982 could have been a recessionary period, with many companies' earnings unduly depressed, giving *X* an unnaturally high *PE* ratio relative to *Y*.

This cyclicality problem can be emphasised in another way. Suppose Crumbly Cakes plc trades on a *PE* of 5 and, when its latest earnings are announced, these are declared to be only half those of the previous year. However, the company confidently expects to recover from the downturn and return rapidly to its normal earnings level. Because of this, the share price does not fall and the *PE* ratio doubles to 10; and yet, Crumbly Cakes has not become a high-growth company overnight. An extreme example is when a company declares zero earnings. Should it have an infinitely high *PE* ratio? So, two companies could have high *PE* ratios for completely different reasons, one because it is a high-growth share and the other due to a sudden – but believed temporary – plunge in profits. One way of getting round this problem is to 'normalise' the earnings, that is, to calculate the *PE* ratio using an earnings figure which the analyst believes to be a reflection of the trend in earnings rather than the peaks or troughs. Another method of avoiding this problem is to compare industries rather than to compare individual companies. This is because companies in an industry are subject to the same economic cycles and commonly have the same year end. Also, because the *PE* ratios in the table are weighted averages for each industry, anomalies caused by individual companies are reduced. Table 5.6 shows the *PE* ratios for each sector or industry.

In the fifth column of Table 5.6, we can see that the average *PE* ratio for the Chemicals industry is 9.03 whereas the average for Electricals is 17.73. Electricals are generally considered to be companies offering good potential for growth, given the advent of electronics, whereas chemical companies are in mature industries, suffering overcapacity problems. In fact, because of the high-growth image of many of the

Table 5.6   FT–actuaries share indices

FT-ACTUARIES SHARE INDICES

These Indices are the joint compilation of the Financial Times, the Institute of Actuaries and the Faculty of Actuaries

EQUITY GROUPS & SUB-SECTIONS — Figures in parentheses show number of stocks per section	Wed March 24 1982 Index No.	Day's Change %	Est. Earnings Yield % (Max.)	Gross Div. Yield % (ACT at 30%)	Est. P/E Ratio (Net)	Tues Mar 23 Index No.	Mon Mar 22 Index No.	Fri Mar 19 Index No.	Thur Mar 18 Index No.	Year ago (approx.) Index No.
1 CAPITAL GOODS (210)	371.62	-0.4	9.50	4.27	13.17	373.06	371.56	372.33	368.46	329.93
2 Building Materials (25)	335.46	-0.5	13.01	5.13	9.23	337.02	334.78	335.28	331.63	299.30
3 Contracting, Construction (28)	618.53	+0.3	14.45	4.66	8.16	616.53	611.43	610.81	606.10	552.61
4 Electricals (31)	1286.12	-0.6	7.21	2.30	17.73	1294.41	1292.33	1294.62	1274.33	1051.32
5 Engineering Contractors (9)	501.32	-0.1	12.88	5.86	9.05	501.97	493.53	495.90	493.62	425.06
6 Mechanical Engineering (67)	191.26	-0.1	11.15	5.79	11.36	191.41	190.50	190.82	190.08	197.89
8 Metals and Metal Forming (12)	164.07	+0.4	9.92	7.47	13.02	163.47	162.03	162.59	160.74	154.44
9 Motors (21)	96.46	-2.6	—	6.91	—	99.07	98.82	99.49	99.57	92.59
10 Other Industrial Materials (17)	382.07	-0.1	9.67	5.50	12.51	382.27	382.09	383.70	381.54	344.56
21 CONSUMER GROUP (199)	299.60	—	12.20	5.57	10.06	299.47	295.29	296.74	293.35	259.00
22 Brewers and Distillers (21)	298.71	+0.9	15.75	6.53	7.64	296.16	292.80	293.75	290.40	278.48
25 Food Manufacturing (21)	276.65	-0.6	15.38	6.55	7.82	278.22	274.41	275.75	271.37	243.50
26 Food Retailing (15)	614.28	-1.4	8.79	3.27	13.86	623.22	614.53	612.61	606.61	505.68
27 Health and Household Products (8)	390.18	-0.1	8.06	4.05	14.57	390.60	387.79	390.71	389.17	272.96
29 Leisure (24)	446.98	-0.6	9.32	4.95	13.46	449.75	445.92	446.60	441.34	395.73
32 Newspapers, Publishing (12)	522.30	+0.7	10.87	6.01	12.31	518.62	518.48	517.93	517.81	477.15
33 Packaging and Paper (13)	149.13	+2.4	13.41	7.23	8.91	145.66	144.17	143.73	142.57	133.44
34 Stores (45)	277.61	+0.5	10.20	4.83	13.16	276.25	270.21	272.30	268.66	262.39
35 Textiles (23)	174.81	+0.6	9.69	5.72	13.31	173.72	173.11	173.30	172.47	144.04
36 Tobaccos (3)	307.82	-0.5	19.90	8.47	5.72	309.49	303.37	308.02	303.87	211.41
39 Other Consumer (14)	290.89	+0.2	0.23	5.82	—	290.45	291.05	289.24	287.08	264.33
41 OTHER GROUPS (78)	258.15	—	13.00	6.03	9.27	258.18	255.78	256.46	253.25	214.43
42 Chemicals (16)	337.23	-0.2	13.23	6.85	9.03	337.95	334.85	336.92	333.58	249.01
44 Office Equipment (4)	129.27	-0.9	12.45	6.65	9.78	130.40	129.42	129.89	128.61	110.50
45 Shipping and Transport (13)	574.15	—	18.66	6.43	6.38	574.20	569.17	573.16	564.33	600.50
46 Miscellaneous (45)	328.59	+0.3	11.26	5.00	10.88	327.51	324.26	323.53	318.75	282.75
49 INDUSTRIAL GROUP (487)	318.93	-0.1	11.31	5.15	10.88	319.32	316.24	317.37	313.81	276.96
51 Oils (13)	679.80	+0.2	18.31	8.52	6.39	678.28	659.61	660.73	643.61	805.18
59 500 SHARE INDEX	348.37	-0.1	12.40	5.68	9.81	348.61	344.28	345.41	340.76	319.02
61 FINANCIAL GROUP (117)	261.65	+0.3	—	6.09	—	260.84	259.36	260.33	257.33	251.71
62 Banks(6)	279.51	+0.7	38.23	7.64	2.87	277.59	278.65	281.09	275.71	233.82
63 Discount Houses (9)	239.89	+1.9	—	9.04	—	235.37	235.15	235.82	234.38	307.62
65 Insurance (Life) (9)	262.06	-0.5	—	6.19	—	263.32	259.51	259.04	257.98	265.91
66 Insurance (Composite) (10)	168.93	-0.3	—	8.18	—	169.43	168.25	168.89	165.89	164.08
67 Insurance Brokers (7)	475.96	+1.7	11.08	5.06	12.32	467.98	453.04	453.45	443.92	342.74
68 Merchant Banks (12)	145.84	+0.7	—	5.38	—	144.87	144.77	144.83	144.83	155.02
69 Property (49)	462.66	+0.4	4.66	3.20	28.63	460.72	458.11	459.11	457.14	496.00
70 Other Financial (15)	181.94	+0.3	15.75	5.99	7.81	181.46	180.54	181.45	180.20	173.44
71 Investment Trusts (112)	297.34	+0.9	—	5.41	—	294.75	292.10	291.94	291.70	294.29
81 Mining Finance (4)	209.72	+1.3	16.15	6.78	7.52	207.03	204.18	204.43	203.57	234.10
91 Overseas Traders (17)	386.48	+0.5	13.55	8.24	9.01	384.47	383.71	382.86	378.95	446.98
99 ALL-SHARE INDEX (750)	326.04	+0.1	—	5.80	—	325.75	322.20	323.16	319.24	305.33

FIXED INTEREST

PRICE INDICES	Wed Mar 24	Day's change %	Tues Mar 23	xd adj. today	xd adj. 1982 to date
British Government					
1 5 years	110.89	+0.16	110.72	—	2.89
2 5-15 years	112.05	-0.56	112.67	—	2.66
3 Over 15 years	116.21	-0.74	117.07	—	2.87
4 Irredeemables	122.34	-0.84	123.37	—	1.62
5 All Stocks	112.77	-0.40	113.22	—	2.77
6 Debentures & Loans	88.47	+0.23	88.27	—	3.09
7 Preference	65.11	+0.53	64.76	—	2.20

AVERAGE GROSS REDEMPTION YIELDS		Wed Mar 24	Tues Mar 23	Year ago (approx.)
British Government				
1 Low	5 years	11.87	11.85	11.41
2 Coupons	15 years	12.63	12.53	12.04
3	25 years	12.44	12.33	12.13
4 Medium	5 years	13.78	13.76	13.09
5 Coupons	15 years	13.59	13.47	13.56
6	25 years	13.14	13.04	13.26
7 High	5 years	13.70	13.69	13.08
8 Coupons	15 years	13.78	13.66	13.76
9	25 years	13.23	13.11	13.37
10 Irredeemables	†	12.19	12.08	11.47
11 Debs & Loans	5 years	14.44	14.44	14.02
12	15 years	14.47	14.51	14.27
13	25 years	14.47	14.51	14.28
14 Preference	†	15.08	15.16	14.28

† Flat yield. Highs and lows record, base dates, values and constituent changes are published in Saturday issues. A new list of constituents is available from the Publishers, The Financial Times, Bracken House, Cannon Street, London, EC4P 4BY.

Source: Financial Times, 25 March 1982.

companies in the Electricals sector shown in Table 5.2, the average *PE* ratio for the Electricals industry is higher than the average *PE* ratio for the stock market as a whole. The *PE* ratio for the stock market can be represented by the *PE* ratio of the 500 Share Index, shown in Table 5.6 as 9.81.

However, a major problem with the *PE* ratio, which affects its use in any context, is the quality of the earnings per share figure. Firstly, as already noted, the *eps* is an accounting approximation to an economic determination of income. It is difficult to know how well accounting earnings reflect the economic profits of a company and how a historic earnings figure can indicate the extent to which future cash flows will be affected by economic changes. Economic profits by definition can only be assessed by taking a view of the future. Accounting profits are the results of calculations based on conventions in which such a view takes only a limited part and which also depend on personal judgements.

Secondly, different companies use different accounting practices to arrive at their earnings figures, and so the earnings and hence *PE* ratios may not be comparable. For example, suppose company *F* and company *G* are identical in all respects save in their method of accounting for depreciation. Table 5.7 shows how they will have different earnings per share and *PE* ratios whilst remaining, in all economic respects, identical.

Thirdly, the earnings per share figure is fraught with problems in its calculation due to the current tax system on dividends. Earnings can be

Table 5.7   Impact of different accounting practices for depreciation on eps and PE ratios

	Company F £m.	Company G £m.
Earnings before depreciation and tax	1,000	1,000
Depreciation*	(100)	(300)
Tax[†]	(400)	(400)
Earnings after tax	500	300
Number of ordinary shares (billion)	10	10
Share price	40p	40p
Earnings per share (eps)	5p	3p
PE ratio	8.0	13.3

* Company *F* uses straight-line depreciation (10% pa); company *G* uses accelerated depreciation (30% of balance pa).
[†] Since the same tax allowances for fixed assets will apply to both companies, their actual tax liabilities will be the same.

calculated either on a 'net' basis, representing earnings which allow for the actual tax charge incurred by the company, or on a 'nil' basis, where an earnings figure is determined independent of the company's dividend policy. For most companies, the 'nil' and 'net' *eps* and *PE* ratio calculations will give the same numbers, but for some companies, for example those with substantial overseas earnings, the payment of a dividend will mean unrelievable ACT (since ACT can only be offset against mainstream corporation tax due on *UK* taxable profits), giving a lower 'net' *eps* than 'nil' *eps*.

For example, in Table 5.8, International Irrigation plc earns profits entirely overseas, but because it pays dividend it incurs additional tax.

In this example, if International had 100 million shares in issue, the 'nil' *eps* would be 50p and the 'net' *eps* 41p. If the share price were 500p, the 'nil' *PE* ratio would be 10.0 and the 'net' *PE* 12.2. The *Financial Times* publishes *PE* ratios calculated by the 'net' method. However, the dilemma of which *eps* figure to use is admitted by bracketing *PE* ratios where the difference in *PE* ratio calculated by the two methods is significantly different (as is the case with Ward & Gold in Table 5.2). Also, certain sectors, such as mining, do not have *PE* ratios given at all,

Table 5.8 *Difference between 'net' and 'nil' earnings*

		International Irrigation plc £m.
Profit before tax		100
Overseas tax at 50% (giving relief from mainstream corporation (tax)		(50)
Profit after overseas tax		50*
Unrelieved ACT on dividend		(9)
Profit after tax		41†
Gross dividend	30	
ACT due $\left\{\dfrac{3}{10}\right\}$	(9)	
Net dividend paid		21
Retained earnings		20

* 'Nil' earnings.
† 'Net' earnings.

since the problems of dividend policy, accounting differences and tax render the *PE* ratios in these instances 'meaningless'.

Despite these fundamental problems with both the meaning of the *PE* ratio and its use for comparative purposes, the *PE* ratio is still commonly used as a summary measure by investors and their advisers, as evidenced by its appearance, however qualified, in the *Financial Times*. Also, the revised statement of Standard Accounting Practice on Earnings per Share states that: 'price-earnings ratios remain one of the most commonly used stock market indicators. Although they are not strictly comparable because of differences between one country's tax system and another's, they are, nevertheless, used on a world-wide basis.'[20] This attitude towards the *PE* ratio's usefulness lies behind the accounting profession's concern over providing clear guidelines for the calculation of earnings per share – despite the fact that there is no empirical evidence to show that a company's past earnings per share can successfully be used to predict its future earnings.[21]

Estimate of *HPR*

We saw in Chapter 2 that the two most important measures describing a share were its expected holding period return and its risk, measured by the standard deviation of the expected returns. The four summary measures discussed so far, net dividend, dividend cover, gross dividend yield and the *PE* ratio, have not proved of much help in estimating either risk or return. We have to find alternative means.

The simplest way to express a one-period expected holding period return is

$$\text{Expected } HPR = R = \frac{D_1 + (P_1 - P_0)}{P_0} \tag{5.1}$$

where D_1 is the expected income to be received during the period, P_1 the expected value of the security at the end of the period, and P_0 the cost of the security.

If the share is held for n periods or years, in each of which income is received, as we saw in Chapter 2, Table 2.5, equation (5.1) could be rearranged and extended to give

$$P_0 = \frac{D_1}{(1 + R)} + \frac{D_2}{(1 + R)^2} + \cdots \frac{D_n}{(1 + R)^n} + \frac{P_n}{(1 + R)^n} \tag{5.2}$$

[20] Revised Statement of Standard Accounting Practice on Earnings per Share (1974), p. 2.
[21] See Brealey (1983), ch. 5.

where P_n is the value of the security at the end of n years and D_i the income to be received in the ith year. We also saw that, since P_n could be viewed as the present value of the future dividends from year $(n+1)$ onwards, the equation for P_0 could be written as the present value of *all* future dividends.

$$P_0 = \frac{D_1}{(1+R)} + \frac{D_2}{(1+R)^2} + \dots + \frac{D_n}{(1+R)^n} + \dots \qquad (5.3)$$

In equation (5.1), R represents the one-period expected holding period return. In equations (5.2) and (5.3), R is the expected *annual* rate of return whatever the holding period. Yet, we saw in Chapter 3 when considering the redemption yield, R, for gilts that there was no reason why R should be the same in year 1 as it is in year n, since interest rates and required rates of return will vary according to time. So, equation (5.2), for example, should be written:

$$P_0 = \frac{D_1}{(1+R_1)} + \frac{D_2}{(1+R_2)^2} + \dots + \frac{D_n + P_n}{(1+R_n)^n} \qquad (5.4)$$

However, in the case of ordinary shares, the future P_n and all the future D_i are uncertain and must be estimated. So, the approximation inherent in using R for all years instead of R_i is less important (since R must of necessity be a rough estimate) than in the case of gilts, where the D_i and P_n (at redemption) are known for certain and an accurate assessment of the implicit R_i can be made.

Dividend valuation models

Equations (5.2) and (5.3) are known as dividend valuation models for shares. How can we use them to estimate the expected annual holding period return R?

If we look at equation (5.2), we know P_0 and so we need to estimate the dividend stream $D_1, D_2,\dots, D_n$ expected during the holding period and the end-of-period share price, P_n. The holding period can be as long or short as desired and will probably reflect how far into the future the investor feels able to predict the cash flows, D_i. This type of dividend valuation model, given in equation (5.2), is known as a finite horizon model, since we consider the cash flows up to a finite horizon in year n.

The dividend stream must be estimated from knowledge of the company's dividend policy and from expectations concerning the company's future prospects, since dividends ultimately depend on the cash flows generated by the company. Even if the company has a declared dividend policy, for example a constant percentage growth or constant payout ratio, it will not be able to maintain this policy if insufficient cash flow is generated.

How can P_n be estimated? It represents the company's share price in n years' time and its value will depend on market views at time n of all future cash flows attributable to the share beyond year n. Since it is impossible to estimate with any degree of accuracy such a share price n years ahead, an alternative would be to estimate the PE ratio and earnings per share n years hence, because

$$P_n = eps_n \times \frac{P_n}{eps_n}$$

so,

$$P_n = eps_n \times PE_n$$

The investor may, despite the problems inherent in the use of PE ratios and earnings per share which were discussed earlier, feel more confident about estimating the future earnings per share figure and PE ratio than their product, the future share price, P_n.

The PE ratio of a company will vary according to expected future growth and risk, and the stage of the economic cycle prevailing. These must be considered from the point of view of year n. The earnings per share figure in year n will also depend on many factors – the company, the industry and the economy as a whole. It has been found, for example,[22] that around 21% on average of changes in company earnings can be attributed to industry factors and a further 21% to economy-wide factors. Of course, earnings will also reflect accounting conventions and policies, and will thus be even more difficult to forecast correctly than cash flows. Unfortunately, as has already been mentioned, there appears to be no strong trend in earnings, so that a study of past earnings cannot be relied upon to give a good prediction of the future pattern of earnings.

As a result of the problems of estimating P_n, either directly or indirectly through PE_n and eps_n, the alternative method for estimating R is to use equation (5.3), obviating the need to estimate P_n. In other words, we consider an infinite horizon model. Since it would be a Herculean task to estimate with any degree of accuracy *all* the future dividends the company will ever pay, simplifying assumptions concerning future dividends must be made. For example, if it can be assumed

---

[22] See Brealey (1983), p. 95.

that all future dividends will grow by a constant percentage, g, equation (5.3) becomes

$$P_0 = \frac{D_1}{1 + R} + \frac{D_1 (1 + g)}{(1 + R)^2} + \frac{D_1 (1 + g)^2}{(1 + R)^3} + \dots$$

which simplifies to[23]

$$P_0 = \frac{D_1}{R - g} \qquad\qquad (5.5)$$

Rearranging gives

$$R = \frac{D_1}{P_0} + g \qquad\qquad (5.6a)$$

or

$$R = \frac{D_0 (1 + g)}{P_0} + g \qquad\qquad (5.6b)$$

This is known as Gordon's growth model.

To use Gordon's growth model, all that is needed to estimate R is last year's dividend, D_0, the current share price, P_0 and the expected dividend growth rate, g. For example, if Battered Biscuits plc has a current share price of 60p, paid a *net* dividend last year of 3p per share, and is expected to increase its dividend by 5% each year, we find from equation (5.6b) that

$$R = \frac{3 (1 + 0.05)}{60} + 0.05$$

$$= 0.05 (1 + 0.05) + 0.05$$

$$= 0.0525 + 0.05$$

$$\boldsymbol{R = 10.25\%}$$

The dividend net of ACT is used since this is what is received by the shareholder. Each shareholder will then reclaim tax, do nothing or pay further tax according to his or her income-tax liability. Thus, the

---

[23] Using the formula for the sum to infinity of an infinite geometric progression

$$S = a + ar + ar^2 + \dots ar^n + \dots = \frac{a}{1 - r}$$

estimated holding period return calculated for shares is net of tax at the basic rate. This should be borne in mind when comparing share returns with, say, the redemption yield on gilts which is quoted gross in the *Financial Times*.

Obviously, the assumption of constant growth in expected dividends is only a model of possible reality. Problems can arise using this model if the company currently does not pay any dividends but is expected to do so in the future, or if it is a small, rapidly growing company with a high dividend growth rate, say 25% per annum. We can see that, in equation (5.5), if g is large, R will not be much greater than g, and so the denominator will be very small, giving a very large (or, when $g = R$, infinite) share price. Since we do not see companies with infinitely large market values traded on the Stock Exchange, we can assume that the very high growth rates currently experienced will not last for ever. This leads us to another form of finite horizon model

$$P_0 = \frac{D_1}{(1 + R)} + \frac{D_2}{(1 + R)^2} + \dots + \frac{D_n}{(1 + R)^n} + \frac{D_n (1 + g^*)}{(R - g^*) (1 + R)^n}$$

$$(5.7)$$

where $D_1, \dots, D_n$ can be assumed to grow at, say, g per annum, but after year n, the dividend growth rate will be a smaller g^*.

An alternative way of using the dividend valuation model is to transform it into an earnings model. Since the dividend payout ratio is defined to be

$$K_i = D_i/eps_i$$

we can write

$$D_i = K_i \, eps_i$$

and equation (5.3) becomes

$$P_0 = \frac{K_1 \, eps_1}{(1 + R)} + \frac{K_2 \, eps_2}{(1 + R)^2} + \dots \frac{K_n \, eps_n}{(1 + R)^n} + \dots \qquad (5.8)$$

This type of model allows the investor to forecast future earnings instead of dividends. However, some assumption still has to be made about dividends. It could be assumed, for example, that the dividend payout ratio will remain constant, say at $K = 40\%$. So, equation (5.8) would become

$$P_0 = \frac{K \ eps_1}{(1 + R)} + \frac{K \ eps_2}{(1 + R)^2} + \ldots + \frac{K \ eps_n}{(1 + R)^n} + \ldots \tag{5.9}$$

where $K = 0.4$.

If the same simplification of constant growth is applied to earnings as was applied to dividends, we get

$$P_0 = \frac{K \ eps_0 \ (1 + g)}{(1 + R)} + \frac{K \ eps_0 \ (1 + g)^2}{(1 + R)^2} + \ldots + \frac{K \ eps_0 \ (1 + g)^n}{(1 + R)^n} + \ldots$$

$$= \frac{K \ eps_0 \ (1 + g)}{(R - g)} \tag{5.10a}$$

or

$$P_0 = \frac{K \ eps_1}{(R - g)} \tag{5.10b}$$

This is obviously the same as Gordon's growth model, since the assumption of constant growth g in earnings and a constant dividend payout ratio must also give constant growth g in dividends. Thus, this constant growth version of the dividend valuation model can either be used by forecasting dividend growth explicitly or by forecasting both earnings growth and a dividend payout ratio. Unfortunately, as we saw earlier, the evidence is that there is in practice no such trend in earnings growth and so the simplifying assumption of constant earnings growth (as well as constant dividend payout and constant dividend growth) must be viewed as an approximation to reality.

Before we leave the earnings version of the dividend valuation model, let us take a further look at equation (5.10a). If we divide both sides by eps_0, we get

$$PE_0 = \frac{K \ (1 + g)}{(R - g)} \tag{5.11}$$

The left-hand side of the equation is simply the PE ratio and the equation, written in this way, allows us to see exactly which factors affect the PE ratio. The term g reflects earnings growth, K shows how much of earnings is paid out as dividends, and R, the holding period return, gives an idea of the riskiness of the share (since the higher the required R, the riskier must be the share). We can now see that the PE ratio will be greater, the higher the earnings growth (as we saw in Table 5.5), but also the higher the dividend payout ratio and the lower the risk of the share. So, despite the limitations of the model, it does allow us an insight into the factors that are likely to affect the value of a share.

All the above methods of estimating holding period return, whether from finite or infinite horizon models, require estimates of future dividends, earnings or share prices. Each model is based on the same fundamental equation for the value of a share, equation (5.2), which simply states that the current value of a share, given by its share price, must be equal to all the future cash flows attributable to that share discounted by the required rate of return given its risk.

Figure 5.1 shows a small sample of the large number of different share valuation models which can be derived from equation (5.2). The choice of model will depend on the investor's subjective estimate of which variables he can best forecast, for example dividends or earnings, growth rates or future *PE* ratios.

Risk

Whichever model is employed to estimate the expected holding period return, R, it is useful to think of R as being made up of a basic return required on a riskless investment, say a very short-term gilt, plus a premium for the uncertainty of the future cash flows. Thus we can write

$$R = R_F + \text{risk premium} \tag{5.12}$$

where R_F is the riskless return, which will change as interest rates and hence required rates of return change. This serves as a useful check to any estimates of R; the figure calculated should always be greater than the redemption yield on gilts because of the greater risk of holding shares.

Of course, the expected holding period return on a share cannot be calculated in isolation from its risk which can be measured, as we saw in Chapter 2, by the standard deviation of the probability distribution of returns. How should the standard deviation be assessed? Strictly, we need to estimate not only all expected future cash flows but the probability distributions of all such flows. This would in practice be a daunting task. Luckily, the risks attached to particular shares have been found in general not to change rapidly over time so that risk can usually be fairly adequately measured by the standard deviation of past returns.

Thus, given the expected *HPR* and risk of, say, two shares being considered as potential investments, the investor can, given his attitude to risk and return (utility function), decide which share he prefers. However, if the investor is considering adding a share to his existing

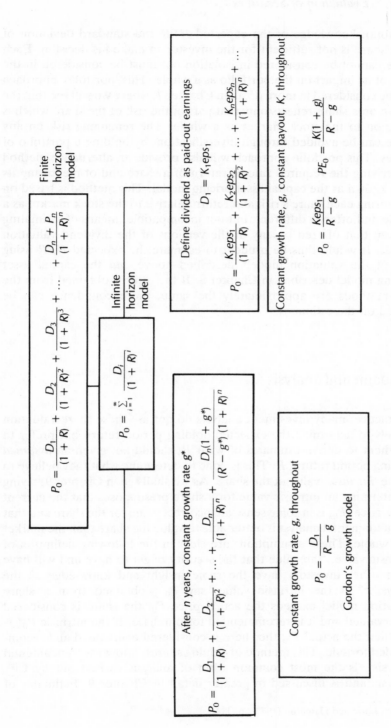

Figure 5.1   Alternative share valuation models

portfolio, knowledge of the expected *HPR* and standard deviation of each share is not sufficient for the investor to make his decision. Each share cannot be considered in isolation but must be considered in the light of its impact on the portfolio as a whole. This 'portfolio' approach will be considered in more detail in Chapter 7, where we will see that the return on a share reflects only that part of the risk of the share which is common to the stock market as a whole. The remaining risk on any share can be avoided through diversification, by holding a portfolio of shares. This portfolio approach will also provide an alternative method of deriving the required rate of return of a share and of measuring its risk, known as the capital asset pricing model. This method is based on measuring each share's risk and return relative to the stock market as a whole and offers a different, but not incompatible, means of estimating R from that offered by any of the versions of the dividend valuation model. It would thus be prudent to estimate the expected *HPR* using one of the valuation models described above *and* the capital asset pricing model described in Chapter 8. If the returns obtained from the two methods are approximately the same, more confidence can be placed on the estimates.

Fundamental analysis

In practice, many investment analysts do not use these share valuation models to determine the expected holding period return but prefer to use them to derive estimates of what P_0 should be, given an *assumed* holding period return, R. This is done to determine what they believe to be the '*intrinsic*' value of the share. As we shall see in Chapter 9, trying to determine an intrinsic value for a share presupposes that the current share price, P_0, is in some sense an incorrect value for the share and that the fundamental analyst is better able to value the share than the market as a whole. These assumptions are clear in the following definition of intrinsic value: 'the value that the security *ought* to have and will have when other investors have the same insight and knowledge as the analyst'.[24] If the intrinsic value, say P_0^*, obtained from a share valuation model exceeds the actual price P_0, the share is considered undervalued and it is recommended for purchase. If the intrinsic P_0^* is less than the actual P_0, the share is considered overvalued and recommended for sale. This method of valuing shares, known as 'fundamental analysis', is the most common form of analysis carried out by City analysts and is discussed in greater detail in Chapter 9. Estimates of

---

[24] From Lorie and Hamilton (1973), p. 114.

future earnings and dividends are still needed, but P_0^* is the unknown as opposed to R.

Thus, estimates of R must be found from other sources. In practice, either the capital asset pricing model estimate of the required rate of return, R, described in Chapter 8, is used, or an arbitrary risk premium, based on intuition or judgement, is added to the current yield on gilts, as in equation (5.12), or it is assumed that the average rate of return achieved over some holding period in the past is a good estimate of the future *HPR*. However, the historic *HPR* is unlikely to be a good estimate of the future *HPR* as earnings and dividends will of course change over time as, more importantly, will the riskless rate of return, R_F, even if the risk *premium* remains constant. The basic premise for fundamental analysis is that the market is not 100% efficient – in the sense that some of the securities sold on it will later prove to have been wrongly priced and that greater returns than expected given the shares' risk can be made from spotting such share bargains. Far more time is spent in the City on such activities as fundamental analysis than on calculating the 'fair' rate of return on a share bought at a fair price, given the risk. Chapter 9 will describe in more detail such commonly used investment techniques as technical and fundamental analysis, and consider whether, for the ordinary investor, such activities are likely to be worthwhile.

Summary

This chapter has examined ways in which ordinary shares and associated securities are valued. The major characteristics of ordinary shares and their methods of issue were described as well as measures used to compare equities – dividend yield, dividend cover and *PE* ratios. The advantages and disadvantages of these measures were discussed, the major disadvantage being that none of them provided an estimate of total holding period return. The next section described how the expected holding period return could be derived from estimates of future earnings or dividends, this model being known as the dividend valuation model. All the different versions of the basic model require subjective estimates of future income from the share and these estimates depend on a multitude of factors, including company, industry and general economic influences. The major use to which these valuation models are put in practice is not, in fact, to determine expected holding period return, but, *assuming* a value for R, to determine an intrinsic share price to see whether the share is under- or over-valued and should be bought or sold.

Appendix: calculation of dividend cover

The simplest way to calculate dividend cover is to divide the *eps* by the *gross dps*. However, as we saw on page 147 when looking at PE ratios, there are different types of *eps*, and the preferred *eps* will depend on the type of comparison between companies being made. For example, the *Financial Times* uses the 'net' *eps* figure for its calculations of PE ratios. However, the *eps* figure used for dividend cover calculations is the 'full distribution' *eps*. This attempts to measure the maximum amount of earnings available for the payment of a *gross* dividend (i.e. *net* dividend plus associated ACT). The *Financial Times* therefore defines dividend cover to be '*full' eps/gross dps*.

Note: The use of different measures of *eps* for PE ratio and dividend cover calculations in the *Financial Times* is the reason why, for many companies

$$\frac{P_0}{PE_0 \times \text{gross } dps_0}$$

(an indirect method of calculating $eps_0/\text{gross } dps_0$) does not equal the dividend cover shown. See problems 1 and 4.

Problems

1. Mr Foot is assessing his investments. He holds £5,000 nominal of gilt-edged stock, Treasury 8½% 1984–6, and 1,000 £1 ordinary shares of National Westminster Bank Ltd. The *Financial Times* gives him the following information on his investment:

	Price £	Dividend net	Cover	Interest yield	Gross yield	Redemption yield	PE
Treasury 8½% 1984–6	80⅝xd			10.54		14.52	
National Westminster £1 shares	408	21.0	4.5*		7.4		3.5

*See the above appendix.

(i) What is the current value of Mr Foot's investments and what annual *gross* income (i.e. before income tax/tax credit) do they provide?

(ii) What does the term 'gross yield' mean for National Westminster shares and how is it calculated? It is lower than either the interest or redemption yield on the gilt-edged stock. Does this mean that National Westminster shares give a lower return?

(iii) Explain why investment in a share such as National Westminster is said to be riskier than investment in a fixed interest government security. How can risk be measured?

2. (i) Bloomington's Boutiques plc has a share price of 68p. It paid a gross dividend of 5p per share last year and is expected to pay 5.5p per share next year. Assuming the dividend is expected to grow at a constant rate in perpetuity, what is the return on the share? (Hint: use Gordon's growth model.)

   (ii) There are 1,000,000 Bloomington's ordinary shares in issue and Bloomington's is expected to earn £117,000 after tax next year. Calculate the expected earnings per share, *PE* ratio, gross dividend yield and dividend cover. Explain the significance of each of these ratios.

  (iii) Suppose the current gross redemption yield on gilts is around 12%. This is higher than Bloomington's gross dividend yield. Does this mean that Bloomington's can raise share capital more cheaply than the UK government can borrow in the gilt market?

  (iv) How would you decide whether to buy Bloomington shares? What further information would you require?

3. Blue Boxes plc has just announced a rights issue of two million new shares. The pre-announcement share price was 145p and the rights issue involves the issue of one new share (for every existing three shares held) at a price of 115p.

   (i) What will be the theoretical ex rights price and the value of the 'rights'?

  (ii) How much new money will be raised (before transaction costs)? What will those transaction costs consist of?

  (iii) Mr Blair already holds 3,000 shares. Outline the main alternatives available to him. Can Mr Blair simply do nothing without financial loss?

4. You are given the following information from the *Financial Times* on two companies in the Electricals section:

	Share price	Dividend net	Cover	Yield gross	PE
Racal	460	5.0	4.2*	1.6	17.6
Plessey	500	8.62	2.4*	2.5	23.7

*See the appendix.

   (i) How would you explain the differences in *PE* ratio?

  (ii) How would you choose which share to purchase from the above information?

5. What is meant by the reverse yield gap? What does it imply about the return on equity relative to the return on gilts?

6. Advanced Electronics Corp. expects to pay a dividend of 20p per share at the end of the present year. The dividend is then expected to grow at a 15% rate for three years, then at a 10% rate for the next three years, and at 5% for ever more.

   (i) What value would you place on the share if a 9% rate of return were required?

  (ii) Would your valuation change if you expected to hold the shares for only three years?

7. How would you expect inflation to affect the value of your equity investments?

Options

Introduction

Although options on ordinary shares have existed in the UK since the seventeenth century, the opening in 1978 of the UK Stock Exchange traded options market has reawakened interest in this type of investment. Also, advances in the techniques of valuing options have encouraged trading in options and in securities incorporating an option element, for example convertible unsecured loan stocks.

Options offer their holders the right to buy (call options) or sell (put options) shares at a fixed price at some time in the future, usually within a few months. At present, the UK traded options market has call and put options on eighteen shares. Early growth in the UK traded options market was not as rapid as had been widely expected. Hopes had been high given the huge success of the Chicago Board Options Exchange set up in 1973, where the 1980 volume in options amounted to ninety-seven million option contracts worth a massive $45b. Reasons for the UK market's relative lack of success included initital teething problems such as the Inland Revenue's treatment of options as a wasting asset (which involved a relatively higher tax on capital gains compared with other securities[1]). This tax disadvantage was removed in the 1980 Budget and the major obstacle to success subsequently appears to have been lack of investor understanding of options, in particular, perhaps, private investors who consider options too risky an investment.

This concept of options as particularly risky and speculative investments is not a recent one. Dealing in options was officially banned on the London Stock Exchange from 1734 to 1860 and again from 1939 to 1958. The first ban was as a result of speculation leading to the South Sea Bubble which burst in 1720.[2] The second was imposed as part of general restrictions on share dealings during wartime but, despite pressure from would-be dealers in options, was only relaxed nearly twenty years later in 1958. The idea that options are used for speculation also appears to be confirmed by the fact that the biggest options market in the world is based in Chicago, the centre of commodity futures markets, rather than in New York, the site of the major US Stock Exchange. Options are similar to futures contracts in that only a small percentage of the value of the underlying security need be paid initially. This type of dealing 'on margin' can, as we shall see later, lead to large gains or losses on relatively small outlays. These kinds of investments will obviously attract speculators.

Also, the major difference between traded options and the types of securities we have considered so far is that options do not represent direct claims on the assets of the borrower. (This is in contrast with corporate securities which have built-in options, such as convertibles and warrants; these securities are issued by companies and therefore represent claims on them.) An ordinary shareholder holds the right to some fraction of the earnings and assets of the company whereas a call option holder merely has the right to buy shares in the future (shares which are already in issue) representing only a potential claim on the company's assets. An ordinary shareholder holds a security issued by the company, providing funds for the company in return for future

---

[1] The value of the option was assumed to depreciate over its life, creating a greater capital gain when sold than if the original cost were used.

[2] The South Sea Bubble was a rush of share speculation which was concentrated on the shares of the South Sea Company. This company was granted a monopoly in the South Seas by the British government in return for taking over the government debt. Its share price during the Bubble rose from £86 to £1,100.

income. A traded option holder has no relationship with the company whose shares he has an option to buy or sell. He has simply entered into an agreement with another party, the option seller or 'writer', concerning the possible future purchase or sale of shares by the option holder to the option 'writer' at a predetermined price. The writing of such options contracts has no impact on the company's issued share capital and neither the writer nor the purchaser has any direct relationship with the company.

As with futures contracts, many traded options contracts are closed (offsetting transactions are made) before exercise takes place. So, many more options will be written than are actually exercised; in other words, the underlying shares will only rarely be bought or sold by the option holder. This is why, as happens on the Chicago Board Options Exchange, the number of shares implicit in the options entered into can exceed the number of shares actually in issue. If every option holder were to exercise his right to buy or sell shares there might not be enough shares to go round. Because only a small fraction of options are exercised, the volume of options in existence, called 'open interest', can be higher than the volume of the underlying shares.

As well as having a rather tenuous relationship with corporate assets, options also have the property of becoming completely worthless, if the share price has moved contrary to the purchaser's expectations by the expiry date of the option. An ordinary share only becomes completely valueless if the company's liabilities exceed its assets so as to have nothing for the shareholders on a winding up. In contrast, a put or call option can become valueless whatever the solvency of the underlying company.

It is these characteristics of options which lead to the view that options are speculative investments. What is often not appreciated is that options enable the investor to vary the risk element in shares in *both* directions. In other words, the investor may either increase *or* decrease expected return and risk by trading in options. For example, institutional investors such as insurance companies, which, as we shall see in Chapter 11, are generally considered to be relatively risk averse in their attitude to investment, are frequent sellers or 'writers' of call options. By simultaneously holding shares and writing call options on those shares, they can reduce their risk to less than that of simply holding the shares.

An understanding of how options work and how to value them also allows investors to analyse securities which have option elements in them, in particular convertible unsecured loan stocks. We saw in Chapter 3 how issues of UK corporate fixed interest debt had declined dramatically after 1973. The major type of fixed interest company security to survive into the 1970s and 1980s was convertible unsecured loan stock (CULS for short), because, not only could it be treated as a straight fixed interest unsecured loan stock but it also offered the holder the right to convert the loan stock at a later date into ordinary shares and thus the *option* to avoid inflation and interest rate risk. Because of this option element, option valuation models can be applied to the valuation of convertible unsecured loan stocks.

This chapter begins with a description of options, in particular those traded on the UK Stock Exchange. It goes on to compare the differences between buying call options on shares and buying the underlying shares themselves. We find that the purchase of a call option contract involves a smaller initial outlay than the purchase of the underlying shares, with a smaller potential loss in money terms but a greater risk overall. Put options are then described, as are various combinations of options (and options with shares) which can increase or reduce risk and expected return. This, combined with an understanding of the various factors which affect the value of options, allows us to derive an option valuation model, known as the Black–Scholes model. The reader is then shown how to use this model to value traded options. The final section of the chapter discusses how option valuation techniques can be applied to corporate securities with built-in options, such as warrants and CULS.

It should be noted that the option valuation model used *looks* difficult to use and it is, probably, the most complex model in this book. However, in practice, this is irrelevant since the calculations can be done by a very simple program on a microcomputer. All that is needed is an understanding of the factors that affect the value of an option. The computer will do the rest.

Description of options

The purchase of a *call* option on an ordinary share entitles the holder to buy the share, on or before some fixed date in the future, at a fixed price. The fixed date is known as the exercise or expiry date and the fixed price as the exercise or striking price. A *put* option, on the other hand, entitles the holder to *sell* an ordinary share on or before the expiry date at a fixed price. Puts or calls which offer the holders the option to exercise *before* as well as on the expiry date are known as American options. European options entitle the holders to exercise their options to buy or sell only *on* the expiry date itself. Traditionally, in the UK, options were of the 'European' type. However, the traded options market has been based on the US options markets and, so, traded options purchased via the UK Stock Exchange are of the 'American' type.

Prior to the opening of the traded options market, options (now known as 'traditional' options) could only be arranged via an options dealer on an individual basis between two parties, the seller or 'writer' of the option and the purchaser. Traditional options could not be traded, since there was no official secondary market, and the purchaser of the option had only two alternatives, to exercise the option (and buy or sell the shares at a fixed price) or to do nothing and let the option expire unexercised. A traded option allows the holder a third alternative, to sell the option to someone else in the secondary market at any time during the option's life.[3]

Table 6.1 gives the details on London traded options provided daily in the *Financial Times*, usually on the bids and deals page. The *Financial Times* also provides price information (on the same page) for the European Options Exchange, based in Amsterdam. This options market, set up just before the London market, is separate from the Dutch Stock Exchange, unlike the London traded options market which is run by the UK Stock Exchange. Options traded in Amsterdam include not only options on Dutch company shares but also on shares from other European countries and on gold.

Information on traditional, non-traded options is also provided by the *Financial Times* on the back pages, that is, with the ordinary share prices. Table 6.2 provides an example of details given on traditional options. The terms of traditional options, such as the date they are set up, are not standardised as for traded options. In fact, non-traded options can be arranged at any time, with the expiry date usually fixed at three months from the date of the contract and the exercise price traditionally fixed around the prevailing offer price for the share.[4]

Traded options are created on a rota system, with options always having nine-month lives and being created at three-monthly intervals. Options on some shares, for example BP, will be in the January, April, July and October series, whereas options on other shares, such as Barclays, will belong to the February, May, August and November series. Only three out of four options in a series will exist at any one time; for example, in Table 6.1, there are no January options in GEC since January is more than nine months from the date of the table. The actual expiry date on a traded option is usually the second Wednesday in the last Stock Exchange account to fall within the nine-month period.

Another difference between traditional and traded options is that traded options are created with a range of exercise prices, including at

---

[3] Also, because a traded option is an American (as opposed to a European) option, the holder has the right to exercise throughout the life of the option. We shall see later that the holder is more likely, in fact, to sell rather than exercise before expiry.

[4] Plus a small premium representing the interest cost to the writer of financing the option for three months.

Table 6.1   Details of London traded options

LONDON TRADED OPTIONS

Mar. 24 Total Contracts 12,406 Calls 1,556 Puts 850

Option	Ex'rcise price	April Closing offer	Vol.	July Closing offer	Vol.	Oct. Closing offer	Vol.	Equity close
BP (c)	260	38	1	44	—	50	—	294p
BP (c)	280	18	105	28	1	36	11	"
BP (c)	300	6	30	16	27	22	34	"
BP (c)	330	1½	4	7	1	10	36	"
BP (c)	360	½	—	3	33	—	—	"
BP (p)	260	6	135	10	26	12	75	"
BP (p)	280	14	5	17	—	20	5	"
BP (p)	300	28	13	28	79	34	125	"
BP (p)	330	56	91	56	—	60	—	"
CU (c)	130	20	27	21	—	25	—	149p
CU (c)	140	10½	13	14½	13	19	—	"
CU (c)	160	3	—	7	5	10	—	"
Cons. Gld (c)	360	42	7	52	3	64	1	312p
Cons. Gld (c)	390	14	5	32	3	42	3	"
Cons. Gld (c)	420	5	38	16	37	25	1	"
Cons. Gld (c)	500	1½	25	4	—	7	10	"
Cons. Gld (p)	360	6	—	13	2	16	—	"
Cons. Gld (p)	390	14	1	24	1	27	1	"
Ctlds. (c)	80	6½	—	12	—	16	4	85p
Ctlds. (c)	90	2	—	5½	14	8½	2	"
GEC (c)	850	10	2	36	—	57	—	822p
GEC (p)	750	5	—	10	2	—	—	"
GEC (p)	800	10	6	20	2	30	—	"
GEC (p)	850	34	—	45	2	50	3	"
Gr'd Met. (c)	180	33	7	41	—	45	—	211p
Gr'd Met. (c)	200	15	2	23	5	28	—	"
Gr'd Met. (c)	220	3	8	10	109	14	100	"
Gr'd Met. (p)	200	6	—	10	20	12	—	"
Gr'd Met. (p)	220	15	—	16	2	21	2	"
ICI (c)	300	30	1	40	—	50	—	326p
ICI (c)	330	9	11	23	—	32	—	"
ICI (c)	360	4	—	10	50	18	—	"
ICI (p)	280	2	—	4	11	—	—	"
ICI (p)	300	3	5	8	5	12	—	"
ICI (p)	330	10	28	18	5	24	5	"
Land Sec. (c)	300	9	—	20	58	31	3	295p
Land Sec. (c)	330	3	5	9	3	18	—	"
Mks & Sp. (c)	120	35	1	39	—	—	—	154p
Mks & Sp. (c)	130	25	—	29	5	33	—	"
Mks & Sp. (c)	140	15½	6	19½	9	23½	4	"
Mks. & Sp. (c)	160	4	23	7	28	11½	—	"
Shell (c)	330	46	—	54	3	62	—	374p
Shell (c)	360	16	1	30	8	38	1	"
Shell (c)	390	5	—	15	5	23	—	"
Shell (p)	330	4	—	8	30	12	—	"
Shell (p)	360	15	2	18	—	24	—	"
Shell (p)	390	36	30	38	—	40	—	"

Option	Ex'rcise price	May Closing offer	Vol.	August Closing offer	Vol.	November Closing offer	Vol.	Equity close
Barclays (c)	460	13	—	28	—	42	5	456p
Barclays (p)	460	15	5	20	—	25	—	"
Barclays (p)	500	47	—	52	—	55	2	"
Imperial (c)	70	24½	1	27½	—	—	—	94p
Imperial (c)	80	14½	180	18	25	20½	—	"
Imperial (c)	90	6	38	10½	91	13	4	"
Imperial (p)	70	½	—	11½	—	—	20	"
Imperial (p)	90	3	15	4½	—	5½	—	"
Lasmo (c)	260	50	6	57	—	67	—	300p
Lasmo (c)	280	35	2	45	1	52	—	"
Lasmo (c)	300	23	16	32	5	37	3	"
Lasmo (c)	330	10	6	18	—	—	—	"
Lasmo (c)	360	3	3	9	5	—	—	"
Lonrho (c)	80	2½	4	5½	3	7½	10	75p
Lonrho (c)	90	1	5	3	—	—	—	"
Lonrho (p)	70	2	8	4	—	5	—	"
Lonrho (p)	80	6	9	8	—	10	—	"
Lonrho (p)	90	16	7	18	—	—	—	"
P & O (c)	120	16	30	24	—	28	—	132p
P & O (c)	130	11	11	17	13	21	—	"
Racal (c)	330	60	4	70	—	77	—	383p
Racal (c)	360	30	1	45	—	57	—	"
Racal (c)	390	12	20	25	—	37	—	"
Racal (p)	360	7	13	10	—	15	—	"
Racal (p)	390	18	5	25	—	30	—	"
RTZ (c)	420	25	44	40	—	47	—	427p
RTZ (c)	460	9	2	22	—	30	—	"
RTZ (c)	500	4	12	12	2	—	—	"
RTZ (p)	390	6	3	13	—	15	—	"
RTZ (p)	420	15	6	24	16	35	—	"
Vaal Rfs. (c)	40	6¾	14	9	—	9½	2	$45
Vaal Rfs. (c)	45	3½	7	5¼	4	6¾	10	"
Vaal Rfs. (c)	50	1	10	3	5	4	—	"
Vaal Rfs. (p)	40	1¼	—	2¾	4	3¼	—	"
Vaal Rfs. (p)	45	3½	2	4¾	10	5½	—	"
Vaal Rfs. (p)	50	5¾	3	7¼	1	7½	2	"

C=Call   P=Put

Source: Financial Times, 25 March 1982.

Table 6.2   Details of traditional options

OPTIONS
3-month Call Rates

Industrials				House of Fraser..	15	Utd. Drapery	7
Allied-Lyons......	8			I.C.I.	24	Vickers..............	16
BOC Intl.	15			"Imps".	8	Woolworths........	5
B.S.R.	$8\frac{1}{2}$			I.C.L.	$5\frac{1}{2}$		
Babcock	10			Ladbroke............	15	**Property**	
Barclays Bank ...	42			Legal & Gen.	19	Brit. Land..........	$7\frac{1}{2}$
Beecham	21			Lex Service	10	Cap. Counties	10
Blue Circle	48			Lloyds Bank........	42	Land Secs..........	28
Boots	19			"Lofs"	$6\frac{1}{2}$	M.E.P.C.	20
Bowaters............	24			London Brick......	7	Peachey	14
Brit. Aerospace ..	17			Lucas Inds..........	20	Samuel Props.....	11
B.A.T.	38			"Mams"...............	12	Town & City	$3\frac{1}{2}$
Brown (J.)...........	7			Mrks. & Spncr	12		
Burton Ord.	15			Midland Bank.....	30	**Oils**	
Cadburys	9			N.E.I.	9		
Courtaulds..........	8			Nat. West. Bank.	38	Brit. Petroleum ..	26
Debenhams.........	7			P & O Dfd.	14	Burmah Oil	10
Distillers	15			Plessey..............	32	Charterhall........	6
Dunlop	$6\frac{1}{2}$			Racal Elect.........	35	KCA	14
Eagle Star..........	31			R.H.M.	$6\frac{1}{2}$	Premier	6
F.N.F.C...............	4			Rank Org. Ord. ...	20	Shell	30
Gen. Accident	28			Reed Intnl.	26	Tricentrol..........	22
Gen. Electric	65			Sears	6	Ultramar............	38
Glaxo	42			Tesco	$5\frac{1}{2}$		
Grand Met...........	17			Thorn EMI	42	**Mines**	
G.U.S. 'A'..........	45			Trust Houses	11	Charter Cons.	25
Guardian	25			Tube Invest.	13	Cons. Gold..........	45
G.K.N.................	15			Turner & Newall.	11	Lonrho...............	7
Hawker Sidd	30			Unilever.............	55	Rio T. Zinc	42

A selection of Options traded is given on the
London Stock Exchange Report page

"Recent Issues" and "Rights" Page 36

This service is available to every Company dealt in on Stock
Exchanges throughout the United Kingdom for a fee of £600
per annum for each security

Source: Financial Times, 25 March 1982.

least one below and one above the current share price. For example, we can see from Table 6.1 that BP call options have exercise prices ranging from 260p to 360p, with a current share price of 294p. Commission charges are also different between traditional and traded options, with commission being charged, at the same rate as for shares, on the *exercise price* of traditional options, and commission being paid on the *option* price (plus a fixed charge) for traded options.[5] The unit in which traded options are bought and sold is a *contract*, usually representing options on 1,000 shares. The total number of contracts traded on 24 March 1982, given in Table 6.1, was 2,406. This compares with an average of 19,620 ordinary share bargains per day for March 1982.

Purchase of call option contract or shares?

We now examine the effect of buying a call option contract. We suppose Mr Choice buys one Marks & Spencer call option contract with an

---

[5] See Appendix 1 for details of these transaction costs.

exercise price of 140p per share and due to expire in April. The price
quoted for such a contract in Table 6.1 is 15½p per share, equivalent to
£155 for the contract. The current M&S share price is 154p and so the
option will entitle Mr Choice to buy M&S shares at below the current
market price. Such an option is termed 'in the money' since Mr Choice
could buy the option, immediately exercise his right to buy the shares at
140p, then sell them at 154p to make 14p per share, before any
transaction costs. Call options such as the 160p April M&S contract,
where the exercise price exceeds the current share price, are referred to
as 'out of money'. Obviously, for an 'in the money' call option to be
traded, its value must exceed the profit which could be made on
immediate exercise. For example, the option purchased by Mr Choice is
worth 15½p per share, compared to the 14p per share profit which could
be made if the shares were exercised immediately.

We ignore for the moment the alternatives that Mr Choice has of
selling the option unexpired or exercising his option *before* expiry and
assume, for simplicity, that he holds the option until expiry. How will
Mr Choice decide whether or not to exercise his option on expiry? If the
M&S shares are quoted at the expiry date of the option at less than
140p, there will be no point in exercising the option, since it would be
cheaper for Mr Choice to buy the shares in the marketplace than at the
exercise price of 140p. His total loss on the contract, if the option is not
exercised, will be 15½p × 1,000 = £155, a 100% loss on his investment
in the option. However, if the M&S shares are quoted at more than
140p on the expiry date, the exercise price will be less than the market
price and it will benefit Mr Choice to exercise. When he has exercised
his option, he can then decide whether to keep the M&S shares he has
acquired or immediately sell them. Suppose the M&S share price on
expiry is 160p. If Mr Choice immediately sells the shares, he will make a
profit of 20p per share (160p − 140p). However, he paid 15½p per share
for the right to exercise at 140p and this must be deducted from the 20p
per share to arrive at his actual profit.

Cost of option contract (1,000 at 15½p)	(£155)
Cost of exercise (1,000 at 140p)	(£1,400)
	(£1,555)
Proceeds on sale (1,000 at 160p)	£1,600
Profit before transaction costs	£45

Of course this profit of £45 would be reduced by the transaction costs
incurred by Mr Choice. These are excluded from our analysis to simplify

the exposition. Note that it would still pay Mr Choice to exercise if the M&S share price on expiry were only, say, 145p, since he would be able to make 5p per share by exercising his right to buy the shares and selling them to offset against the 15½p per share cost of the option.

By purchasing a call option, Mr Choice has limited his maximum potential loss to the cost of the option, £155. His potential profit, however, is unlimited and will depend on the M&S share price when he exercises the option. For it to be worthwhile to exercise, the M&S share price must be greater than the exercise price, in this case 140p.

Table 6.3 compares the alternative investment strategies of buying a call option contract on 1,000 M&S shares as opposed to buying the 1,000 shares themselves at the current market price of 154p. Two possible M&S share prices on the exercise date are considered, $S = 120p$ and $S = 160p$, and, again, transaction costs are ignored.

Table 6.3 highlights the three fundamental differences between buying a call option on shares and buying the underlying shares themselves. Firstly, the investment outlay required for a call option is smaller, in this case £155 as opposed to £1,540 for the shares. Secondly, the downside risk in *money* terms is smaller for a call option. The maximum amount Mr Choice can lose on his option is £155, by leaving the option unexercised. However, Mr Choice can lose much more in money terms on the shares themselves if the price falls substantially below his purchase price. In this example, Mr Choice would lose £340 from holding shares if the share price fell to 120p. Thirdly, the *percentage* gain or loss given by the holding period return is greater on

Table 6.3   Purchase of call option or shares

	$S = 120p$	$S = 160p$
1. Call option on 1,000 shares (exercise price $X = 140p$)		
Cost of option	(£155)	(£155)
Cost of exercise	(0)	(£1,400)
Proceeds of sale	(0)	£1,600
Net profit/(loss)	(£155)	£45
Holding period return	−100%	+29%
2. Buy 1,000 shares		
Cost of shares	(£1,540)	(£1,540)
Proceeds on sale	£1,200	£1,600
Net profit/(loss)	(£340)	£60
Holding period return	−22%	+4%

an option purchase than on share purchase. Relative to the amount invested, Mr Choice stands to make a greater percentage gain or loss on the option than on the shares. This implies, from our knowledge of the relationship between expected return and risk, that the purchase of a call option is riskier than the purchase of the underlying shares.

Graphical presentation of options

Call option

Figure 6.1(a) illustrates the potential gain or loss to Mr Choice on the M&S option just before expiry, depending on the underlying share price, S, and the exercise price, $X = 140p$. We can see that Mr Choice makes a loss on his option investment unless the share price, S, reaches 155.5p, equal to the exercise price, X, of 140p plus the cost of the option, C, of 15½p. Beyond that, his profit amounts to $(S - X)$ per share minus the cost of the option, C, giving a profit of $S - (X + C)$.

Figure 6.1(b) shows the equivalent gain or loss on the underlying shares. This is simply the difference between the cost of the share, in this case, 154p, say S_0, and the share price on expiry, S.

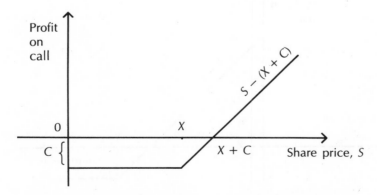

Figure 6.1(a)   Profit on a call option just prior to expiry

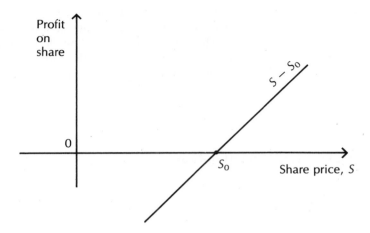

Figure 6.1(b)   Profit on underlying share just prior to expiry

Put option

A put option can be analysed graphically in exactly the same way as a call option. Figure 6.2 shows that the holder of a put will make money on his investment if the share price on expiry is *less* than the exercise price (by at least as much as the cost of the put), since he can then sell at the exercise price, X, and buy back immediately at the lower market price, S. Thus, the holder of a put makes money on a share price fall without actually having to hold shares. All that he has to do on exercise is buy the shares at the share price, S, and immediately sell them for the higher exercise price, X, to make his profit.

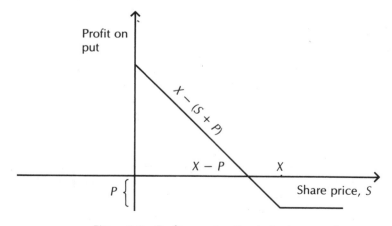

Figure 6.2   Profit on put option just prior to expiry

For example, look at the April ICI put option in Table 6.1 with an exercise price, $X = 300p$. This put is valued at $P = 3p$ with the share price at 326p. In this case, P is 'out of the money' since the shares could be sold in the market at 326p compared with only 300p if the put were exercised. The put is still worth 3p, since there is the possibility that the share price could fall further before the expiry date and the put be worth exercising. If Mr Choice bought the ICI put now at 3p, he would make a profit on expiry if the ICI share price fell to below the exercise price of 300p *minus* the cost of the put, $P = 3p$, that is, to below 297p. Suppose the ICI share price on expiry were 280p. Mr Choice would make the following profit on his investment in the ICI put option.

Proceeds of exercise at 300p per share for 1,000 shares	=	£3,000
less: cost of acquiring shares at 280p per share		(£2,800)
less: cost of put option, (1,000 at 3p)		(£30)
Profit before transaction costs		£170

Buying a put is a way of selling shares 'short', that is, selling shares that you do not have in the expectation that you will be able to buy them back at a lower price before you have to deliver. Short selling is allowed in the US but not in the UK. However, the potential losses from buying puts and short-selling are different. The short-seller is obliged to buy shares for delivery whatever they may cost whereas the put option holder does not have to exercise his right to sell. This limits the put option holder's losses to the cost of the option whereas the short-seller's losses are potentially unlimited.

Combinations of options

This graphical way of looking at options also allows us to examine combinations of different options, all based on the same underlying share. For example, the simultaneous purchase of a put and a call option on a share, with the same exercise price and expiry date, called a

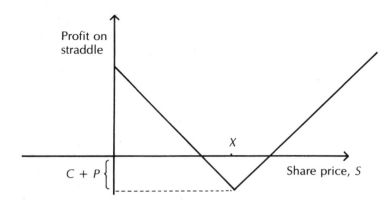

Figure 6.3   Profit on straddle just prior to expiry

'straddle', would lead to the profit pattern shown in Figure 6.3 on expiry.

Since the holder of a straddle will make money if the share price moves substantially up *or* down, an investor in a straddle would be someone who believed that the future price changes in that particular share, whatever their direction, had been underestimated by the market (as reflected in the market price of the straddle).

Other types of option combinations include a 'strip' (the purchase of two puts plus one call) and a 'strap' (two calls plus one put). The number of possible variations is vast, allowing different amounts of risk to be borne, by speculating on or hedging against a variety of possible share price movements.

Use of options to hedge risk

As well as combining different types of option to speculate on share price movements, we can combine options with shares to *reduce* the risk to the investor of substantial price changes in the share. It will be remembered from Chapter 2 that options were mentioned, along with forward or futures contracts, as a means of hedging risk. And yet we have seen that options are risky investments, with possible returns on, say, a call option ranging from a 100% loss to unlimited positive returns. However, options can be used to hedge risk provided they are combined with investment in the underlying shares.

For example, suppose that Miss Pick buys shares in Axe plc and simultaneously sells or writes a call option contract in Axe shares. By writing a call option contract we mean that Miss Pick effectively sells a call option contract to an investor. Suppose, for example, that the Axe share price is currently 100p and that the exercise price of the call option is to be 110p with nine months to expiry. Suppose also that Miss Pick sells the call option contract for 20p per share. (This 20p is known as the premium.) Miss Pick will therefore receive 20p × 1,000 = £200 if she sells a call option contract for 1,000 Axe shares. Now, if the share price never exceeds 110p during the life of the option, the purchaser of the option will not exercise the option and Miss Pick will be left with a clear profit of £200. However, if the option is exercised, Miss Pick will be obliged to sell 1,000 Axe shares at the exercise price of 110p, whatever their market value. If Miss Pick did not already hold 1,000 Axe shares, her written call contract would be 'uncovered' since she would have to buy the shares needed in the market. If she already held the necessary Axe shares, her written call contract would be 'covered'. Note, however, that whether or not her written call contract is covered, her loss per share if the call option is exercised will still be the same, the difference between the current share price, S (the price at which she could have sold the share if there had been no contract) and the exercise price, X (the price at which she is obliged to sell the share) *less* the premium she has already received.

Figure 6.4 illustrates the effect on Miss Pick of buying Axe shares, of

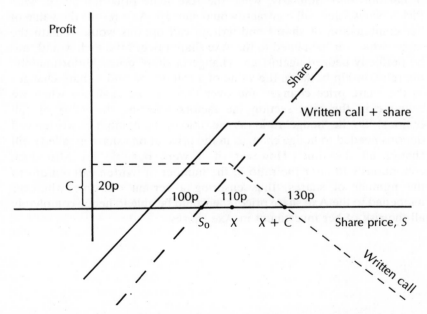

Figure 6.4   Profit just prior to expiry on combination of share purchase and written call option

writing a call contract and of combining the purchase of Axe shares with the writing of a call option contract just prior to expiry.

For simplicity, we look at the profit per share. The impact of this particular combination, compared to simply buying the shares, is to increase the profit if the share price, S, is low on expiry and to reduce the gain if the share price is high on expiry. The break-even point is when the share price on expiry, S, is equal to the exercise price, X, plus the premium received, C, in this case, 110p + 20p = 130p. Thus, the risk of holding shares and writing call option contracts is *lower* than the risk of simply holding shares and, as mentioned in the introduction to this chapter, this combination is frequently employed by risk averse financial institutions.

In fact, if Miss Pick could alter the number of shares and the number of written call contracts in her investment portfolio as she wished, she could actually hedge risk completely not only at expiry but throughout the life of the option contract. So, whatever happened to the share price, the value of her shares *plus* the written contracts would remain constant. For example, suppose that, for every 1p change in the Axe share price, the value of a call option on the share changed by ½p.[6] Miss Pick would then write call options on two Axe shares for every Axe share she held. Every time the share price went up by 1p, Miss Pick would lose 1p on her written call options leaving no change in the value of her portfolio. Similarly, when the Axe share price fell by 1p, Miss Pick's two written call contracts would gain 1p. As a result, the value of her combination of shares and written call options would remain the same, whatever happened to the Axe share price. Miss Pick would thus be perfectly hedged against any change in share price. Unfortunately, the relationship between the value of a call option and a share changes as the share price changes and over time (as we shall see when we examine in the next section the factors affecting the value of call options). So the 'hedge' ratio (as the ratio of the number of written call options needed to hedge changes in the price of one share is called) will change all the time. However, if it were possible for Miss Pick continuously to alter the ratio of the number of written call options to the number of shares, thus ensuring a certain outcome whatever happened to the Axe share price, she would be able to hedge completely all the risk of her investment in Axe shares.

---

[6] For example, if a call option with an exercise price of 40p were priced at 10p when the share price was 40p and 10½p when the share price was 41p.

Comparison of options with futures

If options can be used in this way to hedge completely risk on share investment, how do they compare with the traditional use of forward or futures markets to hedge risk?

Suppose that there were a futures market in shares. Such markets do already exist in other countries in various forms. For example, although there is no official futures market in France, share purchases on the French Stock Exchange can be bought for settlement one month ahead as well as for immediate settlement. Also, in the US, a futures market in the Standard & Poors share index has been in operation since 1982 and the US already has both options and futures markets in fixed interest securities.

Share options and share futures contracts both represent future claims upon shares. The first difference to note is that the share futures contract represents an obligation rather than an option to buy (or sell). Both involve some form of initial payment – the premium for the option and a 'margin' deposit in the case of the futures contract. The futures contract would, in addition, involve daily topping up or reduction of the margin throughout its life, each day's cash flow being equal to the daily change in the value of the future.

The other major difference between options and futures contracts for hedging purposes is that the futures contract more closely mirrors the equivalent spot contract (in this case, simply buying the share) and so is easier to use as a complete hedge. Figure 6.5 shows the values a share futures contract takes as the share price changes. Each share price movement will be exactly mirrored in the value of the futures contract. This is because the value of such a futures contract would simply be the spot value (the current share price) minus the expected return on the share in the period to the maturity date of the future.[7] This direct relationship between a share futures contract and the underlying share allows complete hedging whatever happens to the share price.

On the other hand, a call option is not so directly related to the share price. The number of options which need to be written completely to hedge risk will change over time and as the share price changes. Every time the share price of Axe plc changes, Miss Pick will need to adjust the number of call options she writes. Thus the 'hedge ratio' of written call options to shares held must be constantly adjusted, whereas a

---

[7] Note that in the case of commodity futures, there is no positive expected return on the commodity as there is for shares. The price of a futures contract for a commodity will therefore be the spot price *plus* a premium reflecting the storage and interest costs of holding the commodity for the life of the future. A share futures contract price will in fact be the spot price *minus* the expected return on the share (net of the financing cost of holding the share).

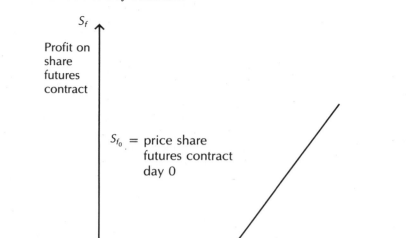

S_f

Profit on
share
futures
contract

S_{f_0} = price share
futures contract
day 0

S_{f_0}

Share price, S

Figure 6.5   Profit on share futures contract

futures hedge needs no alteration except for topping up of the margin as required.

A further complication with an option hedge is that hedging is complete only for relatively small changes in share price. For example, if the Axe share price fell by more than Miss Pick had received in premium (in our example 20p) the loss in the value of the Axe shares that she held would not be counterbalanced by an equivalent gain on the written options. Her gain on the writing of the call options is limited to the 20p premium per share that she received. With a futures hedge, whatever the size of the share price movement, it would be matched by an equivalent movement in the futures price.

Despite the complications encountered in practice for completely hedging risk by using options, it is this property of options which enables us to value them. Before deriving an exact valuation model for options, we first need to consider which factors will affect their value.

Factors affecting value of call option

We now consider the factors which will affect the value of a call option. We can see from Figure 6.1 on p. 169 that the value of a call, C, is greater the greater the underlying share price, S. Also, the call option will be worth more, the lower the exercise price, X. This can be seen to be true in practice by looking at Table 6.1 on p. 165 where the BP July option contract is worth 44p per share with an exercise price, X, of 260p and only 3p per share with $X = 360$p.

Similarly, the longer the call option has to expiry, the more valuable it will be, since there will be more time for the share price to rise. So, in Table 6.1, the BP call contract with $X = 300$p is worth 6p, if expiry is in April, and 22p if expiry is six months later in October. An important corollary to this is that it usually does not pay an investor to exercise a call option before the expiry date, since, even if the current share price, S, exceeds the exercise price, there is still time for S to increase even further. Since shares are expected to have positive returns, share prices must be expected to rise over time (unless there is a dividend imminent).[8] Therefore, the holder of a traded option will usually do better if he wishes to realise his investment before the expiry date by selling his option than by exercising it before expiry. For example, with the M&S May call option contract with $X = 140$p, Mr Choice will do better by selling his contract for 15½p per share than by exercising, buying and selling the shares, and making 14p per share. The 1½p premium, known as the 'time' value element of the option, reflects the potential gain from a further expected rise in the share price in the time remaining to expiry.

Two other factors affect the value of a call option. Firstly, the prevailing rates of interest influence the call's value. The purchaser of a call option acquires the right to buy something in the future. By not having to buy the shares now, he is in effect saving money which he could invest until (possibly) needed at expiry. So, the higher the prevailing interest rates, the more valuable the option. In fact, the relevant interest rate affecting the value of a call option is, rather surprisingly, the *risk-free* interest rate, R_F. This is because we saw that if Miss Pick combined written call contracts on shares with the shares themselves in a suitable hedge ratio, she could completely hedge all the risk of her investment. Whatever happened to the share price, her return from the combination of written call contracts and shares was certain and risk-free. So, since investment in call options *can be*

---

[8] We know that the expected holding period return on a share consists of any dividend plus an expected capital gain. If there is to be no dividend during the holding period, the share price must be expected to rise. See, later in this chapter, pp. 184–6, for more comment on the problem of dividends.

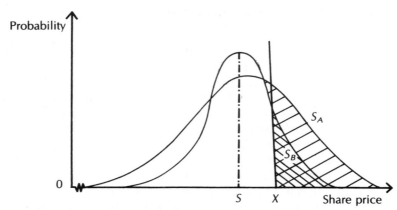

Figure 6.6   Effect of variability of share price on call option value

risk-free (if it is correctly combined with the underlying shares) the rate of return required on such call options will be the risk-free rate.

Secondly, the more risky the underlying share, the more the option is worth. Figure 6.6 considers two shares, A and B, where A is riskier due to the greater variance, V_A, of its share price probability distribution. Suppose that these shares currently have the same share price, S, and that identical call options can be bought on each, with exercise price, X. If X is greater than the prevailing share price on each share when the investor buys the call options on A and B (the options are 'out of the money'), he must hope that, on expiry, the share prices, S_A and S_B, will exceed X. That eventuality is more likely in the case of A, since there is a greater possibility that S_A will exceed X than S_B exceed X, as evidenced by the greater shaded area in Figure 6.6. In the case of put options, it will be the downside risk (also measured by the variance or standard deviation in a normal probability distribution) which affects its value. So again, the higher the risk of the share, measured by the variance or standard deviation, the higher the value of the put option.[9]

It is worth emphasising at this point that, when valuing options, we are concerned with share *prices* and not share returns. The future share *price* is relevant, since this is what determines the future return on the option. Dividends are not paid to option holders and are only of interest in so far as they affect the future share price. (Share prices usually fall when shares go ex dividend.) At this stage, we assume for simplicity that no dividends are paid during the life of the option, although we shall relax this assumption later.

---

[9] We shall see in Chapter 8 that, when considering investing in a share, only part of the total risk of the share is relevant, the part known as beta or market risk, since the remainder can be diversified away. However, when considering investing in options, the *total* risk or volatility is relevant since the value of the option depends on the *total* price movements of the share.

Option valuation model

Knowing the five factors which affect the value of a call option – the share price, S; the exercise price, X; the time to expiry, t; the risk-free interest rate, R_F; and the risk of the underlying share measured by its variance, V – all that remains is to combine these into a formula for the value of the call option, C.

The valuation model most commonly used is one formulated by Black and Scholes, using the technique we considered for Miss Pick of combining written call contracts with the purchase of shares in such a way as to obtain a totally risk-free, hedged investment. Using the hedging strategy devised for Miss Pick, Black and Scholes obtained the formula for the value, C, of a call option:

$$C = S\, N\, (d_1) - PV\, (X)\, N\, (d_2) \tag{6.1}$$

where S is the underlying share price, X the exercise price, $PV(X)$ the present value of the exercise price payable on expiry (discounted to the present by using the risk-free rate of interest) and $N(d_i)$ the value of the cumulative normal probability distribution with a mean of 0 and an area under the curve of 1, evaluated at d_i. The d_i are functions which depend on the five factors, S, X, t, R_F and V.[10] Although equation (6.1) looks complex, it becomes much more comprehensible if, for the time being, we ignore the $N(d_1)$ and $N(d_2)$. By doing this, we get

$$C = S - PV(X) \tag{6.2}$$

In fact, the equality in equation (6.2) only holds at the date of expiry. However, it represents a lower bound for the call option value at any point in its life. We can show that this is so by considering two alternative investment portfolios, as in Table 6.4.

Portfolio A consists of buying a call option with an exercise price of X at a cost of C and of investing risk-free sufficient money, denoted $PV(X)$, which, with interest, will be worth X by the expiry date. If the share price on expiry, S_1, is greater than or equal to the exercise price, X, the call option will be worth the difference, $S_1 - X$, and the risk-free investment will be worth X, giving a total of S_1. If the share price is less than X, on expiry, the call option will be worthless and the value of portfolio A will simply be X.

Portfolio B consists only of the underlying share, purchased for S, which must be worth S_1 on the expiry date, by definition. Thus, if S_1 is

---

[10] For further explanation of the relevance of the $N(d_i)$ and the Black–Scholes model generally, see Elton and Gruber (1981), ch. 17.

Table 6.4   Determining a lower bound for C

Investment portfolio	Value at expiry date	
	$S_1 \geqslant X$	$S_1 < X$
Porfolio A		
Buy call for C	$S_1 - X$	0
Invest $PV(X)$	$\underline{X}$	$\underline{X}$
	$\underline{\underline{S_1}}$	$\underline{\underline{X}}$
Porfolio B		
Buy share for S	$\underline{\underline{S_1}}$	$\underline{\underline{S_1}}$

greater than or equal to X on expiry, portfolios A and B will have identical values. However, if S_1 is less than X on expiry, the value of portfolio A will be greater than the value of portfolio B, since X is greater than or equal to S_1, in that case.

Since in both cases the value on expiry of portfolio A 'dominates' the value of portfolio B, the cost of portfolio B must be less than or equal to the cost of A, which may yield a higher value on expiry. Thus,

$$\text{Cost of } B \leqslant \text{ cost of } A$$

$$S \leqslant C + PV(X)$$

or,

$$C \geqslant S - PV(X) \tag{6.3}$$

We can now see that $S - PV(X)$ is a lower bound for the value of a call option at any point in its life, as predicted by equation (6.2).

In fact, we also know an upper bound for the value of a call option since the value of C can never exceed the value of the underlying share, S. For example, if the exercise price were zero, the value of the option would at most be the value of the free gift – the share. If the exercise price were positive, there would be a cost to acquiring the share and the value of C would be less than S.

The solid lines in Figure 6.7 represent the upper and lower bounds that we have derived for C. The dotted line shows the value of C as given by the Black–Scholes formula in equation (6.1). This diagram shows the value of C at a particular point in time, say T, where there remains a period t to expiry. However, we can see that, as C approaches expiry, it must become less valuable since there is less time for the share

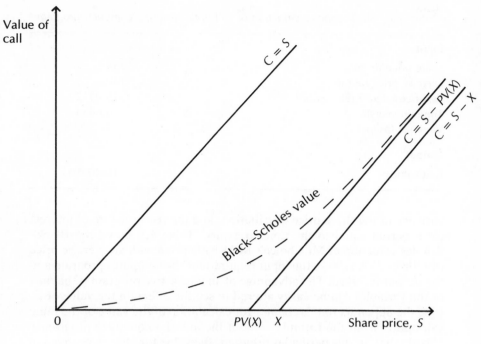

Figure 6.7   Limits on value of call option

price to increase. Thus, the dotted line will get closer and closer to the lower bound, $S - PV(X)$, as the option moves to expiry. Simultaneously, the value of $PV(X)$ will approach X as the expiry date nears, and so the right-hand bound, $S - PV(X)$, will move towards the value $S - X$. On expiry, provided $S \geq X$, the call option will be on the boundary itself, since it will then be worth exactly $S - X$. Prior to expiry the option is worth more than the lower limit (as we saw with the M&S April option worth 15½p), given the potential for the share price to rise further.

Using the Black–Scholes formula

The use of the Black–Scholes formula to obtain an exact value of C requires either a good calculator and some probability distribution tables or, more simply, a computer program which can be used interactively.

If a computer program is used, the program will request details on the current share price, the exercise price, the time remaining to expiry, the

Table 6.5   Black–Scholes valuation of call option using a computer program

Input	
Share price (in p)?	154
Exercise price (in p)?	140
Risk-free interest rate (as %)?	13.03125
Time (in years)?	0.0833
Variance (as %)?	9
Output	
Call value =	16.2005036

variance of the share price distribution, and the risk-free rate of interest for a period equal to the time to expiry. Table 6.5 shows the Black–Scholes valuation of Mr Choice's M&S call option with an exercise price of 140p and also shows the input required for the computer program and the output received. The advantage of an interactive program is that any of the variables can be easily altered to see the effect on the value of *C*. (See the appendix to this chapter for calculation of the value of the same call option from the formula without the aid of a computer program.)

Note that, in this particular program, the value for *t* has to be given in years in the form of a decimal and the risk-free rate and the variance as percentages. In this example, the time to expiry to the nearest month was one month. The risk-free rate used was the one-month Treasury Bill rate (expressed as an annual rate) given in the *Financial Times* of the same day as 13¹⁄₃₂%. Finally, the historic standard deviation of 30% was used.[11] This was found in the *London Business School Risk Measurement Service* which gives historical risk and return information on the shares of UK companies listed on the Stock Exchange and which is discussed further in Chapter 8.

If we compare the value of the M&S call option found using the Black–Scholes model of 16.2p with the actual market price (given in Table 6.1) of 15½p, we see that the two values are very close, with a difference of only 0.7p. In this example, no dividends were due to be paid before expiry. As we shall see later, the Black–Scholes model does not take acount of dividend payments and, unless the model is adjusted for them, can lead to discrepancies from market values. Since there is in this case no complication due to dividends, the difference of 0.7p must arise from an inefficient market in options, from problems with the

[11] Strictly speaking, the standard deviation used in the formula should be that of the continuously compounded rate of return on the share. Instead of returns being calculated annually or six-monthly, the assumption of continuous compounding, although unrealistic, leads to exponential functions which are easier to deal with mathematically than discrete functions.

assumptions underlying the Black–Scholes model, or from different views concerning the inputs.

We will see in Chapter 9 that the UK market for ordinary shares is efficient in the sense that excess profits cannot in the long run be made by using simple trading rules. Similarly, the UK traded options market is efficient enough for arbitrage profits (net of transaction costs) not to be available from trading rules based on the discrepancies of option prices from their Black–Scholes values. Thus, either the assumptions of the Black–Scholes model are not appropriate for realistic option valuation or different inputs to the model are being used. Although we have not derived the Black–Scholes formula from first principles, we are aware of one of the major assumptions – that written call options and shares can be combined in such a way as to produce a perfect hedge against changes in share price throughout the life of the option. We saw with Miss Pick that this was hardly feasible in practice; in any case, the transaction costs involved would be enormous. Other assumptions include continuously compounded rates of return and a particular model of share price behaviour, both of which allow a formula to be derived using calculus.[12] However, despite these problems, the assumptions are not implausible and the Black–Scholes model does allow options to be valued. Given this, and the fact that most investors in the options market are aware of and use the Black–Scholes values, it is more likely[13] that any discrepancies between the market values of the options and their Black–Scholes values are due to different views concerning the inputs.

Given that there is little room for disagreement on S, X, R_F and t, if there is disagreement amongst traders in options about the inputs, this must stem from different expectations concerning the future volatility of the share than that provided by the historical standard deviation. This has an interesting implication. If the Black–Scholes model is used for option valuation, as it appears to be in practice, the model can be used to provide not the option value but an up-to-date forecast of the future volatility of the share. Thus, the market value of the option becomes an input to the model and the standard deviation the output. For example, if we use the data in Table 6.5 to find the standard deviation of the return on M&S shares, inputting the market value of the call option of 15½p, the model gives a variance of 3.5%. This implies that the market believes the future riskiness of the M&S shares will be less than evidenced by their volatility over the past five years.

---

[12] Calculus is a form of mathematics which allows solutions to equations to be found using the properties of functions as they approach limits.

[13] Although, as we shall see later, discrepancies can be due to the fact that dividends are to be paid during the life of the option.

Valuation of put option

Since the values of call options, put options and the underlying shares
are related, the Black–Scholes model can also be used to value put
options. We can find the relationship between the values of put and call
options by returning to the concept of two alternative investment
portfolios, A and B, this time with portfolio A consisting of a share and
a put option P and portfolio B of money on deposit, again PV(X), and a
call option C. Table 6.6 shows the values of both these portfolios on
expiry.

This time the two portfolios have identical values on expiry whichever
value of S_1 prevails. Their initial costs must therefore also be identical,
giving

$$S + P = C + PV(X) \tag{6.4}$$

So, once the value of either a call or a put is known, the price of the
other (provided it has the same exercise price and time to expiry) can be
found from equation (6.4). Calculations by hand or the computer
program used earlier can give the investor the Black–Scholes value of
either type of option without difficulty. Table 6.7 shows the input and
output from the program for the ICI April put option with an exercise
price of 300p. The Black–Scholes value of 1.7p given in the output in
Table 6.7 is, as for the call option, close to the market price given in
Table 6.1 of 3p.

A word of warning before using the Black–Scholes model. Firstly, as
mentioned above, the model ignores the problem of dividend payments.
A call option will probably be worth less when a dividend is to be paid
before expiry since a share price will usually fall when the share goes ex

Table 6.6   *Relationship between put and call values*

Investment portfolio	Value at expiry date	
	$S_1 > X$	$S_1 \leqslant X$
Portfolio A		
Buy share for S	S_1	S_1
Buy put P	0	$X - S_1$
	S_1	X
Portfolio B		
Buy call C	$S_1 - X$	0
Invest PV(X)	X	X
	S_1	X

Table 6.7   *Black-Scholes valuation of put option using a computer program*

Input

Share price (in p)?	326
Exercise price (in p)?	300
Risk-free interest rate (as %)?	13.03125
Time (in years)?	0.0833
Variance (as %)?	8.4

Output

Put value =	1.7389425

dividend. Similarly, the value of a put option will be worth more if a dividend is paid during its life. The options market prices of traded options shown in Table 6.1 have taken this factor into account. So, for example, the value of a BP 300 call option expiring in October is given as 36p by the Black–Scholes formula and 22p in Table 6.1. The lower market value is due predominantly to an expected dividend payment which is not taken into account in the Black–Scholes formula. If an option has a life of at least six months to expiry, as does the BP 300, there will almost certainly be at least one dividend payment during its life.[14] The Black–Scholes formula can to some extent be amended to cope with this problem. Instead of using the current share price, S, in the formula, S is reduced by the present value of the expected dividend. For example, if BP, with a current share price of 294p, is expected to pay a dividend of 10p in three months' time, the share price of 294p can be reduced by the present value of 10p. To be consistent with the continuous compounding assumption, 10p would be multiplied by $e^{-R_{Ft}}$ = $e^{-0.12 \times 0.5}$ = 0.94 if the annual risk-free rate is 12% and $t = 0.5$ of a year, before insertion into the Black–Scholes equation. This adjustment takes account of the timing of the dividend payment but assumes that the share price will fall by the exact amount of the dividend when it goes ex div and assumes that the option will not be exercised before the expiry date.

The second point which must be borne in mind when using the Black–Scholes model is that the formula actually gives the value for a European option, that is, one which can only be exercised on maturity. In the same way as the problem of dividends is ignored in the option valuation model, this assumption is to simplify the option sufficiently to be able to value it at all! However, this difficulty is not insuperable. We can see that the 'American' London traded options must be worth at least as much as equivalent European ones because of their additional

---

[14] Dividends are usually paid at approximately six-monthly intervals.

right to exercise before expiry. However, they may not be worth more than European ones since we saw earlier that it was usually more profitable either to sell the option or to hold the option to expiry rather than to exercise before expiry. For example, the call option held by Mr Choice was worth 15½p unexercised compared to 14p exercised. This was because of the 'time' value of the option. So the Black-Scholes formula which gives the value of European options will usually also give the value of American options provided there are no complications such as dividends. If a dividend is due before expiry, the investor may do better to exercise before the share goes ex dividend and collect the dividend rather than wait till expiry to exercise and thus forfeit the dividend payment. So, in the case of a call option on a dividend-paying share, such as the BP 300 call expiring in October considered above, the option must be valued twice, first assuming that it will be exercised on expiry and, second, that it will be exercised before the shares go ex dividend. It may be that the call option will be more valuable if exercised before the shares go ex div and thus, in this case, an American call option will be more valuable than an equivalent European call.

Convertible unsecured loan stock

The ability to value options, using a model such as the Black–Scholes model described above, is not only of use when investing in the options markets. It also enables us to value other securities, in particular convertibles which are discussed in this section.

The variety of corporate securities has declined dramatically over the past few decades, with the most common securities now being equities, debentures and unsecured loan stocks. However, one 'hybrid' security has survived, *convertible* unsecured loan stock (CULS for short). Other types of convertible security, for example debentures, have not survived to the same extent, partly for tax reasons and partly because the issue of convertible *un*secured loan stock does not disturb the list of precedence of existing creditors as would, say, a convertible debenture. The continued popularity of CULS can be seen by comparing the new issues of convertible debt (mostly, as we have noted, convertible unsecured loan stock) during the period 1971–81 with other forms of corporate debt. New issues of convertible debt in fact exceeded new issues of other corporate debt during that period, with new issues of convertible debt amounting to £993m. compared with £856m. for straight corporate debt.

Convertible unsecured loan stock lies somewhere between straight debt and equity and it has been this compromise in terms of risk and return which has ensured its survival. Companies unwilling to issue debt at high interest rates during the 1970s and yet unhappy about raising equity, were prepared to issue convertible debt. Similarly, investors, worried about the declining value of fixed interest debt in a period of high interest rates and high inflation, were often willing to invest in convertible debt, which offered the comparatively greater security of fixed interest debt if the ordinary shares did not do well combined with the possibility of switching into the shares at a later date if they did do well.

Characteristics of CULS

In order to gain an understanding of how convertibles work and how they are valued, we will examine one particular CULS in some detail, the RTZ 9½% 1995–2000, whose price is quoted in the back pages of the *Financial Times*, next to the ordinary share price. From Chapter 3, we know the significance of the 9½% coupon and the redemption dates 1995–2000. RTZ have contracted to pay the debt-holders interest of £9.50 per annum (in two semi-annual instalments) for each £100 nominal of CULS held and, provided the stock remains unconverted, to continue to do so until redemption some time between 1995 and 2000. The choice of redemption date in the period 1995–2000 is up to RTZ, as it is up to the government for some gilts. This choice gives RTZ what is known as an option to 'call' the stock and, in fact, this option can be valued using the option valuation model described earlier in the chapter.[15]

What the coupon and redemption dates do not tell us is that a holder of the RTZ CULS has the right, in the month of June in any year from 1984 to 1995, to exchange his or her fixed interest stock for ordinary shares, receiving in this case twenty ordinary shares for each £100 nominal of stock given up. This figure of twenty is known as the 'conversion ratio' and the nominal amount of stock given up per share, in this example £100/20 = £5, as the 'conversion price'. These figures will vary from convertible to convertible and may, in some instances, vary over time.[16] The RTZ CULS under consideration has, however, a constant conversion ratio.

---

[15] In this case, the exercise price would be the nominal value of the stock, £100, which would be the price paid by the company to redeem the stock.

Differences between straight options and CULS

Before we attempt to value the CULS using an option valuation model, it would be useful to highlight the major differences between straight options traded on the Stock Exchange and the options to convert implicit in CULS.

Firstly, to exercise an option, cash must be paid equal to the predetermined exercise price, X. In the case of a CULS, no cash changes hands; instead, the fixed interest stock is surrendered in return for shares. The exercise price is the value of the fixed interest stock surrendered. As a result, the exercise price will vary according to the value of this fixed interest stock in the marketplace at the time of exercise.

The second difference between straight options and CULS is the length of time to expiry. As we saw earlier, traded options usually have a maximum life of nine months, whereas the option element of the RTZ CULS, when it was issued in 1980, had a maximum time to expiry of nearly fifteen years since conversion could take place as late as June 1995.

Thirdly, straight options have no impact on the volume of the underlying share capital of the company. We saw earlier that the number of ordinary shares implicit in the options traded on the Chicago Options Exchange could exceed the number of shares in issue. Exercise of all these options would not increase the number of shares in issue. In fact, most of these options will be self-cancelling or will never be exercised; those which are exercised will involve the transfer between investors of existing shares and not the issue of new shares. In contrast, convertible debt does affect the share capital of the company concerned. As debt is given up in exchange for equity, the amount of debt in the balance sheet decreases and the amount of equity increases. New shares are issued and existing shareholders find that they hold a smaller proportion of the company after conversion. This is why earnings per share are calculated both on existing share capital and 'fully diluted' when a CULS is in issue.

---

[16] Since share prices are expected to increase over time, some CULS have an increasing conversion price (and hence a decreasing conversion ratio) to prevent the differential between the conversion price and the actual share price from widening.

For example, suppose that Fast Car plc has earnings of £20m. and share capital of 100 million £1 nominal ordinary shares. If Fast Car has £20m. of 8% CULS in issue, with conversion terms of fifty shares per £100 nominal of stock, full conversion would involve the issue of ten million new shares. Earnings per share before conversion are £20m./£100m. or 20p per share. After conversion, the earnings would be spread between more shareholders, but the interest cost on the CULS would be saved. Earnings after conversion would increase to £21.6m. (to allow for the £1.6m. saving in interest) and would be divided amongst 110 million shares. In this example, 'fully diluted' earnings per share would be 19.6p per share.

Value of CULS

When attempting to value a complex security, a sensible first step is to establish limits to its value. This was done for options and can be done in the case of a CULS by considering its value as a straight fixed interest stock, ignoring the value of the implicit option to convert into equity. As for gilts, the interest yield and the redemption yield can be calculated for a CULS. For example, at a price of £115 for £100 nominal of RTZ CULS, the RTZ interest yield would be 8.3% and the redemption yield in, say, January 1983, assuming redemption will take place in 1995,[17] would be approximately 7.5%. Because the holder of a CULS has the option to convert his fixed interest stock into ordinary shares, the yield he will usually get on a CULS will be lower than he would get on an unsecured loan stock with the same coupon and redemption date but without the conversion option. The more valuable the option to convert into ordinary shares (and this will be a function, as with options, of such factors as the share price), the lower the yield on the CULS will be. For example, the RTZ CULS redemption yield of 7.5% was 5% lower than the average redemption yield on fifteen-year corporate debentures and loan stocks (given in the FT–actuaries indices of the same date) of 12.5%.

Turning the above argument round, we can say that the value of the CULS must be greater than the value of an equivalent unsecured loan stock. Therefore, the value of such an unsecured loan stock with no conversion option must act as a lower limit for the value of the CULS. If the option to convert becomes totally worthless, which it could do if the

---

[17] Redemption will probably take place in 1995 if RTZ can refinance at a lower interest rate than 9.5%.

share price fell to below the exercise price,[18] the CULS would always be worth the value of the fixed interest stock.

To calculate this lower limit, the investor must choose a suitable redemption yield for an equivalent RTZ unsecured loan stock. This will probably be a few points higher than the redemption yield available on a gilt, with the same period to redemption and a similar coupon, to allow for the risk of default by RTZ, a risk which is not present with government stock. If the company already has quoted fixed interest stocks in issue, the redemption yield can be obtained from these stocks. If not, an idea of the required premium can be obtained from the FT–actuaries indices, where the average redemption yields for gilts and for corporate debentures and loan stocks are given. For example, assuming that RTZ unsecured loan stock has approximately average default risk, the average gross redemption yield for fifteen-year corporate debentures and loans already referred to can be used. Once the required redemption yield is determined, the interest and redemption payments must be discounted to give the value of the fixed interest element of the CULS.

So, in January 1983, assuming a required redemption yield of 12.5%, say 6.25% semi-annually, we would get, again assuming redemption in 1995,

Value of unsecured loan stock element of RTZ CULS

$$= \sum_{i=1}^{i=25} \frac{4.75}{(1 + 0.0625)^i} + \frac{100}{(1 + 0.0625)^{25}}$$

$$= 59.30 + 21.97$$

$$= \mathbf{£81.27}$$

This is substantially below the market price at that time of £115. The option to convert into the ordinary shares must be a valuable one. We can see this by considering another potential lower bound for the value of the CULS. This is its conversion value, that is, its value assuming conversion can take place immediately. In the case of RTZ, the holder of £100 nominal would be entitled to twenty shares. These were worth, when the CULS was quoted at £115, 512p per share, giving a conversion value of 20 × 512p = £102.40. This represents a *valid* lower limit value for the RTZ CULS only if conversion can actually take place. The RTZ CULS was not convertible until 1984 at the earliest and so the conversion value in 1983 was only a *potential* lower bound (assuming the

---

[18] However, if the share price fell substantially, this would affect the value of the company's debt as well, because of the increased default risk.

share price did not fall between 1983 and 1984) rather than an actual lower limit.[19]

Thus, the RTZ CULS was standing at that time above both its unsecured loan stock value of £81.27 and its higher notional conversion value of £102.40. We saw when looking at the M&S call option that an option before expiry is always worth more than its conversion value, because of the possibility that the share price will rise even further before expiry. So, the RTZ CULS, with its option to convert into RTZ shares in the future, is worth more than the current value of the shares into which the CULS can be converted.

Traditional approaches to CULS valuation

We have seen that lower limits for the value of a CULS can be estimated with little difficulty. The problem arises when an exact value for the CULS is required. Until the development of option valuation models such as the Black–Scholes model, CULS valuation was primarily determined by income differential methods. This involves, first, the determination of the optimal conversion date. This is calculated by considering the expected dividend growth pattern of the shares and comparing with the fixed interest income.[20] The optimal conversion date is then the first year in which the expected dividend income will exceed the fixed interest income.[21] Given the optimal conversion date, the traditional method of valuing CULS would be to take the conversion value and to adjust for the income forgone. Such a valuation technique assumes that conversion at the time of valuation is a reality (which it is not for RTZ in 1982), concentrates only on cash flows and ignores the value that the *option* to convert confers on the investor. It is also dependent on the dividend growth assumptions made and on the discount rate used to discount those dividends and the interest payments.

---

[19] In the US, convertible stocks tend to be convertible almost immediately after issue whereas recent UK CULS have tended to have a period of a few years before the first conversion date. The company can then be certain of paying interest for a minimum period, and is perhaps better able to forecast its short-term cash flows.

[20] The expected net dividends will be compared with the net interest payments, so that different types of taxpayer may have different optimal conversion dates.

[21] However, the dividend income will be more uncertain and hence riskier than the fixed interest income, although this is not usually taken into account.

Valuing CULS with option valuation techniques

An alternative way of attempting an exact valuation of the CULS would be to use the option valuation model, since the value of a CULS can be written as

Value of CULS = value of equivalent ULS + value of option to convert into equity

We have seen how to value the equivalent ULS by determining the relevant redemption yield and discounting the interest and redemption payments. In a previous section we obtained a value for the equivalent ULS of £81.27. All that remains, therefore, is to value the option element of the CULS.

Unfortunately, the option to convert into equity, in this example RTZ ordinary shares, is a more complex security to value than a straight call option on RTZ shares. Firstly, there are twelve possible expiry dates from 1984 to 1995 instead of just one on a European option. This would not be a problem if dividends were not paid or if the conversion ratio were adjusted for dividends. However, CULS are not in general protected against dividends which are bound to be paid given the long life of the CULS. So, some adjustment for the dividends to be paid on the ordinary shares before the option is exercised must be made. This can be done by deducting the expected present value of the dividends from the current share price, as we saw with traded options. However, with a traded call option, one or at most two dividend payments have to be forecast. In the case of the RTZ CULS, RTZ's dividend policy for up to fifteen years ahead has to be estimated. As we saw above, this disadvantage also applied to the income differential method of valuing CULS.

A third complication which applies to CULS option valuation is the determination of the exercise price. With a straight option, the exercise price is fixed. With a CULS, the exercise price is the value *at conversion* of the fixed interest stock given up. So, not only must the current value of the unsecured loan stock element be determined but also its value at the optimal conversion date.

This optimal conversion date is another problem with CULS. The best solution is to calculate the value of the RTZ CULS option using some sort of iterative program which considers every possible conversion date, taking into account expected dividends. This obviously requires a much more complex option valuation program than do straight options and this is, no doubt, the reason that convertibles are still valued using income differential techniques.

The advantages of the option valuation model over more traditional methods are, however, that it does *not* assume that conversion is possible today, and that it quantifies the advantage of being able to acquire shares in the future by explicitly taking into account the likely future share price and therefore the advantages of conversion, rather than only considering the likely income from the share.

It is beyond the scope of this book to attempt an exhaustive valuation of CULS. The object of this section has been to describe CULS and to show how, as for options, lower bounds can be derived and valuation attempted either from an income differential viewpoint (the traditional approach) or using options. Despite the complexities of the options built into CULS, models can be set up to value them. The increased understanding of the factors affecting option valuation has led to better valuation of hybrid securities such as CULS.

Warrants

Finally a word about share warrants. These are options to acquire ordinary shares and can be valued accordingly. Warrants are securities either issued separately or attached to other corporate securities, such as loan stock, as 'sweeteners', offering the same type of attraction as CULS. In contrast to CULS, warrants usually require the holder to pay a cash exercise price to acquire ordinary shares, although this price may vary (in a predetermined way) over time, especially if there are capital changes such as scrip issues on the shares. Warrants are thus securities which are more closely related to straight options, but they are uncommon in the UK in comparison to CULS, enjoying more popularity in the US.

Summary

This chapter has described the market in both traditional and traded options. A call option offers the investor the right to acquire a share on or before a particular date at a fixed price. A put option offers the holder the right to sell a share at a fixed price on or before the expiry date. Traded options, which now form the bulk of trading in the UK stock market, are American options in the sense that exercise, the taking up of the option, can take place at any time before the option expires. European options, for example traditional options, can only be exercised on the expiry date itself.

Investment in options was then compared with investment in the underlying shares themselves and it was found that combinations of different options or options with ordinary shares allowed the investor to increase or reduce return and risk relative to the return and risk of simply holding ordinary shares. Upper and lower limits to the value of a call option were found and the factors affecting the value of a call option discussed. This led to an explicit valuation model for call options, the Black–Scholes model, which is commonly used by traders in the options markets. A discussion on how to apply the Black–Scholes model to value both call and put options in practice then followed.

The chapter concluded with a look at a corporate security which is a mixture of debt and equity, convertible unsecured loan stock. It was found that CULS could be valued as straight unsecured loan stock plus an option to convert into equity, allowing option valuation techniques to be applied. However, the options built into CULS are more complex than straight options and traditional valuation methods using income differentials are often preferred.

Appendix: calculation of value of call option using Black–Scholes model

If the value of the call option is to be found without the aid of a computer program, we must know the exact Black–Scholes formula:

$$C = S\,N(d_1) - Xe^{-R_F}\,N(d_2) \tag{A.1}$$

where

$$d_1 = \frac{\ln\,(S/X) + (R_F + \tfrac{1}{2}V)t}{\sqrt{Vt}} \tag{A.2}$$

$$d_2 = d_1 - \sqrt{Vt} \tag{A.3}$$

We use e^{-R_F} for the present value of the exercise price, X, since the Black–Scholes model assumes that all returns are continuously compounded. We know, for the M&S April call option, that

$S = 154\text{p}$
$X = 140\text{p}$
$t = 1\text{ month} = 0.0833\text{ year}$
$V = 9\%$
$R_F = 0.1303125$

Substituting these values into equations (A.2) and (A.3) we get

$$d_1 = 1.2694$$
$$d_2 = 1.1828$$

Table A.1 overleaf cumulative normal distribution tables which enable us to determine $N(d_1)$ and $N(d_2)$. (See also a graphical representation in Figure A.1.) We find from Table A.1 that

$$N(d_1) = 0.8980$$
$$N(d_2) = 0.8816$$

Substituting into equation (6.1) (see p. 179) for $N(d_i)$ gives

$$C = 154 \times (0.8980) - 140e^{-0.0108} (0.8816)$$

$$C = 138.3 - 122.1$$

$$C = \mathbf{16.2p}$$

This is the same value as was found using the Black–Scholes formula in a computer program (although there may sometimes be differences due to the accuracy of the normal distribution tables used in either case).

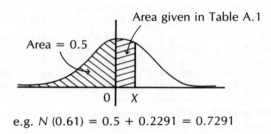

e.g. $N(0.61) = 0.5 + 0.2291 = 0.7291$

Figure A.1   Areas under the standard normal distribution function with mean of 0 and total area of 1

Table A.1   Areas under the standard normal distribution function $\int_0^z f(z)dz$

z	0.00	0.01	0.02	0.03	0.04	0.05	0.06	0.07	0.08	0.09
0.0	0.0000	0.0040	0.0080	0.0120	0.0160	0.0199	0.0239	0.0279	0.0319	0.0359
0.1	0.0398	0.0438	0.0478	0.0517	0.0557	0.0596	0.0636	0.0675	0.0714	0.0753
0.2	0.0793	0.0832	0.0871	0.0910	0.0948	0.0987	0.1026	0.1064	0.1103	0.1141
0.3	0.1179	0.1217	0.1255	0.1293	0.1331	0.1368	0.1406	0.1443	0.1480	0.1517
0.4	0.1554	0.1591	0.1628	0.1664	0.1700	0.1736	0.1772	0.1808	0.1844	0.1879
0.5	0.1915	0.1950	0.1985	0.2019	0.2054	0.2088	0.2123	0.2157	0.2190	0.2224
0.6	0.2257	0.2291	0.2324	0.2357	0.2389	0.2422	0.2454	0.2486	0.2517	0.2549
0.7	0.2580	0.2611	0.2642	0.2673	0.2704	0.2734	0.2764	0.2794	0.2823	0.2852
0.8	0.2881	0.2910	0.2939	0.2967	0.2995	0.3023	0.3051	0.3078	0.3106	0.3133
0.9	0.3159	0.3186	0.3212	0.3238	0.3264	0.3289	0.3315	0.3340	0.3365	0.3389
1.0	0.3413	0.3438	0.3461	0.3485	0.3508	0.3531	0.3554	0.3577	0.3599	0.3621
1.1	0.3643	0.3665	0.3686	0.3708	0.3729	0.3749	0.3770	0.3790	0.3810	0.3830
1.2	0.3849	0.3869	0.3888	0.3907	0.3925	0.3944	0.3962	0.3980	0.3997	0.4015
1.3	0.4032	0.4049	0.4066	0.4082	0.4099	0.4115	0.4131	0.4147	0.4162	0.4177
1.4	0.4192	0.4207	0.4222	0.4236	0.4251	0.4265	0.4279	0.4292	0.4306	0.4319
1.5	0.4332	0.4345	0.4357	0.4370	0.4382	0.4394	0.4406	0.4418	0.4429	0.4441
1.6	0.4452	0.4463	0.4474	0.4484	0.4495	0.4505	0.4515	0.4525	0.4535	0.4545
1.7	0.4554	0.4564	0.4573	0.4582	0.4591	0.4599	0.4608	0.4616	0.4625	0.4633
1.8	0.4641	0.4649	0.4656	0.4664	0.4671	0.4678	0.4686	0.4693	0.4699	0.4706
1.9	0.4713	0.4719	0.4726	0.4738	0.4738	0.4744	0.4750	0.4756	0.4761	0.4767
2.0	0.4772	0.4778	0.4783	0.4788	0.4793	0.4798	0.4803	0.4808	0.4812	0.4817
2.1	0.4821	0.4826	0.4830	0.4834	0.4838	0.4842	0.4846	0.4850	0.4854	0.4857
2.2	0.4861	0.4864	0.4868	0.4871	0.4875	0.4878	0.4881	0.4884	0.4887	0.4890
2.3	0.4893	0.4896	0.4898	0.4901	0.4904	0.4906	0.4909	0.4911	0.4913	0.4916
2.4	0.4918	0.4920	0.4922	0.4925	0.4927	0.4929	0.4931	0.4932	0.4934	0.4936
2.5	0.4938	0.4940	0.4941	0.4943	0.4945	0.4946	0.4948	0.4949	0.4951	0.4952
2.6	0.4953	0.4955	0.4956	0.4957	0.4959	0.4960	0.4961	0.4962	0.4963	0.4964
2.7	0.4965	0.4966	0.4967	0.4968	0.4969	0.4970	0.4971	0.4982	0.4973	0.4974
2.8	0.4974	0.4975	0.4976	0.4977	0.4977	0.4978	0.4979	0.4979	0.4980	0.4891
2.9	0.4981	0.4982	0.4982	0.4982	0.4984	0.4984	0.4985	0.4985	0.4986	0.4986
3.0	0.4987	0.4987	0.4987	0.4988	0.4988	0.4989	0.4989	0.4989	0.4990	0.4990

Reprinted from Copeland and Weston, *Financial Theory and Corporate Policy*, Addison-Wesley Publishing Company, Inc. By permission of the publishers.

Problems

1. XYZ shares are currently quoted at 105–107p. An investor wishes to buy a three-month traded call option contract on 1,000 shares. Explain what a 'call option' means and under what conditions the investor should exercise his option. The call option is priced at 12p per share and the exercise price is 115p.

2. (i) Suppose it is early September and an investor believes the annual results of International Manufacturing, due shortly, will cause a sharp rise in the share price. The shares can be bought at 320p or the October traded options, with an exercise price of 280p, at 50p. If his prediction is correct and the shares rise to 350p while the options rise to 70p, what profit will he have made (allowing for transaction costs) if:

    (a) he has bought 2,000 shares,

    (b) he has bought two October 280p call option contracts for 1,000 shares each?

  (ii) Using your results from part (i), discuss the advantages of buying options rather than shares.

3. (i) Use the Black–Scholes model to determine the value of a European call option with an exercise price of 40p and a maturity date six months from now, if the current share price is 30p, the variance of the share price is 40% and the risk free rate 10%.

  (ii) What would the call option be worth if the current share price were (a) 40p or (b) 50p?

4. (i) Use the Black–Scholes model to value a six-month European put option on a share currently priced at 20p, with an exercise price of 30p, a risk-free rate of 8% and the variance on the share equal to 36%.

  (ii) How good an estimate of the value of an *American* put option would you expect the Black–Scholes model to give if the put option were substantially

    (a) 'in the money'

    (b) 'out of the money'?

5. Look at actual trading prices of BP traded call options to see if they behave as the theory would predict, e.g.

  (i) Follow some BP options as they approach maturity. Do their prices behave in the way you would expect?

  (ii) Compare two BP call options with the same maturity but different exercise prices. Which call option has the highest value?

  (iii) Compare two BP options with the same exercise price but different maturities. Which option is worth more?

  (iv) Use the Black–Scholes model to value any BP call option with the shortest maturity. Does your answer give the same as the market price? If not, why do you think you get a different answer?

  (v) What complications would have to be taken into account if you applied the Black–Scholes model to valuing longer maturity traded call options, say, for example, with an exercise date over six months away?

6. (i) Which variables affect the value of a call option on a share? Derive boundaries within which the value of a European call option must lie.

  (ii) Show how an option and a futures contract can be used to hedge risk. How does an option differ from a futures contract?

7. Brick Bat plc, with ten million ordinary shares priced at 80p (15 May 1983), has just paid a final net dividend at 4.6p per share. The interim dividend, paid six months ago, was 2p net. Brick Bat plc is issuing, in the form of a rights issue, 10½% Convertible Unsecured Loan Stock 1991–6. Each shareholder will be entitled to buy £1 of convertible unsecured loan stock for each eight ordinary shares held. The loan stock can be converted on 15 May in any year 1984–91 and, on conversion, the holder will receive seventy-five ordinary shares for each £100 nominal of convertible unsecured loan stock.

(i) Miss Ball holds 100,000 Brick Bat ordinary shares. How much convertible unsecured loan stock is she entitled to purchase?

(ii) If Miss Ball does not wish to put any new money into the company, how many of her existing Brick Bat ordinary shares will she have to sell to provide sufficient cash to take up her right to the convertible unsecured loan stock in full?

(iii) Assume Miss Ball has taken up rights as in (ii). She wishes to maximise her income and decides to convert when the income to be received from the shares in the form of dividends exceeds the interest from the loan stock. In which year will Miss Ball convert if dividends grow by 10% per annum? Assume Miss Ball pays tax on income at the basic rate of 30%.

(iv) Discuss the factors that Miss Ball would consider when deciding whether to invest in convertible unsecured loan stock.

PART II
INVESTMENT STRATEGY

Portfolio theory

Introduction

In Chapter 2 we discussed how to measure the most important characteristics of a security, its return and its risk. We decided that, for each security, investors would compare the expected return from a range of probable outcomes with the risk of the security, as measured by the standard deviation of the probability distribution of returns.[1] So, investors would only need to consider expected returns and standard deviations when choosing securities for their investment portfolios. They would, since they were assumed risk averse, choose those securities which offered the most return for a given level of risk or the least risk for a given level of return.

However, we did not consider the effects of *combining* securities; we only looked at how to compare them. We did get an inkling that combining them into a portfolio might be sensible when we looked at

---

[1] The variance, V, of a probability distribution of returns measures its total dispersion. The standard deviation, S, is the square root of the variance. If the probability distribution of returns is normal then either V or S is a sufficient measure of the risk of the security in question.

ways of reducing risk, in particular, pooling. Pooling was concerned with *independent* investments. The problem with securities is that they are not independent. If the *Financial Times* Industrial Ordinary 30 Shares Index[2] goes up, an investor will expect most company shares to show an upward trend, whether or not they are in the FT 30 Shares Index. There are market influences, such as changes in interest rates or the imposition of dividend controls, which will affect the prices of all securities to a greater or lesser extent. We shall see that, despite this common market influence, with the few assumptions about investor behaviour described above, it still makes sense to combine securities even if their returns are related. In fact, portfolio theory, as it is known, shows that it is foolish to hold only one security. An investor can always get more return for his risk by holding a portfolio with at least two and possibly many more securities in it.

Portfolio theory enables the investor, given a set of securities to choose from, to decide which combinations of these securities, or portfolios, give him the best return for the risk involved. He can then choose the portfolio which has the optimal risk–return relationship for him, depending on his individual circumstances. For example, an individual investor on the stock market may prefer a high-risk, high-return portfolio whereas a pension fund manager may choose a lower-return portfolio because he feels unable to accept more than a certain level of risk. Each investor will end up with what is known as an efficient portfolio (which provides the best return for the risk involved); but each investor will probably hold a different efficient portfolio according to his individual risk–return preference.

We shall see in Chapter 8 that, with a few additional assumptions such as the existence of a risk-free security, a model which is simpler to use than portfolio theory can be derived, known as the capital asset pricing model. However, the additional assumptions inherent in the CAPM, as it is known, are less realistic than those underlying portfolio theory. For this reason, portfolio theory is still widely used. For example, in the chapter on international investment, Chapter 10, we find that there is no world-wide risk-free security. Because of this, the CAPM cannot easily be extended to an international framework. However, we find that portfolio theory offers us a suitable model for determining optimal international portfolios.

This chapter now goes on to explain how the results of portfolio theory were obtained and what they mean in practical terms to the investor. Some mathematics is involved, since the reader needs it to

---

[2] See the Appendix to Chapter 9 for a description of share indices, including the FT 30 Shares Index.

understand implications of the theories, but this is kept to a minimum.[3] The initial part of the chapter considers a portfolio of only two securities and shows how an investor can decide on a combination of these two securities which is optimal for him, given his utility function. The result is then extended to any number of securities. The chapter concludes with the general implications of portfolio theory for investment and with the problems inherent in its use.

Portfolio theory

In order to understand how combining securities together into a portfolio can reduce risk, we shall start by looking at the simplest case, where two securities are combined, and then extend the results to any size of portfolio. Suppose the investor is considering securities A and B, which have the characteristics detailed in Table 7.1.

Table 7.1   *Portfolio of two securities*

	% Return	
Probability	Security A	Security B
0.25	20	45
0.50	10	25
0.25	0	5
1.00		
Expected return	$E(R_A)$ = 10%	$E(R_B)$ = 25%
Variance of returns	V_A = 50%	V_B = 200%
Standard deviation of returns	S_A = 7.1%	S_B = 14.1%

The investor could choose which of these securities he prefers if he calculates the utility he would derive from the risk–return relationships of each security. However, what would happen if, instead of buying A or B, he bought both A *and* B, say in proportions W_1 and W_2 such that $W_1 + W_2 = 1$?

If we call the resulting combination of A and B, portfolio P, what can we say about P's expected return and risk?

---

[3] For more advanced discussion of portfolio theory and the CAPM, see Elton and Gruber (1981).

Firstly, the expected return of P is simply:[4]

$$E(R_p) = W_1\ E(R_A) + W_2E(R_B) \tag{7.1}$$

That is, the expected return of P is the weighted average of the expected returns of A and B. For example, if the investor had half his portfolio in A and the other half in B, we would have $W_1 = W_2 = \frac{1}{2}$. So,

$$E(R_p) = \frac{1}{2}E(R_A) + \frac{1}{2}E(R_B)$$

$$= \frac{1}{2} \times 10\% + \frac{1}{2} \times 25\%$$

$$\mathbf{E(R_p)} = \mathbf{17.5\%}$$

The variance of any security, as we saw in Chapter 2, can be written as

$$V_i = S_i^2 = \sum_{i=1}^{i=n} (R_i - E(R))^2 p(R_i) \tag{7.2}$$

which is just the sum of the probabilities of each return (R_i) multiplied by the square of the difference of each R_i from the expected return $E(R)$.

In exactly the same way, the variance of the portfolio return can be written

$$V_p = S_p^2 = \sum_{i=1}^{i=n} (R_{pi} - E(R_p))^2\ p(R_{pi}) \tag{7.3}$$

If we allow for the fact that P is made up of $W_1\ A + W_2\ B$ in (7.3) we get

$$V_p = W_1^2 S_A^2 + W_2^2 S_B^2 +$$

$$2W_1W_2 \sum_{i=1}^{i=n} (R_{Ai} - E(R_A))\ (R_{Bi} - E(R_B))\ p(R_i) \tag{7.4}$$

This expression for the variance of P is not quite the weighted average of the variances of A and B, S^2_A and S^2_B, as was the case for the expected return of P. In equation (7.4), the expression for the variance of P includes a complex-looking term at the end which describes the relationship between the returns of A and B. This term (excluding the

---

[4] For a more detailed discussion of the properties of expected values and standard deviations in this context, see Markowitz (1959).

proportions $2W_1W_2$) is called the *covariance* of returns of A and B and is written COV_{AB}:

$$COV_{AB} = \sum_{i=1}^{i=n} (R_{Ai} - E(R_A))(R_{Bi} - E(R_B))p(R_i) \qquad (7.5)$$

What does the covariance of returns between two securities mean? In each state of the world (expressed by different probabilities $p(R_i)$), the return is compared with its expected value for both securities. If the return on A is greater than its expected value and the return on B in the same state of the world is greater than *its* expected value, then that term in COV_{AB} will be positive, and similarly, if the returns on A and B are less than their expected values in the same state of the world. So, if two securities do well (better than expected) or badly (worse than expected) in the same state of the world, they will have a positive covariance. If the returns of A and B are on different sides of the expected value, for each state of the world, covariance will be negative. If they are sometimes on the same side of the expected value and sometimes on different sides, the signs will cancel out to give a covariance of around zero.

The correlation coefficient, written $CORR_{AB}$, is defined to be the covariance divided by the product of the standard deviations of A and B:

$$CORR_{AB} = \frac{COV_{AB}}{S_A S_B} \qquad (7.6)$$

The reason for bothering to define the correlation coefficient is that it can only take values of between -1 and $+1$. It is merely another way of expressing the amount of covariance between the returns of two securities which has the property that it can never be greater than 1. If two shares' returns move together in perfect unison, they will have a correlation coefficient of $+1$. If they move in exactly opposite directions, $CORR_{AB}$ will be equal to -1.

If they are totally independent, so that if they move together it is by chance, they will have $CORR_{AB} = 0$.

Rearranging equation (7.6) to give

$$COV_{AB} = CORR_{AB}S_A S_B$$

and substituting for COV_{AB} in equation (2), we get

$$V_p = W_1^2 S_A^2 + W_2^2 S_B^2 + 2W_1 W_2 S_A S_B CORR_{AB} \qquad (7.7)$$

This is a quadratic equation in S. We now investigate what effect on the variance of the portfolio, V_p, different values of the correlation coefficient will have.

Perfectly correlated securities

First, let us look at the securities A and B described in Table 7.1. We can calculate the covariance and hence the correlation coefficient from the information we have:

$$COV_{AB} = \sum_{i=1}^{i=3} (R_{Ai} - E(R_A))(R_{Bi} - E(R_B)) \, p(R_i)$$

$$COV_{AB} = (0.20 - 0.10)(0.45 - 0.25) \times 0.25 + (0.10 - 0.10)$$
$$(0.25 - 0.25) \times 0.50 + (0 - 0.10)(0.05 - 0.25) \times 0.25$$

$$= 0.10 \times 0.20 \times 0.25 + 0 + -0.10 \times -0.20 \times 0.25$$

$$COV_{AB} = 0.01$$

So,

$$CORR_{AB} = \frac{COV_{AB}}{S_A S_B} = \frac{0.01}{0.071 \times 0.141}$$

$$\boldsymbol{CORR_{AB} = 1.0}$$

This means that the returns of the two securities A and B move perfectly in unison which was intuitively obvious from looking at Table 7.1.[5] Substituting $CORR_{AB} = +1$ into equation (7.7) we get

$$V_p = W_1^2 S_A^2 + W_2^2 S_B^2 + 2W_1 W_2 S_A S_B \tag{7.8}$$

$$V_p = (W_1 S_A + W_2 S_B)(W_1 S_A + W_2 S_B) \tag{7.9}$$

because multiplying out the terms in (7.9) gives us (7.8). Taking positive

---

[5] In fact, the returns of securities A and B are related by a linear equation
$$R_B = 0.05 + 2R_A$$
which shows that they move exactly together.

square roots of both sides,[6] with S_p the square root of V_p

$$S_p = W_1 S_A + W_2 S_B \qquad (7.10)$$

Equation (7.10) tells us that, when $CORR_{AB} = +1$, the standard deviation of P is the weighted average of S_A and S_B. So, when two securities are perfectly positively correlated, the risk and expected return of any combination of these two securities are just the weighted averages of the constituent securities' risks and returns.

In Figure 7.1, any combination of A and B, with particular values of W_1 and W_2, will be on the straight line joining A and B. No particular advantage has been gained by combining A and B in this case.

Let us look again at equation (7.7):

$$V_p = W_1^2 S_A^2 + W_2^2 S_B^2 + 2W_1 W_2 S_A S_B CORR_{AB} \qquad (7.7)$$

If $CORR_{AB} = +1$, the right-hand side of the equation is the square of the weighted average of the standard deviations. What happens if $CORR_{AB}$ is less than +1? The right-hand side of the equation must be *less than* the weighted average and so the risk of the portfolio must be less than the weighted average of the risk of its constituent securities.

This implies that, provided two securities are not perfectly positively correlated, advantages can be gained by combining them. We look first at two specific cases, where $CORR_{AB} = 0$ and $CORR_{AB} = -1$.

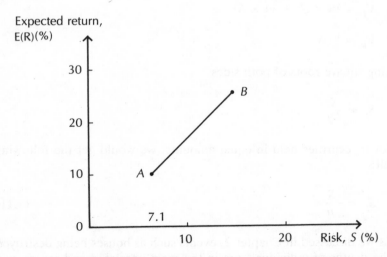

Figure 7.1 *Possible combinations of A and B when* CORR$_{AB}$ = +1

---

[6] The standard deviation is defined to be the *positive* square root of the variance.

Unrelated securities

Suppose that $CORR_{AB} = 0$. In this case, the two securities A and B are completely unrelated – they are not affected by any common factors and any similar movements will be due to chance.

Equation (7.7) becomes

$$V_p = W_1^2 S_A^2 + W_2^2 S_B^2$$

Suppose the investor holds two identical securities (each with standard deviation of 10% and expected return of 10%) in equal proportions.

We get

$$V_p = \tfrac{1}{4} \times 0.01 + \tfrac{1}{4} \times 0.01$$

$$V_p = 0.005$$

$$S_p = \mathbf{7.1\%}$$

The standard deviation of the combination is less than that of the individual securities. This result gives us the principle of pooling discussed in Chapter 2.[7] To be more general, if each security had the same standard deviation, S, the risk of the portfolio would be

$$V_p = \tfrac{1}{4} \times S^2 + \tfrac{1}{4} \times S^2$$

$$V_p = \tfrac{1}{2} S^2$$

Taking square roots of both sides,

$$S_p = \frac{S}{\sqrt{2}}$$

For n securities held in equal amounts, we would get the following result:

$$S_p = \frac{S}{\sqrt{n}} \tag{7.11}$$

As we discussed in Chapter 2, events such as houses being destroyed or the deaths of individuals are in the main unrelated and so any two insurance policies covering such eventualities would have returns which

---

[7] Risk can be reduced by pooling insurance against unrelated events. See Chapter 2, p. 55.

were uncorrelated, that is, have a zero correlation coefficient. As a result, the risk of holding a portfolio of n such insurance policies would be S_p, as in equation (7.11), which would be substantially less than the sum of the risks, S, on the individual policies. The independence between events insured, reflected in zero correlation coefficients, represents the rationale behind the principle of pooling. Unfortunately, the returns of securities quoted on the Stock Exchange are not independent in the same way.

Perfectly negatively correlated securities

In this case, $CORR_{AB} = -1$. The returns of each security react in exactly opposite ways in each state of the world. An example could be company A selling ice cream and company B selling umbrellas. If the weather is fine, A will do well and B badly and, if the weather is poor, A will do badly and B well. Equation (7.7) becomes

$$V_p = W_1^2 S_A^2 + W_2^2 S_B^2 - 2W_1 W_2 S_A S_B$$

This is also a perfect square and can be written

$$V_p = (W_1 S_A - W_2 S_B)(W_1 S_A - W_2 S_B)$$

The square root can be taken to give

$$S_p = |W_1 S_A - W_2 S_B| \qquad (7.12)$$

where the two vertical lines require the absolute value, that is, whichever square root has a positive value.

In fact in this particular case, W_1 and W_2 can always be found to give $S_p = 0$ in equation (7.12). In other words, a riskless portfolio can always be found when combining two perfectly negatively correlated securities.

For example, suppose we have two securities A and B as described in Table 7.2. (Note that they are as in Table 7.1 with the returns of B reversed.) If we choose equal proportions of A and B so that $W_1 = W_2 = \frac{1}{2}$, we will get

$$E(R_p) = \frac{1}{2} \times 10\% + \frac{1}{2} \times 25\%$$

$$E(R_p) = \mathbf{17.5\%} \text{ as before for } CORR_{AB} = +1$$

Table 7.2

Probability	% Return	
	Security A	Security B
0.25	20	5
0.50	10	25
0.25	0	45
1.0		
Expected return	$E(R_A)$ = 10%	$E(R_B)$ = 25%
Variance of returns	V_A = 50%	V_B = 200%
Standard deviation of returns	S_A = 7.1%	S_B = 14.1%

However the risk of the combination will be substantially reduced:

$$S_p = |\tfrac{1}{2} \times 0.071 - \tfrac{1}{2} \times 0.141|$$

$$S_p = 3.5\%$$

This combination is shown as point P in Figure 7.2.

In what proportions must we hold A and B to get a riskless portfolio P, with $S_p = 0$? Equation (7.12) must be set to zero so that

$$0 = W_1 S_A - W_2 S_B$$

Rearranging,

$$W_1 S_A = W_2 S_B$$

$$0.071 W_1 = 0.141 W_2$$

$$W_1 = 2W_2$$

We must choose $W_1 = \dfrac{2}{3}$, $W_2 = \dfrac{1}{3}$

and in this case the expected return of P would be

$$E(R_p) = \frac{2}{3} \times 10\% + \frac{1}{3} \times 25\%$$

$$E(R_p) = 15\%$$

This is a riskless portfolio, so the investor is *certain* of getting a return

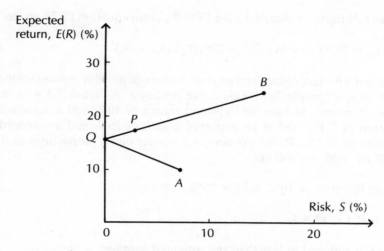

Figure 7.2   Possible combinations of A and B when CORR$_{AB}$ = −1

of 15% whichever state of the world prevails. In this case of perfectly negatively correlated securities, the investor has been able to remove risk altogether whilst still achieving a return in between those expected of *A* and *B*. This riskless portfolio is shown as point *Q* in Figure 7.2.

Small positive correlation between securities

What implications do the above results have for the investor? If he can find two securities which are not perfectly positively correlated, that is, which have $CORR_{AB} < +1$, then he can combine them into a portfolio and expect to get the weighted average of their expected returns with less than the weighted average of their risk. In other words, he will have reduced risk without sacrificing return. Provided two securities do not have $CORR_{AB} = +1$, he can always do better than just holding one risky security.

The less correlated the returns of two securities, the more the investor can reduce risk by combining them. If he can find two securities which have $CORR_{AB} = −1$, he can reduce his risk to zero whilst still getting a weighted average of expected returns.

Unfortunately, risky securities are not usually negatively correlated or even independent since they are subject to common influences. The correlation coefficient between two securities will probably be small and positive, for example $CORR_{AB} = 0.3$.

If we substitute a value of 0.3 for $CORR_{AB}$ into equation (7.7), we get

$$V_p = W_1^2 S_A^2 + W_2^2 S_B^2 + 2W_1 W_2 S_A S_B \times 0.3$$

This is not a perfect square and so gives a *curve* of possible combinations rather than a straight line. This curve is shown in Figure 7.3 with *A* taken, as before, to have an expected return of 10% and a standard deviation of 7.1% and *B* an expected return of 25% and a standard deviation of 14.1%. If, for example, we assume equal proportions of *A* and *B* are held, we still get

$$E(R_p) = \tfrac{1}{2} \times 10\% + \tfrac{1}{2} \times 25\%$$

$$E(R_p) = 17.5\%$$

but risk is reduced to less than the weighted average:

$$V_p = \tfrac{1}{4} \times 0.005 + \tfrac{1}{4} \times 0.02 + 2 \times \tfrac{1}{2} \times \tfrac{1}{2} \times 0.071 \times 0.141 \times 0.03$$

$$V_p = 0.0078$$

$$S_p = 8.8\%$$

This particular combination is shown as *P* on Figure 7.3.

We have shown how the investor can reduce risk by holding different combinations of two securities instead of just one on its own. It is likely that the securities he will consider will provide a curve of possible combinations as in Figure 7.3. The investor then has to decide which

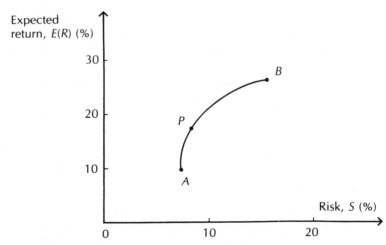

Figure 7.3   Possible combinations of A and B when CORR$_{AB}$ = 0.3

point on the curve AB he prefers, that is, which portfolio maximises his utility. To show how this can be done we first discuss how indifference curves can be derived for each investor from knowledge of his utility function. These indifference curves will then be used to determine the investor's *optimal* portfolio.

Indifference curves

As we saw in Chapter 2, each investor has a utility function which quantifies his attitude towards risk and return at different levels of wealth. If we consider a risk averse investor, his utility of wealth function will describe a curve as in Figure 7.4.

This curve implies a certain trade-off relationship between risk and expected return. For example, we found in Chapter 2 that Mr Black, armed with his utility function, could distinguish between two securities which offered different expected returns and different risks.

An investor's risk–return trade-off can be expressed more directly by using the utility function to determine the investor's indifference curves.

For example, if the investor requires a 10% return for accepting a

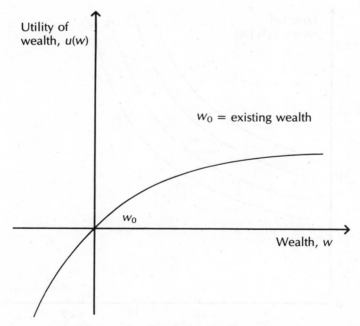

Figure 7.4   Utility curve of a risk-averse investor

standard deviation of 12% and for each additional 3% of standard deviation he requires an additional 4% of return, we can draw his 'indifference curve' – by identifying the risk–return combinations between which he is indifferent. From the above information we know he is indifferent between a security which offers 10% expected return and has $S = 12\%$ and a security which offers 14% and has S 3% higher at 15%. If we plot these and other points on a graph we will get a curve I_1 as shown in Figure 7.5. We know that I_1 will curve upwards because we are dealing with a risk averse investor who requires more return for taking on more risk – as measured by standard deviation. Each investor will have a different curve, although of the same basic shape, because each investor will differ in how he trades risk and return.

In fact each investor will have an infinite number of parallel indifference curves I_1, I_2, I_3 and so on. He will be indifferent between any point on I_1, say between A and B, but he will *not* be indifferent between a point on I_1 and a point on I_2. Compare points A and A_2. Both have the same risk but A_2 has a higher expected return. The investor will obviously prefer to be on I_2 rather than I_1. In fact, he will aim to get on the highest possible indifference curve, in order to maximise his utility, but once there he will be indifferent to where he is on that curve.

Once the utility function of an investor is known, his indifference curves can be drawn. These curves are used in deciding which portfolio

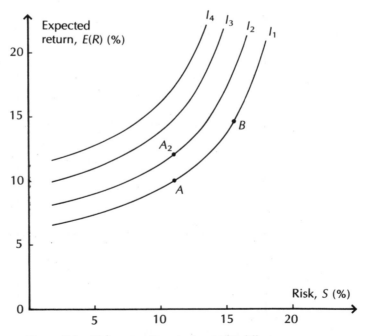

Figure 7.5   *Risk-averse investor's set of indifference curves*

the investor should choose to maximise his utility. Suppose A and B are the only securities the investor can buy and that they are as described in Figure 7.3 with $CORR_{AB} = 0.3$. Any combination of securities A and B lies on the curve AB. If the investor plots his indifference curves on this graph, as is done in Figure 7.6, we can see that he would prefer A to B because A is on a higher indifference curve than B.

We also know that the investor could do better than buying A on its own by investing in P, a portfolio containing equal quantities of A and B and with a standard deviation of 8.8%, as described earlier. However, the investor can maximise his utility in this case by investing in portfolio Q. At this point, one of his indifference curves is a tangent[8] to the curve AB. This is the highest indifference curve he can reach (any higher one would not touch a portfolio on AB) and so Q must be his optimal portfolio.

So, unless securities A and B are perfectly positively correlated, an investor can always reach a higher indifference curve and hence achieve greater expected utility (a better risk–return trade-off) by investing in a combination of the two securities.

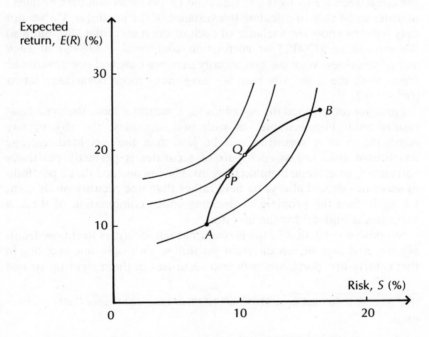

Figure 7.6   Optimal combination of A and B where CORR$_{AB}$ = +0.3

---

[8] A tangent is a line or curve which only touches another line or curve at one point.

Extension to *n* securities

We can extend all the above results that we have shown hold for two security portfolios to any size of portfolio. If we assume that we have a combination of *n* securities, it can be shown[9] that the resultant portfolio has an expected return and variance as follows:

$$E(R_p) = \sum_{i=1}^{i=n} W_i E(R_i) \tag{7.13}$$

$$V_p = \sum_{i=1}^{i=n} W_i^2 S_i^2 + \sum_{\substack{i=1 \\ i \neq j}}^{i=n} \sum_{j=1}^{j=n} W_i W_j COV_{ij} \tag{7.14}$$

Although daunting to look at, equation (7.13) says, as for two securities, that the expected return of the portfolio is the weighted average of the expected returns of the constituent securities. Similarly, equation (7.14) is the sum of the variance terms $W_i^2 S_i^2$ plus the sum of the covariance terms COV_{ij}.[10] Equation (7.14) looks complex because, in order to be able to calculate the variance of the portfolio, V_p, we not only have to know the variance of each of the *n* securities, S_i^2, but also the covariance (COV_{ij}) or correlation coefficient $(CORR_{ij})$ of *each pair of* securities. With the two security case, we only had one covariance term. With the *n* security case we have many more covariance terms $[(n^2 - n)/2]$.[11]

However complicated the equations for *n* securities look, the same basic results hold. For example, as with two securities, the risk of any combination of *n* securities will be less than the weighted average constituent risks unless *each pair* of securities is perfectly positively correlated, an extremely unlikely event. Having decided that a portfolio of securities should always be held rather than one security on its own, we again face the problem of deciding which combination of these *n* securities is optimal for the investor.

Suppose *n* = 10, that is, the investor has ten securities to choose from. He has a choice of ten different portfolios with only one security in them, forty-five portfolios with two securities in them right up to one

---

[9] For proof of these results, see Markowitz (1959) or Elton and Gruber (1981).

[10] N.B.

$$COV_{ii} = CORR_{ii} S_i S_i = S_i^2$$

(since $CORR_{ii}$ must equal 1). So equation (7.14) consists only of covariance terms with the special cases where $i = j$ separated out.

[11] See p. 219 below for an explanation of how we calculate this.

portfolio with ten securities in it. He thus has a choice between 1,023 possible portfolio combinations of the securities[12] and, of course, an infinite variation in the proportions in which he can hold the securities in each possible portfolio.

If we draw these possible portfolios on a graph, as in Figure 7.7, we find that they all fit into a shape which resembles an umbrella. This is because each pair of the *n* securities is likely to have a small positive correlation coefficient and so the possible combinations of each pair of securities will lie on a *curve* joining the securities. This will give the serrated edge *AB, BC* and so on. Combinations of more than two securities will similarly lie on curves inside or on the umbrella. All possible portfolios are said to make up the 'opportunity set' available to the investor.

The curve *XY* is called the efficient frontier. This means that all the portfolios lying on the curve joining *X* and *Y* are efficient in the sense that they are superior to any other portfolios in the opportunity set. A

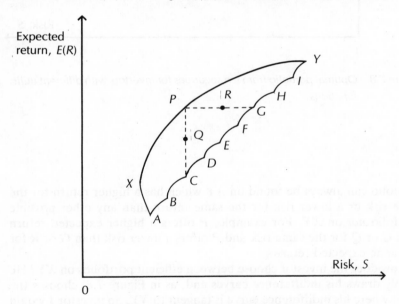

Figure 7.7   Opportunity set with ten securities

---

[12] The formula for the number of possible combinations of *m* securities out of a choice of *n* securities is

$$nCm = \frac{n!}{(n-m)!m!}$$

where *n*! represents the multiple of all numbers from 1 to *n*. For example, $6! = 6 \times 5 \times 4 \times 3 \times 2 \times 1$.

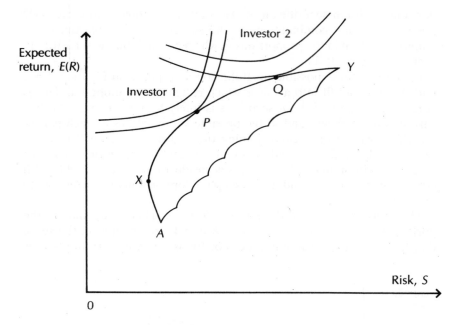

*Figure 7.8   Optimal portfolio from ten securities for investors with different utility
functions*

portfolio can always be found on *XY* which has a higher return for the
same risk or a lower risk for the same return than any other possible
portfolio *not* on *XY*. For example, *P* offers a higher expected return
than *C* or *Q* for the same risk and *P* offers a lower risk than *G* or *R* for
the same expected return.

How does the investor choose between efficient portfolios on *XY*? He
simply draws his indifference curves and, as in Figure 7.8, chooses the
point where his indifference curve is tangent to *XY*. So investor 1 would
choose portfolio *P* as optimal and investor 2, portfolio *Q*.

Investors 1 and 2 would probably choose different portfolios from the
same efficient frontier because they no doubt have different attitudes to
the relationship between risk and return (although both risk averse)
which will be reflected in different utility functions and indifference
curves. Also, investor 2 may not even have the same opportunity set and
efficient frontier as investor 1, because he may have different views on
the expected returns and risks of the ten securities in question. This
would lead him to a different umbrella altogether.

Practical implications for the investor

Portfolio theory therefore allows the investor, given a set of securities, to choose the particular combination of securities which will maximise his utility. How is this done in practice? For each security, the investor has to estimate its expected return $E(R_i)$, its variance V_i, and its covariance COV_{ij} or correlation coefficient $CORR_{ij}$ with every other security in the set. For example, suppose the investor is considering three securities, A, B and C, whose characteristics are detailed in Table 7.3.

Table 7.3   Determination of optimal three-security portfolios

Security	Expected return (%)	Standard deviation (%)	Covariances (%)		
A	6	4	$COV_{AA} = 16$	$COV_{AB} = 12$	$COV_{AC} = 16$
B	8	6		$COV_{BB} = 36$	$COV_{BC} = 12$
C	10	8			$COV_{CC} = 64$

The section between vertical lines is called the variance–covariance 'matrix'.[13] Variances are just a special case of the covariances COV_{ij} where $i = j$. (For example, $COV_{AA} = CORR_{AA}S_AS_A = S_A{}^2 = V_A$.) So we need n expected returns, n variances and just under half the matrix of covariance items (since $COV_{AB} = COV_{BA}$), giving $(n^2 - n)/2$ covariances. In the example of Table 7.3, we need a total of nine values, three expected returns, three variances and $(9 - 3)/2 = 3$ covariances.

Given these figures, the portfolios on the efficient frontier can be calculated (equivalent to the curve XY in Figure 7.8) and some are shown in Table 7.4. With this example, the efficient portfolios can be calculated manually but for any larger number of securities a computer program is needed.[14]

How will the investor choose between these efficient portfolios? If he knows his utility function he has two choices. He can either calculate the utility he will get from each efficient portfolio and choose the one which offers him the highest utility or he can plot his indifference curves

---

[13] A matrix is simply a rectangular array of numbers or symbols. Matrices allow multiple equations to be solved more simply than ordinary algebra. Covariances are often expressed in matrix form since this helps computation of, for example, the efficient frontier or the optimal portfolio.

[14] Details on how the efficient frontier can be calculated using graphical analysis (by hand), calculus or quadratic programming can be found in Elton and Gruber (1981).

Table 7.4   Some efficient portfolio combinations of A, B and C

	Proportions held of A,B,C			Expected return $E(R_p)$ (%)	Standard deviation S_p (%)
	W_A	W_B	W_C		
(1)	0.46	0.33	0.21	7.5	4.3
(2)	0.41	0.35	0.24	7.7	4.4
(3)	0.3	0.4	0.3	8.0	4.6
(4)	0.13	0.48	0.39	8.5	5.1
(5)	−0.19[15]	0.63	0.56	9.5	6.1

against the efficient frontier and choose the portfolio where the tangent indifference curve touches the efficient frontier (as in Figure 7.8).

In practice, the investor will probably not know his utility function or be able to plot his indifference curves. What he can do is specify a minimum acceptable level of expected return or a maximum acceptable level of risk. For example, he could require his portfolio to have minimum risk given an expected return of at least 8.5% – pension funds, for instance, may have the objective of doing at least as well as inflation – or be unwilling to accept a higher level of risk than 20% measured by variance – the investor may be acting as trustee for someone who cannot afford to lose more than a certain amount. If the former requirement held, portfolio (4) in Table 7.4, which yields an expected return of 8.5%, would be chosen as optimal. If the latter restriction held, portfolio (2), with a standard deviation of 4.4%, would be preferred.

Size of optimal portfolio

The investor, given a set of n securities, can now choose the combination of those securities which is optimal for him. It may include only two securities or it may include all n, depending on the correlations of the securities. The question that the investor will now no doubt ask is how many securities should he consider in the first place? What would n be? He knows that he should diversify to gain the benefits of risk reduction,

---

[15] In this example, we allowed negative amounts of securities to form part of the portfolio – in other words, it is assumed that securities can be sold short (see p. 171). In practice, this may not be possible. However, the computer program used to determine the efficient frontier can be adjusted to incorporate the requirement that all $W_i \geqslant 0$.

but to what extent? The small investor will be particularly concerned to know the answer to this question since he will have higher transaction costs the more securities he buys.

We now examine what happens to the risk of a portfolio as we increase its size. If we look at the equation for the variance of a portfolio of n securities, equation (7.14), we can see that

$$V_p = \text{weighted variance terms} + \text{weighted covariance terms}$$

If we assume that the n securities are all held in equal amounts, that is, $W_i = 1/n$ for each i, it can be shown that the variance terms diminish in importance as we increase n. For larger n, the risk of the portfolio will depend on the average covariance between the securities. Obviously, as n becomes large enough to include all securities in the stock market, so the risk of the portfolio will become the risk of the stock market.

How quickly does the risk of a portfolio decrease and tend towards the average market risk as we increase n? Experiments have been carried out on different sizes of *randomly* selected portfolios of UK

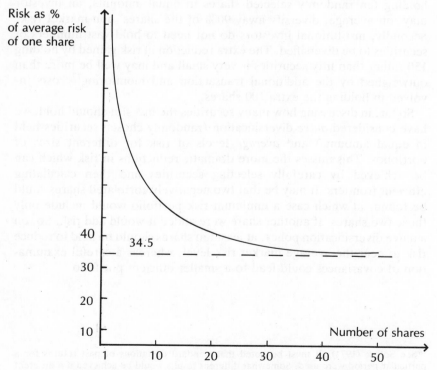

Figure 7.9   The effect on risk of number of securities in portfolio

Source: Solnik (1974). By permission of the *Financial Analysts' Journal*.

222 *Investment Strategy*

shares.[16] Portfolios from one to fifty securities were chosen and the
average risk of each size of portfolio calculated. This average risk was
then expressed as a percentage of the average risk of holding only one
share. The results are as shown in Figure 7.9.

We can see from Figure 7.9 that average risk decreases fast as we
increase the number of securities held from one upwards. Each time
another security is added, risk is reduced by a smaller amount, and no
matter how many securities are held, risk cannot be reduced on average
to below 34.5% (in this particular study) of the risk of holding only one
share. This reinforces the view we already held that there is a certain
amount of risk common to all shares quoted on the UK stock market
which cannot be diversified away. This is intuitively obvious since if an
investor held all quoted UK shares, he would not be holding a riskless
investment!

These results have two major implications for investors. Firstly small
investors need only diversify by holding ten to fifteen shares to have
substantially reduced risk from holding one share and to have removed
most of the non-market risk from their portfolios. For example, by
holding ten randomly selected shares in equal amounts, an investor
may, on average, diversify away 90% of the shares' non-market risk.
Secondly, institutional investors do not need to hold vast numbers of
securities to be diversified. The extra reduction in risk gained by holding
150 rather than fifty securities is very small and may well be more than
outweighed by the additional transaction and monitoring[17] costs involved in holding the extra 100 shares.

So far, in discussing how many securities the investor should hold, we
have considered *naïve* diversification (randomly chosen securities held
in equal amounts) and *average* levels of risk for different sizes of
portfolios. This misses the more dramatic reductions in risk which can
be achieved by carefully selecting securities and then calculating
efficient frontiers. It may be that two negatively correlated shares could
be found, in which case a minimum risk portfolio would include only
those two shares. If another share were added it would add risk. So, on
a naïve diversification policy, at least ten shares should be held to reduce
risk to near the average market risk level, whereas a careful examina-
tion of covariances could lead to a smaller efficient portfolio.

---

[16] See Solnik (1974). It must be noted that standard deviations of past returns for a
particular period were used. Somewhat different results would be achieved if a different
period were to be examined.

[17] By monitoring costs, we mean the cost of keeping up to date with all information on the
shares.

Problems with portfolio theory

When portfolio theory was first discussed in the 1950s, it was not widely accepted by analysts and investors. There were two main reasons for this. Firstly, if n securities are to be considered, estimates of the value of n expected returns, n variances and $(n^2 - n)/2$ covariances have to be made. As can be seen from Table 7.5, the number of figures required soon gets extremely large and computers in the 1950s and 1960s were slow and expensive to run.

Table 7.5   Comparison of data requirements for different sizes of portfolio

Number of securities	3	30	300
Number of data items required for calculation of efficient frontier	9	495	45,450

Secondly, the investment research departments were usually organised on an industry basis and who was to determine the covariance of returns of a timber company with those of a shoe retailer? In any case, the only way such variances and covariances could be estimated was by looking at past data and assuming that underlying factors affecting the securities would be the same in the future so that values based on past frequencies could be used for future probabilities. This was relatively straightforward for returns and variances but calculations were messy for covariances.

One further potential problem with portfolio theory is that it is only a one-period model. Investors usually consider investment policy for several years (or periods) ahead and wish to maximise their expected utility of wealth at the end of the whole period. However, it can be shown that, if certain assumptions concerning the utility function of the investor are made,[18] the investor will maximise his overall expected utility by considering each period separately. Thus, he can use the portfolio theory approach in each individual period.

So, despite the problems in using portfolio theory which derive from the cumbersome nature of the required input data, as computers evolved and acceptance of more quantitative techniques in investment analysis grew, portfolio theory began to be used in determining optimal portfolios.

Portfolio theory does offer a framework for each investor to determine his optimal portfolio from inputs which he can derive subjectively or from past data. For example, the theory can be applied to net of tax returns, thus allowing for the particular tax position of the investor. This would lead to different optimal portfolios for each investor even if they

---

[18] For example, if the utility function is a logarithmic one, $U = f(ln (W))$.

started off with the same expected *gross* returns and risk for each security. Also, as was mentioned in the introduction to this chapter, portfolio theory can be applied to the determination of optimal portfolios in an international context. Provided the expected returns and risk can be estimated in sterling (again usually relying to some extent on past data), optimal international portfolios can be found for UK investors.

Summary

This chapter has looked at how the investor can decide on an optimal *portfolio* of securities. It was discovered that, not only should the expected return and risk (measured by standard deviation) of each security be considered, but also its correlation or covariance with the other securities in the portfolio.

Since most shares quoted on the UK stock market are correlated positively, but less than perfectly, with each other, combining them into a portfolio will actually reduce the risk to the investor to less than the weighted average of the individual risks of the securities. However, the expected *return* on a portfolio is equal to the weighted average of the expected returns of the constituent securities. Thus, it will always pay the investor to diversify, provided the securities in his portfolio are not perfectly positively correlated.

The investor, knowing his utility function and indifference curves, can then find a portfolio which is optimal for him from the efficient frontier of portfolios, that is, from those portfolios which offer the best expected returns given their risk. This method of finding the optimal portfolio is termed 'Markowitz' diversification, and involves careful consideration of all the securities and how they relate to each other. The investor can also reduce risk by going for 'naïve' diversification where he simply invests equal amounts in randomly selected securities. 'Naïve' diversification will reduce risk substantially, but will involve a portfolio with more securities and a worse risk–return ratio than the more rigorous 'Markowitz' diversification.

Problems

1. Shares *A* and *B* have the following characteristics:

	E(R)	S (%)	CORR$_{AB}$
A	10	10	0.5
B	20	20	

   (i) Calculate the expected return and risk of the portfolio consisting of
      (a) ¼A, ¾B
      (b) ½A, ½B
      (c) ¾A, ¼B
  (ii) Plot these portfolios on a graph of expected return against risk.
      Which proportions of *A* and *B* do you think will maximise expected
      return given the risk?

2. The expected returns and variance–covariance matrix of 3 shares are
given below:

	E(R)	COV$_{ij}$		
A	8	25	100	150
B	10	100	120	180
C	12	150	180	300

   (i) Calculate the expected return and variance of equally weighted
      portfolios of
      (a) *A* and *B*
      (b) *A* and *C*
      (c) *B* and *C*
      Why is the variance of the *B, C* portfolio greater than the variance
      of the *A, B* portfolio?
  (ii) Calculate the expected return and variance of a portfolio consisting
      of equal amounts of *A, B* and *C*. Compare with the two security
      portfolios.

3. Suppose two shares *P* and *Q* have perfectly negatively correlated
returns.

	E(R)	S
P	13	25
Q	18	40

   (i) What will be the expected return and risk of an equally weighted
      portfolio?

    (ii) What portfolio weights for *P* and *Q* will lead to a perfectly hedged portfolio?

    (iii) Plot your results on an expected return and risk graph.

    (iv) Can you suggest any securities whose returns might, in practice, be negatively correlated.

4. Mrs Peach intends to invest in three securities, *J, K* and *L*, each with expected return of 15% and variance of 150%. The three securities all have returns which are totally uncorrelated with each other.

    (i) What will be the expected return and risk of Mrs Peach's portfolio if she holds the three securities in equal amounts?

    (ii) What if Mrs Peach puts 40% in *J*, 40% in *K* and 20% in *L*?

    (iii) Estimate the weights for *J, K* and *L* which would lead to a minimum risk portfolio for Mrs Peach.

    (iv) Would Mrs Peach be right to go for a minimum risk portfolio?

5. 'Three hundred equities, if they are rightly chosen, are sufficient as a selection ground for most portfolios. I feel that increasing the number of shares under consideration to an unmanageable number is no way of diversifying.' Does this statement conflict with the results of portfolio theory?

The capital asset pricing model

Introduction

We saw, towards the end of Chapter 7, that finding an optimal portfolio using portfolio theory requires a computer program and a rather large variance–covariance matrix. This has hindered general acceptance of portfolio theory, despite its usefulness. We also saw, in the section called 'Size of Optimal Portfolio', that however much we diversify and however many securities are included in the portfolio, risk cannot be reduced, using a naïve diversification policy, to less than a certain amount. This is because as we hold more and more securities, we end up holding the whole stock market, and thus bearing the risk of that stock market, which cannot be diversified away. This concept of undiversifiable market risk, as it is known, is fundamental to the development of the more rigorous capital asset pricing model (or CAPM), which is described in this chapter. The CAPM shows that the risk of any security can be divided into two parts – the element which reflects that undiversifiable market risk and an element which is specific to the share and which can be diversified away when the share is held as part of a large portfolio.

The capital asset pricing model is a much stronger model than portfolio theory in that it not only prescribes optimal portfolios for investors but also derives an equation relating the expected return and risk of any security.

For example, if we consider the optimal portfolio prescribed by the CAPM and compare it to that derived by portfolio theory, we find that the CAPM, with further assumptions about the market in which securities are traded, including the introduction of a risk-free security, shows that all investors will hold, not different portfolios derived from different opportunity sets, but different amounts of the *same* portfolio. The portfolio of securities which all investors will hold is the market portfolio, that is, the portfolio consisting of all securities in the market. Each investor will adjust to his particular risk–return requirements by combining his holding of the market portfolio, M, with positive or negative amounts of the risk-free security. For example, the individual investor wishing to take on more risk than the stock market for shares offers will borrow money and invest further in M. This will increase the risk of his investment through 'gearing up'. In contrast, a more cautious investor, not wishing to bear all the risk of ordinary shares, will put only a small part of his money into M and will invest the rest in risk-free securities, for example gilts.[1]

The relationship between the risk and return of any security, which is found in the capital asset pricing model, is an equally strong result. The equation, known as the securities market line, shows that there is a *linear* relationship between the risk and expected return of any security but that the risk for which the investor is to be rewarded by return is *not* the total risk (represented by the standard deviation or variance of returns) but only a proportion of it – that element referred to earlier which reflects the undiversifiable market risk. Any risk arising from holding the share on its own and not as part of a diversified portfolio will not be rewarded.

The implications of the CAPM for investment decision-making are far-reaching. Investors who assume that securities are valued according to the capital asset pricing model will not attempt to select investments according to techniques such as fundamental analysis (mentioned in Chapter 5), but will simply select securities on the basis of the risk and expected return predicted by the CAPM. Such investors will expect only a 'fair' return for the risk they bear, as opposed to fundamental analysts who expect to earn better than average returns from their share selection skills. These differing investment strategies are discussed in greater depth in Chapter 9.

---

[1] As we saw in Chapter 2, gilts are not in reality truly risk-free.

The chapter starts with the empirical basis of the CAPM, the market model. The assumptions underlying the capital asset pricing model are then introduced and the results of the CAPM are derived. A whole section is then devoted to how the results of the CAPM can be applied in practice, for example how the notion of market risk, called beta, should be used, and the chapter concludes with a discussion of more complex models than the CAPM which are currently being tested, including arbitrage pricing theory.

Market model

It was inevitable that a simplification of portfolio theory would be proposed, especially given the fact that securities do seem to be subject to common influences – we have noted their tendency to move up or down together. Sharpe (1963) postulated that the returns of securities, which we have seen are usually positively correlated, were only so related because of their common 'market' response. This led him to suppose that the expected return of any security could be expressed as a linear function of the expected return of the market as a whole. (The expected return of the market could be approximated by using the return on a suitable stock market index.) This would lead to an equation of the form

$$E(R_i) = a_i + b_i \, E(R_m) \tag{8.1}$$

for each security i, where $E(R_i)$ was the expected return on security i, a_i and b_i were constants specific to that security and $E(R_m)$ the expected return on the market as a whole. In practice the return R_i would not necessarily turn out to be equal to its expected value, $E(R_i)$, and so, if past data on returns were used, an equation of the form

$$R_i = a_i + b_i \, R_m + e_i \tag{8.2}$$

would be found where R_i and R_m were the actual returns for security i and the market as a whole, and the residual term, e_i, was the difference between the actual and expected result. The expected value of e_i would be zero. Such a model obviously has quite strong assumptions. It presupposes that the *only* common factor affecting all securities is the return on the market.[2] Other common influences such as industry

---

[2] Mathematically, this is expressed by requiring the covariances between all values of e_i to be 0 $COV(e_i, e_j) = 0$ for all i, j. Sharpe's model also requires $COV(e_i, R_m) = 0$ for all i which means that the size of the error term e_i is unaffected by the size of the market return.

factors or economic influences affecting only some securities are ignored.

Obviously, it would be nice if Sharpe's market model worked in the real world but, as yet, we have no theoretical foundation for such a model. However, as we shall see in the next section, such a market model can be proved theoretically if certain additional assumptions are made about the stock market and investor behaviour.

Advantages of the market model

How does this market model help us? It radically reduces both the number of variables needed to determine efficient portfolios and the calculations to find these variables. For each security to be considered, all that is needed is a_i, b_i and the variance of the error term $V(e_i)$. These can be calculated using regression[3] by plotting actual past values of R_i and R_m against each other, as in Figure 8.1.

For example, monthly returns[4] over the past five years could be plotted. The intercept of the line fitted to the points by regression would give a_i, the slope of the line b_i, and the variance of the error terms would

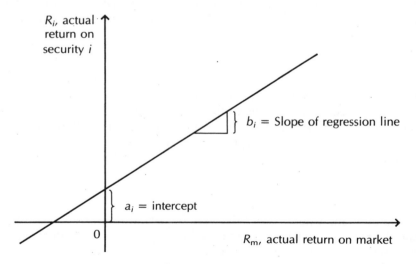

Figure 8.1   Calculation of coefficients in $R_i = a_i + b_i R_m + e_i$

---

[3] Regression (of Y on X) is used to plot a *line of best fit* through a set of points by minimising the sum of the vertical distances of the points from the line. It is an attempt to find a linear relationship between two variables, using empirical data.

[4] Return = dividends received plus any capital gains or losses.

be calculated from the regression analysis by the computer. It must then be assumed that these values will hold in the future for each security. If any specific changes are anticipated, a_i, b_i and $V(e_i)$ can be subjectively estimated. The variance of the market V_m and its expected return $E(R_m)$ must also be estimated. In all, a total of only $3n + 2$ data items are required for an n-security portfolio. For example, with thirty securities, portfolio theory requires 495 data items and the market model ninety-two.

The expected return and variance of any portfolio P are then simply

$$E(R_p) = a_p + b_p \, E(R_m) \tag{8.3}$$

$$V_p = b_p{}^2 V_m + \sum_{i=1}^{i=n} X_i^2 \, V(e_i) \tag{8.4}$$

where a_p and b_p are the weighted averages of the constituent securities' a_i and b_i and the X_i are the weightings.

$$a_p = \sum_{i=1}^{i=n} X_i a_i$$

$$b_p = \sum_{i=1}^{i=n} X_i b_i$$

and

$$\sum_{i=1}^{i=n} X_i = 1$$

The attractions of the simpler model are obvious.

Capital asset pricing model

The market model's attempt at explaining security returns is attractive in its simplicity but we have as yet no theoretical foundation for believing that we can cut corners in this way. Portfolio theory, provided we accept its assumptions and the fact that it is a one-period rather than a multi-period model,[5] leads to some interesting results. However, to

[5] The one-period model restriction means that all investment decisions must be made at the beginning of the period and no changes can be made during the period. (A multi-period model would allow changes at the beginning of each period and so perhaps achieve greater utility.) The period considered can be as long or short as desired. But see p. 223 for a reconciliation of the multi-period and single-period models.

get any further we need to introduce some *additional* assumptions:

(1) a perfect securities market; that is, perfect competition in a friction-less securities market which is also in equilibrium;[6]

(2) all investors agree on a period under consideration for investment purposes (say one month or one year) and have identical expecta-tions regarding the probability distributions of security returns for that period;

(3) unlimited amounts of money can be borrowed or lent by all investors at the risk-free rate. If inflation exists, it is fully anticipated in interest rates.

The first assumption, which requires the absence of such possible distorting factors as taxes and transaction costs, is obviously unrealistic and far from the 'real world'. However, if too many realities are introduced into a model at an early stage, no analysis of the basic return relationships of securities or of how investors behave can be made. The validity of the model can be tested empirically[7] and, if necessary, complexities can be added at a later stage.

Assumption (2) is important since the capital asset pricing model requires investors to have the same opportunity set of portfolios and the same efficient frontier. Portfolio theory does not require this – each investor can derive his own set of efficient portfolios, map his own indifference curves on to them and choose his own optimal portfolios without concerning himself with other investors' beliefs.

Assumption (3) is also crucial to the derivation of the capital asset pricing model, because the existence of risk-free lending and borrowing extends the range of opportunities available to the investor. Before we continue, what do we mean by 'risk-free'? We mean without any of the risks described in Chapter 2. Suppose the investor buys government fixed interest securities (equivalent to lending money free of default risk); he may still be subject to inflation risk and interest rate risk. The former is dealt with in this instance by the assumption that inflation is fully anticipated in interest rates. The latter can be avoided if a zero coupon[8] fixed interest security is chosen which matures exactly at the

---

[6] The underlying assumptions for a perfect frictionless market are:
  (i) no taxes, no transaction costs and no restrictions on short-selling (selling shares you do not have);
  (ii) information is free and simultaneously available to all investors;
  (iii) securities are infinitely divisible (can be bought in any quantity) and they all have a market price;
  (iv) no individual can affect the market price by buying or selling securities;
  (v) investors are all rational, expected utility maximisers.

[7] In other words, the model can be tested to see if it reflects what actually happens in the stock market.

[8] A zero-coupon bond is one which pays no interest during its life. The price is therefore low to allow the required return to be made entirely through capital gain.

end of the period in question. However, the assumption that any investor can also *borrow* money at the 'risk-free' rate is more difficult to envisage being possible in the 'real' world.

Given these assumptions, over and above those needed for portfolio theory, we can derive interesting results both as to how the risk and return of securities are related and as to how investors should behave.

First of all, we can say that all investors face the same opportunity set of risky securities and portfolios and the same efficient frontier, XY, as shown in Figure 8.2. They may, however, choose different optimal portfolios according to their different indifference curves, for example P and Q.

The introduction of the risk-free borrowing and lending possibilities widens the alternatives available to each investor. For example, the investor who initially chose P can now, as well as choosing P, also move up and down the line $R_F PP^1$. If he borrows money at the risk-free rate of interest, R_F (or 'gears up'), he can move along PP^1, say to P_2, having increased the risk of his investment in P by using some borrowed money. If he lends, he can move along $R_F P$ say to P_1, having reduced the amount of his investment in the risky portfolio P and hence his overall risk.

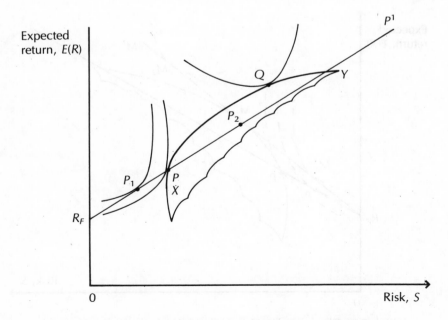

Figure 8.2 Optimal portfolios with risk-free borrowing and lending

In fact, the possibility of moving up and down $R_F PP^1$ enables the investor to increase his utility by moving to a higher indifference curve. For this particular investor, if he lends and moves to P_1, he will have reached a higher indifference curve and thereby increased his utility.

Let us look at other alternatives available to our investor. He does not have to restrict himself to portfolio P which was optimal without the borrowing and lending possibilities. It can be seen from Figure 8.3 that he would do better still by investing in portfolio M and then lending until he reached M_1 on the line $R_F MM^1$. M is the point on the efficient frontier where the line from R_F is a tangent to the frontier.

In fact, it can be shown that *every* investor would maximise his utility by choosing portfolio M and then moving up or down $R_F MM^1$ until he reached the point where $R_F MM^1$ touched his indifference curve, M_1 in the case of one investor, M_2 in the case of another. So every investor will hold some proportion of M and either positive amounts of R_F (lend) or negative amounts of R_F (borrow).

What will M be? If all individuals hold M in equilibrium, M must be the total of all risky assets in the market place. So individuals will hold small amounts of all risky securities in proportion to their market values. If they want higher risk than that offered by the market, they will borrow to buy more of M and move to the right up $R_F MM^1$. If they want less than the market risk, they will hold less M and lend some money at R_F (say, buy gilts).

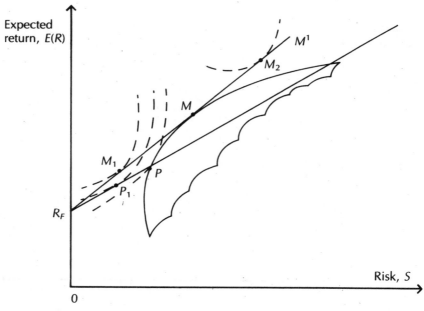

Figure 8.3   The optimal portfolio with risk-free borrowing and lending

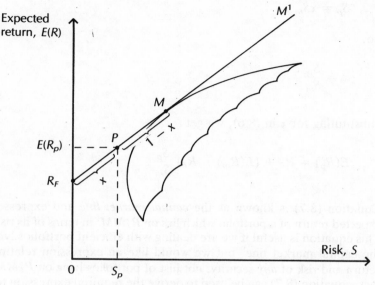

Figure 8.4   Capital market line

The model we have built up from our assumptions has told us how investors ought to behave. The staggering result is that all investors should hold not different portfolios, but different amounts of the *same* portfolio *M* combined with positive or negative amounts of money invested at the risk-free rate. Unlike portfolio theory which expects each investor to hold his own tailor-made portfolio, the capital asset pricing model says we should hold the same security portfolio made up of all risky securities in the market in proportion to their market value – not ten or fifteen shares but several thousand securities.

The capital asset pricing model does not stop there. It also tells us about return and risk. Suppose an investor holds a portfolio *P* on the line $R_F M M^1$, made up of fraction x of *M* and fraction $(1 - x)$ of R_F, as in Figure 8.4.

The expected return on his portfolio will be

$$E(R_p) = R_F (1 - x) + xE(R_m)$$

Rearranging gives

$$E(R_p) = R_F + x(E(R_m) - R_F) \qquad (8.5)$$

The variance of this portfolio will be

$$V_p = x^2 V_m$$

because the variance of a risk-free investment in R_F must be zero, giving

$$S_p = xS_m$$

So,

$$x = \frac{S_p}{S_m} \tag{8.6}$$

Substituting for x in (8.6), we get

$$E(R_p) = R_F + (E(R_m) - R_F)\frac{S_p}{S_m} \tag{8.7}$$

Equation (8.7) is known as the *capital market line* and expresses the expected return of a portfolio which lies on R_FMM^1 in terms of its risk, S_p. This equation is useful if we are dealing with efficient portfolios lying on the capital market line[9] but we would like an expression relating the return and risk of *any* security, not just of portfolios lying on R_FMM^1. In fact, equation (8.7) can be used to derive the required expression for the expected return of any security in the market:

$$E(R_i) = R_F + (E(R_m) - R_F)\frac{COV_{im}}{S_m^2} \tag{8.8}$$

Equation (8.8) is known as the *securities market line* since it relates the expected return of any security to its risk. This equation is similar to the capital market line but instead of expressing $E(R_i)$ in terms of its standard deviation, S_i, we see that the return of a security is a function of its *covariance* with the market, COV_{im}.

If we consider a risk-free security, COV_{im} will be zero[10] and so $E(R_i)$ will be equal to R_F. If the security is risky, a premium will be required over and above the risk-free rate, which will increase with the covariance of the security with the market. $(E(R_m) - R_F)/S_m^2$ is sometimes called the unit market price of risk. For each 1% increase in COV_{im}, the expected return required of the security will increase by the market price of risk.

This has serious implications for the investor when considering adding a security to his portfolio. The only risk for which he will be rewarded will be the *covariance* of the security with the market and not its total risk measured by variance or standard deviation. This can be seen more

---

[9] Any portfolio lying on R_FMM^1 must be efficient in the sense that it must be perfectly positively correlated with the market portfolio M (because it is joined to M by a straight line).

[10] Since $COV_{im} = S_iS_mCORR_{im}$ and S_i, the standard deviation of a riskless security must be zero.

clearly if we simplify equation (8.8). If we let $\beta_i = COV_{im}/S_m^2$ (different for each security i) the equation can be written

$$E(R_i) = R_F + \beta_i \, (E(R_m) - R_F) \tag{8.9}$$

or

$$E(R_i) = a_i + b_i \, E(R_m)$$

where a_i is equal to $R_F - \beta_i R_F$ and b_i is equal to β_i.

This looks like the market model that Sharpe suggested might hold. We have shown that, under certain conditions, it does hold and that the return of a security depends on its relationship to the market return. β_i is a measure of sensitivity to the market and it is for this sensitivity that the holder of the security is rewarded. The market portfolio M will have a β of 1; this can be seen by substituting $\beta_i = 1$ into equation (8.9). Securities with βs less than 1 will be less risky than the market as a whole and yield less return. For example, companies in stable industries such as food manufacturers, whose profits and hence returns vary less than the average, will have shares with low βs. Securities with high βs, greater than 1, will be those of companies in cyclical industries, such as construction, with returns fluctuating more than the market average. For example, Table 8.1 on p. 239 shows Armitage Brothers to have a low β of 0.73 and Applied Computer Techniques to have a higher β than average˙of 1.14.

How do we calculate the β (or beta as it is more usually written) of an individual security? Ideally, we would need to look at the future to determine beta. If, as with standard deviation, we assume that a past figure will be a good surrogate for the future, we can, as for the market model, plot historical returns R_i against R_m, as in Figure 8.1. β_i will then be the slope of the regression line

$$R_i = \alpha_i + \beta_i R_m + e_i$$

where e_i is the error term of the regression.
The risk of the security will be

$$V_i = |\,\beta_i^2 S_m^2 + S^2(e_i) \tag{8.10}$$

Equation (8.10) splits the total risk of a security, measured by its variance, into two parts – risk relative to the market, measured by the sensitivity factor β_i, and specific risk or diversifiable risk, $S^2(e_i)$. The latter risk is called diversifiable because it can be diversified away. We saw when looking at portfolios of n securities that risk was quickly reduced to market risk as n increased. The risk specific to individual securities could easily be reduced through diversification.

What the securities market line, equation (8.8), tells us is that the holder of a security is *only* rewarded for the risk, sometimes known as systematic risk, of his security, and not for his diversifiable risk. In other words the market assumes all investors hold diversified portfolios and thus have diversified away the specific risk of securities, $S^2(e_i)$.

Practical application of the CAPM

How does all this help the investor? In so far as we have derived a theoretical foundation for the market model, so the calculations for determining the risk and return of any portfolio are much simplified. Once the β (or beta) risk and diversifiable risk, $S^2(e_i)$, are known for each security, the risk and return of any combination of securities can be calculated, provided the risk and return characteristics of the stock market are known, as well as the risk-free rate, R_F.

This information is now readily available for all shares quoted on the US, UK and other major stock exchanges. Table 8.1 gives an extract from the London Business School *Risk Measurement Service*, published quarterly, which provides all the information needed to be able to use the CAPM on UK quoted share portfolios. The betas provided in the London Business School publication are derived from historical data (monthly returns for the past five years) using regression analysis. The use of these betas therefore assumes that the shares' past risk characteristics are relevant for the future. This assumption is usually referred to as requiring betas to be 'stationary' over time. Evidence supporting this assumption for both UK and US shares is reasonably strong, in particular for the betas of portfolios rather than of individual shares.[11] In fact, it is always true that the CAPM works better on portfolios of shares than on individual shares. For example, if we compare the standard error terms,[12] in Table 8.1, of Ashdown Investment Trust (which represents a portfolio of shares) with Arensen Group shares, we can see that the standard error term for the investment trust is much lower, 0.09 compared with 0.23. The standard error is a measure of how much reliance we can place on the beta estimate provided. The lower it is, the more confidence we have in the beta.

Now, suppose that an investor, Miss Divine, holds equal money amounts of the four securities starred (*) in Table 8.1, Anglo Metropoli-

---

[11] See, for example, Blume (1975) and the Editorial to the London Business School, *Risk Measurement Service*, July–September 1982.

[12] For a definition of the standard error term and an explanation of regression analysis applied to beta estimates, see Fogler and Ganapathy (1982).

Table 8.1 Extract from the London Business School Risk Measurement Service

SEDOL Number	Company Name	S.E. Industry Classification	Market Capit'n	Market-ability	Beta	Vari-ability	Specific Risk	Std Error	R-Sq'rd	Qly Ab Return	Ann Ab Return	Ann Act Return	Gross Yield	P/E Ratio	Price 30:6:82
32069	ANGLIA TELEVSN 'A' N.V.	LEISURE	17	2TA	.98	30	23	.13	43	-1	51	58	7.0	6.4	128
32100	ANGLO-AFRICAN FIN.	FIN.TRST	2	4	.91	37	32	.17	27	-4	-8	-1	6.4	1.6	25
33608	ANGLO-AMER.SECS.	INV.TRST	74	3TA	1.04	26	16	.10	62	-3	-4	-2	5.6	22.0	129
37989	ANGLO-INDONES. PLANT.	RUBBER	3	3	.28	30	29	.16	4	-28	-49	-39	2.1	.0	68
38067	ANGLO INTL INV PLC'ASS'	INV.TRST	5	3T	1.21	30	71	.10	71	-1	-6	-1		.0	214
38045	ANGLO INTL INV PLC'DIV'	INV.TRST	3	4T	.80	26	21	.14	34	-7	-12	-4	17.7	8.5	42
38410	ANGLO METROPOLTN HDGS	PROPERTY	4	3	1.13	65	61	.25	11	-10	-41	-35	2.1	.0	67
39606	ANGLO-SCOT.INV.TR.	INV.TRST	20	3TA	1.05	26	17	.11	60	-9	-12	-6	5.7	22.0	60
43715	ANSBACHER (HENRY)& CO	MRCH.BNK	19	2 A	1.66	40	38	.19	11	-26	-51	-42	5.0	15.9	10
62248	ANVIL PETROLEUM	OIL	3	2	1.16	55	50	.24	16	-7	-65	-59	5.0	.0	83
46305	APEX PROPERTIES STK 10P	PROPERTY	11	4TA	.93	29	22	.14	41	-15	-33	-25	2.8	32.5	103
46509	APPLEYARD GROUP	MTR.DIST	3	2T	.92	45	41	.20	17	-53	-53	-46	.5	.0	30
46587	APPLIED COMPUTER TECHNIQ	OFFC.EQP	21	2TA	1.14	47	40	.26	27	1	42	48	.5	29.2	183
1508	A.P.V.HOLDINGS LTD	IND.PLNT	79	2TA	.90	28	31	.14	11	0	-13	-5	5.3	7.4	258
46725	AQUASCUTUM GRP PLC 'A'	STR.MULT	5	2TA	1.15	38	31	.18	32	-3	12	18	10.1	8.1	29
46703	AQUASCUTUM GRP PLC	STR.MULT	2	4T	.86	34	29	.16	26				8.1	10.0	36
46800	AQUIS SECURITIES LTD.	PROPERTY	8	2T	.66	30	27	.18	18				4.9	19.6	29
47308	ARBUTHNOT LATHAM HLDGS	MRCH.BNK	25	3T	1.74	46	31	.18	54	-3	-7	0	5.4	14.6	320A
47386	ARCHIMEDES INV TR 'CAP'	INV.TRST	3	1	.66	19	16	.17	29	-13	-3	4	15.0	9.6	54
47364	ARCHIMEDES INV TR 'INC'	INV.TRST	1	4						6	-11	-2			76
47524	ARCOLECTRIC HDGS'A N V'	ELECTRCL	1	4	.84	62	59	.29	9	3	-35	-28	6.5	11.3	11
47502	ARCOLECTRIC HLDGS	ELECTRCL	0	5										13.4	13
47609	ARDEN & COBDEN HTLS LTD	HOTL&CAT	3	3	.62	20	16	.19	34	1	16	26	3.9	9.7	200
47900	ARENSON GROUP PLC	OFFC.EQP	3	3	.52	49	48	.23	4	-13	-53	-43		.0	25
306087	ARGYLL FOODS LTD	FOOD.RET	31	A	.92	65	62	.25	8	-24	-35	-28	7.2	10.3	74
49207	ARIEL INDS. LTD.	FAST&PRT	2	3T	.76	58	56	.25	6	23	13	21	7.1		27
49456	ARLEN ELECTRICALS	ELECTRCL	1	4	1.07	54	48	.24	15	-4	-39	-33	9.9	63.7	25
49467	ARLINGTON MOTOR	MTR.DIST	3	3T	.78	41	31	.19	17	10	-18	-6	7.8	5.7	72
49809	ARMITAGE BROTHERS	FOOD.MAN	2	5	.73	23	20	.25	23	4	-3	6	1.5	40.0	495
49661	ARMOUR TRUST LTD	IND.HOLD	2	4	.81	57	55	.24	8	-20	28	36			12
50005	ARMSTRONG EQUIPMNT	MTR.COMP	10	2TA	.81	39	35	.19	17	-29	-65	-57	7.6	94.7	18
50878	ARNCLIFFE HLDGS. LTD.	CONSTRCT	2	4	.96	43	38	.22	21	-10	-7	3	10.5	4.1	36
51644	ARROW CHEMICAL HLDGS	GEN.CHEM	3	2T	.86	71	69	.26	6	-24	-8	5	5.4	25.7	45
53101	ASHDOWN INV.'TR.	INV.TRST	20	3TA	.99	22	13	.09	66	-5	-1	-1	5.9	27.3	184
52807	ASH & LACY LIMITED	METALLGY	14	3T	.41	22	21	.14	11	17	15	25	5.9	8.4	336
53491	ASHLEY INDUSTRIAL TST	TIMBER	1	3	.69	37	35	.22	11	-9	-14	-6	13.9	.0	36
54030	ASPREY & CO	STR.MULT	26	3						-12			4.6	8.4	1075
54706	ASSAM DOOARS HLDGS	TEA	3	4	.48	23	21	.15	14	-6	-29	-18	3.5	9.3	245
55141	ASSAM FRONTIER TEA	TEA	3	4	.51	33	31	.18	10	-13	-35	-44	3.5	.0	260
55237	ASSAM TRADING 'B'	OVSE.TRD	6	4	.71	34	31	.22	14	-16	-22	-11	3.5	.0	61

Source: London Business School, *Risk Measurement Service*, July–September 1982. By permission of the publishers.

tan Holdings, Anvil Petroleum, Argyll Foods and Arlen Electricals. The only additional information required for a complete risk–return analysis of her portfolio is the return on the market and the risk-free rate of interest. A way round having to estimate the expected return on the market is to calculate the 'market premium', $E(R_M) - R_F$. This has averaged around 9% in the UK over the past sixty years. The use of 9% for the market premium thus avoids a direct assessment of $E(R_M)$.

So, all that remains to be estimated is the risk-free rate of interest. We saw in the assumptions of the CAPM that a true risk-free security would be hard to find. Two possible approximations are either a very short-term, government-backed security, such as a three-month Treasury Bill, to reduce inflation risk and interest rate risk to a minimum, or a longer-term gilt which matches Miss Divine's expected holding period.

Analysing past performance

In fact, the CAPM can be used, as well as for estimating expected return and risk on any portfolio, for the purpose of assessing the past performance of the portfolio. For example, the portfolio performance can be compared with the performance which would have been achieved by following the recommended CAPM strategy of holding a proportion of the market portfolio, M, with a beta of 1, and adjusting to the required level of risk by holding positive or negative amounts of R_F. Such a comparison will show Miss Divine whether or not she was wise to restrict herself to a small, relatively undiversified portfolio, which still has diversifiable (or specific) risk attached, instead of completely diversifying away all specific risk.

So, let us first examine the past. What were (and will be[13]) the risk characteristics of the portfolio?

The beta of the portfolio is simply the weighted average of the constituent shares' betas:

$$\beta_p = \frac{1}{4} \times 1.13 + \frac{1}{4} \times 1.16 + \frac{1}{4} \times 0.92 + \frac{1}{4} \times 1.07$$

$$\beta_p = 1.07$$

If we know that the market risk, S_m, was 19% over the past year,[14] we can calculate the market element of the portfolio's risk, $\beta_p^2 S_m^2$:

---

[13] Since we assume that the risk characteristics of the securities (and hence the portfolio) derived from past data are also relevant to the future.

[14] This can be found by using the standard deviation of a surrogate for the market, say the FT All Share Index.

$$\beta_p^2 S_m^2 = (1.07)^2 \, (0.19)^2$$

$$= (1.145) \, (0.036)$$

$$= \mathbf{0.041}$$

The other element of risk of the portfolio, the diversifiable or specific risk will be the weighted averages of the specific risks of the constituent shares. (Remember that we have to square and add when dealing with risk – we use variances and not standard deviations.)[15] So,

$$(\text{Portfolio specific risk})^2 = S^2(e_p) = \sum_{i=1}^{n} (W_i S(e_i))^2$$

We know that $W_i = \frac{1}{4}$ for each i, giving

$$S^2(e_p) = \frac{1}{16} (0.61)^2 + \frac{1}{16} (0.50)^2 + \frac{1}{16} (0.62)^2 + \frac{1}{16} (0.48)^2$$

$$= \mathbf{0.077}$$

So, the portfolio specific or diversifiable risk is

$$S(e_p) = \mathbf{0.28}$$

Note that the portfolio's diversifiable risk is lower than the diversifiable risk of any of the individual constituents of the portfolio. However, diversifiable risk is still present and represents an unrewarded element of risk according to the CAPM. We shall see below whether or not Miss Divine was rewarded for taking on this unnecessary risk.

To complete the picture of the portfolio's risk, we calculate the portfolio's total risk, V_p, which is the sum of the market element of risk plus the specific risk. From equation (8.10), we can write

$$V_p = \beta_p^2 \, S_m^2 + S^2(e_p)$$

$$= 0.041 + 0.077$$

$$V_p = \mathbf{0.118}$$

$$S_p = \sqrt{V_p}$$

$$S_p = \mathbf{34\%}$$

---

[15] This derives from the statistical properties of the variance as opposed to its square root, the standard deviation.

So, we know that the total standard deviation of Miss Divine's portfolio is 34% compared with an equivalent figure for M of 19%. (Note that the standard deviation for each security in the *Risk Measurement Service* is given under the heading 'variability'.)

We can now compare Miss Divine's portfolio's performance last year with what she could have achieved under a CAPM strategy. If we know that the return which could have been achieved on a gilt bought one year ago with one year to maturity was 10%, and the return on the market last year (using the surrogate of the FT–Actuaries All-Share Index) was 7%,[16] we can calculate the return on the benchmark portfolio. Note that the benchmark portfolio is designed to have the same beta risk and Miss Divine's portfolio, that is, a beta of 1.07.

$$R_B = (1 - \beta_p) R_F + \beta_p R_m$$

$$= -0.07 \times 10\% + 1.07 \times 7\%$$

$$\boldsymbol{R_B = 6.8\%}$$

We can now compare this with the return Miss Divine actually achieved on her portfolio. We do this by looking at the column labelled annual actual return in Table 8.1 and finding the weighted average of the returns for each of the securities:

$$R_p = \tfrac{1}{4} \times -35\% + \tfrac{1}{4} -59\% + \tfrac{1}{4} -28\% + \tfrac{1}{4} -33\%$$

$$\boldsymbol{R_p = -38.8\%}$$

Although the stock market as a whole did not do well, Miss Divine would have done better to stick to the CAPM strategy. The diversifiable risk she retained by not holding a diversified portfolio led to her underperforming the benchmark portfolio which had the same amount of beta risk, by $6.8 + 38.8 = 45.6\%$. This is known as the 'abnormal return' and is given in the *Risk Measurement Service* for each share.

The returns shown above remind us of the meaning of the term 'risk'. According to the CAPM, we expect to earn a premium over the risk-free rate when investing in shares. In fact, the return on the market in the period considered above was actually 7%, *below* the risk-free rate of 10%. Although we expected to earn more than 10%, we actually did not. Over a sufficient number of years, we would expect to earn on average (as the empirical evidence shows) 9% per annum more than the risk-free rate. This does not stop us earning much less in some years and much more in others.

---

[16] The one-year gilt 'matches' the one-year holding period and so is relatively risk-free. Last year's R_m can be found in the *Risk Measurement Service*.

Estimating future performance

As far as estimating the *expected* return on her portfolio, all that Miss Divine needs to know is the future risk-free rate. Suppose she again wishes to consider a one-year horizon. She can use the one-year spot interest rate implicit in gilt prices, which can be derived, as we saw in Chapter 4, as her risk-free rate. Suppose this is 11%. The market premium can be estimated at 9% again, giving the expected return on the portfolio, $E(R_p)$ as

$$E(R_p) = R_F + \beta_p(E(R_m) - R_F)$$

$$= 11\% + 1.07\ (9\%)$$

$$= \mathbf{21\%}$$

Note that Miss Divine can only expect to be rewarded for the element of market risk, measured by the beta of 1.07, of her portfolio. She can expect no additional reward from bearing diversifiable risk.

How to construct a benchmark portfolio

Before we leave this example, let us consider how Miss Divine could follow the recommended CAPM strategy in practice. First of all, she should hold a proportion of the market portfolio. Obviously, it would be difficult in real life for her to hold small amounts of each risky security in issue, in proportion to its total market value, because of the enormous transaction costs involved. She would also have to buy and sell securities continually, as share prices moved, to maintain her weightings.

An alternative strategy would be to buy shares in an index fund, a fund set up specially to mirror the market portfolio as closely as possible. This type of fund restricts itself to shares (although strictly it should include all marketable assets) and it does not contain all the shares in the market, or even, say, all the 750 shares in the FT All Share Index (discussed in the appendix to Chapter 9). This is because a reasonably good approximation to the share market as a whole can be obtained by holding only a few hundred shares. With that number, a beta of 1 can be achieved and there is hardly any specific risk.

Such index funds have been set up in the US, where the CAPM has been accepted much more as a model for portfolio investment decisions. In the UK, index funds are as yet barely established.

An alternative would be to invest in an investment trust or unit trust (both discussed in greater detail in Chapter 11) with betas of 1. To achieve a beta of 1.07, Miss Divine would have to borrow a small amount to 'gear up' her investment in the index fund or investment trust.

Another alternative strategy for Miss Divine would be to invest in a portfolio much better diversified than her present one and which has the beta that she requires of 1.07. She would thus avoid having to borrow to reach her required level of risk. In fact, she would not need to hold many more shares than she holds at the moment, since we saw in Chapter 7 that a portfolio equally divided amongst ten shares will on average eliminate 90% of the diversifiable risk of the individual securities.

Miss Divine must therefore be holding her present portfolio either because she has not heard of portfolio theory and the capital asset pricing model or because she believes that she can pick shares that will do better than predicted by the CAPM. In other words, she believes that she can 'pick winners'. She appears not to have succeeded last year. It remains to be seen whether she will exceed her expected return of 21% next year. Chapter 9 discusses her chances in the light of the efficiency of the stock market.

Problems with CAPM

We have seen how simple the CAPM is to apply in practice to portfolio investment. And yet, we do not see all investors holding index funds (or investment trusts) with betas of 1 and positive or negative amounts of some risk-free security. In practice, each investor holds a different portfolio of shares, as predicted by portfolio theory but not by the capital asset pricing model. So what is wrong with the CAPM?

First of all, we must remember the restrictive assumptions of the model, for example no taxes or transaction costs. The small investor will be unwilling to buy a proportion of all the securities in the stock market when he has only £2,000 to invest although the unit trust or investment trust will, as we saw with Miss Divine, offer him a surrogate for M. Also, M in theory should contain all marketable assets, including the works of art and property we excluded in Chapter 1. For practicalities' sake, a market index including most company shares is used to represent M but this excludes a substantial number of marketable assets.

Another problem with the assumptions which immediately springs to mind is that all investors cannot borrow and lend at the risk-free rate. If we assume that the lending rate R_L, is lower than the borrowing rate, R_B, we get the result shown in Figure 8.5.

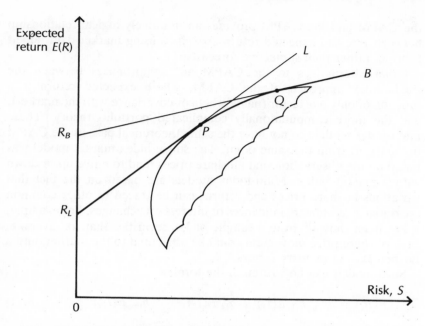

Figure 8.5   Efficient portfolios with different borrowing and lending rates

There is no longer only one efficient portfolio M. The investor will choose either a point on one of the two lines $R_L P$ and QB or any efficient portfolio from the efficient frontier PQ. We can see that, with a relaxation of one of the assumptions of the CAPM, we have the result that investors will not necessarily all hold the market portfolio. However, it has been shown that other assumptions underlying the CAPM can be relaxed *without* affecting its major results.[17]

Alternatives to CAPM

Despite the problems associated with the assumptions underlying CAPM, there are few simple alternatives to the CAPM which can provide estimates of the future expected return on a share. One method, already mentioned in Chapter 5, is to forecast all future dividends to be paid on the share or, more simply, to assume constant growth of such dividends (Gordon's growth model). The assumptions underlying Gordon's growth model are as restrictive as those underlying

---

[17] For example, the CAPM can still be derived without the need for a risk-free asset. A zero beta security (or combination of securities) can be used instead. See Black (1972).

the CAPM and the CAPM provides an intuitively logical relationship between risk and expected return as well as using market data, albeit historic, rather than subjective forecasts.

Other alternatives to the CAPM are compromises between the single-index approach of the CAPM, where expected return is a function of only *one* factor (namely beta or covariance with the market), and the more computationally complicated portfolio theory. These multi-index models do not have the same theoretical base as the CAPM but start off from the same point. The single-index market model was based on the observation that all share prices tend to move up or down with a market index. Multi-index models are based on the fact that variations in share prices and returns can be traced to other common factors such as industry influences or interest rate changes. For example, it has been shown[18] from a sample of US securities that, on average, 21% of share price movement could be attributed to the market, and a further 21% to industry factors.

Such models can be written in the form

$$E(R_i) = a_i + b_{i1} E(I_1) + b_{i2} E(I_2) + \dots b_{im} E(I_m) \tag{8.11}$$

where the a_i and b_{ij} are constants and $I_1, I_2, \dots, I_m$ are the indices used to measure the different influences on share returns. I_1 could be a market index, I_2 an industry index and so on. Equation (8.11) can always be stated so that I_i and I_j are independent of each other [$(COVI_i, I_j) = 0$ for all i, j] and this considerably simplifies the computations for calculating efficient portfolios.[19]

Multi-index models are generally derived by putting in possible explanatory factors such as industry or interest rate indices and seeing how well the data can be explained. Historic data are used to calculate the coefficients of the equation and the equation can then be used to forecast expected returns, as with the CAPM. The problem with more complex models, which have more explanatory variables, is that although they explain the historic data better than simpler models (achieve a good 'fit') they may in doing so include random 'noise' from the data and actually explain less than a simpler model when used on other sets of data. A regression model always involves a compromise between explaining as much variation as possible and running the risk that the 'noise' included will spoil its predictive powers.

A multi-index model which statistically derives the explanatory factors affecting share returns from the actual data (rather than taking economic factors and seeing how well they fit) is that of arbitrage pricing

---

[18] See Brealey (1983), p. 95.
[19] When considering a portfolio of *n* securities and *m* indices, $2n + 2m + nm$ data items are needed for a multi-index model.

theory. Proposed by Ross in 1976 this provides a theoretical foundation for a multi-index model with independent indices. Firstly, it shows that with the possibility of diversification available to any investor, any non-common causes of risk ('specific' or 'unique' risk) can be diversified away as with CAPM. Secondly, it proves that, if shares are assumed to form an efficient market where no arbitrage profits[20] can be made, expected return of a share must be a *linear* expression of its sensitivities to the factors affecting it.

So,

$$E(R_i) = a_i + b_{i1}\beta_1 + b_{i2}\beta_2 + \ldots \tag{8.12}$$

where the β_j are the sensitivities of security i to the factors or indices affecting its returns, and the a_i, b_{ij} are constants specific to security i. These indices can be statistically derived from the data rather than by indices suggested by the researcher as in the earlier multi-index models.

Arbitrage pricing theory (or 'APT' as it is known) has gained popularity as the empirical tests of CAPM have come under increasing criticism. It has been shown reasonably successfully[21] that a security's return is an increasing and linear function of its beta but the foundation for such tests has been criticised by Roll who argues that the surrogates used for 'the market' are not good enough and the tests in fact show whether or not the surrogates are efficient portfolios rather than proving or disproving CAPM. The implication of Roll's criticism is, in fact, that the CAPM is untestable. However, empirical testing of the newer APT is as yet at a very early stage.

Despite the problems associated with the CAPM and the possible shifts in research emphasis to a multi-index model of the form suggested by the APT, the CAPM is simpler in conception than the newer multi-index models, such as APT. It is therefore unlikely to hold as well as these in the real world but it is computationally simple and easy to understand and apply in practice. Although its results should be treated with caution, it offers a framework for investment decision-making to the investor which 'gut feel' does not.

---

[20] Arbitrage profits are those which can be made without any risk at all – in this case, if there were some securities which were cheaply priced relative to others with the same risk. In efficient markets, where no arbitrage profits can be made, there would be no 'free lunches' of this kind.

[21] For further discussion on both empirical evidence on CAPM and Roll's critique, see Elton and Gruber (1981), ch. 13.

Summary

We saw in Chapter 7 that portfolio theory provides a basis for determining efficient portfolios for each investor taking into account his risk–return preferences. However, the determination of these portfolios requires a substantial amount of data and calculation and simpler models explaining the risk and return relationship of securities have been put forward which enable a much quicker analysis of portfolios to be undertaken.

The capital asset pricing model provides a theoretically based single index model. It shows that the reward for holding a risky security is not based on the security's total risk (its standard deviation) but only on its beta, or systematic risk – that risk which remains, assuming the security is held as part of a well-diversified portfolio. The CAPM also shows (unlike portfolio theory which assumes each investor has his individually designed portfolio) that all investors should hold the same market portfolio (all marketable assets) combined with borrowing or lending at the risk-free rate. The only difference between portfolios would be the different proportions held of M and risk-free borrowing or lending. However these results can break down if the assumptions underlying CAPM are relaxed.

CAPM allows the expected return and risk of a security or portfolio to be estimated so that alternative investments can be easily compared. Empirical tests of the CAPM have been carried out but criticism of the methodology and a desire for more complete explanations of security returns have led to multi-index models. Arbitrage pricing theory is one such model which is as yet in its early stages of development.

However, the CAPM has gained acceptance, first in the US and now in the UK, as a helpful investment decision-making tool, facilitating the choice of portfolios for the investor, whether investing hundreds or millions of pounds.

Problems

1. (i) If the expected return on a share is 15%, when the risk-free rate is 10% and the expected return on the market is 20%, what is the share's beta?

   (ii) Suppose you know that shares A and B are correctly priced according to the capital asset pricing model. Share A is expected to have a return of 19.8% and has a beta of 1.2. A return of 17.1% is expected on share B, which has a beta of 0.9. Derive the securities market line.

(iii) Suppose that the following securities market line was derived for last year

$$E(R) = 10 + 9\beta$$

You see that two unit trusts X and Y achieved returns of 17 and 20% with betas of 0.8 and 1.3 respectively. Can you say anything about their performance?

2. Sharpe postulated that a portfolio's expected return and risk could be expressed as in equations (8.3) and (8.4)

$$E(R_p) = a_p + b_p E(R_m) \tag{8.3}$$

$$V_p = b_p{}^2 V_m + \sum_{i=1}^{i=n} X_i{}^2 V(e_i) \tag{8.4}$$

where the X_i are the proportions in which securities are held.
  (i) What is the main argument behind the market model?
 (ii) How many data items are needed using the market model for a ten-security portfolio compared with portfolio theory?
(iii) As the size of the portfolio is increased (n gets larger) which *part* of the risk, V_p, will become dominant and why? What will happen to the overall risk V_p?

3. (i) Shares with betas below one are sometimes referred to as 'defensive' whereas those with betas above one are known as 'aggressive' shares. Which industries do you think will have defensive shares and which aggressive? Can you think of any shares which might have a negative beta?
 (ii) You are trying to construct two well-diversified portfolios, one with a beta of 0.6 and one with a beta 1.4. How would you go about constructing these portfolios?

4. Mr Quick has inherited the following portfolio from a great-aunt:

Share	Number of shares	Current share price p	Beta	Specific risk (%)	Annual abnormal return (%)
African Mountains Corp.	1,000	28	0.77	34	−39
Board Timber Co.	2,000	41	1.22	28	−23
Millers Mechanical Engineering	1,000	40	0.80	67	−33

(i) What is the beta of the portfolio? Given a risk-free rate of 12% for the next twelve months, and an expected market premium ($E(R_m)$) − R_f) of 9%, what should Mr Quick *expect* to earn next year?

(ii) Calculate the total risk and the specific risk of the portfolio. (Suppose the standard deviation or variability of the market index is 10%.) What can you say about the riskiness of the portfolio?

(iii) Explain the meaning of the term 'annual abnormal return'.* Can you explain why it was negative for Mr Quick's portfolio? If the return on the FT–Actuaries All-Share Index was 20% last year and the risk-free rate was 10%, what was the *actual* return on Mr Quick's portfolio? Does the annual abnormal return figure help you say anything about *next* year's expected return?

(iv) Can you make any suggestions to Mr Quick as to how he can improve his portfolio, bearing in mind that he is employed by a rival of Board Timber Co., Pine Panels plc.

5. (i) Explain how you would use the information provided by a Beta Book service to evaluate an individual security, for example, Lennons Group:

Extract from Risk Measurement Service

SEDOL No.	Company name	SE industry classn	Market capn	Marketability
521464	Lennons Group	Food Ret.	16	3A

Beta	Variability	Specific risk	Standard error	R^2	Quarterly Ab. return	Ann Ab. return	Act. return
0.82	32	26	0.14	30	10	34	38

Gross Yield	PE ratio	Price
6.9	9.0	50

(ii) How has the beta of Lennons Group been calculated and what assumptions underlie its use?

Hint: Annual abnormal return is the difference between the actual return and what would have been achieved on a benchmark portfolio with the same beta.

Efficient markets

Introduction

So far, in this book, we have concerned ourselves primarily with how securities can be valued. For example, forward rates in Chapter 4 gave us a method for forecasting future gilt prices and estimating their expected holding period returns. Particular gilts could then be chosen according to investor expectations about future interest rates. Also, in Chapter 5, it was shown how Gordon's growth model could be used to estimate the expected *HPR* on a share, given assumptions concerning the company's future dividend policy. The shares with the best prospects for high returns or those which were considered undervalued could then be acquired. This type of investment strategy, where securities are evaluated and selected on their individual merits, we shall call 'picking winners'.

Chapters 7 and 8, on the other hand, concentrated on the characteris-

251

tics of securities in the context of a portfolio. For example, portfolio theory suggested that a diversified portfolio of securities be held, and that securities should be valued not in isolation but in relation to their impact on the remainder of the investor's portfolio. The capital asset pricing model went further and recommended all investors to hold appropriate proportions of the market portfolio M (consisting of all risky securities) combined with an appropriate positive or negative holding of a risk-free security, such as a gilt. Thus, both portfolio theory and the capital asset pricing model take the individual risk and return characteristics of each security as given and concentrate on the optimal risk–return profile of the investor's portfolio. Investment strategies based on these models could be termed 'fair return for risk' strategies, by which we mean that the investor following such a strategy expects to get a return on his portfolio which is equal to that predicted by the CAPM, given the level of risk in his portfolio.

The essential difference between the two approaches is that, when picking winners, the investor's underlying assumption is that he can 'beat the market' without incurring extra risk, whereas an investor using, say, the CAPM as a basis for his investment strategy is expecting only to beat the market if he takes on more risk than the market. Gilt and share prices already incorporate market expectations concerning interest rates, dividends, discount rates, and so on. By considering that some securities will offer higher returns than others, allowing for their relative risk, investors trying to pick these winners must be assuming that they know something about these securities *either* that the market does not yet know *or* has not yet incorporated into the share price. The 'fair return for risk' approach, on the other hand, embodied in portfolio theory and CAPM, *accepts* market expectations for *all* securities as the best estimates available, and merely attempts to combine holdings of securities, given their expected return and risk characteristics, in an optimal way for each investor.

This chapter examines these alternative investment strategies both in terms of what happens in practice and what should happen in theory on the basis of given assumptions about investor behaviour. The type of investment strategy to pursue will be shown to depend on how 'efficient' securities' markets are. If these markets are efficient, and we shall see later how this can be defined, trying to pick winners will be a waste of time and effort. This is because, in an efficient market, the prices of securities will reflect the market's best estimates of their expected return and risk, taking into account all that is known about them. There will thus be no undervalued securities offering a higher than deserved expected return, given their risk. So, in efficient markets, an investment strategy concentrating simply on the overall risk and return characteristics of the portfolio will be more sensible. If, however, securities' markets are not efficient, and excess returns can be made by correctly picking winners, then it will pay investors to spend time finding these undervalued securities. By excess returns, we mean returns consistently[1] achieved which are above those predicted by the CAPM, given the level of risk incurred.

This concept of markets as efficient or inefficient has caused much emotion and argument in investment circles. This is no doubt partly because, in practice, the great majority of investment advisers act as if markets are 'inefficient' and therefore attempt to make 'excess' profits. If markets are, in fact, fully efficient in the above sense, the rationale on which most investment advice and policy is based can be shown to be invalid.

This debate has become more heated as investment has become more indirect. Individual investors have, in a sense, only themselves to blame if they try to pick winners and are unsuccessful at it. However, if, say, pension fund managers adopt a 'picking winners' strategy when, in fact, securities markets are efficient, beneficiaries of the fund will suffer. Firstly, the turnover of the fund (and hence transaction costs) will be unnecessarily high, as the pension fund managers think they see opportunities to invest in 'winners'. Secondly, the portfolio may well be badly diversified if the managers have concentrated on holding a few potential 'winners'. Thus, unnecessary and unrewarded (according to CAPM) risk will be incurred, to the detriment of the beneficiaries of the fund who may be unable to indicate their disapproval by moving their funds elsewhere.

As the amount of indirect investment has grown, a need to monitor the investment strategy and performance of financial intermediaries, such as pension funds, has developed. Given that these institutions could adopt the 'fair return for risk' strategy prescribed by the CAPM, this model offers a suitable benchmark against which to assess their actual investment strategies. In fact, the CAPM has been used to develop a series of performance measures, adjusted for risk, which can be used to assess any portfolio's performance and hence investment managers' ability, if any, to 'beat the market'. Prior to the development of the CAPM, performance was often misleadingly judged solely on return with little direct account being taken of risk. Even today, tables on investment trust performance show only the cumulative returns on investment for the past five years, with no indication of the riskiness of each of the trusts. Similarly, unit trusts are ranked according to the last, say, five years' return, again ignoring risk.

In view of the current importance of financial intermediaries for Stock Exchange investment, the whole of Chapter 11 is devoted to a description of the major institutions involved and how they affect the invest-

---

[1] By 'consistent' or 'long-run' returns we would normally mean returns achieved over a period of years.

ment scene. Chapter 12 considers how performance can be measured using the CAPM. This chapter concentrates on whether or not the security markets are efficient and discusses the implications of the different levels of efficiency – weak, semi-strong and strong – on investment strategy.

The chapter begins with a description of the random walk theory of share price changes, which was first discussed at the turn of the century and is the precursor of the more modern concept of efficient markets. Three possible strengths of efficient markets are then discussed, with the evidence supporting the validity of each and the implications for investment decision-making outlined. In particular, the implications for technical analysis and fundamental analysis are considered.

An appendix to this chapter describes the main stock market indices, and considers which indices can most suitably be used as surrogates for the 'market', whether attempting to measure performance from a 'picking winners' strategy or whether holding the 'market' in a 'fair return for risk' CAPM strategy.

Random walk

The efficient markets hypothesis (or EMH as it is known) and its predecessor, the random walk theory, are perhaps the most misunderstood concepts in the theory of investment. This is due partly to the back-to-front way in which the theory of efficient markets has evolved and partly to the misleading and emotive statements often ascribed to these theories, for example 'Investment analysis is a total waste of time' or 'No one can beat the market'. The term 'random walk' is also disturbing with its connotations of share prices determined by chance.

The idea that security prices in an organised market might follow a random walk was first put forward by Bachelier in 1900 for commodities traded on the French commodities markets. The term 'random walk', in this context, is used to refer to successive price changes which are independent of each other. In other words, tomorrow's price change (and therefore tomorrow's price) cannot be predicted by looking at today's price change. $P_{t+1} - P_t$ is independent of $P_t - P_{t-1}$. There are no trends in price changes. In the same way as the best place to look for a drunken man previously abandoned in the middle of a field is where he was left, so the best estimate of tomorrow's commodity price is today's. Both the drunken man and commodity prices follow a random walk, being as likely to go in one way as the other.

In the 1950s and 1960s, the random walk theory was also tested on company share prices and, as we shall see, share prices do appear to follow a random walk. One difference to note between share prices and commodities is that, in so far as shares have a positive expected return, share prices will exhibit an upward trend. So, whereas the statement 'The best estimate of tomorrow's price is today's' holds for commodities with zero expected return, it does not hold for shares. In the case of shares, we can say that tomorrow's price change is as likely to be above the price change expected by the market as below it.

Proofs of the random walk theory can take several forms. As with all tests of theories involving *future* expected prices or returns, *past* actual prices or returns are used for the tests (since these are easier to measure). So, for the random walk theory, sets of past share prices are tested for dependence. One such test involves calculating the correlation coefficients of consecutive (or lagged)[2] share price changes over daily and longer intervals. Tests have been carried out on both UK and US share data bases and the serial correlations, as correlation coefficients for time series data are called, have been found to be around zero. For example, Moore (1962) looked at weekly share price changes from 1951 to 1958 on twenty-nine US shares selected at random and found an average serial correlation coefficient of −0.06.

Another intuitive test of the random walk theory is based on one of the standard arguments used against it – that share price charts *do* show trends. For example, again using US share prices, Figure 9.1(a) shows the Dow Jones Industrial share index plotted weekly during 1956. This reveals two clear peaks and troughs during the period. However, if a series of price changes is generated randomly (for example, from random number tables) and then, starting from an arbitrary base number, say the same initial value as in Figure 9.1(a), the prices so derived are plotted on a graph, they too appear to have trends and patterns in them. Figure 9.1(b) shows just such a randomly generated graph which exhibits trends which are as clear as those in Figure 9.1(a).

Other, more rigorous methods of testing the random walk theory, for example runs tests,[3] have been applied to many sets of share prices, in the US, the UK and the other major stock markets. These, too, have confirmed that share prices do on the whole follow a random walk.

---

[2] For example, a comparison of price changes every second or third day. For a discussion of such tests, see Brealey (1983), ch. 1.

[3] A runs test is a comparison of the plus and minus *signs* of the price changes with the signs that would be expected from a random pattern.

Figure 9.1   Actual and randomly generated share index

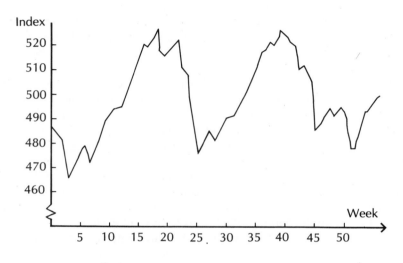

(a) Actual Dow Jones industrial share index 1956

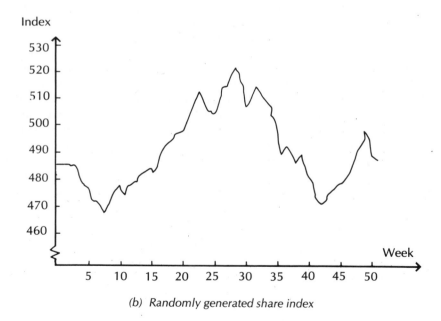

(b) Randomly generated share index

Source: Roberts (1959). By permission of the *Journal of Finance*.

Model of share price behaviour

That share prices appear to follow a random walk is an interesting result and proving it occupied many researchers throughout the 1960s. But what remained to be shown was *why* share prices followed a random walk. There was plenty of evidence but a formal theory was missing. What was needed was a model of share price behaviour to explain the random walk. This gap has now been filled by a more general model based on the concept of efficiency of the markets in which shares are traded – the efficient markets hypothesis.

If we go back to the idea of a perfect market (which was assumed when deriving the capital asset pricing model), with information freely and instantaneously available to all, a homogeneous product, no taxes, perfect competition amongst investors and no transaction costs associated with trading, we can see that, under these conditions, each share will be 'correctly' valued, in the sense that all information will be fully absorbed into the share price and investors will be in agreement that the current share price will be as likely to go up as go down. Thus, the share price can, until new information is released, be considered to be at an equilibrium value. As new items of information about the company's prospects come in, the company's share price will absorb this information and move to a new equilibrium value. It can be shown that in such a perfect market, successive price changes will be independent and prices will follow a random walk. This follows, firstly because the news inherent in the new piece of information concerning the company may be either good or bad, but it will certainly be *independent* of the last piece of information (otherwise it would not be new) and so the price change towards the new equilibrium value will be independent of the last price change. Secondly, because of the number of traders in the market and the lack of barriers to trading, the information (known to everyone) will be absorbed so quickly that the new equilibrium value will be achieved straightaway.

However, in a market where transaction costs were high enough to deter trading or where information was slow to reach the majority of investors, and speculative dealing by those who had the new information was in some way prevented, it might take several days or weeks for new information to be impounded in the share price. There would then be a trend in the share price as it moved towards its new equilibrium value. In such an imperfect and inefficient market, share price changes would be serially dependent rather than random, and excess returns could be made either by spotting the trends from charts or by trading on new information before it was fully impounded into the share price.

So, a random walk theory for share prices reflects a securities market where new information is rapidly incorporated into prices and where abnormal or 'excess' returns cannot be made from spotting trends or from trading on new information. Of course, we know such securities markets are not in practice *perfect* in the sense of having no transaction costs, no taxes, and so on. We also know that it is an impossible task to make all information immediately available to everyone and to give everyone the ability to interpret instantaneously the information correctly. Nevertheless, judging from the evidence on random walks, securities markets do appear to be *relatively* efficient at reflecting new information in prices. The question then becomes one of *how* efficient the markets are.

Fama (1970) decided to define different markets in terms of their level of efficiency, where the level reflected the *type* or *scope* of information which was quickly and fully reflected in price. He defined three levels of efficiency, each level designed to correspond with the different types of 'picking winners' investment strategies which were used in practice to try to achieve excess returns.

Table 9.1 shows the three different 'strengths' of the efficient markets hypothesis corresponding to different levels of efficiency. In the weak form of efficiency, each share price is assumed to reflect fully the information content of all past share prices. In the semi-strong form, the information impounded is assumed to include not only that given by all past share prices, which are of course public knowledge, but *all* publicly available information relevant to the share value. This includes, for example, company announcements, brokers' reports, industry forecasts and company accounts. The strong form of the EMH requires all known information to be impounded in the current share price, whether publicly and generally available or not. The strong form will thus include what is known as 'insider' information, for example details of an impending takeover bid known only to senior management of both parties to the bid.

As we saw earlier, markets which are efficient in quickly reflecting new information prevent investors from making excess profits using that information. Thus, in a weak-form efficient market, investors would be unable to pick winners by looking at charts of past share prices or by

Table 9.1   Efficient markets hypothesis

Efficient markets hypothesis
Prices fully reflect all available information

Weak form	Semi-strong form	Strong form
Prices fully reflect past prices	Prices fully reflect all publicly available information	Prices fully reflect all information

devising trading rules based on share price movements. In a semi-strong form efficient market, investors with access only to publicly available information would not be able consistently to make excess profits by buying shares, say on announcement of favourable new information. For example, if an investor decided to buy shares on each announcement of unexpectedly high earnings, this information would be available to all and the share prices concerned would quickly reflect that information and increase. Even if the shares did not reach their new equilibrium values immediately (because it can take time for new information to be fully analysed), the prices at which the investor could buy the shares would be unbiased estimates of these new equilibrium values, as likely to be above as below them. Finally, if the strong form of the EMH held, no investor could generate excess returns whatever information he used, whether a 'new' analysis of the company accounts or a hot tip from the managing directors, since in a market with this level of efficiency, share prices would already reflect all information relevant to the shares, whether publicly available or not.

It can be seen from the above that the ability of investors to pick winners and make excess returns using new information is directly related to the speed and efficiency of a market at absorbing that information. So, efficiency can be considered in terms of the 'fair game' concept. A market can be regarded as efficient with respect to a particular set of information if investors using that information are faced with a fair game, that is, they receive *on average* the return expected for the risk involved and make no consistent abnormal returns. This can be expressed in the following way. If ϕ_t is defined to be a particular set of information concerning security j available at time t, then any abnormal or excess return achieved at time $t + 1$ on security j can be written

$$\epsilon_{j,t+1} = (R_{j,t+1} - |(E(R_{j,t+1})/\phi_t)) \qquad (9.1)$$

Equation (9.1) shows that the excess return will be the difference between the return actually achieved and the return expected given the risk. The solidus / simply means that the returns are achieved or expected *knowing* information ϕ_t at the time t.

The EMH does not say that investors will never beat the market and will never make large profits. In other words, $\epsilon_{j,t+1}$ can be large and positive. What it does say is that, on average, over a period of time, investing is a fair game. 'You win some, you lose some.' So, the $\epsilon_{j,t+1}$ will sometimes be positive and sometimes negative, with the result that the sum of the excess returns over a number of periods of time will average zero:

$$\sum_{t=1}^{t=n} \epsilon_{j,t+1} = 0 \qquad (9.2)$$

The fair game for investors is an outcome of a market being efficient. *If* a market is efficient, *then* investing is a fair game. This fair game concept is useful in that it allows the different levels of the EMH to be tested. Instead of trying to measure the amount of information impounded in share prices, we can look to see if, by using different pieces of information, excess returns can be made. If they can, the market is not efficient with respect to that information. If they cannot, it is one piece of evidence supporting efficiency, but not a conclusive proof. However much evidence is piled up in its favour, the EMH can never be formally proved, leaving open the possibility that some investor may have an as yet untested way of picking winners consistently over time.

The EMH, as described above, is a more comprehensive model of share price behaviour than the random walk theory, referring not just to past share price movements but to all information pertaining to the share. It is a model which helps us to understand how markets operate in practice and how closely they approximate to theoretically perfect markets. Figure 9.2 places the EMH in perspective relative to the other models of share price behaviour.

In Figure 9.2, the perfect market has the most stringent requirements concerning market behaviour. The attraction of the perfect market is that it is an assumption underlying the major securities pricing models, such as the capital asset pricing model. In the real world, we know that the conditions assumed in perfect markets do not prevail. There are transaction costs associated with trading in securities and information concerning securities is not freely and instantaneously available to all. However, if transaction costs are not excessive, information is fairly

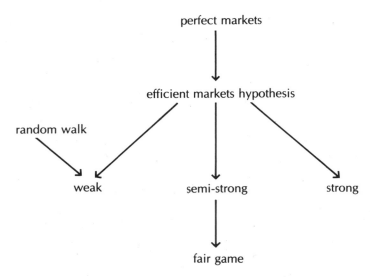

Figure 9.2   Models of share price behaviour

readily available and there is sufficient competition among investors, markets will be reasonably efficient in the sense that the securities' prices will reflect the information available and reflect it quickly enough to prevent excess returns being consistently made through trading on that information.

It can be seen from Figure 9.2 that the original random walk theory is most closely related to, but slightly stronger than, the weak form of the EMH. This is because the weak form implies that excess profits cannot be made by using past share price information whereas the random walk theory, whilst confirming the uselessness of studying past share prices, also says something about the shape of the pattern of share price movements. For example, it requires successive share price changes to be independent with zero serial correlation. The weak form of the EMH does not require any particular pattern of share price movements. So the random walk theory is stronger than the weak form of the EMH but less extensive than the full EMH.

Technical analysis

Since we have noted that, for the major stock markets of the world, the random walk theory appears to hold, the weak form of the EMH must also hold in practice. Thus, excess profits cannot be made in the long run by using past share price information.

Despite the evidence against them, investment strategies using past share price information do still exist; they are called technical analysis. There are two main types of technical analysis strategies, chartism and mechanical trading rules.

Chartism

Chartists specialise in analysing charts and graphs of share price information, spotting past trends and patterns and using these to forecast future price movements. For example, the shape in the centre of Figure 9.3 is known as a 'head and shoulders' formation. Other commonly occurring patterns include the 'neckline', 'congestion areas' and 'triangles'.

The charts can be plotted in various forms, one of the most common being the 'point and figure' chart, an example of which is shown in Figure 9.4, which emphasises trends (if there are any) in price changes.

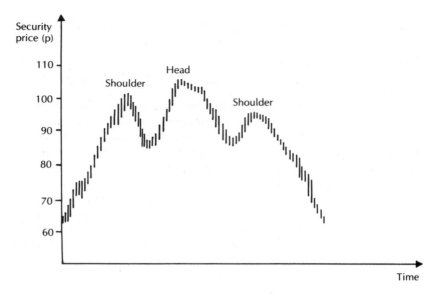

❙ = Price range for each sub-period (e.g. day).

Figure 9.3   Head and shoulders pattern

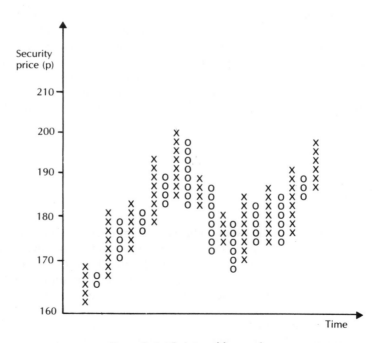

Figure 9.4   Point and figure chart

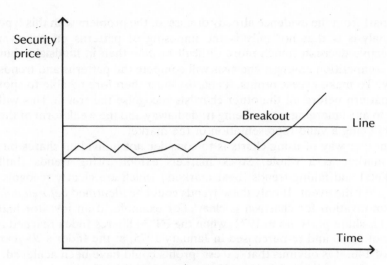

Figure 9.5   Example of line and breakout patterns

In point and figure charts, consecutive price increases of at least Yp (where Y is determined by the chartist) are plotted as X in the same column. A price decrease of at least Yp implies a move to the next column where consecutive price decreases of at least Yp are marked with a 0, and so on.

Of course, the difficult part of the analysis is the forecasting of the *future* share price pattern. This is based on study of past patterns, an assessment of whereabouts in a particular pattern the share is at the moment and therefore what pattern will occur in the future. The standard patterns which are believed to exist, such as head and shoulders, triangles or lines (which could all, as we saw earlier, be generated by random numbers) are explained by trading activities in the share. For example, a line, shown in Figure 9.5, is where buyers and sellers are evenly matched. At some stage, trading at this level will cease as would-be buyers or sellers dominate at that price level. At this stage, there will be a 'breakout' as in Figure 9.5. It is believed that the longer the share price remains within the line, the bigger will be the breakout.

Notice how chartists are completely uninterested in the fundamental characteristics of a share, such as, for example, the prospects for the company's high technology project in the US. They are concerned only with price movements and also volume of trading in the share (when available).[4] These are then translated into patterns reflecting the elusive 'mood of the market'.

---

[4] The Stock Exchange daily official list gives the prices at which shares were traded on a particular day, but not the *number* of shares which were traded at each price.

Apart from the evidence already discussed, the problem with this type of analysis is that not only is the imposing of patterns on charts a subjective decision, much more difficult *ex ante* than in hindsight, but also competition amongst chartists will compete the patterns and trends away. To make excess profits, a chartist must therefore be able to spot the pattern before all the other chartists recognise the trend. This will lead to any emerging trends being traded away and the weak form of the EMH being a valid representation of the market.

Another way of using charts is to consider not individual shares but the market as a whole. Stock markets exhibit rising trends (bull markets) and falling trends (bear markets) which are clearly recognisable after the event. If only these trends could be identified *beforehand*. The motivation for chartism is clear! For example, if an investor had sold his share portfolio in 1972, when the FT 30 Shares Index reached a peak of 543.6 and re-purchased in January 1975, at the Index's 20-year low of 146, it is obvious that 'excess' profits could have been achieved.

A similar realisation in the US at the end of the nineteenth century led to the Dow Theory. Charles Dow, editor of the *Wall Street Journal*, suggested that the stock market was influenced by three cyclical trends – a primary, long-term trend, a secondary trend lasting months and minor trends lasting days. Bull markets could be identified when successive highs in a suitable market index had been reached after secondary corrections, provided the secondary advances were greater and longer in direction than the secondary downturns. Figure 9.6 gives an example of a bull market trend. A bear market would be identified by exactly opposite trends. Dow used two indices, the Dow Jones Industrial Average, started in 1884 (its nearest UK equivalent being the FT Industrial Ordinary Share Index of thirty shares) and the Transportation Index, mostly railway company shares. Similar trends in both indices had to be noted before a bull or bear market could be confirmed.

In reality, these secondary trends cannot be stringently defined. They cannot be identified objectively before the event, and can turn out after the event to be only minor trends. To confirm this, try covering up half a graph of a suitable share index and then guess, from the first half of the graph, what the market will do next.

Mechanical rules

The other major form of technical analysis attempts to convert subjective impressions of trends or patterns in charts into objective trading rules. However objective the rules may sound, they are still based on a theory of share price movement in a weak-form inefficient market.

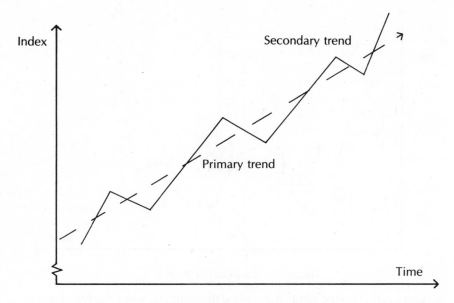

Figure 9.6   Dow Theory

For example, filter rules are designed to catch the breakout from a line, shown in Figure 9.5. Within the line, the share is assumed to be trading at around its equilibrium value. As a piece of new information is absorbed, the price will break out towards its new equilibrium value. The filter rule is designed to catch the share at the breakout point as it moves from the old to the new equilibrium value. In an efficient market, this would not be possible, since the price would move too quickly – there would be no trend.

The object of a filter rule is to buy before the share reaches its new, higher value and sell before its new, lower value. The dilemma is which size filter to choose. Figure 9.7 shows a filter of 5%. The wider the filter, the more likely the investor is to trade only on 'true' breakouts, but the later he will be in catching the trend. The smaller the filter, the likelier the investor is to catch the trend early enough. However, he may be misled by false breakouts and his transaction costs will doubtless outweigh any gains he makes from trading in and out of the share as opposed to simply buying the share and holding it.

Another mechanical trading rule often employed is one based on a share's relative strength. This is defined to be $P_t/\bar{P}$, where P_t is a particular share's current share price and $\bar{P}$ the share's average share price over the past x weeks (x is subjectively chosen by the analyst, a common period being twenty-six weeks). The higher P_t relative to $\bar{P}$, the higher the relative strength. Trading on relative strength also

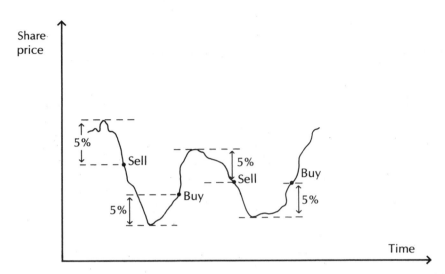

Figure 9.7   Example of filter rule

assumes serially dependent share price movements, since the idea is that if a share exhibits high relative strength it should be purchased because it will continue to do well. A typical trading rule is to buy in equal amounts say the top 5% of shares ranked by relative strength. As soon as a share's relative strength falls below the relative strength of say 70% of the shares, it should be sold and the proceeds reinvested in the new top 5%. Of course the percentages and the time periods can be varied as desired.

Two characteristics of these trading rules should be mentioned. Firstly, where individual shares are concerned, they ignore relative risk, the shares being chosen purely on the basis of past price movements, their fundamental and economic characteristics being ignored. Chartists believe they can afford to do this because they are looking for short-term gains, moving in and out of shares relatively frequently, rather than choosing long-term investments.[5] However, because shares with the biggest price changes will usually be chosen under these trading rules, there may well be an emphasis on shares with higher volatility and therefore higher risk, leading the investor to hold a portfolio which is riskier than he is, perhaps, aware.

Secondly, use of these rules will involve high transaction costs and, perhaps for this reason, are popular with stockbrokers whose commission depends on share turnover. This is no doubt one of the reasons why, when these trading rules have been tested and compared with a simple 'buy and hold' strategy over a period of months or years, the buy

---

[5] Although mostly concerned with short-run investment, chartism is also used for the optimal timing of a long-run investment.

and hold strategy has been found to yield higher returns, net of transaction costs.[6]

As was mentioned earlier, no form of the EMH, including the weak form, can conclusively be shown to hold, for any stock market, since it is an impossible task to test every possible trading rule on every possible set of share prices for excess returns. However, the weight of evidence in favour of the weak form of the EMH is generally accepted by academic opinion to be overwhelming, both in the UK and, more particularly, in the US. In the US, legal requirements may place more constraints on investment managers than in the UK; for example, US pension fund managers are required to make investment decisions 'with the care, skill, prudence and diligence...that a prudent man...familiar with such matters...would use'.[7] US investment managers therefore take more account of the results of tests of the EMH than do their UK counterparts. I quote from a US text aimed at US investment managers for the last word on the use of technical analysis:

> Thus a situation exists in which a stock selection technique that has been so thoroughly researched – and debunked – that it would no longer be a fitting subject for an investment seminar at any leading business school can nonetheless form the basis for an investment management approach just a few blocks away. Unquestionably, employing such analysis is *illogical*. What constitutes imprudence is a matter which, in the final analysis, must be decided by the courts.[8]

Fundamental analysis

In a sense, the semi-strong form of the efficient markets hypothesis is the most interesting of the three forms. As we saw above, there is now wide agreement that the weak form holds and that the use of technical analysis on its own is most unlikely to enable anyone consistently to make excess profits.

However, belief in the validity of the semi-strong form in its fullest sense calls into question not just the activities of chartists but the

---

[6] Transaction costs are high since, for example, if the shares are held for a period longer than the account, transfer stamp duty of 2% must be paid on each purchase. See Appendix 1 for details of share dealing transaction costs.

[7] See Section 404(a)(1) of the US Employee Retirement Income Security Act, 1974.

[8] See Hagin (1979), p. 36.

investment strategy of the majority of investment analysts in the City – fundamental analysis – briefly touched on in Chapter 5.

Most investment analysts act as industry specialists, spending their time forecasting future earnings, dividends or returns (according to preference[9]) for the companies within their chosen sector, using anything from a naïve model, such as $eps_1 \times PE_1 = P_1$, to a complex regression model. They do this by studying economic forecasts, industry reports, visiting the company, analysing company accounts and statements and generally forming a view on the company's prospects. This view is usually translated into an estimate of what they believe to be the share's intrinsic or 'correct' value (discussed in Chapter 5) which is then compared with the current share price, and generates a 'buy', 'sell' or 'hold' recommendation to clients.

There are over 1,900 members of the Society of Investment Analysts, and many more professional and amateur analysts who are non-members. There are approximately 2,000 UK company equity securities currently listed on the Stock Exchange,[10] of which around 950 have a market capitalisation of under £5m. This leaves approximately 1,100 shares with a market capitalisation of over £5m. to be analysed by *at least* 1,900 analysts. Each major British company will be 'followed' by a good many analysts, who have available to them the same public information, can make the same company visits, and presumably pore over the same company accounts. With this in mind, the semi-strong form of the EMH, which postulates that share prices at any time fully reflect all relevant publicly available information, becomes readily believable. Any new piece of information made public will be so quickly analysed and absorbed into a new market estimate of the company's value that an investor trading on each announcement, say, of unexpectedly good earnings, will act too late to be able to make consistent excess returns. Even if the market does not initially fully absorb the new information, the new share price is as likely to be an overestimate as an underestimate of the equilibrium share price reached once the information has been correctly interpreted and impounded.

It is perhaps useful at this point to compare the behaviour of technical analysts and fundamental analysts at the time new information believed to justify a change in price is announced. The fundamental analysts will trade as they evaluate the impact of the announcement. The technical analysts, by looking *not* at the announcement but at the share price and

---

[9] We saw in Chapter 5 that although dividends are actual cash flows and earnings are accounting figures, earnings are the more popular variable to forecast (despite their limitations as predictors) since less account need be taken of management's dividend payout policy.

[10] This includes both ordinary and deferred ordinary shares but excludes the unlisted securities market which has a further 150 (approximately) UK company shares quoted on it.

trading volume movements due to the fundamental analysts, will also trade.

The implications of the semi-strong form of the EMH for fundamental analysis, if it closely reflects reality, are far-reaching. Not only does it follow that trading on announcement of new information will not on average and taken over time produce excess returns, but it also implies that the best available indicator of a share's so-called intrinsic value is its current market price. So a fundamental analyst's search for undervalued shares within his sector using publicly available information is a waste of time. For example, a study of the inflation accounts of companies could lead an analyst to believe that certain companies were undervalued and others overvalued. However, if the inflation accounting information is publicly available in the accounts, other analysts will already have impounded whatever additional knowledge was contained in the inflation accounts into the share price. Not all analysts and investors need to have fully digested and analysed the inflation accounts. All that is required is for a sufficient number of analysts and their clients to have traded in the share with that knowledge. Thus, if the semi-strong form of the EMH does hold, no investor or analyst will be able consistently to make abnormal returns from the analysis of such publicly available information.

If the semi-strong form (but not the strong form) is a good approximation to reality,[11] the market value of a share will only be as good an estimate of the share's intrinsic value as the quality of the publicly available information concerning the company permits. If the information available is meagre, the market price of the share will be a correspondingly poor approximation to the share's worth. If, on the other hand, most relevant information is disclosed, the market value will be a good estimate of the share's worth. The implication for those concerned with corporate disclosure and accounting standards is therefore that careful consideration should be applied to *what* information is disclosed rather than *how* it is disclosed, since each new item of information not previously available may improve the market's estimate of the share's worth.

Reasons for fundamental analysis

We shall see later that the empirical evidence regarding the semi-strong form of the EMH as a good approximation to reality in the major stock

---

[11] In other words, if all publicly available information is impounded in the share price, but not 'insider' information.

markets is quite strong. If this is so, why has so much time and effort been devoted – and is still being devoted – to fundamental analysis?

There are at least two main reasons why fundamental analysis is such a popular form of investment decision-making, despite published results of research on the validity of this form of the EMH. The first is that, during the 1960s, the stock markets in both New York and London experienced considerable rises. Fundamental analysis which led to the buying of high growth shares was interpreted as success in 'beating the market'. Fundamental analysis was therefore seen as a successful investment strategy. The catch was that no account was taken of risk in deciding the investment portfolio. What were in fact being recommended were high beta shares, which *should* outperform the market in a bull phase. Apparent success at picking winners was really only a 'fair return for risk' and when markets fell in the early to mid-1970s, the high beta shares underperformed the market as a whole, as would be expected.

A second reason for the continued use of fundamental analysis is probably psychological. Looking at the stock market in hindsight, the investor can see many investments which, had he picked the right ones at the right time, would have made him rich. Abnormally large profits seem only just beyond his grasp. This huge apparent potential for making profits is highlighted by some research carried out by Niederhoffer and Regan. They compared analysts' published forecasts of changes in 1970 earnings per share (the favourite variable to forecast, as we saw in Chapter 5) with *actual* changes in 1970 earnings per share and actual share price changes in 1970. They examined three groups of fifty shares from the New York Stock Exchange. The first group consisted of the shares with the biggest 1970 price rises, the next fifty were randomly chosen and the third group of fifty were the worst price performers. The results outlined in Figure 9.8 have two major implications.

Firstly, earnings are very difficult to forecast accurately. We saw in Chapter 5 that earnings appear to follow a random walk (as do share prices) and so forecasts based on past earnings performance (which, by substituting earnings instead of dividends into the share valuation model to get estimates of *HPR* or intrinsic value, is the most common method used by analysts[12]) are unlikely to do well. For example, in Figure 9.8, we can see that the fifty worst performing shares had a median 15% *increase* in earnings forecast by analysts compared with an actual earnings *decrease* of 83%.

The second point to note from the results in Figure 9.8 is how much money could have been made by analysts who got it right. If an analyst had correctly forecast higher than expected earnings for the top fifty performers and had bought accordingly, he would certainly have made

---

[12] See footnote 9, p. 268.

greater than average returns given the risk. This is the motivation behind fundamental analysis.

Figure 9.8 also highlights the kind of investment analysis which will most likely lead to long-run excess returns. What is needed is not simply forecasts of high or low earning but forecasts which can be assessed relative to market expectations. To be successful at fundamental analysis, the analyst has to forecast better than others in the market

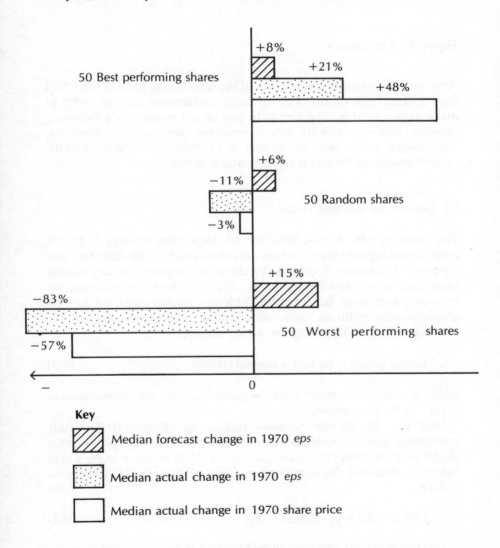

Figure 9.8   Forecast versus actual earnings

Source: Niederhoffer and Regan (1972). By permission of the *Financial Analysts' Journal.*

(using the same information). Forecasting such variables as earnings per share can be likened to forecasting exchange rates (discussed in Chapter 10). The market estimates of future earnings and future exchange rates are the 'best' estimates but they are not necessarily good estimates. This leaves plenty of apparent potential for excess returns. The question in both cases is how to achieve them and, having done so, how to continue to achieve them consistently over time.

Empirical evidence

Attempts to investigate the validity of the semi-strong form of the EMH have concentrated on two ways of using fundamental analysis to try to make excess returns. The first is to buy or sell immediately following announcements containing new information (for example dividends, scrip issues, etc.), and the second is to follow particular analysts' recommendations based on fundamental analysis.

(i) TRADING ON ANNOUNCEMENT

The problem with testing this type of investment strategy is that it involves buying the shares on announcement and holding them for, say, a period of a month. It cannot therefore be compared, as can trading rules, with a buy and hold strategy. So, the returns from trading on announcement must be compared with the returns expected had no announcement (with its 'new' information) been made, denoted the 'normal' returns. This allows the excess return,

$$\text{Excess return} = (\text{actual} - \text{normal}) \text{ return} \tag{9.3}$$

which is usually examined over the period around the announcement date,[13] to be determined.

How can the normal expected returns be calculated? The only practicable method, which adjusts for risk, is either Sharpe's market model or its theoretical counterpart, the CAPM. Once a share's beta has been estimated, the normal return expected from the CAPM can be written

$$E(R_j) = R_F + \beta_j \left(E(R_m) - R_F \right) \tag{9.4}$$

---

[13] For example, in Fama, Fisher, Jensen and Roll's study of the effects of scrip issues, they examined the period thirty months before to thirty months after the month of the actual scrip.

and from Sharpe

$$E(R_j) = \alpha_j + \beta_j|(E(R_m)) \tag{9.5}$$

The coefficients for equations (9.4) or (9.5), the α_j and β_j, have to be calculated from a set of data different from that actually used in the EMH tests, to avoid using the same data twice and rendering the tests meaningless. Nevertheless, this type of test of the EMH will involve a joint test of both the CAPM and the EMH. In other words, it assumes that the CAPM (or the market model) is an accurate representation of a share's risk–return relationship.

Most studies of such announcements,[14] using this risk-adjusted technique to calculate the normal return, have shown that, on average, the excess returns available from trading on announcement were nil. One reason for this could be that the information provided in the announcement adds nothing new to analysts' knowledge. For example, accurate expectations of dividends may have been formulated long before announcement, or a scrip issue already more than hinted at. However, these expectations are much harder to test since it is difficult to ascertain exactly when they became publicly available.

Despite deficiencies arising from the quite complex technical problems inherent in such tests,[15] the evidence, such as it is, points to the semi-strong form holding in general in the major stock markets, in particular those of the UK and the US. In other words, the evidence suggests that these markets adjust rapidly to new information that is publicly available, so that prices change before most people can deal.

(ii) Trading on recommendations

As well as brokers' individual share recommendations which are circulated to clients and published in the press, advisory services also exist which depend upon particular investment strategies, based on some kind of fundamental analysis.

For example, in the US, Value Line is a well-known advisory service. Although it keeps the exact details of its strategy secret, it is known that the strategy is based on the four aspects of a company's performance outlined in Table 9.2.

New rankings are issued every week and investors are expected to adjust their portfolios accordingly. Tests which have been carried out on

---

[14] Including, in the UK, tests of announcements of newly built-up large shareholdings, takeovers, earnings announcements and scrip issues. See Firth (1977).

[15] For example, the need to calculate betas from a different set of share returns than that being examined.

Table 9.2   Basis of Value Line recommendations

Companies are ranked 1–5 according to the following:

Last year's earnings and average price relative to the earnings and price performance over the last ten years and the average price over the last ten weeks relative to last year

The current *PE* ratio relative to the market compared to the last five years' relative *PE*s

'Earnings momentum' – the most recent quarter's[16] earnings compared to twelve months ago

'Earnings surprise' – the most recent quarter's earnings compared to the Value Line forecast

---

Source: Sharpe (1981). By permission of Prentice-Hall Inc., Englewood Cliffs, New Jersey and Value Line, Inc., New York.

various US broker recommendations and advisory services show that Value Line has provided better than average results. For example, if equal money amounts had been invested in Rank 1 shares in April 1965 and the portfolio had been adjusted each month for the new Rank 1 shares until December 1970, an excess return of 10% per annum (allowing for risk) could have been achieved.[17] However, once transaction costs are taken into account (and these are high given the monthly turnover), excess returns are no longer likely.

Implications of the semi-strong form

The evidence from tests of returns achieved from trading on announcement, or following an adviser's recommendations, point then to the US and UK stock markets being semi-strong form efficient. This would imply that the search for consistent excess returns net of transaction costs through fundamental analysis is a waste of time.

---

[16] Companies in the US have to provide quarterly statements of earnings under the Securities Exchange Commission rules compared to the UK Stock Exchange's six-monthly requirement.

[17] See Black (1973).

Implications for investors

Such a conclusion is particularly significant for the small investor whose proportionate transaction costs are high. The implication is that the individual investor should not worry about investment analysis. He should simply choose a diversified portfolio of shares or an index fund and concentrate on his optimum risk–reward ratio and other considerations, such as tax, liquidity and inflation-proofing (which will be considered in greater detail in Chapter 12). Index funds have only recently been established in the UK but are well accepted in the US. They are funds set up to mirror rather than beat the market: that is, reflect as closely as possible the market portfolio of the CAPM. Unfortunately, in practice, individual investors cannot ignore fundamental analysis, since they pay for it, indirectly, through the minimum commission system of the UK Stock Exchange. If, as has happened on the New York Stock Exchange, minimum commissions were to be abolished, investors would in principle no longer have to pay for any fundamental analysis they did not want.

Implications for analysts

The implications of the semi-strong form of the EMH are less reassuring for investment analysts than for investors. Their main *raison d'être* is put into question. And yet, if the evidence supports the semi-strong form, why do so many people still manage to make a living out of fundamental analysis? By analysing information and trading (or recommending to clients) on that information, they ensure that share prices fully reflect the information. But if everyone believed the semi-strong form and ignored fundamental analysis, the market would become inefficient.

This paradox, which is not really resolved by the EMH, leads us to consider more recent work on markets for information. These theoretical models[18] attempt, as the EMH does not, to take account of the role of 'information intermediaries', such as fundamental analysts, by assuming asymmetry of information. In these models, information is not freely available to everyone since, if this were so, security prices would obviously fully reflect all that information. Instead, they assume that information can be purchased at a cost by any investor and that this information improves estimates of securities' expected returns. Informed investors will thus have valuable information not known to uninformed investors. Asymmetry of information will prevail.

---

[18] For further discussion on this area of research, see Beaver (1981).

Within this framework, let us consider the role of the fundamental analyst. He acquires information, say by studying publicly available information, but at a cost. For example, there is the opportunity cost of his time and the possible need for qualifications (such as an accounting qualification to be åble to understand inflation accounting). The fundamental analyst will then make use of that information by selling it (as a broker) or by trading in the shares himself. Either way, share prices will then reflect that information. This appears to lead us straight back to the paradox inherent in the EMH. If the information acquired at a cost by the analyst is fully reflected in share prices, why should investors buy information or the analyst incur costs when the price will reflect the information anyway?

In order to avoid this problem, the models have to assume that prices do not clearly reflect the information for some reason. For example, they assume that there is a certain amount of 'noise' in share prices, which no amount of information can dispel. When studying share price movements, investors will not be able to tell how much of the price changes are due to information and how much to noise. This assumption allows for an equilibrium situation in which certain investors (and analysts) are informed and others choose to remain uninformed. No investor can improve his expected utility by changing from uninformed to informed. Certain investors will prefer to remain uninformed and to protect themselves by holding a well-diversified portfolio or index fund. Others will prefer to buy information and to use it to 'pick winners'. On average, the cost of acquiring the information will equal the benefit from using it. So, for example, informed investors will not in the long run make excess returns *after* transaction costs which include the cost of acquiring information. Similarly, following the recommendations of an investment strategy based on fundamental analysis will not on average yield excess returns after transaction costs. However, informed investors may do better, on average, than uninformed investors *before* transaction costs, and some may on occasion do better than the average.

For example, tests have found that the average level of forecasting ability amongst analysts (measured by the correlation coefficients between forecast and actual share price changes) is of the order of 0.15.[19] A coefficient of zero would imply no ability, so a coefficient of 0.15 implies that analysts taken as a whole (but not necessarily individually) do seem able to offer better than a risk-adjusted random choice of shares. So, fundamental analysts appear to be able to produce valuable information, albeit at a cost. The paradox thrown up by the EMH has under this framework been to some extent explained away.

---

[19] See Hagin (1979), ch. 29.

Conclusions for analysts

Trying to explain the role of fundamental analysts has led us to consider models which have a stronger theoretical background than the EMH. However, the EMH does have a substantial body of empirical evidence to support it, both at the weak and semi-strong levels.

Although our understanding of exactly how information is impounded into share prices is limited, we can still draw useful conclusions from the EMH for fundamental analysts.

Firstly, it would appear to be a waste of time to study standard, publicly available information and come up with a simple forecast of next year's earnings. What would seem to be a more fruitful approach would be to consider forecasts derived from publicly available information in the light of market expectations already impounded in the share price. Analysts would then be forced to consider whether their forecasts differed from the market consensus and, if so, why.

The second conclusion concerns the identifying of investment analysis ability and its best use. The use of such measures as the correlation coefficients mentioned above enables analysts to determine where their strengths and weaknesses lie. It may be that such forecasting ability as they do have is frittered away by analysing too many shares and by wasting time on shares where they have no such forecasting ability. However, the measurement of individual forecasting ability is as yet rare in the City. Nevertheless, the implication for analysts is clear. By measuring their abilities, they can decide, for example, whether to adopt a low transaction cost, index fund approach or whether to specialise in sectors where they believe they have a competitive edge.

Strong form

The strong form of the efficient markets hypothesis states that share prices fully reflect *all* knowable information, whether publicly available or not. This would imply that, if only a few people knew something about a company (for example, if only a handful of senior managers and civil servants were aware that the company had just been awarded a lucrative government contract), even they would not be able to make excess profits by trading on this knowledge.

There are far fewer tests of the strong form of the EMH than of the weak or semi-strong form, because of the difficulty in obtaining share trading information on the kind of people likely to have access to non-public information. Such people are known as 'insiders'. However, certain groups of potential insiders can be identified, such as directors and associates of US companies and New York Stock Exchange brokers on whom there is a certain amount of information available. For example, in the US, insiders are obliged to register all their share dealings in the companies to which they are insiders and studies of these share dealings have shown that excess returns are possible. Another type of insider dealer is the 'specialist' broker on the New York Stock Exchange who has access to a different kind of non-publicly available information – the orders to buy and sell at particular prices of his clients. The specialist can buy and sell on his own account with no time lag, and tests have shown that he too can, at least occasionally, make excess returns.

In the UK, neither of these types of tests is possible since, as mentioned earlier, information on market trading is not available in sufficient detail. Similarly, although UK company directors have to register their shareholdings at the company year end in the accounts and although insider dealing is now illegal in the UK,[20] insiders are not yet required, as in the US, to register full details of all their share dealings.

An alternative way of testing whether the strong form holds is to examine the behaviour of investing intermediaries or institutions. The economies of scale they can achieve in investment analysis and transaction costs should mean that they, of all investors, stand the most chance of being able to earn consistent long-run returns from publicly available information. Also, the relatively close relationships with the companies in which they invest (due to, for example, company visits) could lead to their obtaining information on these companies which is not generally available. So, examining the performance of such institutions would provide some evidence for and against both the semi-strong and the strong forms of the EMH. Since information on the performance of UK financial institutions is most readily available for unit and investment trusts, these are the institutions which have been studied for evidence of the possibility of long-run excess returns – the ability to pick winners. No such evidence has been found, which provides further support for the semi-strong form. As far as the strong form is concerned, the evidence is less clear-cut, however. If these institutions do not have access to non-publicly available information, a study of their performance is *not* a test of the strong form. In so far as they *do*, the validity of the strong form is supported by the lack of apparent long-run excess returns achieved by the investing institutions. However, it might be that excess returns are achieved but counterbalanced by losses on other investments, although this hypothesis is not testable given current levels of disclosure.

A final point on the strong form of the EMH. Although the evidence

---

[20] Since the Companies Act, 1980, pt V.

appears to be against the strong form, implying that insider dealing can be a profitable activity, the amount of inside dealing must be perceived by the market as a whole to be relatively insignificant or rational, risk averse, 'outsider' investors would not be prepared to invest in such a market. Indeed, regulation aimed at preventing insider dealing and providing for the rapid disclosure of information is common to all the major stock markets where turnover and investor interest is high.

Summary

This chapter has looked at the level of efficiency of stock markets with respect to information. The more quickly and completely information is impounded into share prices, the less likely that investors will be able to earn excess returns from using that information to pick winners.

The EMH has had a confusing history. It started out as the random walk theory, concerned only with trends in share prices. In its present form, it is concerned with a wide range of information, from past share prices to 'inside' information, and with whether investing in shares is a 'fair game' with respect to each particular set of information.

Fama defined three main levels of efficiency with respect to three types of information. The weak form considers past share prices (as does the random walk theory). The semi-strong form is concerned with all publicly available information and the strong form with *all* information, including information known only to a few insiders.

The evidence in general supports both the weak and the semi-strong forms, but not the strong form. Publicly available information, therefore, appears to be quickly impounded into share prices, so quickly that excess returns, given the risk, cannot consistently be made over a substantial period of time. This result suggests that the use of both chartism and fundamental analysis will not in the long run produce undeserved (in terms of risk) rewards. The role of fundamental analysts appears to be to produce information for a cost which matches any benefits derived therefrom.

The implication of the EMH for investors, in particular 'naïve' investors, is that they can, without needing to analyse or acquire costly information, adopt a 'fair return for risk' strategy, either by holding a well-diversified portfolio or an index fund. Investment analysts, on the other hand, should switch emphasis from a straight 'picking winners' approach to concentrating on analysing shares in the light of market expectations already impounded into share prices and of their ability to select winners. They should also construct share portfolios for investors which take into account the investors' risk–return preferences rather than trying to earn excess returns for everyone, regardless of risk.

Appendix: stock market indices

When we discuss the subject of efficient markets, and the alternative strategies of 'picking winners' to attempt to beat the market or the 'fair return for risk' strategy prescribed by the CAPM, we need to clarify what we mean when we talk about the 'market' and how we measure it in practice.

For example, the 'picking winners' route can involve trying to forecast market movements. Similarly, investment intermediaries may claim to have beaten the 'market'. How do they measure this? Alternatively, the 'fair return for risk' strategy recommended by the CAPM requires investors to hold the 'market' portfolio and betas are measured by comparing security returns with 'market' returns. Again, how is this done in practice?

The 'market' should in theory include all marketable assets, for example works of art and property. In practice, it is confined to the stock market since quoted securities have easily determined market values. So, given that the 'market' for risky assets is usually restricted to shares, how many of them does it include – all of them or a representative sample? Also, how are the share values aggregated into a representative index which can be used for calculating betas, as a benchmark portfolio or as a basis for constructing an index fund?

FT 30 Shares Index

The most frequently quoted share index is the *Financial Times* 30 Shares Index, started in 1935 and based on thirty major industrial shares. This is the index quoted on the news and printed on the back page of the *Financial Times*. Similarly, in the US, the most famous index is the Dow Jones Industrial Average, also based on thirty shares, although originally based on eleven shares when started in 1884. The limited size of these indices is a function of their age, since both predate the era of computers, and their long history is responsible for their influence.

The original purpose of both indices was to measure market movements over the short term and not to provide any estimates of market return (they ignore dividends) or to act as benchmark portfolios. Their object was to help predict market trends and to provide measures of market volatility. To this end, the FT 30 Shares Index was constructed as an unweighted geometric mean. All the shares in the index are given equal weighting and the same emphasis is given to a 10% increase in price to 55p of a share quoted at 50p as to a 10% increase in price to 550p for a 500p share. The relative sizes of the companies and the relative share prices are ignored. What counts is the percentage change in share price, that is to say, the share's volatility.

Despite only having thirty shares, the FT 30 Shares Index represents around 25% of the market value of all UK equities. This shows that a small sample can mirror movements of the whole market quite effectively. The FT–Actuaries All-Share Index, for example, which includes 750 shares, represents 80% of the total market value of all UK equities.

FT–Actuaries All-Share Index

The FT–Actuaries All-Share Index is calculated as an arithmetic average and weights the shares according to their market value. This index is suitable as a benchmark portfolio, against which real-life portfolios can be compared, since the FT All Shares Index represents a share portfolio which can actually be held.

Table A.1 gives the FT–Actuaries share indices (one of which is the FT All-Share Index), as shown in the *Financial Times*. As can be seen, there are also a

Table A.1   FT–actuaries share indices

FT-ACTUARIES SHARE INDICES

These Indices are the joint compilation of the Financial Times, the Institute of Actuaries and the Faculty of Actuaries

EQUITY GROUPS & SUB-SECTIONS Figures in parentheses show number of stocks per section	Thur Jan 13 1983 Index No.	Day's Change %	Est. Earnings Yield % (Max.)	Gross Div. Yield % (ACT at 30%)	Est. P/E Ratio (Net)	Wed Jan 12 Index No.	Tues Jan 11 Index No.	Mon Jan 10 Index No.	Fri Jan 7 Index No.	Year ago (approx.) Index No.
1 CAPITAL GOODS (208)	426.27	+0.4	9.37	4.03	13.28	424.64	430.08	440.00	444.90	351.14
2 Building Materials (24)	402.82	−0.4	10.45	4.67	11.52	404.52	416.68	426.30	426.76	299.95
3 Contracting, Construction (30)	726.71	+1.2	12.12	4.54	9.83	717.95	742.44	756.89	756.02	542.60
4 Electricals (32)	1653.79	+0.2	7.21	2.08	17.77	1651.26	1657.91	1708.10	1754.85	1205.68
5 Engineering, Contractors (10)	416.52	+0.6	17.03	7.48	7.20	413.85	423.03	435.42	439.14	504.57
6 Mechanical Engineering (66)	196.23	+1.4	12.30	6.03	9.95	193.61	195.33	198.11	197.45	190.30
8 Metals and Metal Forming (11)	159.10	+1.1	13.61	7.82	8.83	157.42	158.77	163.20	158.52	161.80
9 Motors (18)	78.96	+0.7	1.08	8.05	—	78.45	79.54	79.89	79.22	94.72
10 Other Industrial Materials (17)	365.73	+0.2	9.58	5.83	13.00	365.03	369.71	371.65	372.60	370.75
21 CONSUMER GROUP (201)	398.43	+0.8	10.46	4.42	11.58	395.44	401.74	411.03	416.68	269.35
22 Brewers and Distillers (23)	442.54	+0.9	11.40	4.82	10.71	438.48	444.15	453.40	455.95	261.83
25 Food Manufacturing (21)	333.69	+1.9	13.47	5.45	8.70	327.45	332.25	334.21	336.50	269.36
26 Food Retailing (14)	847.27	+1.2	7.39	2.79	16.99	837.36	856.54	878.73	893.33	555.85
27 Health and Household Products (8)	689.74	+0.5	5.72	2.64	20.75	686.09	689.34	694.22	708.16	351.23
29 Leisure (24)	451.89	—	9.38	5.13	13.57	451.80	459.83	471.75	477.01	410.50
32 Newspapers, Publishing (13)	652.04	+0.1	9.71	4.97	12.98	651.24	657.20	654.53	653.34	472.39
33 Packaging and Paper (14)	147.27	+0.9	14.88	7.61	7.95	145.91	147.46	150.48	150.63	132.54
34 Stores (47)	350.39	−0.5	8.67	3.91	15.23	352.22	361.31	378.45	384.99	243.86
35 Textiles (23)	176.83	−0.3	13.44	6.06	9.01	177.42	179.23	180.43	180.12	155.74
36 Tobaccos (3)	460.76	+3.0	19.04	6.01	5.80	447.20	453.01	463.10	477.62	257.58
39 Other Consumer (11)	341.19	−0.1	2.47	4.07	—	341.62	346.32	351.03	349.54	257.29
41 OTHER GROUPS (77)	290.98	+0.8	11.80	5.72	10.21	288.55	292.65	296.27	297.38	235.31
42 Chemicals (15)	381.92	+0.5	12.62	6.33	9.46	379.93	384.00	388.27	391.71	314.18
44 Office Equipment (5)	85.55	+2.4	16.02	8.63	7.67	83.54	85.31	87.35	89.03	117.88
45 Shipping and Transport (13)	535.50	+0.6	16.18	7.95	7.36	532.25	537.76	544.63	537.33	540.97
46 Miscellaneous (44)	413.48	+1.0	9.66	4.38	12.61	409.35	416.50	421.55	422.04	290.13
49 INDUSTRIAL GROUP (486)	393.76	+0.6	10.25	4.45	11.91	391.26	396.99	405.63	410.34	292.68
51 Oils (14)	742.61	+2.1	17.03	7.78	6.92	727.25	720.41	722.46	732.51	697.10
59 500 SHARE INDEX	422.73	+0.9	11.27	4.95	10.75	419.14	423.79	431.85	437.01	325.54
61 FINANCIAL GROUP (121)	273.21	+1.3	—	6.46	—	269.62	271.25	274.67	274.46	245.86
62 Banks(6)	285.15	+2.4	35.36	8.46	3.09	278.52	274.28	277.25	275.56	271.68
63 Discount Houses (8)	276.00	+0.6	—	8.58	—	274.44	277.59	288.01	293.82	212.85
65 Insurance (Life) (9)	337.46	+1.4	—	5.67	—	332.67	338.81	344.08	350.43	244.79
66 Insurance (Composite) (10)	185.17	+0.8	—	7.68	—	183.62	184.96	187.49	187.04	150.24
67 Insurance Brokers (7)	530.82	+1.4	12.11	5.14	11.47	523.38	528.49	531.62	530.18	418.19
68 Merchant Banks (13)	155.86	−0.2	—	5.54	—	156.14	156.59	158.28	156.55	149.19
69 Property (54)	412.26	+0.5	6.25	4.32	21.14	410.37	418.08	424.20	424.29	437.02
70 Other Financial (14)	195.69	+3.0	14.26	5.94	8.32	189.95	190.67	191.73	188.80	175.66
71 Investment Trusts (109)	383.66	+0.5	—	4.38	—	381.88	386.22	389.50	380.19	284.14
81 Mining Finance (4)	263.39	+0.5	7.79	5.40	17.18	261.96	267.85	263.53	262.04	218.25
91 Overseas Traders (16)	437.65	+1.8	11.41	8.27	11.57	429.82	425.86	417.28	406.76	404.00
99 ALL-SHARE INDEX (750)	386.90	+0.9	—	5.20	—	383.41	387.37	393.64	396.42	306.67

Source: *Financial Times*, 14 January 1983.

number of sub-indices, each dealing with a particular industry or sector, which aggregate to give the FT All-Share Index, and which allow benchmark portfolios to be created excluding certain sectors of the market. For example, if a fund under consideration is not permitted to invest in oils, the Industrial Group Index, containing 486 shares excluding oils, can be used as a benchmark.

Unlike the FT–Actuaries share indices, the FT 30 Shares Index cannot be held in practice. And yet, some investors compare their performance with this index. One problem with it is that poor performance shares are slow to be replaced, which tends to depress the index. Another, more important characteristic is that, since it is a geometric mean, it rises more slowly and falls more quickly than would an equivalent arithmetic average. Thus, a real-life portfolio will always appear to do better when compared with the FT 30 Shares Index than with the more suitable benchmark FT All-Share Index. Table A.2 illustrates this phenomenon with a simple example of unweighted arithmetic and geometric means of three shares over three years. The geometric mean is lower than the arithmetic mean in years 1 and 3.

Because of these characteristics, the FT 30 Shares Index should not be used either as a benchmark portfolio or as a means of determining betas. Its use should be confined to that of an indicator of market movements, in particular for industrial shares.

The FT All-Share Index and the comparable Standard & Poors 500 Index in the US are the indices used as surrogates for the UK and US markets both for calculating betas and as benchmark portfolios. Index funds also base their portfolios on the constituents of these indices.

Table A.2   *Comparison of arithmetic and geometric indices*

	Price		
	Year 1	*Year 2*	*Year 3*
Security *A*	120	100	120
B	30	100	300
C	110	100	110
Arithmetic mean	87	100	177
Geometric mean	73	100	158

FT–SE 100 Shares Index

The most recently developed index is the FT–SE 100 Index, designed to enable futures and options contracts to be based on the UK equity market. The FT–Actuaries All-Share Index was considered too large and too sluggish for such a purpose. The FT 30 Shares Index, although more active, suffers from the disadvantages of being a geometric index and from being biassed towards the manufacturing sector. The FT–SE 100 Index is a weighted arithmetic index of the top 100 (in terms of capitalisation) companies; it thus mirrors a real portfolio, includes both service and manufacturing companies, and is small enough to be calculated on a continuous basis.

Dividends

When calculating returns on indices, dividends usually have to be added to the index changes to give an overall return. This highlights a potential problem when comparing indices on an international basis, as may be done when considering an international investment portfolio (see Chapter 10). Indices usually represent only price changes and not dividends. If shares in different countries tend to follow different dividend policies, a comparison of the share indices will not give a true picture of either the relative capital gains or the relative holding period returns available in each country.

Problems

1. You are an investment analyst in the 'electricals' sector for the Cautious Assurance Company. You have been asked to prepare a report for the weekly investment meeting on ABCD Electronic, stating whether the holdings of this share in the various portfolios under the management of Cautious should be increased, maintained at their present level, or reduced.
   Describe
   (i) the information you would require to make a fundamental analysis of the company,
   (ii) how you would determine whether the share was of a 'buy', 'hold' or 'sell' type.

2. (i) To what extent does empirical evidence support the efficient markets hypothesis in its various forms?
   (ii) Discuss the implications of the EMH for stock market investment analysis.

3. Evaluate Value Line's ranking system for equity. Would you subscribe? Why or why not?

4. Describe a possible mechanical trading rule which you think might lead to possible excess returns. How would you test whether the market is efficient or inefficient with respect to your rule?

5. Mr Dither is undecided between two investment alternatives. His stockbroker has recommended that he invest £10,000 in a portfolio of nine shares and one gilt with an overall beta of 0.9. Mr Dither is also impressed with the Report and Accounts of an investment trust which has the same beta of 0.9. Discuss the advantages and disadvantages of each of these investment alternatives.

6. You have been asked to address a group of pension fund advisers and investment analysts on the subject of efficient markets. Outline the main points you would make.

7. An efficient market implies that the net present value of any security's future cash flow is *zero*, whatever its risk. And yet, finance managers of companies are expected to find *positive* NPV projects to invest in. Is there a contradiction here?

PART III

INTERNATIONAL INVESTMENT AND INVESTING INSTITUTIONS

International investment

Introduction

So far in this book we have restricted ourselves to securities issued in sterling by a UK company, UK institution or the British government. This emphasis is misleading, as we saw in Chapter 1, since over half the market value of securities quoted on the UK Stock Exchange is made up of overseas securities, quoted in London but not necessarily in pounds and pence. For example, IBM shares are quoted in US dollars and Deutsche Bank shares in German deutschemarks. However, opportunities for overseas investment are not restricted to these securities.

Investment can be made directly through overseas Stock Exchanges in such securities as US government bonds quoted on Wall Street or shares in Japanese companies quoted on the Tokyo Exchange.[1]

Also, indirect investment has long been available through the medium of investment trusts,[2] set up originally in the mid-nineteenth century to enable small investors to invest in such securities as South American railway stocks. In fact, even investment in UK company shares may represent a form of overseas investment, given the high proportion of foreign earnings of many UK companies, for example those in mining, such as RTZ, or overseas traders, such as Inchcape.

International investment in overseas securities, both direct and indirect, has become more attractive to UK resident[3] investors since the relaxation of exchange controls in 1979. From 1939 to 1979, investment in securities denominated in foreign currencies was strictly controlled by the Bank of England. The foreign currency needed for such investments had to be bought from a special pool of funds known as investment currency, and this pool was made up of the proceeds of sales of foreign currency investments by UK residents.[4] Thus, if the demand for foreign currency investment exceeded the supply from sales, the price of the investment currency would rise to a premium over the normal exchange rate, raising the cost of any investment in foreign currency securities. Although the proceeds from such international investment could be sold at the investment currency rate, the investor ran the risk not only of an adverse change in the exchange rate but also of an adverse change in the level of the premium. This was a real risk since the premium was as high as 80% during its life. In addition, a further penalty was imposed in the form of a requirement (introduced in 1965 and abolished in 1977) to sell 25% of the proceeds from any foreign currency investment at the normal exchange rate, without premium. This had the effect of reducing the return on investment of the international investor and of shrinking the pool of investment currency for future investors.[5]

These exchange control regulations naturally dampened investors' enthusiasm for foreign currency securities. Even investment trusts, whose rationale for existence had been a spread of international

---

[1] UK stockbrokers will deal with either kind of overseas investment although, for investment via overseas stock exchanges, transaction costs will be higher due to the increased number of intermediaries involved.

[2] For a more detailed discussion on investment trusts, see Chapter 11.

[3] UK investors who are subject to the rules of the Bank of England concerning overseas investment.

[4] In fact, the investment currency pool was always in dollars. If another currency was needed, say French francs, dollars could then be converted at the normal dollar/French franc exchange rate.

[5] If exchange rate changes reduced the value of the foreign currency or overseas investments fared badly, the investment currency pool would shrink anyway.

investments, reduced their holdings of overseas securities from 53% in market value terms of their total investments in 1938 to 32% in 1978. Their overseas investments were either financed by purchases of investment currency from the 'pool' or by foreign currency loans[6] when these were allowed by the Bank of England. Private investors, however, had no alternative but to use investment currency for their direct overseas investments.

Since 1979, the attitude to international investment has changed dramatically with the removal of the costs and complications of exchange control. Any foreign currency investment can now be financed with a straightforward foreign currency purchase. The present enthusiasm for international investment can be seen by examining the flow of funds of the major UK investing institutions.

Institutions such as pension funds may be constrained in their investment policy as to how much they can invest overseas (until recently by law in the case of local authority funds and by recommendation in the case of private sector funds) and, as will be mentioned in Chapter 11, pension fund liabilities are sterling liabilities. So, after an initial overseas surge, they will most probably maintain their overseas investment at around 10–15% of their portfolios. Other institutions, such as unit trusts or investment trusts, can be up to 100% invested overseas, enabling the investor to acquire a share in an internationally diversified portfolio. The investor can choose between investments such as Foreign and Colonial Investment Trust, with investments spread between UK, US and Japanese markets, a specialist unit trust such as Crescent Life Tokyo (100% invested in the Japanese market), or a fund specialising in the fairly new market of eurobonds such as JF Currency and Bond Fund.[7] Thus, he can invest directly or indirectly in specific overseas securities or specific overseas markets.

Despite the ease with which international investments can now be made, there are additional factors, such as exchange risk, not usually relevant when deciding on domestic security investment, which the investor must consider when making foreign currency investments. This chapter is designed to give an understanding of the additional risks and benefits of international as opposed to domestic investment as well as an explanation of the techniques required for any foreign currency investment.[8]

---

[6] For example, a 'back-to-back' loan which involved investment trust X lending sterling to the UK subsidiary of US company Y, and, in return, US company Y lending dollars to investment trust X in the US.

[7] See the appendix to this chapter for a description of eurobonds. Note that this type of fund is usually in the form of a unit trust but registered and managed overseas.

[8] Although this chapter, as does the whole of the book, concentrates on quoted securities, unquoted international investments can be made in the same way as sterling ones; for example, by putting money on deposit for three months with a clearing bank, not in sterling but in, say, deutschemarks.

The chapter begins with a discussion of the major factor which differentiates any foreign currency investment from a sterling investment – exchange risk. This derives from the effect of changes in exchange rates, which have become a dominant factor affecting returns on overseas securities as the major currencies have moved from a fixed to a floating exchange rate regime in recent years[9] and as the volatility of exchange rates has increased. (For example, during 1981, the end-of-month sterling/dollar exchange rate varied between £1 = $1.81 and £1 = $2.38.) The workings of the foreign exchange markets are then explained (in particular spot and forward exchange rates), and the ways of reducing exchange risk by hedging and matching are outlined. This leads to a discussion of the economic factors causing exchange rates to change and hence exchange risk to exist.

The next part of the chapter shows how the underlying concepts of portfolio theory, described in Chapter 7, have been extended to international investment decisions. It will be shown that any investor should hold, not just a domestically diversified portfolio, but an internationally diversified one. This holds true whether fixed interest securities or equities are being considered. The chapter concludes with a discussion of how to apply the techniques of portfolio theory to international investment in practice.

Exchange risk

What additional factors do we have to consider when making international investments, factors which do not have to be considered when investing in sterling securities issued by UK institutions?

Transaction costs, as mentioned earlier, may well be higher, as may the tax burden on any proceeds from the investment. For example, dividends paid on a US share owned by a UK resident are liable to both US and UK tax. However, most countries which allow foreign investors to buy their securities (and some do not[10]) have signed what is known as a double taxation treaty with the UK. Under these tax treaties, each government undertakes not to charge tax on such items as dividends paid to investors who will be liable to equivalent taxes in their own

---

[9] With a fixed exchange rate, the government of the country maintains its currency at a particular exchange rate against specified foreign currencies. When the level can no longer be maintained due to market pressure, a devaluation or revaluation takes place. With a floating exchange rate, the market determines the exchange rates of that currency with other currencies and these rates will constantly fluctuate.

[10] For example, before 1961 and during 1972–3, Japan restricted non-residents' purchases of Japanese quoted securities.

country. Despite these treaties the tax burden on an overseas investment may still be higher than on its UK equivalent for a UK investor.

A third factor to be considered when investing overseas is the risk
that, for political reasons, an overseas government may withhold
dividends, impose additional taxes or expropriate (for little or no
compensation) assets belonging to UK investors. Although unlikely to
happen in countries with a long history of political stability as, for
example, the US, an uprising in a country such as occurred in Iran in
1978 could lead to the nationalisation of companies and to the exprop-
riation of the assets of overseas shareholders.

Transaction costs, taxes and political risk can all be incorporated into
the estimate of the holding period return for any overseas security –
transaction costs and taxes directly by adjusting the cash flows and
political risk indirectly by altering the probability distribution of returns.
However, one other factor, which has a potentially much greater impact
on holding period return than do those already mentioned, must be
explicitly considered. This is the effect of changes in exchange rates,
known as exchange risk, on holding period return. An example will
illustrate the potential effect of exchange risk.

Suppose Mr Cook buys 100 shares in Travelog Inc., a US company,
for \$50 each[11] and holds them for one year. At the end of the year,
Travelog Inc. pays a dividend of \$5 per share and Mr Cook sells the
shares for \$60 each.

The holding period return on his dollar investment, $R_\$$, calculated on
each share, is then

$$R_\$ = \frac{60 + 5 - 50}{50}$$

$$R_\$ = 30\%$$

Mr Cook has had to buy dollars to make his investment in Travelog.
Also, since he wishes to spend the proceeds of his investment in the UK,
he will convert the dollars he receives back into pounds.

If the exchange rate at the time of purchase was £1 = \$2, the
investment in Travelog would have cost Mr Cook \$50/2 = £25 per share,
a total of £2,500. Let us now imagine two scenarios for the exchange
rate on disposal of the dollar proceeds. In the first, the exchange rate at
the end of the year is £1 = \$2.50; in the second, the exchange rate is £1 =
\$1.80.

---

[11] As can be seen from the *Financial Times*, shares in US companies (or stocks, as they are
known) trade at much higher prices per share than UK companies. Coupled with the fact
that brokers like to trade US shares in lots of 100, this reduces the attraction to the small
investor of direct investment in US shares.

The holding period return in sterling terms, $R_£$, will thus be:

Scenario (1)

$$\text{Cost of investment per share} = \textbf{£25}$$

$$\text{Proceeds per share} = \$60 + \$5$$

$$= £\frac{65}{2.50}$$

$$= \textbf{£26}$$

So

$$R_{£,1} = \frac{26 - 25}{25}$$

$$\textbf{R}_{£,1} = \textbf{4\%}$$

Scenario (2)

$$\text{Cost of investment per share} = \textbf{£25}$$

$$\text{Proceeds per share} = \$60 + \$5$$

$$= £\frac{65}{1.80}$$

$$= \textbf{£36.11}$$

So

$$R_{£,2} = \frac{36.11 - 25}{25}$$

$$\textbf{R}_{£,2} = \textbf{44\%}$$

The change in the exchange rate has had a dramatic impact on the return on investment on the Travelog shares. Whereas, for an American investor, the return would have been 30%, for Mr Cook, who invested sterling and required sterling in return, the return was either 4 or 44%. On any such dollar investment, the probability distribution of returns for Mr Cook will also be affected by exchange risk, involving greater risk than for a US investor.

This is true no matter what the original risk of the investment. If Mr Cook chose to invest in a UK gilt to maturity, his return would be certain in nominal terms. If, however, he invested in a US government bond, his sterling return in nominal terms would vary according to the exchange rate prevailing on the day he realised his investment and converted back to sterling. For example, suppose he bought a US government bond for \$960, with a nominal value of \$1,000 and a coupon of 6% maturing in exactly one year, when the interest will be paid. His dollar return would be

$$R_\$ = \frac{1000 + 60 - 960}{960}$$

$$R_\$ = 10.4\%$$

If the exchange rate on purchase was £1 = \$2, but on sale was £1 = \$2.50, that is, the dollar had depreciated in value against sterling (it took more dollars to buy £1), the sterling return $R_£$ would be

$$\text{Cost of investment} = \frac{\$960}{2} = \textbf{£480}$$

$$\text{Proceeds} = \frac{\$1060}{2.50} = \textbf{£424}$$

$$R_£ = \frac{424 - 480}{480}$$

$$= \frac{-56}{480}$$

$$R_£ = -11.7\%$$

The positive return in dollars would actually be a loss in sterling terms.

The problem of exchange risk is not as daunting as appears from the above examples, but, before we can discuss how exchange risk may be reduced, we need to know more about how the foreign exchange markets work, in particular the spot and forward markets.

Spot and forward exchange rates

The dollar/sterling exchange rates which we used in the examples were *spot* exchange rates, that is, the price paid today to receive a currency now (on the spot).[12] This is to differentiate from *forward* exchange rates

---

[12] In fact, delivery on a spot contract is two business days after the transaction is agreed.

which are prices *agreed* today for payment and delivery at some future date, say one, three or six months from now. Table 10.1 shows an extract from the *Financial Times* giving spot, one month forward and three months forward exchange rates for the major currencies – against sterling and against the dollar. Note that the exchange rates against sterling are in the form of how much £1 will buy in each foreign currency. For example, the sterling/dollar exchange rate is quoted in London, say at $2, that is, how many dollars £1 will buy. In other countries it is usual to quote how much of the domestic currency one unit of foreign currency will buy. For example, in France, an exchange rate for the dollar could be 6 FFr, meaning that $1 (foreign currency) will buy six French francs. The reason for the difference is that, before sterling was decimalised, it was difficult to express how much one US dollar or one French franc was worth in pounds, shillings and pence.

Table 10.1 Spot and forward exchange rates

THE POUND SPOT AND FORWARD

Aug 6	Day's spread	Close	One month	% p.a.	Three months	% p.a.
U.S.	1.7920-1.8090	1.7975-1.7985	0.82-0.92c dis	−5.81	2.20-2.30dis	−5.00
Canada	2.2240-2.2350	2.2265-2.2275	1.60-1.70c dis	−8.89	4.20-4.35dis	−7.68
Nethlnd.	5.02-5.06	5.02½-5.03½	¼c pm-¼ dis	—	1⅛-⅝ pm	0.69
Belgium	74.10-74.60	74.20-74.30	57-67c dis	−10.02	122-132 dis	−6.84
Denmark	14.25-14.31	14.26-14.27	3¼-4½ore dis	−3.26	10½-12¼ dis	−3.19
Ireland	1.2380-1.2455	1.2395-1.2415	0.24-0.38p dis	−3.00	0.81-0.95dis	−2.84
W. Ger.	4.52-4.56	4.53-4.54	⅝-⅛pf pm	0.99	1⅞-1⅜ pm	1.43
Portugal	119.20-120.20	119.80-120.00	70-145c dis	−10.76	200-375 dis	−9.59
Spain	180.00-181.00	180.55-180.75	85-120c dis	−6.81	225-265 dis	−5.42
Italy	2,236-2,247	2,239-2,241	30¼-32¼lire dis	−16.74	86-89 dis	−15.62
Norway	11.16-11.22	11.17½-11.18½	½ore pm-¾ dis	−0.13	1 pm-½ dis	0.09
France	10.78-10.84	10.79-10.80	5-6c dis	−6.11	16-17 dis	−6.11
Sweden	9.59-9.64	9.62½-9.63½	⅛-1⅛ore dis	−0.78	¾ pm-⅛ dis	0.13
Japan	430-438	431-432	2.25-1.95y pm	5.84	7.15-6.85 pm	6.49
Austria	31.80-32.00	31.88-31.93	6-1gro pm	1.32	12-2 pm	0.88
Switz.	3.92½-3.96½	3.93-3.94	1¾-1¼c pm	4.56	4½-4 pm	4.32

Belgian rate is for convertible francs. Financial franc 80.35-80.45. Six-month forward dollar 4.15-4.25c dis, 12-month 6.25-6.40c dis.

THE DOLLAR SPOT AND FORWARD

Aug 6	Day's spread	Close	One month	% p.a.	Three months	% p.a.
UK†	1.7920-1.8090	1.7975-1.7985	0.82-0.92c dis	−5.81	2.20-2.30dis	−5.00
Ireland†	1.4450-1.4560	1.4500-1.4520	0.30-0.40c dis	−2.90	0.75-0.85dis	−2.21
Canada	1.2348-1.2397	1.2385-1.2389	0.43-0.48c dis	−4.41	0.86-0.91dis	−2.86
Nethlnd.	2.7855-2.8055	2.7950-2.7980	1.39-1.29c pm	5.73	4.05-3.95 pm	5.71
Belgium	41.10-41.43	41.27-41.29	10-15c dis	−3.62	15-25 dis	−1.93
Denmark	7.8990-7.9550	7.9400-7.9450	1.80-1.55ore pm	2.53	3.65-3.15 pm	1.71
W. Ger.	2.5050-2.5280	2.5200-2.5210	1.46-1.40pf pm	6.81	4.04-3.98 pm	6.36
Portugal	66.30-66.85	66.60-66.80	10-40c dis	−4.49	30-120 dis	−4.49
Spain	100.13-100.55	100.38-100.44	20c pm-par	1.19	10pm-15dis	−0.10
Italy	1,243-1,247¼	1,245-1,246	11-12½ lire dis	−11.32	32-35 dis	−10.76
Norway	6.2060-6.2265	6.2150-6.2200	3.30-2.80ore pm	5.89	8.20-7.70 pm	5.11
France	5.9770-6.0300	6.0025-6.0075	0.20c pm-0.20 dis	—	1.30-1.90dis	−1.06
Sweden	5.3130-5.3500	5.3450-5.3500	1.85-1.65ore pm	3.93	6.30-6.10 pm	4.64
Japan	239.00-240.75	239.85-239.95	2.55-2.40y pm	12.38	7.20-7.05 pm	11.88
Austria	17.63-17.78	17.73½-17.74½	11-9½gro pm	6.93	28½-24½ pm	5.97
Switz.	2.1720-2.1970	2.1870-2.1880	1.94-1.84c pm	10.37	5.29-5.19 pm	9.58

† UK and Ireland are quoted in U.S. currency. Forward premiums and discounts apply to the U.S. dollar and not to the individual currency.

Source: *Financial Times*, 7 August 1981.

The rates quoted are the buying/selling spreads (known as bid/ask spreads). For example, from Table 10.1, a foreign exchange dealer would have sold, at close of business, 1.7975 dollars for £1, but would have required 1.7985 dollars per £1 if buying dollars.

The spot and forward exchange markets are not situated in one place as is the Stock Exchange. Dealers, mostly in banks, communicate with each other by telephone on an international basis. Individuals can deal in foreign currencies through their bank although the average sizes of transactions on the forward market are large. In the UK, a currency futures[13] market was established in 1982, where standard amounts of currency can be traded in *relatively* small amounts (for example, a sterling contract is for £25,000).[14] A similar market has existed in the US since 1972. However, both the forward and the futures currency markets are based on the same principles, discussed below.

Consistent exchange rates

Both the spot and forward markets in foreign exchange are efficient in the sense that any discrepancies in pricing which would allow arbitrage profits to be made are quickly adjusted. Any apparent anomalies are due to restrictions in trading, for example restrictions on the purchase or

Table 10.2   Consistent exchange rates*

(1)	**Spot**	
	Direct	£1 buys FFr 10.79
	Indirect	£1 buys $1.7975
	and	$1 buys FFr 6.0025
	so	£1 buys FFr (1.7975 × 6.0025) = FFr 10.79
(2)	**One month forward**	
	Direct	£1 buys FFr (10.79 + 0.05 disc) = FFr 10.84 forward
	Indirect	£1 buys $(1.7975 + 0.0082 disc) = $1.8057 forward
	and	$1 buys FFr (6.0025 − 0.0020 pm) = FFr 6.0005 forward
	so	£1 buys FFr (1.8057 × 6.0005) = FFr 10.84 forward

* All rates used are those at close of business and the bid or ask rate is used, whichever is relevant.[15]

---

[13] See Chapter 2, pp. 57 and footnote 18 for a discussion of the differences between forward and futures markets.

[14] For further details of the currency futures contracts traded in the UK, see the information published by the London International Financial Futures Exchange.

[15] For all examples in this chapter.

sale of a particular currency or the lack of an active market in the currency.

So, exchange rates are consistent. In other words, it costs the same to buy French francs directly with sterling as it does to buy French francs indirectly through the dollar. Table 10.2 shows this for both spot and one month forward rates, using the close of business exchange rates given in Table 10.1.

As you can see from the table, a forward rate is quoted at a premium or a discount on the relevant spot rate. For example, the French franc is quoted in Table 10.1 at a forward *discount* to sterling, implying that the French franc is worth less relative to sterling on the forward market than on the spot. To calculate the forward rate, the relevant (bid or ask) discount must be *added* to the spot rate. So the FFr 10.84 to £1 forward rate shows the French franc to be worth less than on the spot market where it is FFr 10.79 to £1.[16] In the case of a premium, as exists for the French franc relative to the dollar in Table 10.1, this must be *subtracted* from the spot rate. This rule cannot be applied in every country since it depends on how exchange rates are quoted; the way exchange rates are quoted in the UK is different from, say, the method employed in Belgium.

Hedging exchange risk

The existence of forward markets in foreign currencies allows exchange risk to be hedged, exactly as the risk of changes in commodity prices or interest rates can be hedged. A UK importer due to pay for goods in dollars in, say, one month's time, can fix *now* the amount he will have to pay in sterling terms by buying the dollars forward. Suppose he owes $150,000. He could buy dollars forward, assuming the rates are as in Table 10.1, at a one month forward rate of £1 = $(1.7975 + 0.0082) = $1.8057. In other words, he has contracted now to pay £(150,000/1.8057) = £83,070 in one month's time for dollars to be received at that time which he will immediately use to pay his dollar invoice. Similarly, a UK exporter, due to receive payment in dollars, might sell dollars forward to fix his proceeds in sterling terms.

---

[16] The figures in brackets next to the forward rates in Table 10.1 show the appreciation or depreciation of forward rates relative to spot rates on an annualised basis. For example, the *average* one month forward depreciation of the dollar relative to sterling of $0.0087/1.7980 or 0.484% is multiplied by 12 to give 5.81%.

Hedging exchange risk on equity investment

As we saw earlier, not only traders but also international investors are subject to exchange risk. How can they use the forward markets to hedge exchange risk? Could Mr Cook have eliminated exchange risk and fixed his return on Travelog Inc. shares in sterling terms?

Investment in equities is risky because of the uncertainty of income to be received from the investment. Every such investment has a probability distribution of returns, with one return being the mean or expected return from the investment. The best that Mr Cook could do, without the advantage of perfect foresight, would be to hedge the *expected* return on his Travelog shares. Suppose he had expected the dividend to be $5 per share and the share price on sale $55 per share. He could have financed the cost of $50 per share by buying dollars spot and fixed the expected proceeds in sterling terms by selling $60 per share twelve months forward. If the current spot rate for buying dollars was £1 = $2 and the twelve month forward rate for selling dollars was £1 = $2.10, Mr Cook could have fixed his *expected* return in sterling terms.

Cost of investment per share   **£25**

Expected proceeds per share = $55 + $5

$$= \frac{£60}{2.10}$$

$$= £28.57$$

Expected sterling
return on investment $E(R_£) = \dfrac{28.57 - 25}{25}$

$$E(R_£) = \textbf{14.3\%}$$

However, suppose the *actual* dollars received at the end of the year were $5 per share dividend and $60 per share (ex div), a total of $65. Mr Cook only sold $60 forward and so would have to sell the remaining $5 at the prevailing sterling/dollar exchange rate. Only if his *actual* return in dollar terms had equalled his *expected* return would he have completely eliminated exchange risk.

In practice, it is even more difficult to use the forward market to hedge exchange risk on risky foreign currency investment. The investment may be held for more than twelve months (usually the longest period for which forward rates are quoted), dividends may be received periodically involving a series of forward contracts, and the series of cash flows involved may not be large enough to be able to use the forward market at all.

An alternative method of hedging exchange risk is to borrow the currency in which the desired security is denominated. In Mr Cook's case, he would borrow dollars to buy Travelog shares. This method of hedging risk (already discussed in Chapter 2) is known as 'matching',[17] since Mr Cook is matching the currency and holding period of his asset (the shares) to the currency and maturity of the liability (the debt). Suppose Mr Cook borrowed dollars. To minimise exchange risk, he would borrow sufficient so that, after interest, his debt would equal the expected proceeds from the Travelog shares. Mr Cook expects to get $5 dividend per share and $55 per share on sale, totalling $6,000 for 100 shares. If the interest payable on the loan is 10%, Mr Cook can borrow x, where

$$x(1 + 0.10) = \$6,000$$

$$x = \$5,454^{18}$$

At the end of the year, Mr Cook would simply use the proceeds of the Travelog investment to repay the loan (plus interest). Having borrowed $5,454, Mr Cook would owe $6,000 (including interest). The proceeds from the Travelog shares actually turn out to be $6,500, so that the $500 not expected would have to be sold at the prevailing sterling/dollar exchange rate. As with hedging a risky investment in the forward market, Mr Cook bears exchange risk to the extent that the *actual* proceeds of the investment in Travelog shares are not equal to the *expected* amount of $6,000.

Hedging exchange risk on investment in fixed interest securities

Although investment in most types of risky foreign currency securities cannot be fully hedged against exchange risk, investment in some fixed interest securities held until maturity, or money placed on fixed interest deposit, can be fully hedged. The necessary conditions are that the term

---

[17] The system of 'back-to-back' loans used when exchange controls were in force (see footnote 6) is a form of matching.

[18] This example ignores the problems of what Mr Cook will do with the dollars and the different *risks* of the loan and the shares.

Table 10.3   Eurocurrency interest rates

EURO-CURRENCY INTEREST RATES (Market closing Rates)

Aug. 6	Sterling	U.S. Dollar	Canadian Dollar	Dutch Guilder	Swiss Franc	West German Mark	French Franc	Italian Lira	Belgian Franc Convertible	Japanese Yen
Short term	$11\frac{7}{8}$-$12\frac{1}{8}$	$18\frac{3}{4}$-19	21-23	$13\frac{5}{8}$-$13\frac{5}{8}$	$5\frac{1}{2}$-$6\frac{1}{2}$	$11\frac{7}{8}$-12	$17\frac{1}{2}$-$18\frac{1}{2}$	19-22	17-19	$6\frac{1}{4}$-$6\frac{3}{4}$
7 days' notice	$12\frac{1}{2}$-$12\frac{3}{4}$	$18\frac{7}{8}$-$19\frac{1}{8}$	21-23	13-$13\frac{1}{4}$	$4\frac{1}{2}$-5	12-$12\frac{1}{8}$	$17\frac{1}{2}$-$18\frac{1}{2}$	$29\frac{1}{2}$-$33\frac{1}{2}$	25-$31\frac{1}{2}$	$6\frac{1}{2}$-7
Month	$13\frac{7}{8}$-$13\frac{5}{8}$	19-$19\frac{1}{4}$	22-$22\frac{5}{8}$	$13\frac{3}{8}$-$13\frac{5}{8}$	$8\frac{3}{4}$-$8\frac{7}{8}$	$12\frac{1}{4}$-$12\frac{3}{8}$	19-$19\frac{3}{4}$	30-$31\frac{1}{2}$	$25\frac{1}{2}$-28	7-$7\frac{1}{4}$
Three months	$14\frac{1}{4}$-$14\frac{7}{8}$	19-$19\frac{1}{4}$	$21\frac{1}{2}$-$21\frac{7}{8}$	$13\frac{3}{8}$-$13\frac{5}{8}$	$9\frac{1}{4}$-$9\frac{3}{8}$	$12\frac{1}{2}$-$12\frac{5}{8}$	$19\frac{3}{4}$-$20\frac{1}{2}$	30-$31\frac{1}{2}$	22-$23\frac{1}{4}$	$7\frac{1}{4}$-$7\frac{1}{2}$
Six months	$14\frac{1}{4}$-$14\frac{7}{8}$	19-$19\frac{1}{4}$	$20\frac{7}{8}$-$21\frac{1}{4}$	$12\frac{3}{4}$-$12\frac{7}{8}$	$9\frac{3}{8}$-$9\frac{7}{8}$	$12\frac{5}{8}$-$12\frac{7}{8}$	$19\frac{3}{4}$-$20\frac{1}{2}$	30-31	$20\frac{5}{8}$-$21\frac{5}{8}$	$7\frac{3}{8}$-$7\frac{5}{8}$
One Year	$14\frac{5}{8}$-$14\frac{7}{8}$	18-$18\frac{1}{4}$	$19\frac{7}{8}$-$20\frac{1}{4}$	$12\frac{3}{4}$-$12\frac{7}{8}$	$9\frac{1}{8}$-$9\frac{3}{8}$	$12\frac{7}{16}$-$12\frac{7}{8}$	$19\frac{3}{4}$-$20\frac{1}{2}$	$28\frac{1}{2}$-$29\frac{1}{2}$	$18\frac{1}{4}$-$19\frac{1}{2}$	8-$8\frac{1}{4}$

SDR linked deposits: one-month $15\frac{11}{16}$-$16\frac{1}{16}$ per cent; three-months $15\frac{13}{16}$-$16\frac{1}{16}$ per cent; six-months $15\frac{13}{16}$-$16\frac{5}{16}$ per cent; one-year $15\frac{1}{2}$-$15\frac{7}{8}$ per cent.
ECU linked deposits: one-month $15\frac{3}{4}$-$16\frac{3}{8}$ per cent; three-months $16\frac{1}{4}$-$16\frac{5}{8}$ per cent; six-months $16\frac{1}{4}$-$16\frac{5}{8}$ per cent; one-year $15\frac{11}{16}$-$16\frac{5}{16}$ per cent.
Asian $ (closing rates in Singapore): one-month $19\frac{3}{8}$-$19\frac{1}{4}$ per cent; three-months $19\frac{1}{16}$-$19\frac{11}{16}$ per cent; six-months $18\frac{7}{8}$-19 per cent; one-year $18\frac{1}{8}$-$18\frac{1}{4}$ per cent.
Long-term Eurodollar two-years 17-$17\frac{1}{4}$ per cent; three-years $16\frac{3}{4}$-$17\frac{1}{4}$ per cent; four-years $16\frac{3}{4}$-$16\frac{7}{8}$ per cent; five-years $16\frac{1}{2}$-$16\frac{1}{4}$ per cent; nominal closing rates.
The following nominal rates were quoted for London dollar certificates of deposit; one-month 18.55-18.65 per cent; three-months 18.45-18.55 per cent; six-months 18.30-18.40 per cent; one-year 17.55-17.65 per cent.

Source: *Financial Times*, 7 August 1981.

of the security or deposit is equivalent to a period available on the forward or futures market (say one, three or six months) or the maturity available on a matching loan, and that the proceeds of the investment at maturity are certain in nominal terms.

Let us consider the example of money placed on deposit in eurodollars for one month. (For a brief description of eurodollars and eurocurrency, see the appendix to this chapter.) All eurocurrency interest rates are given in annual equivalents, for comparative purposes. However, they are the simple multiples of, say, the relevant one month rate. So, to calculate the actual interest payable on a one month deposit, the annual interest rate given should be divided by 12. Table 10.3 gives an extract from the *Financial Times* of the same day as the exchange rates in Table 10.1, showing eurocurrency rates for deposits and loans with terms of up to one year in the major eurocurrencies.

Table 10.4   Hedging of exchange risk on fixed interest investment

---

Investment = £100,000

(1) **Use £100,000 to purchase dollars on spot market**

£1 at $1.7975 gives **$179,750**

(2) **Place dollars on one month eurodeposit**

One month eurodollar rate 19% pa equivalent to $19/12\%$

	= **1.583%** for one month
Proceeds at end of one month	= $179,750 (1.01583)
	= **$182,595**

(3) **Sell dollar proceeds forward**

One month forward rate for sale of dollars

	= $(1.7985 + 0.0092)$
	= **$1.8077**
Sterling proceeds of investment	$= \dfrac{£182,595}{\$/£1.8077}$
	= **£101,010**

(4) **Calculate holding period return**

$$R_£ = \frac{101,010 - 100,000}{100,000}$$

$R_£$ = **1.0%**

We use the example of a one month eurodollar deposit to show how a fixed interest investment can be completely hedged against exchange risk. To do this, a UK investor will purchase dollars on the spot market, place them in a one month eurodollar deposit with a fixed interest rate and sell forward the known dollar proceeds on the one month forward market. We use the data in Tables 10.1 and 10.3 and suppose that £100,000 is invested. Table 10.4 shows how the investor can achieve a certain *sterling* return of 1% despite having made a foreign currency investment.

Interest rate parity

In Table 10.4, we have shown that the investor, using the eurocurrency and forward currency markets could ensure a completely certain *sterling* holding period return, in this case 1%, from a short-term, fixed interest dollar investment. As a result, he should be indifferent between investing in this way in eurodollars and investing in eurosterling, which will also give him a certain sterling holding period return. We can check this from Table 10.3. If the investor had instead placed his money on eurosterling deposit for one month, Table 10.3 tells us that he would have been given interest of 13$\frac{9}{16}$% per annum, equivalent to 13$\frac{9}{16}$%/12 or 1.130% for one month. Thus, his one month return would have been the same[19] (1%) whether he invested his £100,000 in eurodollars and sold forward (as in Table 10.4) or simply invested it in eurosterling.

This phenomenon of equal returns from equal risk, *hedged* investments in different currencies is known as *interest rate parity*. In a perfect world, interest rate parity would always hold since, if investors could obtain different returns from investing fully hedged in different currencies, they would arbitrage the differences away[20]. Interest rate parity does hold in the eurocurrency markets and in fact, forward exchange rates are determined by comparing interest rate differentials. We can derive the interest rate parity formula as follows:

If the investor places £Y on eurosterling deposit he will earn interest of $R_£$, say, yielding

$$Y (1 + R_£) \tag{A}$$

---

[19] The returns in this example are not *exactly* the same, the difference being £120 or 0.12% of the investment. This difference would be absorbed in transaction costs.

[20] This type of arbitrage, using the forward currency markets and the money markets, is called 'covered interest arbitrage'.

If he buys dollars spot, he will receive

$$Y(X_0)$$

where X_0 is the spot exchange rate.

If he places these dollars on eurodollar deposit for the same period at $R_\$$ interest and sells forward the proceeds at X_f (the forward exchange rate), he will get

$$\frac{Y(X_0)(1 + R_\$)}{X_f} \qquad\qquad (B)$$

Interest rate parity says that the returns from these two equal risk strategies must be equal, so that (A) must equal (B).
    Thus,

$$Y(1 + R_£) = Y\frac{(X_0)(1 + R_\$)}{X_f}$$

Y cancels out and rearranging gives

$$\frac{X_f}{X_0} = \frac{1 + R_\$}{1 + R_£} \qquad\qquad (10.1)$$

Forward exchange dealers can use equation (10.1) to set forward rates. For example, if the spot dollar/sterling exchange rate is £1 = $2, and the eurodollar and eurosterling one year interest rates are 15 and 10% respectively, the twelve month forward rate must be

$$\frac{X_f}{2} = \frac{1.15}{1.10}$$

$X_f = \$2.09/£$

Interest rate parity will always hold when currency forward markets and money markets are efficient. Because eurocurrency markets are free, unregulated markets, interest rate parity does hold for the major currencies in the eurocurrency markets as we saw in Table 10.4. However, interest rate parity does not necessarily hold with other types of fixed interest investment which have returns certain in nominal terms (such as UK and US Treasury Bills) or with less internationally traded currencies, since exchange controls, taxes and other government intervention may prevent investors from arbitraging away any differences in return.

The fundamentals of exchange risk

We have seen that the major additional problem in making foreign currency as opposed to sterling investments appears to be that of exchange risk. Although for certain types of short-term, fixed interest investments, exchange risk can be fully hedged, most types of investment in risky foreign currency investments can only be partly hedged against exchange risk, if at all.

Forecasting future exchange rates

Exchange risk is the risk that exchange rates will change and adversely affect the expected sterling return on investments. Of course, if future exchange rates could be perfectly forecast by the investor, exchange risk would no longer be such a problem. He would be able to calculate his expected sterling returns, allowing for forecast changes in exchange rates, and choose those investments which offered him his preferred risk and return characteristics. There are two potential sources of forecasts of future exchange rates. Firstly, and more simply, there may be market consensus forecasts and, secondly, forecasts can be obtained from studying the fundamental causes of changes in exchange rates (presumably the basis for any market forecasts).

In Chapter 4, when analysing fixed interest securities, we found that forward interest rates implicit in the spot interest rate term structure could be used to forecast future spot interest rates. In the simplest case, the expectations hypothesis stated that forward interest rates were the market's best estimates of future spot rates. This leads to the question of whether, in the foreign exchange markets, forward exchange rates are the best market estimates of future spot exchange rates. Can Mr Cook or any investor in foreign currency securities use forward rates to forecast expected future exchange rates?

The empirical evidence appears to show that, on average, forward exchange rates are unbiased estimates of future exchange rates.[21] In other words, the expectations hypothesis holds for exchange rates. Unlike forward interest rates, which appear to include a liquidity or inflation premium in their estimates of future spot interest rates, there seems to be no premium to pay for the use of forward markets to hedge exchange risk. Forward exchange rates represent the market's best estimates of future spot rates, without any adjustment needed for a

<hr>

[21] See, for example, Aliber (1974), Giddy and Dufey (1975), Bilson (1976), Bilson and Levich (1977), Levich (1977) and Stockman (1978).

charge for allowing investors and traders to hedge. The only additional cost to Mr Cook of hedging is the slightly wider bid/ask spreads he has to pay in the forward market. For example, the spread on the close of business one month forward sterling/dollar exchange rate in Table 10.1 on p. 294 is $1.7975 + 0.0082 to $1.7985 + 0.0092, equivalent to 0.2 cents, compared with $1.7975 to $1.7985, or 0.1 cents, for the one month sterling/dollar spot exchange rate.

Having established that there is no bias in the forward exchange rate estimates of future spot exchange rates, the next question to ask is how good these estimates are. If they are perfect estimates, forward rates will provide the investor with the future exchange rates needed to estimate holding period returns and to make investment decisions. Unfortunately, forward rates are in practice fairly poor predictors of future exchange rates and economic forecasting models appear no better at forecasting than the market-determined forward rates.[22] The factors influencing exchange rate changes are complex and, as yet, inadequately understood. So, Mr Cook does take on exchange risk if he cannot or does not hedge.

However, exchange risk is not as great as it seems. Although there is no exact understanding of how exchange rates change, there are certain relationships between exchange rates, interest rates and inflation rates which ought to hold in a world where there were no barriers to trade or investment and which do hold to a lesser extent in the real world. Using these relationships, we can predict in broad terms what will happen in the long run to exchange rates, although shorter run movements are more difficult to forecast.

Purchasing power parity theory

The first of these relationships is known as the purchasing power parity theory, derived from the law of one price. If a product is freely internationally traded, with negligible transportation costs, the law of one price says that the product should be traded for the same price everywhere. For example, if a microchip sells for $1 in the US and 50p in the UK, then $1 must be worth 50p and $2 worth £1. The purchasing power parity theory, PPPT for short, extends the law of one price to overall price levels in each country, measured, for example, by a retail prices index. The PPPT is usually expressed in terms of *changes* in exchange rates, and says that, given the assumption of free international

---

[22] See ch. 5 of Levich and Wihlborg (1980).

trade, the change in an exchange rate over a period will be equal to the relative change in inflation rates of the two countries concerned.

This can be written as

$$\frac{X_1}{X_0} = \frac{P_{f1}/P_{f0}}{P_{d1}/P_{d0}} = \frac{1 + \textit{infl}_f}{1 + \textit{infl}_d} \tag{10.2}$$

where X_0 is the exchange rate at the beginning of the period and X_1 the exchange rate at the end of the period; the P_f and P_d are the price levels in the foreign country and domestic country respectively, and the $\textit{infl}_f$ and $\textit{infl}_d$ their equivalent inflation rates during the period. For example, suppose inflation over a period is 15% in the UK and 5% in the US, with the exchange rate at the beginning of the period $2 = £1.

We know that

$$P_{f1}/P_{f0} = 1 + \textit{infl}_f = 1.05$$

$$P_{d1}/P_{d0} = 1 + \textit{infl}_d = 1.15$$

$$X_0 = 2$$

PPPT says that the exchange rate will adjust over the period to give

$$\frac{X_1}{2} = \frac{1.05}{1.15}$$

So,

$$X_1 = 1.83$$

In other words, the pound would be expected to depreciate against the dollar to £1 = $1.83, reflecting its relatively reduced purchasing power.

PPPT cannot hold exactly as in equation (10.2) since not all goods included in a general measure of inflation are internationally traded. Also, such factors as transportation costs, time lags in price adjustments, government controls and taxes on international trade mean that, although exchange rate changes may in the *long* run be expected to reflect relative changes in purchasing power parity, the PPPT relationship cannot be used for accurate short-run forecasts of future exchange rates.

International Fisher effect

The PPPT is concerned with the connection between inflation and exchange rates. However, we saw in Chapter 2 that inflation also affects interest rates, with Fisher postulating that interest rates fully take account of *expected* (as opposed to *actual*) inflation. Fisher suggested an expression relating the nominal interest rate, R, and the real interest rate, r, as follows:

$$(1 + R) = (1 + r)(1 + E(infl)) \qquad (10.3)$$

where $E(infl)$ is the inflation rate expected over the period.

The second fundamental relationship concerning exchange rate changes is the extension of equation (10.3) to an international context, sometimes referred to as the International Fisher effect. If the expression holds in each national financial market, there will be a real interest rate in each currency. If investors can freely choose in which currency to invest their money, this real interest rate must be the same everywhere, otherwise investors would arbitrage the differences away. If we consider the US dollar and sterling, for example, we can write equation (10.3) for each of them:

$$(1 + R_£) = (1 + r_£)(1 + E(infl_£)) \qquad (10.3a)$$

$$(1 + R_\$) = (1 + r_\$)(1 + E(infl_\$)) \qquad (10.3b)$$

If the real interest rate in dollar terms is equal to the real interest rate available in sterling, we must have

$$1 + r_£ = 1 + r_\$$$

So,

$$\frac{1 + R_£}{1 + E(infl_£)} = \frac{1 + R_\$}{1 + E(infl_\$)} \qquad (10.4)$$

Rearranging equation (10.3) and subtracting 1 from each side, we get

$$\frac{R_\$ - R_£}{1 + R_£} = \frac{E(infl_\$ - infl_£)}{1 + E(infl_£)} \qquad (10.5)$$

Both equations (10.4) and (10.5) are different ways of expressing the International Fisher effect. Let us, as before, suppose that inflation is expected to be 15% in the UK and 5% in the US. If nominal interest rates in the UK are 20%, we can use equation (10.5), or (10.4), to derive the level of nominal interest rates in the US

$$\frac{R_\$ - 0.20}{1 + 0.20} = \frac{0.05 - 0.15}{1 + 0.15}$$

Rearranging,

$$R_\$ = 0.20 + \frac{(1 + 0.20)\ (-0.10)}{1 + 0.15}$$

$$R_\$ = 9.6\%$$

Interest rates will be lower in the US, because of the lower rate of expected inflation. In both countries, however, the *real* interest rate will be the same:

$$(1 + r_\$)\ (1 + 0.05) = (1 + 0.096)$$

$$r_\$ = 4.3\%$$

$$(1 + r_£)\ (1 + 0.15) = (1 + 0.20)$$

$$r_£ = 4.3\%$$

The assumptions underlying the existence of a single real interest rate world-wide include, as for PPPT, that of completely free international trade, this time in interest-bearing securities. However, interest rates are often manipulated by governments as part of their economic policies and, as mentioned earlier, foreign investors may not be allowed to hold fixed interest government securities, or may be taxed more highly than domestic investors. The Fisher relationship between expected inflation and interest rates is most likely to hold in the eurocurrency market, where interest rates are not directly government-influenced. Studies of how interest rates and *actual*[23] inflation rates are related in the eurocurrency markets do show that higher interest rate currencies do experience higher inflation. However, netting out actual inflation does not give the same real rate for each eurocurrency. As with PPPT, there are too many barriers and costs to international investment for capital markets to be totally integrated and for all to offer the same real interest rate.

---

[23] Actual inflation is usually used as a surrogate for expected inflation which is more difficult to measure. See, for example, Alamouti (1979) for further details of this work.

Exchange risk with PPT and International Fisher

If these two fundamental relationships, PPPT and International Fisher, did hold, the international investor would not need to concern himself with exchange risk; there would be no *additional* risk to international as opposed to domestic investment.[24] Table 10.5 shows how, if these relationships did hold, Mr Cook would achieve the same sterling return, without hedging, whether he invested in a sterling eurobond with one year to redemption or an equivalent dollar eurobond with the same maturity.

Unfortunately, neither of these fundamental relationships holds in the real world exactly as in Table 10.5, although exchange rates do, to some extent and in the long run, adjust for differences in inflation and nominal interest rates, and so exchange risk remains a factor to be considered when investing in foreign currency securities. As we have seen, hedging on the forward market or borrowing in the currency of the investment can provide a solution to the problem of exchange risk when investing in fixed interest government securities but these techniques only provide a partial solution to the problem of exchange risk for risky investment.

Advantages of exchange risk

However, exchange risk may not be such a disadvantage to international investment as now appears. For example, although there are barriers and costs to international investment, there will be many instances when the two fundamental relationships do hold to a certain extent. In such cases, the correlation between exchange risk and returns will be negative. These instances will occur more often in the case of fixed interest securities than in the case of equities since interest rates and levels of inflation are more directly reflected in fixed interest security returns than in the returns on company shares which are affected by many other factors. For example, if the UK experiences high inflation and high nominal returns relative to the US, the pound will eventually depreciate against the dollar. Thus, differences in nominal returns will be counterbalanced by a change in the exchange rate, reducing variability on *real* returns. In other words, the more the International Fisher effect holds, the closer together will be all risk-free interest rates. The investor may receive very different nominal returns in sterling or dollar fixed interest investments, but his real returns will be similar. The

---

[24] Ignoring political risk and any differentiation between foreign and domestic investors. Of course the fundamental riskiness of the investment (which may vary between countries) will still exist.

Table 10.5   International investment without exchange risk

Suppose PPPT and International Fisher hold

Assumptions

Current exchange rate $X_0 = \$2$

Real interest rate on eurobonds $= 2\%$

Expected inflation, 15% in UK, 5% in US

PPPT gives

$$\frac{X_1}{2} = \frac{1.05}{1.15}$$

where X_1 = year-end exchange rate

$$X_1 = \$1.826$$

International Fisher gives the nominal interest rates which will prevail on sterling and dollar eurobonds, $R_£$ and $R_\$$

In the US

$$(1.02)\,(1.05) = |(1 + R_\$)$$
$$R_\$ = 7.1\%$$

where $R_\$$ = nominal return on dollar bond

In the UK

$$(1.02)\,(1.15) = (1 + R_£)$$
$$R_£ = 17.3\%$$

where $R_£$ = nominal return on sterling bond

Sterling eurobond

The return, $R_£$, on the sterling eurobond will be 17.3%
£100 invested at 17.3% gives **£117.30**

Dollar eurobond

The return, $R_\$$, on the dollar eurobond will be 7.1%
The current spot exchange rate is $2 = £1
The year-end exchange rate will be $1.826 = £1
So, £100 converted at $2 gives $200
$200 invested at 7.1% gives $214.20
$214.20 converted at $1.826 gives **£117.30**

investor can then decide whether to hedge against exchange risk and ensure a certain *nominal* return in sterling or whether to remain unhedged and reduce variation in his overall *real* sterling return.

Alternatively, the changes in exchange rates could be independent of security returns; in other words, there would be zero correlation between returns on securities and changes in exchange rates. This is more likely to hold true for returns on equities. If this is the case, the second method of reducing risk without sacrificing return discussed in Chapter 2 can be employed, namely diversification. If equities in a number of different currencies are held, the risk of one currency depreciating against sterling will be balanced by another's appreciation against sterling and exchange risk will be diversified away.

Consequently, exchange risk is only an additional risk to international investment if it is strongly positively correlated with security returns. Given the above, this is unlikely and thus exchange risk can effectively be an advantage to international investment, leading to the conclusion that overseas investments need not always be hedged.

International diversification

Having considered exchange risk, we are now free to examine whether international investment is in fact worthwhile, in terms of risk and return. Should the UK investor add foreign currency securities to his portfolio, and if so, which securities should he consider?

Portfolio theory

We saw in Chapter 7 that the investor is not only concerned with the expected return and standard deviation of each security, but also with its impact on the overall risk and return of his existing portfolio, measured by its correlation coefficient with the other securities held. This portfolio theory approach can be used in exactly the same way to examine the impact of adding overseas securities to a domestic portfolio. Table 10.6 gives the correlation coefficients between stock market returns, expressed in sterling terms, of thirteen major stock markets for the period 1972–9. The returns, calculated monthly, allow for changes in exchange rates and therefore include exchange risk.

In Figure 7.9 on p. 221, we saw that a naïve diversification policy on UK equities could reduce the risk of a portfolio to around 30% of the

Table 10.6 Correlation coefficients between returns on various stock markets, 1972–9

Country	Austr	Belgm	Canda	Denmk	Franc	Germy	Italy	Japan	Neths	S.A.	Switz	UK	US
Australia		.43	.54	.11	.36	.28	.31	.25	.26	.32	.45	.35	.57
Belgium	.43		.39	.29	.43	.61	.33	.46	.60	.16	.62	.38	.47
Canada	.54	.39		.05	.27	.18	.03	.27	.20	.30	.33	.25	.67
Denmark	.11	.29	.05		.08	.21	-.10	.09	.33	.13	.29	.12	.22
France	.36	.43	.27	.08		.32	.24	.18	.23	.08	.42	.37	.34
Germany	.28	.61	.18	.21	.32		.17	.39	.60	.18	.60	.20	.29
Italy	.31	.33	.03	-.10	.24	.17		.18	.10	.17	.31	.27	.10
Japan	.25	.46	.27	.09	.18	.39	.18		.42	.05	.32	.11	.26
Netherlands	.26	.60	.20	.33	.23	.60	.10	.42		.21	.53	.03	.30
South Africa	.32	.16	.30	.13	.08	.18	.17	.05	.21		.22	-.09	.32
Switzerland	.45	.62	.33	.29	.42	.60	.31	.32	.53	.22		.36	.47
United Kingdom	.35	.38	.25	.12	.37	.20	.27	.11	.03	-.09	.36		.35
United States	.57	.47	.67	.22	.34	.29	.10	.26	.30	.32	.47	.35	

Source: Dimson, Hodges and Marsh (1980).

average risk of holding one share. Risk could not be reduced much below this figure because it represented the systematic, undiversifiable risk of the UK stock market. Figure 10.1 shows the effect on risk of a naïve (by country) international diversification policy, compared to simply holding a UK stock market index. Risk can be reduced to a variability (standard deviation) of around 12% compared with 29% for the UK market as a whole, simply by investing equal proportions of the portfolio in the thirteen stock market indices used in Table 10.6.

The extent of the benefit of international diversification will vary according to the diversification potential of the investor's own stock market. For example, the risk of the German stock market has been found to be 44% of the average risk of holding one German share, whereas the comparable figure for the US is 27%.[25] US market risk is lower because the US stock market is larger and offers greater diversification opportunities than its German or UK counterpart. Thus, the German investor would benefit more than the US investor from international diversification. This is one reason why European investors in general have a greater international content in their investment portfolios and why US investors have only recently begun to take an interest in the opportunities offered by investment in foreign currency securities.

Investors in each country will also be faced with different correlation coefficients in Table 10.6. Returns for US investors would be calculated in dollars and returns for German investors in deutschemarks, and so correlation coefficients will vary according to the base currency used. This would lead one to expect investors in different countries to have different opportunity sets, efficient frontiers and optimal portfolios as was the case in Chapter 7.

Capital asset pricing model

Having seen that portfolio theory can be successfully applied to the problem of international investment, this leads us naturally to look at the role of the CAPM in an international context. As we saw in Chapter 8, the CAPM was derived in a purely national framework by US researchers with the largest Stock Exchange in the world and the least to gain from international investment. Can it be extended to an international framework?

There are two main ways in which the CAPM could be viewed in an international framework. One would be to assume that all capital

---

[25] See Solnik (1974), Figures 1 and 4.

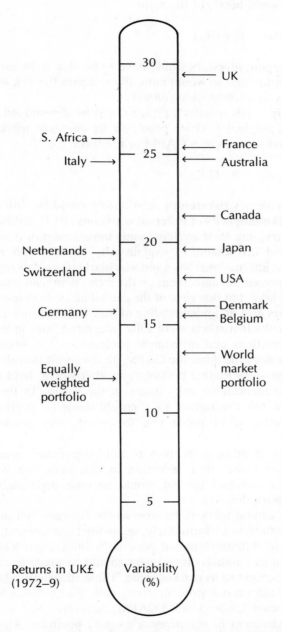

Figure 10.1   Risk reduction from international diversification

Source: Dimson, Hodges and Marsh (1980).

markets were integrated, meaning that all securities were priced relative to a world capital market. In this case, the CAPM would be a 'world' CAPM, with world betas, of the form

$$E(R_j) = \alpha_j + \beta_j\, E(R_w) \tag{10.6}$$

For this to happen, investors would have to be able to invest freely in any capital market and so would naturally compare the risk and return of any security in a world-wide context.

Alternatively, each security's return could be determined, as postulated by the original CAPM, purely in its domestic market. Each country *i* would have its own CAPM of the form

$$E(R_{ji}) = \alpha_{ji} + \beta_{ji}\, E(R_{mi}) \tag{10.7}$$

where each country's risk–return relationship could be different. For there to be this multiplicity of different equations (10.7), a different one for each country, one must envisage some impediment or disadvantage to international investment to explain why investors do not value securities on an international basis and why markets are thus segmented.

There is at present no agreement on the form, if any, an international CAPM would take, but this view of the capital markets as integrated or segmented does give an understanding of how international diversification reduces risk. If markets were fully integrated, and investors had identical expectations and investment preferences,[26] a world CAPM would lead, as does the domestic CAPM, to the result that all investors should hold the same market portfolio, in other words, hold a proportion of all the marketable risky assets in the world. In this case, if investors restricted themselves to a purely domestic portfolio, they would be bearing diversifiable risk for which they would not be rewarded.

On the other hand, if markets were fully segmented, international investment would also offer reduction in risk since risk which was systematic in a national context would become diversifiable in an international portfolio.

In practice, capital markets lie somewhere between full integration and full segmentation. Unfortunately, segmented and integrated capital markets lead to different optimal portfolios. Integration leads to the world portfolio as optimal – investment should be made in each stock market in proportion to its market value. Table 10.7 shows the relative importance of the various stock markets, with the US being by far the largest for equities. Under a world CAPM, therefore, the US should be the largest investment in *any* investor's equity portfolio. The optimal

---

[26] Plus the other CAPM assumptions such as no taxes and no transaction costs.

portfolio will include countries according to the size of their stock markets rather than their low correlation coefficients. The extent of risk reduction obtained by diversifying internationally will therefore not be as great under integrated capital markets as the correlation coefficients in Table 10.6 would lead one to expect. This is evident from Figure 10.1, where the risk of the 'world market portfolio' is greater than that of the equally weighted portfolio. A portfolio consisting of securities with the lowest correlation coefficients would have even less risk.

Segmented markets lead to a more selective approach for the investor. Each investor should determine his efficient frontier from data

Table 10.7   Relative importance of major stock exchanges

Stock exchange	1980 Market value of domestic equities £bn.	Percentage of total (%)
New York American	540	50
Tokyo	151	14
Montreal * Toronto	88	8
UK	86	8
Johannesburg	42	4
Zurich * Geneva	35	3
Germany	30	3
Australia	25	2
Paris	23	2
Hong Kong	16	1
Amsterdam	12	1
Milan	11	1
Singapore	11	1
Madrid	7	⎫
Kuwait	7	⎪
Brussels	4	⎬ 2
Copenhagen	2	⎪
Tel Aviv	2	⎭
TOTAL	1,092	100

* 1979 figures.

Source: *Stock Exchange Fact Book*, March 1981.

on expected returns, standard deviations and correlation coefficients for the securities and countries in which he is *able* to invest. Investors from each country may have different efficient frontiers, due to differences in opportunities and costs (for example, taxes) of international investment. Also, individual investors will choose different optimal portfolios according to risk preference.

International investment in practice

The recommendations of the CAPM in a domestic context are not carried out in practice; investors do not all hold a fraction of the market portfolio. In an international context, with the additional difficulties of differential transactions costs, taxes, and information between domestic and overseas investment, it would be unrealistic to hold a proportion of the world market portfolio. However, Figure 10.1 showed that naïve diversification in only thirteen different stock markets could reduce variability to around 12% of the average risk of one UK share. Diversification in only a few overseas securities or stock markets, whose returns had the lowest correlation with the return on UK shares, would still achieve substantial reduction in risk. For example, looking at the correlation coefficients in Table 10.6, one could surmise that, for the UK investor, securities from the US, Japanese, South African and one or two of the European Stock Exchanges would be sufficient to form a reasonably efficient portfolio.

Of course, there is little point in trying to reduce risk to a minimum if returns are substantially reduced as well. If, say, returns on all overseas investment were substantially less than those available on equivalent

Table 10.8   Returns from international investment

% pa	1970	1971	1972	1973	1974	1975	1976	1977	1978	1979	Ave 70-79
USA	4.2	7.2	29.2	−13.9	−27.3	59.3	46.8	−17.9	0.0	8.5	6.5
Japan	−11.1	44.0	146.2	−19.3	−16.6	39.2	49.3	3.2	44.0	−19.3	18.1
UK	−3.5	47.1	16.4	−28.6	−51.3	150.8	2.0	48.6	8.4	10.2	10.1
Canada	14.9	6.8	44.9	−1.7	−27.7	33.9	30.3	−13.0	13.2	39.1	11.7
Germany	−22.7	16.5	29.0	−3.5	16.0	51.2	26.6	10.5§	16.3§	−12.3§	10.9§
France	−4.3	−5.2	36.0	8.9	−25.8	68.1	−5.2	−6.1	62.2	17.9	11.1
Switzerland	−12.7	19.0	39.5	−2.1	−12.8	63.3	31.4	15.3	13.9	2.3	13.6
Australia	−19.3	−7.3	34.2	−13.0	−32.8	72.7	6.7	−0.8	14.7	31.2	4.9
Netherlands	−5.6	−5.1	40.8	−3.6	−16.7	74.8	38.8	3.8	13.0	9.6	12.2

§Excluding German tax credit.

Source: Phillips & Drew, *World Capital Markets* (1980).

UK investments, it might be the case that the benefit of reduced risk obtained from international diversification was more than offset by reduced returns. However, this is not the case, as.can be seen from Table 10.8, which shows the average annual returns which would have been achieved in sterling terms by investing in the top ten stock markets during 1970–9. The levels of return are, on average, greater than were achieved in the UK. Thus, the reduction in risk achieved through international diversification would not have been gained at the expense of return.

In practice, the investor is concerned with *expected* returns and risk rather than historical figures and it must be remembered that the correlation coefficients given in Table 10.6 are based on historic and not forecast returns. Table 10.6 uses returns in the period 1972–9 and, although such correlation coefficients do show a certain measure of stability, care should be taken to use recent returns, which will most likely reflect similar relationships between exchange rates and economies to those occurring in the future. It would also be appropriate to include any expectations concerning future exchange rate changes and security returns which would alter the correlation coefficients matrix. However, as we have already noted, exchange rate changes are difficult to forecast with any accuracy and detailed information on individual overseas securities may be unavailable (although UK brokers do have overseas offices in the major financial centres and many US brokers have London offices).

Any such difficulties or lack of ability in forecasting can be overcome by adopting an approach of choosing securities randomly or, perhaps more sensibly, adopting an index approach. This would mean buying shares in several funds or trusts, each of which specialised in the securities of a different country, and whose portfolio was a kind of 'index fund' for that particular stock market. Alternatively, the small investor, unwilling to invest separately in purely overseas funds, can achieve some international diversification by buying shares or units in, say, UK investment trusts which have only a proportion of their portfolio invested in other stock markets. Similarly, it might be thought simpliest to invest overseas by buying shares in UK based multinationals such as RTZ or Inchcape. However, research into US multinationals[27] has shown that the gains to US investors from direct overseas investment appear not to be replicated by indirect international investment through US multinationals. Nevertheless, it may be that investors from countries which have strict exchange controls can only diversify internationally by investing, via their domestic market, in multinationals.

Finally, throughout this chapter it has been assumed that the UK investor will wish to receive sterling returns. It may be that his

---

[27] See Jacquillat and Solnik (1978).

consumption preference will lead him to wish to receive part of his income in dollars or Swiss francs. In such a case exchange risk is no longer necessarily a problem and the investor will calculate his expected returns in dollars or Swiss francs.

Summary

This chapter has looked at the advantages and disadvantages to the UK investor of international investment which, since the relaxation of UK exchange controls in 1979, has become an increasingly important part of stock market investment.

The major additional factor to be considered when investing in foreign currency securities is exchange risk, the risk that the return on investment, when converted back into sterling, will be different from expected, due to changes in exchange rates. Exchange risk can be partially hedged by using the spot and forward foreign exchange markets, both of which are efficient, or by borrowing the expected proceeds in the foreign currency. Forward rates are also the best available, albeit poor, estimates of future spot exchange rates.

Although the factors determining changes in exchange rates are as yet inadequately understood, two basic relationships ought to hold in a world with no barriers or costs to international trade. These are purchasing power parity and the International Fisher effect. If these hold, even if only in the long term and approximately, exchange risk is not as great as originally appears. Also because exchange rate changes, for both fixed interest securities and equities, reduce the correlation of returns in different stock markets, exchange risk can be an advantage to international investment.

Exchange risk alters returns on different stock markets and reduces the correlation of these returns with those of the UK stock market. As a result, investment in these overseas stock markets can substantially reduce the risk of the investor's portfolio. This international extension of portfolio theory shows that, unless expected returns are *much* lower on overseas securities (due to transaction costs, taxes or political risk), investors should not restrict themselves to domestic investment. This result holds true whether capital markets are integrated or segmented. A practical approach to overseas investment is to hold a diversified portfolio of fixed interest securities and equities, chosen according to their expected returns, risk and low correlation coefficients with the returns on comparable UK securities. If there are information difficulties or the investor has no forecasting ability on equity returns, an index approach can be adopted.

Appendix: the euromarkets

Eurocurrency

A eurodollar bank deposit is simply dollars placed on deposit outside the US. It is exactly the same as a normal bank deposit except that it represents money placed outside the US national banking system.

This type of bank deposit was first developed during the 1950s and 1960s when dollars became available for lending outside the US for various reasons. For example, persistent US balance-of-payments deficits meant that there was a surplus of dollars held by other countries. Also, the US government chose to restrict the level of interest rates payable on dollar bank deposits placed in the US. Demand for these dollars offered outside the US came from US companies unable to borrow in the US to finance overseas expansion and from a general upsurge in international trade. Since these early days, the eurodollar market has grown dramatically with the eurocurrency liabilities of European banks estimated at over $750b. in 1980, including, as well as eurodollars, other currencies such as eurosterling and eurodeutschemarks. Eurocurrency is thus a general term for a currency available for lending in a centre which is not its home centre.

Borrowing and lending in eurocurrency constitutes what is known as an offshore banking system, in the sense that it is outside any national boundaries and unregulated by any national authorities. Despite its lack of a 'lender of last resort' (such as the Bank of England in the case of the UK banking system), the eurocurrency market has experienced very few defaults. London is the main centre with most major international banks in London being actively involved.

Eurobonds

A market for euro*bonds* has developed in the wake of the eurocurrency market. Instead of eurodollars always being in the form of bank loans, they can be issued as fixed interest securities or bonds. Thus, eurobonds are fixed interest securities issued in several countries at once by a syndicate of banks. Eurobonds are similar in type of security to gilts and corporate fixed interest securities, since they are issued by governments and companies, except for their international character and, as for eurocurrency bank deposits, their freedom from national regulation.

Eurobonds are issued in bearer form with interest usually paid annually. They were originally bought by individual investors through their banks and held until maturity. (The archetypal eurobond investor is said to be a Belgian dentist seeking to avoid payment of tax!) As the market has grown, institutional investors have acquired eurobonds and a secondary market, run by banks in the main financial centres, has evolved. Prices of eurobonds are given monthly in the *Financial Times*. Table A.1 gives an extract showing some *Financial Times*

Table A.1 *Eurobond prices*

FT INTERNATIONAL BOND SERVICE

The list shows the 200 latest international bond issues for which an adequate secondary market exists. For further details of these or other bonds see the complete list of Eurobond prices which will be published next on Wednesday August 18. Closing prices on July 14

U.S. DOLLAR STRAIGHTS	Issued	Bid	Offer	Change on day	Change on week	Yield
Aetna Life 15 86/97 ...	150	102⅞	103⅜	−0¼	+1⅞	13.81
Amax Int. Fin. 16¼ 92	75	97¼	97¾	−0⅛	+0½	16.73
Amex O/S Fin. 14¼ 89	75	94⅜	94⅞	−0¼	+0⅞	15.54
ATT 14¼ 89	400	103⅛	103⅝	−0¼	+1⅜	13.41
Baker Int. Fin. 0.0 92	225	25¾	26¼	−0¾	−0⅛	15.04
BHP Finance 14¾ 89 ...	150	95⅛	95⅝	−0⅜	+0¾	15.87
Bk. Amer. NT SA 12 87	200	90½	91	−0¼	+0⅞	14.80
Bk. Montreal 14½ 87 ...	100	93⅞	94⅜	−0½	−1⅛	16.30
Bque. Indo Suez 15 89	100	95¾	96¼	−0½	+1	15.97
British Col. Hyd. 14¾ 89	200	97⅜	97⅞	−0⅛	+1¼	15.30
Burroughs Int. 15¾ 88	50	99⅞	100⅜	−0⅝	+0⅞	15.65
Canada 14⅜ 87	750	97½	98	−0½	+0¾	15.03
Canadair 15½ 87	150	99⅞	100⅜	−0¼	+0⅞	15.38
Canadian Pac. 14⅝ 92	75	94⅜	94⅞	−0½	+0¼	15.71
Carolina Power 16½ 89	60	101⅛	101⅝	−0¼	+0⅞	16.07
CIBC 16 87	100	97⅜	97⅞	−0⅜	−2¼	16.68
Citicorp O/S 15 84/92	100	99⅝	100⅛	−0⅜	−0⅛	14.95
Citicorp O/S 15½ 85/97	125	100	100½	−0⅜	+0¼	15.25
CNA 15⅞ 97	75	96⅜	96⅞	−0⅜	+1	16.45
Con. Illinois 15¾ 89 ...	100	97⅝	98⅛	−0⅛	−2¼	16.23
Duke Pwr. O/S 15½ 89	60	95¾	96¼	−0¼	+1⅜	16.47
Dupont O/S Cap. 0.0 90	300	34⅝	35⅛	−0⅜	+0½	14.92
ECSC 14¾ 87 (April) ...	80	96⅞	97⅜	−0¼	+0¾	15.59
EIB 15½ 89	150	99	99½	−0½	+0½	15.63
Eksportfinans 14½ 89 ...	50	96¼	96¾	−0¼	+1¼	15.32
Gen. Elec. Credit 0.0 92	400	27⅝	28⅛	−0¾	+0⅝	14.25
Gen. Elec. Credit 0.0 93	400	23¾	24¼	−0⅜	+0½	14.42
Getty Oil Int. 14 89 ...	125	97⅞	98⅜	+0⅛	+1⅛	14.41
GMAC O/S Fin. 16 88	150	101	101½	−0½	+0¾	15.57
GMAC O/S 15¼ 85/97	100	98¾	99¼	−0¼	+0⅛	15.62
GMAC O/S Fin. 15 89	125	97⅜	97⅞	−0⅜	+1¼	15.55
GMAC O/S Fin. 15 87	100	99⅜	99⅞	−0⅛	+1⅛	15.07
Gulf Canada Ltd 14¾ 92	100	95⅞	96⅜	−0⅜	+1	15.50
Gulf Oil 14¼ 94	175	97½	98	−0⅜	+0½	14.63
Gulf Oil Fin. 0.0 92 ...	300	27	27½	−0¾	+0½	14.45
Gulf States O/S 16 90	60	†94¾	95¼	−0⅜	−0½	17.16
Int-Am. Dv. Bk. 15⅛ 87	55	97⅜	97⅞	−0⅜	+1⅜	15.73
Japan Dev. Bk. 15½ 87	50	101¾	102¼	−0⅜	+0½	14.79
New Brunswick 16¼ 89	75	101½	102	−0¼	+1⅛	15.74
Ontario Hydro 14¾ 89...	150	97⅞	98⅜	−0⅛	+1	15.17
Pac. Gas & El. 15½ 89	45	100⅝	101⅛	−0½	+1¼	15.23
Phillips Petrol 14 89 ...	200	96	96½	−0¼	+1⅝	14.88
R. J. Rynlds. O/S 0.0 92	400	26¾	27¼	−0⅜	+0⅜	14.62
Saskatchewan 16 89 ...	125	101½	102	−0¼	+1	15.50
Shell Canada 14⅜ 92 ...	125	95½	96	−0⅜	+0⅝	15.21
Spain 15¾ 87	100	98⅜	98⅞	−0½	−0¼	16.11
Superior O/S Fin. 14 89	125	94⅝	95⅛	0	+1	15.23
Swed. Exp. Cr. 15¼ 89	100	97⅝	98⅛	−0½	+0⅛	15.73
Swed. Exp. Cr. 14¾ 90	100	93½	94	−0⅜	+0¼	16.18
Swed. Exp. Cr. 0.0 94	200	19⅛	19⅝	−0½	−0⅜	15.12
Texas Eastern 15¾ 89...	60	100¼	100¾	−0½	−0⅛	15.60
Union Carbide 14¾ 89	150	98⅝	99⅛	−0⅜	+1¾	14.98
Wells Fargo I. F. 15 87	75	98⅛	98⅝	−0¼	+0½	15.44
World Bank 14¼ 87 ...	500	96¼	96¾	−0¼	+1⅛	15.28
World Bank 15¼ 88 ...	250	99¼	99¾	−0¼	+1¼	15.32

Average price changes... On day −0⅜ on week +0⅝

OTHER STRAIGHTS	Issued	Bid	Offer	Change on day	Change on week	Yield
Bell Canada 16 89 C$...	100	†97	97½	−0¼	+0¼	16.65
Can. Pac. S. 16⅜ 89 C$	50	†98	98½	+0¼	+1	16.77
Crd. Foncier 17⅛ 89 C$	30	†98½	99	0	−0¼	17.39
Gaz Metro. 17¼ 90 C$	20	†97¼	98	+0⅛	+0¾	17.75
OKB 16¼ 88 C$	63	†97¼	97¾	0	+0¼	16.93
Q. Hyd. 16½ 89 (My) C$	50	†99	99½	0	−0¼	16.65
Quebec Prov. 16½ 89 C$	50	†99¼	99¾	0	−0¼	16.58
U. Bk. Nwy. 9½ 90 EUA	18	92½	93¾	0	+0¼	10.85
Amro Bank 10 87 Fl ...	150	100⅛	100⅝	+0½	+1⅜	9.88
Bk. Mees & H. 10 87 Fl	75	98	98½	−0¼	+0⅜	10.46
Eurofima 10½ 89 Fl	50	100⅛	100⅝	−0⅝	+0¾	10.40
Ireland 10½ 87 Fl	75	98⅛	98⅝	−0⅛	+0¼	10.91
Phil. Lamps 10¼ 87 Fl...	100	100⅝	101⅛	−0⅛	+1	9.99
World Bank 10 87 Fl ...	150	98	98½	−0¼	+0⅜	10.46
OKB 14 86 FFr	400	92¾	93¾	+0¼	+0⅛	16.54
Solvay et C. 14¾ 86 FFr	200	92½	93½	+0¼	+0¼	17.39
Beneficial 14¼ 90 £ (D)	20	87¾	88½	0	+0⅛	16.94
BFCE 14½ 87 £	30	99⅜	99⅞	−0½	+0⅜	14.60
BNP 13½ 91 £	15	94⅝	95⅜	0	+0⅝	14.51
CECA 13½ 88 £	20	95⅜	96⅛	−0½	+0⅜	14.53
Fin. Ex. Cred. 13¾ 86 £	15	97⅛	98⅛	0	+0½	14.55
Gen. Elec. Co. 12½ 89 £	50	94⅛	95⅛	−0⅛	+1½	13.75
Hiram Walker 14¼ 86 £	25	98⅜	99⅜	0	+0⅜	14.60
Norsk Hydro. 14½ 87 £	30	99¼	99¾	−0½	+0⅛	14.64
Privatbanken 14½ 88 £	12	96⅞	97⅝	+0⅜	+1⅛	15.20
Quebec 15½ 87 £	35	102¼	103	−0¼	+0⅝	14.63
Reed (Nd) NV 16¾ 89 £	25	105	106	+0¼	+1⅛	15.30
Royal Trustco 14 86 £...	12	98⅞	99⅞	0	+0⅝	14.15
SDR France 15½ 92 £...	30	100¼	101	−0⅛	+0⅜	15.33
Swed. Ex. Cr. 13¾ 86 £	20	98⅛	99⅛	−0⅛	+0¾	14.18
Eurofima 10½ 87 LuxFr	500	95⅜	96⅜	+0¼	+0⅛	11.56
EIB 9¾ 88 LuxFr	600	92⅝	93⅝	0	0	11.46

FLOATING RATE NOTES	Spread	Bid	Offer	C.dte	C.cpn	C.yld
Allied Irish 5¼ 92	0¼	98	98½	15/10	15.69	15.97
Bk. of Tokyo 5¼ 91 (D)	0⅛	99	99½	8/12	15¼	15.37
Bk. Nova Scotia 5¼ 93	0⅛	98½	99	29/10	15⅛	15.32
BFCE 5¼ 88	0¼	98⅝	99⅛	28/10	15	15.17
BFCE 5¼ 87	0¼	99¼	99¾	27/7	16¼	16.33
BNP 5¼ 89 WW	0⅛	*†98⅜	98⅞	6/11	15.19	15.40
Caisse Nat. Tele. 5¼ 90	0¼	99	99½	21/10	15¾	15.87
CCCE 5¼ 2002	0⅜	98¼	98¾	11/12	15⅜	15.61
CEPME 5¼ 92	0¼	99⅛	99⅜	10/12	15.44	15.55
Chemical NY 5¼ 94 ...	‡0¼	99⅛	99⅝	23/9	16.69	16.79
CIBC 5¼ 94	0¼	†97	97½	15/7	5¼	5.40
Cont. Illinois 5¼ 94 ...	‡0¼	99⅝	100⅛	24/9	16⅜	16.40
Credit Agricole 5¼ 97...	0¼	99	99½	24/9	15.44	15.55
Credit du Nord 5¼ 92...	0¼	99¼	99¾	23/12	16.81	16.90
Credit Lyonnais 5¼ 97...	0¼	99¼	99¾	1/10	16	16.08
Credit Lyonnais 6¼ 94...	0¼	99⅞	100⅜	1/1	16.94	16.92
Credit Nat. 5¼ 94	‡0¼	98¼	98¾	9/9	14.69	14.91
Ireland 5¼ 89/94	0¼	†98¼	98¾	25/11	14¾	14.97
Kansallis Osake 5½ 92	0¼	99⅛	99⅝	6/11	15.31	15.41
Lloyds Eurofin 5¼ 93 ...	§0¼	98⅞	99⅜	29/10	17⅛	17.28
Long Term Cred. 5¼ 92	0⅛	98	98½	29/11	14⅝	14.89
J. P. Morgan 5¼ 97 ...	§0¼	98¾	99¼	12/8	14⅝	14.77

DEUTSCHE MARK STRAIGHTS	Issued	Bid	Offer	Change on day	Change on week	Yield
Asian Dev. Bank 9¼ 92	150	98⅜	98⅞	−0⅛	+0⅛	9.46
Australia 9⅜ 91	200	103	103½	0	+0¼	8.80
Austria 8⅜ 92	100	94⅞	95⅜	−0⅛	+0¼	9.14
Barclays O/S In. 8⅜ 94	100	95¼	95¾	−0⅛	+0⅛	9.00
Bowater Int. Fin. 8½ 89	50	95¼	95¾	−0⅜	−0⅛	9.41
Canada 8½ 89	200	102	102½	+0⅜	+1	8.05
Comp. Tel. Esp. 10½ 92	100	100½	101	−0⅜	−0⅛	10.35
Cred. Foncier 8¾ 92 ...	100	95¾	96¼	−0⅛	−0⅛	9.38
Denmark 10⅛ 92	100	†102½	103	+0½	+0⅛	9.66
EDF 9⅞ 92	100	†100¼	101¼	+0¼	+0⅜	9.74
EIB 8⅜ 92	100	94⅞	95⅜	−0⅜	+0¼	9.14
Int.-Am. Dev. Bk. 9 92	150	96¾	97¼	−0½	−0⅜	9.47
Nacnl. Financiera 11 90	150	96¾	97	−0⅜	0	11.61
Norsk Hydro 8½ 92	100	97⅞	98⅜	−0⅛	+0¼	8.79
Philips Lamps 8½ 92 ...	100	97⅞	98⅜	−0⅛	+0¼	8.79
Philip Morris 8¼ 90 ...	100	99½	100	−0¼	0	8.29
Quebec 10⅛ 92	150	102¾	103¼	−0¼	+0½	9.61
Renfe 10 92	100	99⅞	100⅜	−0⅛	+0⅜	9.97
SNCF 8⅝ 92	100	95½	96	−0¼	−0⅛	9.29
Tauernautobahn 9⅞ 94	50	†101½	102½	−0¼	0	9.57
Tenneco Int. 9 92	100	97½	98	−0⅜	−0⅛	9.35
World Bank 9½ 89	100	100¼	100¾	0	+0⅛	9.38
World Bank 8½ 92	200	94⅞	95⅜	−0⅝	0	9.27

Average price changes... On day −0⅛ on week +0⅛

SWISS FRANC STRAIGHTS	Issued	Bid	Offer	Change on day	Change on week	Yield
Air Canada 6¼ 92	100	100⅞	101⅛	0	+0⅞	6.11
Asian Dev. Bank 7 92...	100	101⅞	102⅛	+0¼	+1	6.71
Aucalsa 7¾ 92	80	98¼	98½	+0¾	+1½	7.99
Australia 6½ 94	100	104½	104¾	+0¼	+0⅛	5.94
BNP 6¾ 92	100	97¼	97½	+0⅛	+0⅛	7.13
Cse. Nat. l'Energie 7 92	100	100⅞	101⅛	+0⅛	0	6.85
CFE-Mexico 8¼ 92	50	97¾	98¼	+0⅝	+1¼	8.55
Co-op. Denmark 8⅜ 92	25	104⅞	105⅛	0	+0½	7.62
Crown Zellerbach 6¾ 92	100	99⅝	99⅞	0	0	6.78
Europarat 7¼ 92	100	100¾	101	−0⅛	+0⅞	7.12
Ind. Fund Finland 6¾ 92	30	98¼	99	−0⅛	−0⅛	6.94
Japan Dev. Bank 6 94...	100	100⅜	100⅝	−0⅛	+1	5.94
Kobe City 6⅛ 92	100	100⅝	101⅛	0	+0¾	6.00
Kommunlane 7¼ 92 ...	35	101	101½	+0⅛	+0¾	7.06
Lonrho Int. Fin. 7½ 92	80	94⅞	95⅜	−0⅛	0	8.23
Mitsui OSK 6½ 92	100	99⅞	100⅛	−0⅛	+0⅝	6.50
Nafinsa 8¼ 92	80	94	94½	−0¾	−0¾	9.15
New Zealand 6 92	100	101	101¼	−0⅛	+0¾	5.85
Philip Morris 6⅝ 92 ...	100	103	103¼	+0⅛	+0⅛	6.18
Philip Morris 6¼ 94 ...	100	101¼	101½	0	+0⅛	6.08
Renfe 7¾ 92	80	97¼	97½	+0⅛	+0⅝	8.14
Sekisui Pre. 5¾ 92 WW	70	103⅞	104⅛	−0⅛	+0⅝	5.21
Soc. Lux. de Cnt. 8⅜ 92	80	105¼	105½	+0⅛	−0½	7.20
Svenska Handels. 6¾ 92	100	98⅛	98⅜	+1⅛	+0½	7.00
Tiroler Wasser 6¼ 92	100	97⅜	97⅝	+0⅛	+1	6.60
Vorarlberg Kraft 6¾ 92	50	102⅜	102⅝	+0⅛	−0⅝	6.39

Average price changes... On day +0⅛ on week +0½

Nat. West. Fin. 5¼ 91...	§0¼	99⅛	99⅝	15/7	15.19	15.28
New Zealand 5¼ 87 ...	0⅛	99¼	99¾	7/10	‡15.56	15.64
Nippon Credit 5¼ 90...	0⅛	99	99½	10/8	16.06	16.18
Offshore Mining 5¼ 91	0¼	98¾	99¼	2/12	14.19	14.33
PKbanken 5 91	0¼	99	99½	17/12	15.81	15.93
Scotland Int. 5¼ 92......	0⅛	98½	99	23/9	15⅜	15.57
Sec. Pacific 5¼ 91	0⅛	98⅞	99⅜	24/11	15	15.13
Societe Generale 5¼ 95	0¼	99	99½	1/9	15.31	15.43
Standard Chart. 5¼ 91	0⅛	98⅜	98⅞	18/11	14⅞	15.08
Sweden 5¼ 89	0¼	99⅛	99⅝	26/8	15.31	15.41
Toronto Domin'n 5¼ 92	0⅛	98½	99	11/8	16⅜	16.58

Average price changes... On day 0 on week +0⅛

CONVERTIBLE BONDS	Cnv. date	Cnv. price	Bid	Offer	Chg. day	Prem
Ajinomoto 5¼ 96	7/81	933	84⅛	85⅝	−1⅜	8.94
Bow Valley Inv. 8 95...	4/81	23.12	95	96½	−0¾	71.96
Bridgestone Tire 5½ 96	3/82	470	83⅛	84⅝	0	0.80
Canon 6¾ 95	1/81	829	84	85¾	−2¼	14.85
Canon 7 97	7/82	748.2	92½	94	−2⅝	−1.60
Chugai Pharm. 7¼ 96...	7/82	709.6	99¼	100¾	+1⅝	7.24
Fujitsu Fanuc 4½ 96......	10/81	5641	76¾	78¾	−3	12.27
Furukawa Elec. 5¾ 96...	7/81	300	78	79½	0	−11.97
Hitachi Cable 5¼ 96......	2/82	515	78⅝	80⅛	−2⅜	1.93
Hitachi Cred. Cpn. 5 96	7/81	1612	73¾	75½	−1⅞	12.90
Honda Motor 5½ 97......	3/82	841	83	84½	−1	3.24
Kawasaki 5¾ 96	9/81	229	62	63½	−1	19.21
Marui 6 96	7/81	846.4	94	95½	−0½	2.81
Minolta Camera 5 96...	10/81	826.4	61	62½	+0¾	33.60
Minorco 9¼ 97	5/82	8.16	†78	80	+2½	21.67
Murata 5¼ 96	7/81	2168	66⅛	67⅝	−0⅜	17.83
NKK 6½ 96	7/81	188	72⅝	74⅛	+0¼	−17.67
Nippon Chemi-C. 5 91...	10/81	919	†70	72	−1	42.60
Nippon Electric 5¼ 97...	2/82	846	85	86¼	−2	5.55
Orient Finance 5¼ 97 ...	3/82	1205	85¼	86¾	+0⅛	10.10
Sanyo Electric 5 96......	10/81	652	62½	64	−0½	15.23
Sumitomo Elec. 5½ 97...	3/82	577.3	81½	83	−0⅝	7.44
Sumitomo Met. 5¼ 96...	10/81	296.1	60½	62	−0⅞	40.38
Swiss Bk. Cpn. 6¼ 90...	9/80	191	73	75	0	31.85
Konishiroku 6 90 DM ...	2/82	585	99	100	−1	4.18
Mitsubishi H. 6 89 DM	2/82	263	90⅛	90⅞	+0¼	34.20

* No information available—previous day's price.

† Only one market maker supplied a price.

Straight Bonds: The yield is the yield to redemption of the mid-price; the amount issued is in millions of currency units except for Yen bonds where it is in billions. Change on week = Change over price a week earlier.

Floating Rate Notes: Denominated in dollars unless otherwise indicated. Coupon shown is minimum. C.dte = Date next coupon becomes effective. Spread = Margin above six-month offered rate (‡ three-month; § above mean rate) for U.S. dollars. C.cpn = The current coupon. C.yld = The current yield.

Convertible Bonds: Denominated in dollars unless otherwise indicated. Chg. day = Change on day. Cnv. date = First date for conversion into shares. Cnv. price = Nominal amount of bond per share expressed in currency of share at conversion rate fixed at issue. Prem = Percentage premium of the current effective price of acquiring shares via the bond over the most recent price of the shares.

Source: *Financial Times*, 15 July 1982.

eurobond price quotations. Because of their freedom from government regulation, eurobonds have developed in many different forms in response to the
requirements of the market, with some eurobonds having floating-rate interest
payments and others offering the holders the option to convert into ordinary
shares. See, for example, in Table A.1, Allied Irish 1992 eurodollar bond with a
minimum coupon of 5¼% but a current coupon of 15.69% and Bridgestone Tire
5½% 1996 eurodollar bond, convertible into Bridgestone Tire equity. Despite
the secondary market, eurobonds are still not as marketable as Stock Exchange
securities, with higher bid–ask spreads.

Eurobonds can have a range of maturities, with terms from, say, six to over
fifteen years. Eurocurrency deposits are shorter-term than eurobonds with
terms of up to one year although both deposits and loans can be 'rolled-over' to
extend their maturity. For example, a eurodollar loan can have an overall
maturity of five years, but the interest rate will be based on the three- or
six-monthly eurodollar borrowing rate. So, every three or six months, the loan
will be 'rolled-over' and the interest rate will change.

This very brief introduction to the euromarkets should be supplemented with
further reading. For example, see Dufey and Giddy (1978).

Problems

1. Mr Brooks is trying to calculate the expected return in £ sterling from
   two investments, one in Etiquette plc, a UK company, and the other in
   Protocol Inc., a similar US company. The current share prices are 114p
   for Etiquette and $26 for Protocol and the prevailing £/$ exchange rate
   is £1 = $2.25.
   Mr Brooks has asked his stockbroker for advice on the likely dividends and future share prices for the two companies in exactly one
   year's time. He has been given the following estimates:

	Share price in one year's time	Dividend to be received in one year's time
Etiquette plc	120p	9p
Protocol Inc.	$28	$3

   The broker is unwilling to commit himself on the future exchange rate;
   he is only prepared to give the following probability distribution:

Exchange rate in one year's time	Probability
$1.50	0.2
$2.00	0.2
$2.50	0.3
$3.00	0.3

   £1 =

   (i) Calculate the expected one year sterling return for Mr Brooks on both Etiquette plc and Protocol Inc.

  (ii) If the most pessimistic exchange rate forecast turns out to be true, how much does Mr Brooks stand to lose in £ sterling if he invests £1,000 now in Protocol?

 (iii)| If the expected earnings per share for Etiquette and Protocol are 12p and $5.14 respectively, calculate the *PE* ratio, dividend yield and dividend cover for each company. Explain the meaning and relevance of each of these terms for investment decision-making and comment on the figures you have calculated for Protocol and Etiquette.

2. Miss King wishes to buy 100,000 shares in a US company, BBB Inc., which are currently quoted at $46 per share. She expects BBB to pay a dividend of $3 per share in three months' time and she wishes to sell the shares three months later for an expected price of $55. Miss King wishes to hedge exchange risk as much as possible and her bank has provided her with the following quotations. The bank also states that it will charge ¼% commission.

	£	$
Three month eurocurrency rates (% pa)	11	9
Six month eurocurrency rates (% pa)	12	9.5
Spot exchange rates	$1.50/£1	

   (i) Does Miss King wish to buy or sell forward dollars?

  (ii) Use the interest rate parity theory to determine the equilibrium three and six month forward rates.

 (iii) Will the commission charged increase or decrease the number of $/£ in the transaction?

 (iv) What return in sterling can Miss King expect to get and to what extent can she hedge exchange risk?

3. In January 1983 (when £1 = FFr 10.50), the inflation rate for 1983 expected in the UK was 7% and in France was 10%. Suppose the required real interest rate in both countries is 3%.

   (i) Use the Fisher relation to estimate the nominal interest rates which will prevail in each country.

  (ii) Use the purchasing power parity theory to determine the expected spot French franc/sterling exchange rate in one year's time.

 (iii) Use the interest rate parity theory to estimate the one year forward French franc forward rate.

 (iv) Compare your estimate of the current forward rate with the expected spot rate in (ii). What does this imply about the need to hedge using the forward markets?

4. Describe the different ways in which an investor can invest internationally and the advantages of each.

5. (i) What does the interest rate parity theory state? What are the implications for transactions in the forward foreign exchange and money markets?

(ii) Suppose you are a UK investor considering purchasing one of the following securities on 1 April 1982. Each security is redeemable at par on 30 September 1982, at which date the last semi-annual coupon is also payable.

Government bond	Coupon (%)	Nominal value	Price on 1 April 1982 (ex interest)	Spot exchange rate (FX/£)	Six month forward exchange rate (FX/£)
US$	20	$100	$102.50	1.9185–1.9195	1.64–1.44c pm
UK£	12	£100	£98.50	—	—
German DM	8	DM 1,000	DM 990	4.33–4.34	13¾–12¾ pf pm

   (a) If you wished to make a riskless investment, which security would you choose? Do your results comply with the interest rate parity theory?

   b) If, however, the securities do not mature on 30 September 1982, but have a ten-year life from 1 April 1982, what, if any, exchange risk would you incur by purchasing the US or German security?

6. Mr Crunch wishes to buy shares in a company in the food manufacturing industry. Mr Crunch's stockbroker advises either Beastly Biscuits in the UK or Weavil Wafers in the US, both of which have the same beta in their respective markets. Mr Crunch expects to spend £1,000 on whichever shares he chooses and to hold them for one or three months. Neither share is expected to pay a dividend within the next three months. Mr Crunch's broker and a study of the *Financial Times* have provided the information in the table below.

  (i) Calculate which of the four possible investments (BB or WW for one or three months) offers the highest expected return, explaining your calculations.

  (ii) State which investment opportunity you personally would choose, bearing in mind the advantages and disadvantages of overseas investment and the problems of comparing investments for different holding periods.

Shares	Current share price	Expected share price in	
		1 month	3 months
Beastly Biscuits	$30	$32	$34
Weevil Wafers	90p	95p	101p
Exchange and interest rates		**1 month**	**3 months**
Eurocurrency interest rates	$	17¼–17½%	17¹¹/₁₆–17¹⁵/₁₆%
	£	14¼–14⅝%	14¼–14½%
	Spot	**1 month**	**3 months**
Spot and forward rates $/£	1.7945–1.7955	0.45–0.55c dis (≡ −3.34% pa)	1.50–1.60c dis (≡ −3.45% pa)

Investing institutions

Introduction

This chapter stands apart from the others in this book, in the sense that it is not directly concerned with how to value particular securities or with how to value an investment portfolio. It is concerned instead with a group of principal actors on the Stock Exchange investment stage, that is, with those financial institutions which are the major investors in

Table 11.1   Ownership of listed UK securities by financial institutions, 1957–78

	At end year; per cent of total market value in issue					
	1957	1962	1967	1972	1977	1978
All financial institutions*						
British government securities	44	49	56	61	63	68
UK local authority securities†	39	39	50	70	56	59
UK company securities						
Loan capital	75	79	77	53	49	47
Preference shares	36	38	59	53	72	76
Ordinary shares	21	26	33	37	47	50
Investing institutions‡						
British government securities	17	24	27	34	41	46
UK local authority securities†	23	26	21	10	16	20
UK company securities						
Loan capital	75	79	77	51	45	42
Preference shares	36	37	59	52	69	72
Ordinary shares	19	24	31	35	44	47

* Investing institutions, banks in UK and discount market, building societies, saving banks' investment accounts, finance houses and special finance agencies.
† Listed stocks and negotiable bonds.
‡ Insurance companies, pension funds, investment trust companies and unit trusts.

Source: Wilson Report (1980). By permission of the Controller of Her Majesty's Stationery Office.

Stock Exchange securities. No book on investment can ignore these institutions – pension funds, insurance companies, investment trusts and unit trusts – firstly, because they are the intermediaries through which the vast majority of people knowingly or unknowingly invest in stock market securities and, secondly, because their presence is now so major that every facet of investment, from performance measurement to the role of stockbrokers and jobbers, is affected by their existence.

The role of these institutions as the major investors in all forms of securities quoted on the Stock Exchange is clearly highlighted in Table 11.1.

Table 11.1 differentiates between financial institutions and investing institutions. This is because all financial institutions, whether they be banks, building societies or insurance companies, etc., need to hold a proportion of their assets in a liquid form, either in cash or in easily saleable securities such as certificates of deposit[1] or gilt-edged stock,

---

[1] A certificate of deposit is a short- to medium-term bearer security, say for £1m., issued by a bank and held by other financial institutions. It represents a liquid asset since it is easily traded amongst financial institutions.

whereas only those financial institutions which are so-called investing institutions specialise in the holding of the long-term securities quoted on the Stock Exchange with which this book is predominantly concerned.

Table 11.1 chronicles the growth in importance of the investing institutions throughout the period 1957–78 by examining the percentage of the total market value of each major type of security held by these institutions. For example, they held 17% in market value of all gilts in 1957, and, although the value of the gilts market had hardly increased in real terms by 1978, the percentage held had by then increased to 46%. The increase in their holdings of UK company ordinary shares has been equally dramatic, from 19 to 47% of the total market value of these equities over the same period. This growth, which represents a substantial increase in the assets of these institutions, for reasons which will be described later in the chapter, has led to their being the most powerful securityholders in the stock market today.

Table 11.2 breaks the investing institutions down into the four main types – pension funds, insurance companies, investment trusts and unit trusts – to show their relative importance as investors in UK securities at the end of 1980. Pension funds and insurance companies are now the two major types of institution, with pension funds poised to overtake insurance companies in terms of the value of assets under their control. Investment trusts have suffered a decline since the early 1970s whereas the more recently introduced unit trusts are still on an upward trend. The reasons for these changes in relative importance will be discussed in the separate sections devoted to each type of investing institution.

Tables 11.1 and 11.2 also document the simultaneous decline in importance in the stock market of the individual investor, a decline which is most marked in the ordinary share sector. However, as we saw in the introduction to Chapter 5, the individual investor has not abandoned Stock Exchange investment. He has merely moved from direct to indirect investment of his savings in quoted securities, either because he has had no choice, as in the case of an employee required to contribute to a pension fund, or because of the tax and other advantages of investment in, say, a unit-linked life assurance scheme.[2]

This growth in the use of intermediaries for channelling private sector savings has many implications in the investment field. For example, there may be duplication of investment analysis by stockbrokers and by the investment institutions. Also, demand for regulation and performance measurement of these intermediaries will arise. A private investor who deals direct with a stockbroker, and listens to his advice without having to take it, is largely responsible for his own investment decisions.

---

[2] Such a scheme involves the policyholder contributing most of his payments towards the purchase of units in a unit trust, with only a small part going towards life assurance.

Table 11.2 UK security holdings of the investing institutions

(1980)	Listed UK company Equities £m	(%)	Listed UK company Fixed interest securities £m	(%)	UK gilts £m	(%)	Total £m	(%)
Insurance companies	16,248	(18.9)	2,092	(45.5)	17,409	(24.6)	35,749	(22.2)
Pension funds*	22,846	(26.6)	865	(18.8)	11,286	(16.0)	34,997	(21.7)
Investment trusts	3,759	(4.4)	70	(1.5)	232	(0.3)	4,061	(2.5)
Unit trusts	2,977†	(3.4)	56†	(1.2)	55	(0.1)	3,088	(1.9)
Total institutional holdings	45,830	(53.3)	3,083	(67.0)	28,982	(41.0)	77,895	(48.3)
Other investors	40,080	(46.7)	1,511	(33.0)	41,671	(59.0)	83,262	(51.7)
TOTAL	85,910	(100.0)	4,594	(100.0)	70,653	(100.0)	161,157	(100.0)

* Provisional.
† Including unlisted securities.

Note: the percentages given do not tally completely with those in Table 11.1 because of the different sources of information used.

Source: *Stock Exchange Fact Book*, March 1982.

An investor in a unit-linked life assurance policy, on the other hand, transfers the responsibility for investment decisions to a third party. As a result, he will wish to know that the intermediary is not likely to commit fraud – hence the demand for regulation – and that the intermediary is competent to make the necessary investment decisions – hence the demand for performance measurement.

The influence and scope of these institutions has to a certain extent taken the City and the government by surprise. There was no official enquiry into the workings of the financial institutions between the Radcliffe Committee which reported in 1959 and the Wilson Committee which reported in 1980. However, during that time, there had been a major change both in the types of investment institution and in their size. For example, Harold Wilson, in the parliamentary debate following the publication of the Wilson Report, referred to 'the pension fund revolution having occurred with no formal notice, and without debate or decision in this House'. One of the points made by the Wilson Committee, of which he was chairman, was the lack of accountability of the pension funds to their beneficiaries (compared with, say, the accountability of the companies by which they were formed to their shareholders), despite the volume of assets under their control.[3] In 1980, pension funds controlled assets of approximately £55b. and had an estimated net cash inflow during 1980 of £6.6b., and yet many did not provide annual reports and accounts to present or future pensioners.

Despite the fact that their growth has to some extent gone unnoticed, the increase in importance of the two largest type of investment intermediaries, pension funds and insurance companies, has been largely a result of government fiscal and other policies. Insurance companies have benefited from the requirement for compulsory insurance in certain sectors but, more particularly, from the tax advantages inherent in investment schemes tied to life assurance policies. This dates from the days when pension schemes were not widespread and pension benefits, such as they were, did not provide an adequate retirement income. Individuals catered for their own retirement through savings schemes related to life assurance and, to encourage this, the government accorded tax relief on such investments. The government now encourages the use of pension funds as the major form of retirement saving and, since 1975,[4] companies have been obliged, as well as contributing to the state's basic pension scheme, either to subscribe to the state's additional, earnings-related pension scheme for their employees or to provide their own pension scheme. Many companies chose

---

[3] For example, companies such as GEC and Dunlop Holdings have pension funds whose assets have, at certain times, been worth more in market-value terms than the shares of the companies themselves.

[4] Through legislation incorporated in the Social Security Pensions Act 1975.

to 'contract out' and these privately organised pension schemes are either run as pension funds separate from the company or are provided for the company by an insurance company. Thus, as pension schemes have spread and as benefits and hence contributions have been increased, so the assets of the pension funds (and insurance companies) have grown. Since contributions to pension schemes are tax-deductible and the returns on investments made by pension funds are not liable to tax, 'investment' in a pension fund can offer a more tax-efficient method of saving to the individual investor than does direct investment in Stock Exchange securities.

Investment trusts and unit trusts, on the other hand, did not develop as tax-efficient forms of saving for retirement. They were set up to offer small investors a way of holding a stake in a diversified portfolio of fixed interest securities and ordinary shares, an opportunity which was otherwise unavailable (without high transaction costs). Perhaps because investment and unit trusts have not had the same advantages of government support as insurance companies and pension funds, and also because investment trusts (as limited liability companies) have had to comply with company disclosure requirements, a greater tradition of disclosure of investment policy and investment performance has been established for these types of intermediary. For example, both the Unit Trust Association and the Association of Investment Trust Companies publish *Year Books* giving brief details of the past performance and the spread of each unit or investment trust.

The next section of the chapter considers each of the four main types of investing institution – pension funds, insurance companies, investment trusts and unit trusts – in more detail. A brief description of each type of institution will be given, how it arose, what its investment objectives are and how these determine its investment strategy. The final part of the chapter will be devoted to a discussion of the main areas of investment which have been affected by the growth of these investment institutions, for example the efficiency of the stock market, the role of stockbrokers and jobbers, regulation, and, last but not least, the impact on the individual investor.

Pension funds

The growth of the pension funds has been the fastest of the four investing institutions, rising from £2b. of assets invested in 1957 to approximately £55b. at the end of 1980, equivalent to over 15% annual average growth in nominal terms or 7.5% annual average growth in *real* terms. The net new inflow of cash in 1980 to be invested was around

£6.6b. and is still rising. This volume of new money is seen to be very large if we compare it with, say, the market value of UK equities quoted on the Stock Exchange of £92b. at the end of 1980. Unfortunately, one of the problems in talking about the pension funds and their investments is the lack of data concerning them. One reason for this is that, as we saw above, pension funds are not accountable to their beneficiaries in the same way as investment trusts are to their shareholders, and, to date, the level of disclosure of pension funds does not reflect the volume of funds under their control.

This rapid increase in pension assets, whether controlled by insurance companies or pension funds, is due, as we have already seen, to the extension of pension schemes to a greater proportion of the working population as a result of legislation, to the improved benefits provided (and hence contributions required), and to the tax advantages attached to pension schemes. Pension funds are at present net receivers of income, with contributions and investment income far exceeding their current pension payments. Pension funds are designed to grow or mature to the point where their total income only just matches their outgoings, and so after some point the net income available for investment should fall. However, the point at which this will happen in the aggregate is still many years distant and is receding as pension contributions are increased to cope with inflation and to provide greater benefits.

The way in which a pension fund works is as follows. The employer and, in many cases, the employees of an organisation pay contributions into a separate pension fund. This usually operates as a legal trust, with the present and future pensioners as beneficiaries. The trustees invest the contributions to provide pensions as required by the terms of the trust. The amounts of the contributions to be made by the employer are determined by an actuary, bearing in mind the benefits promised, the characteristics of the workforce with respect to age, sex, retirement dates, etc., and the expected return on the investment of the contributions over time. Thus, the actuary has to be an expert in investment as well as in such matters as expected labour turnover and death rates. Actuaries will vary in their estimates of future cash flows according, for example, to the return they expect to be achieved from the pension fund investments over the next ten or twenty years. The more conservative the actuary's estimates of future returns on investment, the higher will be the employer's contributions to the pension fund. Less conservative actuaries will require lower contributions in the early years of the fund, with a higher probability that the employer will have to 'top up' the fund in later years. Although employers are not required by law to take the advice of their actuaries, it is usual for them to do so.

Before we go on to discuss the investment objectives and policies of pension funds, it is useful to note that pensions do not have to be provided for through the setting up of pension funds such as exist in the US and the UK. An appendix to this chapter discusses how employers in other countries provide for pensions without creating pension funds, in particular through the use of the Pay as You Go system.

Investment objectives and policy

Given that non-government[5] pensions in the UK are usually funded through a separate pension fund, how are the contributions invested to provide in the best manner possible for future pension liabilities? What factors do pension fund managers take into consideration when making investment decisions?

(i) Liabilities

Pension funds have very long-term liabilities. For example, an employee joining a company at the age of twenty will not in general become eligible for a pension for a further forty or forty-five years. We saw in Chapter 2 that one way of reducing risk is to 'match' assets and liabilities; so, if, say, a pension liability will fall due in twenty years' time, an asset can be bought which will also mature in twenty years' time and which will exactly cover the liability. It is thus likely that pension funds, with substantial long-term liabilities, will hold long-term assets. For example, as can be seen in Table 11.3, in so far as pension funds hold gilts, these are long-term, that is, gilts with maturities of at least fifteen years or undated gilts. Note that the statistics for pension funds in Table 11.3 include figures for the three main groups of pension funds – local authorities, other public sector (mostly nationalised industries) and private sector (mostly companies).

However, this risk-reduction strategy only works if the liabilities and the assets are subject to the same economic effects. If, for example, a liability is fixed in real terms and the matching asset in nominal terms, there is a risk that the asset will not be worth enough in real terms to match the liability. Pensions in the UK are nowadays usually calculated on the basis of final earnings, before retirement, which, to a greater or lesser extent, increase with the cost of living (usually measured by the retail prices index). So, if pension funds invest in ordinary gilts, where the redemption value is fixed in nominal terms, the gilts may not yield

---

[5] By specifying non-government pensions, we exclude the government basic and earnings-related pensions which are operated on a Pay As You Go basis. (See appendix to this chapter.)

Table 11.3   Portfolio holdings of investing institutions

(End 1980*) (£m.)	Pension funds	Insurance Companies		Investment trusts	Unit trusts
		General	Long-term		
Short term assets	1,954	1,248	1,616	—	—
UK gilts					
Mt≤5	319	1,101	513	61	8
5<M≤15	3,296	1,113	3,602	87	38
M>15	8,110	563	10,517	118	26
	11,725	2,777	14,632	266	72
UK securities					
Ordinary shares	24,065	2,227	14,602	4,620	3,357
Other	1,143	696	2,706	227	95
	25,208	2,923	17,308	4,847	3,452
Overseas securities					
Ordinary shares	4,216	411	1,994	3,042	1,081
Other	128	526	192	124	24
	4,344	937	2,186	3,166	1,105
Unit trust units‡	1,722	13	1,380	50	—
Loans and mortgages	305	297	3,472	—	—
Land, property and ground rents	8,170	1,280	12,362	23	—
Agents' balances	—	1,936	607	—	—
Other	1,308	105	183	—	—
TOTAL	54,736	11,516	53,746	8,352	4,629

* Local authority pension funds at 31 March 1981.
† Maturity in years of gilts.
‡ Of which, for pension funds, £1,460m. was in property unit trusts.

Source: *Financial Statistics*. By Permission of the Controller of Her Majesty's Stationery Office.

enough to cover the ultimate pension liabilities. This is why there was a demand for index-linked gilts during the 1970s (a period of high inflation), a demand which began to be met in March 1981 with the issue of Treasury 2% Index-Linked Stock 2006, initially available *only* to pension funds.[6]

Another consequence of the need to match assets with liabilities which are increasing with the rate of inflation has been the investment by pension funds in assets which are believed to provide a hedge against inflation – equities and property. Table 11.3 shows that, in 1980, pension funds held 18% of their assets in property or property unit trusts and a further 52% in both UK and overseas equities. We will examine in Chapter 12 whether either of these types of investment has proved to be a good hedge against inflation but it is worth mentioning here the role of overseas investments in reducing inflation risk. One of the arguments raised against pension funds investing overseas (apart from the political question of where pension funds ought to invest for the good of the economy) is that UK pension funds' liabilities are expressed in sterling terms and that assets denominated in foreign currencies cannot be matched with these liabilities because of exchange risk. However, as was discussed in Chapter 10, it may well be that, by investing in overseas bonds and shares, pension funds will be able to achieve returns more certain in real terms than if they had restricted themselves solely to sterling.

(ii) TAX

As already mentioned, pension funds are completely exempt from income and corporation tax on their investments. Thus, they should be indifferent, other things being equal, between high- and low-coupon gilts and between dividends and capital gains on shares. Of course, other factors will influence the decision on which securities to choose but, unlike the individual investor with a high marginal tax rate, pension funds need not, in principle, take tax into account when making investment decisions. However, in practice, gilt prices will reflect the *net* yields available to investors with different tax rates and so certain gilts will be attractive to 'gross' pension funds in exactly the same way as other gilts will be attractive to taxpaying investors. For example, Table 11.4 shows two one-year gilts (for simplicity) offering different *net* returns according to the tax rate of the investor. (Remember that no capital gains tax is payable if the gilts are held for a year and a day, as we assume here.)

---

[6] This issue, and subsequent issues, of index-linked gilts were made available to the general public as of 3 March 1982.

Table 11.4 Effect of tax on choice of gilts

Gilt	Coupon (%)	Price £	One-year net holding period return to pension fund (%)	One-year net holding period return to 60% tax-payer (%)
A	3	94	9.6	7.7
B	12	98	14.3	6.9

The tax-payer with a marginal rate of 60% would prefer the low-coupon gilt *A* whereas the pension fund would prefer the 12% gilt *B*. This is because the tax advantages of the low-coupon gilt for high-rate taxpayers have led to its offering a lower gross yield of 9.6% than the high-coupon gilt's gross yield of 14.3%.

As far as dividend yield and capital gains on shares are concerned, pension funds do *not* appear to be indifferent between them. They seem to prefer dividends, despite the fact that they do not at present need current income, perhaps because dividends give the pension fund managers more funds to invest without having to incur transaction costs by selling shares. This preference for dividends was seen when Coats Paton passed its 1974 final dividend. Although the passing of the dividend actually increased the firm's immediate cash flow (by not having to pay ACT on the dividend when there was insufficient mainstream corporation tax against which to offset it), the pension fund and other institutional shareholders were extremely displeased by this move. Another factor which may affect a company's dividend policy is that if neither an interim nor a final dividend is paid in any one financial year, the ordinary shares can no longer be held by trusts governed by the Trustee Investments Act 1961.[7]

(iii) TIMING AND SELECTION

Employee and employer contributions represent a form of contractual saving, certainly from the employee's point of view. The employee has no choice as to where his contributions are invested nor can he usually decide how much to contribute; his payments are automatically deducted from his pay. This enables the pension fund manager to be more or less certain of how much new money he will have to invest each

[7] See section (iv) below on asset mix for further requirements of this Act. Trusts subject to the Act are likely to include the smaller pension funds.

month or quarter. This regular inflow of new money has two effects on investment strategy. Firstly, it allows the investment manager to alter the balance of his portfolio with the new money, without having to sell part of his existing holdings. This should lead to lower portfolio turnover and transaction costs than, say, investment trusts, which have no regular new inflow of funds. Secondly, the pension fund manager can follow, if he so wishes, a form of investment strategy, known as 'pound averaging'. By spreading the purchases of securities over the peaks and troughs of the market, the pension fund manager can ensure that the average cost of these securities will be at their average prices, rather than at their peak prices, over a period. In practice, pension funds may not do this, preferring instead to keep the new money in cash until they judge that the moment is right for investment in shares or gilts, whatever the efficient markets hypothesis may say. For example, pension funds in general withheld from investment in ordinary shares during the fourth quarter of 1974, despite the fact that share prices were at a fifteen-year low, believing that share prices would fall still further and thus attempting to time correctly their share purchases.

(iv) ASSET MIX

The trust deed of a pension fund usually allows for the overall investment policy to be left to the discretion of the trustees, in consultation with the company and the investment advisers. A few trust deeds make no specific statement on investment policy, and, in these cases, the trustees must conform to the investment policy laid down in the Trustee Investments Act 1961, which, amongst other things, restricts investments to at least 50% in fixed interest stock (excluding preference shares) and up to 50% in ordinary and preference shares, shares in building societies and units in authorised unit trusts. Another constraint on pension funds governed by Act is that they cannot invest directly in real property.

The investment policy will usually be concerned with the asset mix, that is, the proportions which can be invested in each type of security, and possibly a list of approved securities. Day-to-day decisions will be taken by the pension fund managers who can be employees of the company, or may be financial institutions such as merchant banks or insurance companies. The pension funds managed by insurance companies will usually not be in the form of a trust fund but in the form of a contract between the company and the insurance company. In these cases, the insurance company will normally have discretion over the investment policy.

The traditional view on asset mix in periods of low inflation, reflected in the Trustee Investments Act 1961, was that it was advisable to place the bulk of the funds in fixed interest securities such as gilts. As the rate of inflation increased in the 1960s and 1970s, asset mixes were adjusted to allow higher proportions to be invested in equities and property, which, as mentioned earlier, were viewed as better inflation hedges.

A common way of deciding on the asset mix, taking the impact of inflation into account, is to fund the liabilities which have crystallised, such as the future pensions of employees who have left (whose pensions will be based on their known leaving salaries) with assets having future values fixed in nominal terms and to fund the uncertain future liabilities with assets which should maintain their value in real terms. This method of determining the optimal asset mix appears to ignore the implications of the capital asset pricing model which suggest that the equity portfolio should approximate as nearly as possible to the market portfolio, and that the amount of fixed interest securities held should not be related to the ratio of known to unknown liabilities but rather to the required level of risk of the fund.

However, before the optimal level of risk in the fund and, hence, the optimal asset mix can be determined, the question must be asked as to who will benefit or suffer from the risks and returns of the pension fund portfolio. If, as is most common, pension benefits are fixed in relation to final earnings, the company will benefit from good performance by being able to make reduced contributions in the future, and correspondingly suffer from poor performance by being asked to make increased contributions in the future.[8] So, in the cases where pension rights are linked to salary and not pension fund performance, the risk that the assets of the pension fund will be less than or greater than its liabilities will be felt more by the shareholders of the company than by the legal beneficiaries of the fund.[9]

Given that, in these instances, the shareholders of the company may be more concerned with the risk and return of the pension fund than are the pensioners, the question of optimal asset mix should perhaps be considered from the shareholders' point of view. For example, it is likely that when the stock market as a whole does badly, and hence the pension fund's equity portfolio suffers, the company will be required to top up its contributions at a time when it, too, is suffering and is least able to do so. In this way, equities in a pension fund portfolio will increase the volatility of the company's earnings and hence the risk

---

[8] It is worth noting that a company is not *legally* bound to follow an actuary's recommendation to make good any deficit which may occur (based on the actuary's valuation of the assets and liabilities of the fund at a given date) although, provided the company is solvent, it is usual for the company to do so.

[9] Where pension rights *are* linked to fund performance (that is, where pensions are increased when the fund does well and vice versa), it will be the beneficiaries of the pension fund who suffer or benefit from the risk and return of the pension fund portfolio.

borne by the shareholders of the company. In contrast, fixed interest investments in the portfolio would reduce this risk without affecting the pensioners' *expected* benefits. So, by considering who actually benefits or suffers from pension fund performance in the long term, we may reach a different view of what constitutes the optimal asset mix from that usually held. Instead of investing in risky equities and property, perhaps pension fund managers should be concentrating on investing in lower risk fixed interest securities. However, this brings us back to the inadequacy of most fixed interest investments as hedges against inflation.

A similar dilemma arises when we consider how the risk of the pension fund portfolio should be measured. In Chapter 2, we chose to measure the riskiness of securities and portfolios by their standard deviations, whereas, in Chapter 8, we saw that, according to the capital asset pricing model, investors are only rewarded for the beta element of risk in their portfolios, due to the fact that the remaining risk of their portfolios can largely be diversified away. Applying this approach to the pension fund problem, if the shareholders of the company effectively bear the portfolio risk, the pension fund's beta will be the appropriate measure of risk, since it can be assumed that the shareholders hold these shares as part of a diversified portfolio. However, if the pensioners bear the risk, as they may do if their pensions are linked to the fund's performance, it must be remembered that the assets of the pension fund probably represent the major portion of their savings, especially if they are not home owners. In this case, the standard deviation, as a measure of *total* risk, may be a more appropriate measure of risk. As we shall see in Chapter 12, a risk measure appropriate to the persons at risk must be chosen before any comparable estimates of performance can be made.

Before any conclusions concerning optimal asset mix or suitable measures of risk can be drawn, it must be said that the whole area of what the financial objectives of a pension fund should be in practice and how these should be translated into investment decisions is, unfortunately, still a matter for much debate and disagreement.

Insurance companies

We now turn to the second fastest growing type of investing institution, insurance companies. UK insurance companies had assets invested of £4.9b. in 1957 (they were then twice the size of pension funds) compared with £65.3b. in 1980, of which, say, £18b. was pension business.

The benefits of reducing risk through pooling have long been obvious.

We saw, in Chapter 7, that if the independent risks of an event occurring are pooled, the combined risk is less than if risks were separately borne. For example, the risk of a house being destroyed by fire is fairly easily quantified by looking at past experience. Now, if an insurance company takes on several thousand fire insurance policies, it can be reasonably certain of the level of claims from those policies and the premium charged can take account of the fact that the risk borne by each individual house owner has been reduced through pooling. Of course, the insurance company will have to cover expenses and, if it is profit-making,[10] will require a return for its shareholders. So the premium charged will not reflect the entire statistical benefit of pooling.

As well as carrying out their insurance role, insurance companies have also evolved as investment intermediaries. This is partly because of the nature of life *as*surance,[11] where the policyholder seeks to protect his dependants from financial loss caused by his premature death and perhaps also to provide for his old age. Most life policies provide benefit on expiry of the term of the policy, say at age sixty, or on earlier death – known as 'endowment' policies. This contrasts with non-life policies, where no benefit is paid if the event does not occur, that is, in the majority of cases. So, life assurance policies can be thought of as long-term savings schemes with an element of insurance attached to provide the benefits earlier in the case of premature death. As has already been mentioned, the success of life assurance policies as a means of long-term saving has been encouraged by government tax reliefs accorded to these policies.

The activities of insurance companies can thus be split into two, general business and long-term business[12] (the latter mostly life assurance-related). To give an idea of their relative sizes, insurance companies held assets related to general insurance of £11.5b. in 1980 compared to £53.7b. for long-term business. Many insurance companies carry out both activities, indeed most of the major UK insurance companies are 'composites'. However, they are required by law to manage and report the two activities completely separately, to prevent cross-funding of two basically very different types of business.

---

[10] Mutual insurance companies aim to distribute profits by way of increased bonuses to the 'with profits' policy-holders or by way of reduced premiums. So, these policyholders can be regarded as the equivalent of shareholders.

[11] The term *as*surance is used where a benefit is always going to be paid (for example, if not on death then on expiry of the policy) as opposed to *in*surance where a benefit is only paid *if* an event such as theft occurs.

[12] Long-term business includes life assurance, pensions business, insurance-related long-term savings policies and long-term sickness insurance.

General insurance

In this field, which includes motor and fire insurance, policies are usually taken out for a period of one year. Claims related to these policies are mostly settled fairly quickly, reducing the insurance companies' ability to build up long-term reserves except out of profit. Also, the funds held to meet these claims have to be in fairly liquid form. Thus, in Table 11.3 on p. 333, we can see that 13% of the total assets related to general insurance business (net of agents' balances[13]) were held in short-term assets in 1980 compared with an equivalent figure of 3% for long-term business. Similarly, the gilts held for general business were of shorter maturity, and lower proportions of equities and property were held, than for long-term business. Nevertheless, substantial long-term investments are held to back the risks of general insurance.

Long-term funds

As mentioned above, this is mostly life assurance-related business. However, the type of policy varies from the 'term' policy, where a benefit is payable only on death (or injury) within the period stipulated, to the 'unit-linked' policy, where the life assurance element may be only a minor addition to investment in a unit trust. The UK is one of the most heavily insured countries in the world, with four out of five households having some life assurance cover and over 100 million policies in issue. The reasons behind this amount of life assurance are the tax relief available, possibly the lower level of state benefits available compared to other developed countries, and the method of sale of these policies; for, life assurance is the only form of saving which agents have been allowed to sell 'on the doorstep'. This has led to anomalies; for example, unit trusts cannot sell units in this way, but unit-linked life assurance policies can be so sold. The ability to market products directly through the use of agents in this and other ways has given insurance companies an advantage over such institutions as investment trusts which are not allowed to promote the sale of their shares in the same way.[14]

Given the long-term nature of life assurance policies, insurance companies often have funds to invest for long periods. If we look at

---

[13] Agents' balances represent premiums owing to the insurance companies but still held by the agents who collected them.
[14] Since investment trusts are limited liability companies.

Table 11.3, we can see that this is reflected in the type of securities held for long-term business. For example, in 1980, 31% of total assets were invested in equities and a further 23% in property and land. Similarly, the gilts held were mostly those with a maturity of at least fifteen years.

Investment objectives and policy

In the same way as for pension funds, we now examine in more detail the factors affecting the investment decisions of insurance companies.

(i) LIABILITIES

We have seen that the nature of insurance companies' liabilities varies according to whether they do general or long-term business. The long-term business includes a proportion (estimated at one-third) of pensions business, which is a major growth area for insurance companies. The remainder is life assurance policies linked to different savings packages.

Originally, insurance companies concentrated on offering fixed benefits from long-term savings plans, for example a fixed sum or an agreed annuity. The maturities of these policies could be matched with those of long-term, fixed interest securities, enabling the insurance companies to provide benefits fixed in nominal terms (subject only to the risk of changes in market rates at which future premiums could be invested). As increased inflation and interest rates eroded the value of these fixed benefits during the 1960s and 1970s, insurance companies began to offer more 'with profits' policies linked to investments in equities, since equities were expected to increase in value in real terms. It must be remembered that insurance companies act predominantly as intermediaries for the savings element of these policies, passing on the majority of the investment risks to the policyholders. If they cannot fix exactly the benefits by matching, insurance companies prefer not to commit themselves on the actual benefits to be paid, usually guaranteeing a low fixed benefit plus a bonus related to 'investment performance' – a 'with profits' policy. However, competition between insurance companies ensures a wide range of tax-efficient investment packages, all envisaging high benefits. Despite this shift to growth investments, a substantial proportion of the long-term business liabilities of insurance companies is still fixed in nominal terms. This is reflected in the higher proportion of assets invested in gilts in Table 11.3 than is the case for pension funds, whose liabilities are not in general fixed in nominal terms.

(ii) TAX

The two types of insurance business are treated differently for tax purposes. Corporation tax is payable on the profits of non-life business whereas, for life business, tax is payable on the investment income (net of management expenses) at a reduced rate of 37.5%.[15] Life assurance policyholders were also entitled to tax relief at half the basic rate of income tax on their premiums (until March 1984 when such relief was withdrawn).

This tax treatment for life assurance business has had two effects. Firstly, as already mentioned, the tax relief available on life assurance policies renders saving through this medium relatively more attractive than some other forms of investment, other factors being the same. Also, because the intermediary, in this case the insurance company, is charged a low basic rate of tax, so in effect is the policyholder (except in the case of certain types of policy where he has a higher tax rate and has to pay additional tax). However, the individual with a lower effective tax rate than that paid by the insurance company, allowing also for the tax relief on his premium, might be able to achieve higher net returns through alternative forms of investment if he does not want life cover. Secondly, insurance companies, because they do pay tax, are not generally 'gross' investors like the pension funds (except on pensions business which is tax exempt).

(iii) LEGISLATION

The insurance industry is heavily controlled by law, as evidenced, for example, by the careful separation of general and long-term business. The aim of the legislation is to try to prevent insurance companies from being unable to meet claims and to minimise the risk of fraud, a potential problem with any form of investment intermediary.

For example, UK insurance companies involved in general business are required to maintain certain solvency margins. These are the ratio of shareholders' capital plus free reserves (in other words, the excess of their assets over their liabilities) to net premium income. Although the legislation does not specify exactly which securities insurance companies

---

[15] This rate is applicable to profits allocated by insurance companies to policyholders or annuitants.

must invest in,[16] certain types of security are not admissible when computing solvency margins. Thus, in effect, these insurance companies are wholly free to choose their investment policy only to the extent that their solvency margins are more than satisfied.

During the early 1970s, insurance companies found that nominal premiums and claims were increasing due to inflation. They therefore tried to ensure that the market value of their assets also increased with inflation, in order for solvency margins to be maintained and to allow them to expand as they wished. As a result, they switched emphasis from fixed interest securities to investments more likely to maintain their value in real terms. However, too great a dependence on risky assets increases the probability of reduced solvency margins (as happened in 1974).

In terms of profits, general insurance companies, say, depend to a greater extent than in the days of low interest rates on their returns from investment. No longer do they automatically expect premium income to cover claims. An underwriting loss is acceptable provided the returns from investment are sufficient. Portfolio performance can make all the difference between a profit-making and a loss-making insurance company.

Investment trusts and unit trusts

We will treat these two types of investing institution in the same section since, although they have different histories and structures, they both have similar investment objectives and policies.

Investment trusts

Investment trusts have been in existence for more than 100 years. Promoted to offer the small investor a way of holding a diversified portfolio, the portfolio emphasis of investment trusts has switched from over 50% in fixed interest securities in 1930 to over 90% in equities by 1980. There has always been a tendency towards a strong international flavour to their portfolios, as can be seen in Table 11.3, where 38% of total assets in 1980 were invested in overseas securities. Assets have

---

[16] This is in contrast to the US where insurance companies are restricted in their investments predominantly to fixed interest securities.

grown from £1.1b. in 1957 to £8.4b. in 1980, representing an annual average growth rate of only 9% per annum. This conceals rapid expansion during the 1960s followed by decline in real terms during the 1970s.

Investment trusts (or ITCs as they are known for short) are limited liability companies and are not trusts in the legal sense. Investors in these trusts acquire the ordinary shares and their return is therefore in the form of dividends and capital gains or losses from their shares. ITCs use the funds raised from shareholders to invest in a diversified portfolio of securities. New money for investment can only come from a rights issue or from borrowing, either from the bank or by issuing fixed interest debt such as debentures or loan stock. This ability to raise fixed interest debt capital was exploited in the 1960s and allowed the ITCs to 'gear themselves up'. However, the collapse of the quoted fixed interest new issue market in the early 1970s has led to a fall in the average level of gearing of ITCs, some now having negative gearing, where the amount of fixed interest debt held in their own portfolios exceeds their own debt. Table 11.5 illustrates the impact of positive gearing on the ordinary shareholders of Wary Investment Trust.

Because of the fixed interest debentures in issue, an increase of 20% in the market value of the share portfolio held by Wary would lead to a 27% increase in the net assets belonging to the shareholders of Wary. A decline in the value of Wary's portfolio would have a similarly magnified detrimental effect on the value of Wary ITC's ordinary shares.

Since investment in ITCs is via the purchase of ordinary shares, which are quoted on the Stock Exchange, one might expect the ITC share price to approximate the market value of the underlying investment portfolio which is held on behalf of the shareholders. However, this has not been the case in practice and ITC share prices usually stand at a discount or a premium to their underlying portfolio value, more often the former. Recent discounts have been of the order of 20–30% to net

Table 11.5   Effect of gearing on Wary Investment Trust shareholders

	£m.
Market-value portfolio (all equities)	20
less: 5% Debentures 1990	(5)
Net assets for ordinary shareholders	15
Suppose that market-value portfolio increases by 20% to:	24
less: 5% Debentures 1990	(5)
Net assets for ordinary shareholders	19
Representing an increase of	**27%**

asset value. Many reasons have been put forward to explain this phenomenon, which implies that shares held through the medium of an investment trust are less valuable in some way than if they were held directly. Reasons have included the limited marketability of some ITC shares, contingent capital gains tax liabilities (no longer a factor[17]) which would have crystallised on disposal of particular investments, and the fact that investment trusts do not distribute 100% of the income they receive from investments, some being absorbed by management costs and some reinvested. (To qualify as an ITC, with its attendant tax advantages, ITCs must distribute at least 85% of the investment income they receive.) There is still no agreement on which of these and other factors lead to the discounts frequently observed on ITC shares.

Premiums on net asset value, which occasionally exist on investment trust shares, are just as difficult to explain. In these cases, investors appear to be paying a premium for management of the portfolio. This either implies that investment trust managers are believed to have superior 'picking winners' skills (although this is unlikely to be a permanent feature – see the discussion in Chapter 9 on efficient markets) or that they have information on or access to, say, overseas securities which is not readily available to individual investors.

Whatever the reasons for the discounts or premiums on net asset values of ITC shares, one effect is to add an extra dimension of risk to investment in ITC shares compared to buying shares direct. An investor in ITC shares takes on not only the risk of the underlying investments but also the risk that the level of the premium or discount will change. So, future changes in the level of the discount or premium to net asset value of ITC share prices add another risk factor to investment in ITC shares, in the same way as changes in the investment currency premium added an extra dimension of risk to investment in foreign currency securities in the days of exchange control.

The existence of quite large discounts on ITC share prices led to a mini-takeover boom by pension funds in the late 1970s.[18] By incorporating the investment trust portfolio into their existing investments, the pension funds could acquire in one go a substantial equity portfolio possibly at a price discount. However, the level of any gain to the pension fund from such a move depended on the price paid for the ITC shares.

Aware of their vulnerability to takeover and of the depressing influence on marketability of the discount, investment trusts have tried several methods of relating their share price more closely to the

---

[17] For an explanation, see the section on tax under 'Investment Objectives and Policy' on p. 349 of this chapter.
[18] For example, the acquisition by the Post Office Staff Superannuation Fund of Investment Trust Corporation for around £90m. in 1978.

underlying net asset value. For example, some set a fixed date for redemption of the shares, at which time the underlying assets will be sold and distributed to shareholders. Others have chosen to convert themselves into unit trusts which, as we shall see, are not quoted at a discount to net asset value. The ability to buy in their own shares, first allowed by the 1981 Companies Act, now provides investment trusts with another possible partial solution to the problem.

Another important effect of their being organised as limited liability companies is that ITCs are not allowed to promote the sale of their own shares. Unit trusts, on the other hand, can and do spend substantial amounts on marketing their units and on commission to agents. This is one reason for the relatively greater success of unit trusts in recent years, despite their consequently higher running costs.

Unit trusts

Unit trusts are a more recent phenomenon than ITCs, only really taking off in the 1960s. Assets managed by unit trusts have grown from a mere £60m. in 1957 to £4.6b. in 1980, a much faster growth rate than with ITCs. Although the total assets of unit trusts are still less than those of the ITCs, there are more than twice the number of unit trusts in existence, with over 400 'authorised' unit trusts compared with approximately 200 investment trusts. Unit trusts have concentrated on equity investment, with 96% of assets invested in UK and overseas ordinary shares in 1980 (see Table 11.3), 23% overseas and 73% in the UK. However, as we shall see in the section on tax, there has been a move towards gilts since 1980. Unit trusts do not have such a strong tradition of investment in overseas securities as do ITCs although unit trusts have become more internationally oriented in recent years.

An investor in a unit trust invests by buying units from the managers. Unit trusts are also known as 'open end' funds (as opposed to ITCs which are known as 'closed end') because of the fact that the size of a unit trust varies with the number of units in issue. If investors wish to invest in the trust, new units are created to meet demand, which increases the size of the fund. The managers invest the money (less a management charge) by adding to the fund portfolio. If investors wish to disinvest, they will sell their units back to the managers and the trust will shrink in size, the managers in principle[19] being forced to realise

---

[19] In practice the managers will keep part of the portfolio in cash to meet such requests and will, in fact, often be able to 'match' purchasers and sellers of units on a day-to-day basis without having to touch the portfolio.

part of the portfolio in order to buy back the units from the holders. The managers of the unit trust buy and sell units at prices based on the underlying market value of the portfolio at the time. There is thus no discount or premium on net asset value except for the equivalent (charged by the managers) of the jobber's turn and broker's commission between the buying and selling price.

From this description of unit trusts, we can see the major difference between unit trusts and investment trusts. The capitalisation of ITCs is fixed in size (unless they borrow or have a rights issue), with the discount or premium of the share price to net asset value reflecting current demand and supply for the shares. The units of unit trusts, on the other hand, are bought and sold at prices based on the underlying net asset value, so that there are no discounts or premiums. Thus, demand in the case of unit trusts is reflected in the number of units in issue, which defines the size of the unit trust.

Investment objectives and policy

In the case of an investment trust company, the board of directors will determine investment policy. In the case of a unit trust, although the board of trustees will check that the investment policy is being properly carried out, the actual policy itself will usually be chosen by the unit trust managers. Management of both types of trust is mostly delegated to a management company, sometimes an outside organisation, sometimes owned by the trust. Some management companies run a whole 'stable' of trusts. For example, in 1978, four unit trust management groups managed ninety-seven unit trusts while nine investment trust management groups looked after sixty-eight ITCs. Each trust is characterised by its own investment policy, which may be geographic specialisation as with Crescent Tokyo Unit Trust, or a stress on income or capital gain as with Gartmore Extra Income Unit Trust, or like many trusts, simply offer a diversified portfolio spread geographically and/or across different market sectors.

A number of ITCs have a 'split capital' structure, separating income from capital growth. The income shares usually receive the income earned on the trust investments and paid out by way of dividends and the capital shares are usually entitled to the assets on final winding up (which will be on a pre-specified date). For example, Altifund ITC has income and capital shares, with the income shares entitled to

$$\frac{30}{31}$$

of the profits available for distribution and to a 50p capital payment plus a 50p premium on winding up. The winding-up date will be between 31 March 1986 and 31 March 1988, the exact date to be fixed by shareholders. The capital shares are entitled to

$$\frac{1}{31}$$

of the profits available for distribution plus all surplus assets on winding up.

(i) LEGISLATION

Unit trusts, as a special kind of intermediary not subject to company and Stock Exchange regulation (as are investment trusts), are tightly controlled by the Department of Trade under separate legislation. Indeed, the 1982 Gower Report on the regulation of financial institutions criticised the burden of regulation on unit trusts compared to other financial institutions as an example of legislative 'overkill'.[20] To achieve certain concessions, unit trusts have to be 'authorised' by the Department of Trade, although there are now a number of 'exempt' trusts set up specifically to make investments not available to 'authorised' trusts, for example in property. 'Exempt' trusts are so-called because they are exempt from capital gains tax and their units can only be held by gross investors such as pension funds and charities. Since 1980, authorised unit trusts have also been exempt from capital gains tax on their disposals and the major difference between the two types now lies in their investment policies and the right held only by authorised unit trusts to advertise and promote their units.

Management charges for unit trusts average around 5% initial charge and an annual charge of, say, 1% and are higher than the effective management costs of running ITCs. In addition, managers also charge a turn between the 'bid' and 'offer' price for units, which averages around 7%,[21] although, of course, this spread will also be implicit in the purchase of ITC shares via the stock market, which have the additional burden of stamp duties.

Both types of trusts have traditionally had restrictions imposed on their investment policies. These restrictions are on the type of security which can be held (for example, they have to hold marketable securities which excludes direct investment in property) as well as on the amounts invested in any one security. For example, ITCs are not allowed to

---

[20] See the Gower Report (1982), p. 69.
[21] This is lower than the spread allowed by the Department of Trade because, as mentioned in footnote 19, unit trust managers can usually 'match' buyers and sellers.

invest more than 15% of their assets in any one company.[22] This type of restriction ensures a reasonable amount of diversification, a sensible policy according to portfolio theory. Interestingly, ITCs, which have the longer history of the two, have reduced the average number of securities they hold (with an ITC perhaps holding as many as 1,000 securities twenty years ago compared with several hundred now). This suggests they realise that they can have efficient portfolios in the portfolio theory sense without incurring the huge transaction and monitoring costs associated with holding large numbers of securities.

(ii) Tax

It will be noted from Table 11.3 that only 4% of unit trusts' assets and 6% of ITCs' assets were invested in UK government or corporate fixed interest securities in 1980. This reflected a tax disadvantage to trusts of investing in these securities, a disadvantage which was removed in 1980. Prior to that, both types of trust paid corporation tax on 'unfranked income', that is, income from securities which do not have an associated tax credit to show that tax has already been paid. Franked income, such as the dividends from UK company shares, is not liable to tax payable by the trusts, and the tax credits are passed on to the ultimate investors. Interest from gilts and corporate debentures represents unfranked income and, prior to 1980, was liable to corporation tax before being passed on to the investors. As a result, until recently, trusts preferred to concentrate on equity investments. Since 1980, however, several trusts specialising in fixed interest securities have been set up.

A basic problem of any intermediary is to provide benefits, whether from economies of scale, pooling of risk or diversification, without these benefits being eroded by tax disadvantages. For example, we saw that non-tax-paying investors might be at a tax disadvantage if they invested through certain types of life assurance policies. Similarly, investors would be reluctant to invest via investment or unit trusts if they were taxed twice, once in the hands of the trust and once in their own hands. However, we have seen that, in the case of trusts, potential double taxation is avoided by, for example, the tax credit attached to dividends from UK shares being able to be passed on intact, and by trusts not being liable to capital gains tax on their own disposals, any such liability being incurred only by the ultimate investor. Of course, intermediaries will benefit from any tax *advantages* attached to investment through their particular medium. For example, pension funds, life assurance companies and, indirectly, unit trusts, all benefit from tax concessions.

---

[22] This and other requirements are imposed by the Inland Revenue on approved ITCs before they can qualify for certain tax concessions (some of which are discussed in the next section on tax).

(iii) Timing and selection

A growing unit trust will have a regular inflow of cash to invest from the sale of new units, although it must retain a certain proportion of its portfolio in liquid assets to be able to buy back units on demand. A unit trust which suffers a decline in popularity may well find itself with a shrinking number of units and a net cash outflow. Unit trusts can thus have an unpredictable cash flow, which will complicate the planning of investment strategy. One way round this has been for unit trusts to set up schemes for the purchase of their units by instalments to create some form of long-term savings plan (often with the tax advantages obtained by linking the scheme with life assurance), thereby ensuring a regular monthly cash inflow over a period of years.

Unit trusts have the highest portfolio turnover[23] of the four types of institution, with sales of ordinary shares averaging 40% of the value of the share portfolio in 1978. Many unit trusts are therefore not unduly inhibited by any lack of new money, being prepared if necessary to sell existing securities in their search for high performance. Investment trusts have a lower portfolio turnover than unit trusts (22% in 1978). These figures compare with the average for all investing institutions in 1978 of under 15%. We saw in Chapter 9 that, given the applicability of the semi-strong form of the efficient markets hypothesis, it is unlikely that any investing institution will, on the basis of security analysis, be able consistently to achieve abnormal returns over the long run. This implies that a high level of portfolio turnover will be unproductive, merely resulting in unnecessarily high transaction costs. Studies of UK unit trusts and investment trust have not found evidence of long-term abnormal returns, leading one to conclude that the higher than average levels of portfolio turnover in both unit trusts and ITCs may waste some of the benefits they provide in the form of diversification.

(iv) Asset mix

As we have already seen, the objectives of both investment and unit trusts are to provide the advantages of diversification, predominantly in equity investment. Most investment trusts have a beta of around 1, with an average for the industry in 1982 of exactly 1.0. Those with a high overseas content should have somewhat lower betas[24] since returns on overseas investments will be less correlated with returns on the UK

---

[23] Defined as sales during the year as a per cent of the average of beginning- and end-year holdings at market value.

[24] For example, G.T. Japan Investment Trust had a historical beta in 1981 of 0.7.

stock market. Investment trusts with a high element of gearing (described in Table 11.5) have relatively higher betas, because of the increased volatility of the ordinary shareholders' assets.

Impact of the investing institutions on the stock market

Having looked at each of the above types of investing institution separately, we can now consider their overall impact on Stock Exchange investment. As we have seen, the investing institutions are now the dominant investors in the stock market, both in terms of the proportion of securities held and in terms of turnover. By 1978, the four main types of investing institution were responsible for over 60% of all Stock Exchange turnover in value terms. As they have increased the size of their investment portfolios, so they have also increased their portfolio turnover rates (security sales as a percentage of the value of the security portfolio). For example, their portfolio turnover in equities increased from an average of 6.5% in 1963–7 to an average of 19.3% in 1973–7. This dominance of the investing institutions as traders in the market has led to larger average bargain sizes for all types of security and to the increasing dependence of stockbrokers and jobbers on the institutions for business.

Investment analysis

The effects of this dependence are manifest in many areas. For example, stockbrokers now often give priority to their institutional clients when circulating research reports and recommendations. The small investor may be regarded as a less important client. Such privileged treatment for the institutions is no doubt due to their importance as clients.

However, some of the larger institutions also employ their own investment analysts and advisers. This has two implications. Firstly, because these institutions do their own investment research, they are reluctant to subsidise through their commission payments the general market research carried out by stockbrokers. There have therefore been complaints about the minimum commission system, which covers not only dealing charges but also the cost of the stockbrokers' research activities. The institutions have had some success in this area by developing their own secondary market through ARIEL (described in

Chapter 1).[25] ARIEL has not become as important as was originally forecast, probably because the Stock Exchange responded to the threat by reducing commission charges on various large transactions three times between 1970 and 1982 and offering to phase out minimum commissions completely by 1986.

Secondly, the institutions are often the dominant shareholders in any company whose shares they hold, even though they may each hold a relatively small percentage. As a result, it has become commonplace for the institutions' own analysts to keep in close touch with these companies' managements, through the medium, for example, of regular company visits. This privileged treatment could lead to the institutions gaining access to 'inside' information, information which may not be generally available to all investors. If this were the case, there would be a two-tier shareholder information structure, with the smaller shareholders less well informed. However, as we saw in Chapter 9, whether they have access to privileged information or not, the investing institutions do not appear to earn long-run excess returns with it. Similarly, their greater economies of scale in investment analysis (in the sense that only one chemical industry analyst, say, is needed whether thousands or millions of pounds are being invested) do not seem to show up in their performance.[26]

Relationships with company managements

The importance of the investing institutions as the major shareholders in many large UK quoted companies has caused much discussion.[27] If they have close relationships with the companies concerned, so the argument goes, surely the institutions could offer help and advice to the companies as well as placing resources at their disposal when needed? However, many company managements, used to the advantages of a well-dispersed, numerous body of shareholders, may be unwilling to spend time liaising with institutional shareholders. Also, the expertise of the institutional investors may not lie in the management area.

From the point of view of the investing institutions, it should be in their interests, in so far as they are long-term shareholders, to develop close links with company managements. That these links have not yet been forged can be seen by the eagerness with which institution

---

[25] ARIEL is a computerised system which matches institutions' buying and selling orders for ordinary shares with a minimum of £5,000 per transaction.

[26] There is no evidence to suggest that individual investors on average do worse than the institutional investors.

[27] For example, the whole of ch. 19 of the Wilson Report is devoted to it.

managers sold their 'long-term' investments in the dawn raids of the early 1980s without the prior knowledge of the companies' managements. A dawn raid takes place when a purchaser quickly builds up a large equity stake in a quoted company (usually before the Stock Exchange officially opens in the morning). Substantial shareholdings can be built up within minutes precisely because only a handful of institutional shareholders, each holding a few per cent of the equity, need to be persuaded to sell. The Council for the Securities Industry has attempted to stop this practice,[28] believing that company managements should have time to defend themselves from what is, in effect, a partial takeover, but 'dawn raids' reflect two things. Firstly, the long-term objectives of the investing institutions do not appear to affect their search for short-run profits and, secondly, it is certainly in the interest of company managements to have an amicable relationship with their institutional shareholders so that they can prevent sudden transfers of share ownership occurring without their knowledge.

Impact on share prices

The institutions may also affect the relative pricing of different types of share. For example, it has been argued that because investing institutions are investing on other people's behalf, they are reluctant to take risks and therefore avoid high-risk investment. Similarly, it has been suggested that because of the large sums at their disposal, they will avoid investment in small companies because of the high monitoring costs of a myriad of small investments and because they would then be forced into the position of largest shareholder, with all its attendant responsibilities. The shares of small companies will probably also be less easily and quickly marketable than the shares of the major companies, especially if large amounts are held. Also, it may be that the institutions as a whole, as we saw with the pension funds, have distinct preferences in such areas as dividend policy. All these factors could affect share prices in the sense that shares for which there was considerable institutional demand would have higher prices relative to the shares for which there was little institutional demand.

Finally, since the majority of investment decisions are now made by perhaps a few hundred institutional investment managers, there may well be greater homogeneity of beliefs in respect of future expectations of return and risk on particular securities than when large numbers of

---

[28] By issuing Rules Governing Substantial Acquisitions of Shares in 1980 (revised in 1982).

individual investors dominated the stock market. If this is so, one of the assumptions of the capital asset pricing model would more nearly hold, but it could also imply greater volatility of share prices and relatively lower liquidity in the stock market if institutional investors all wished to buy and sell at the same time.[29] However, the evidence discussed in the Wilson Report could find no direct relationship between increased institutional investment over time and this may well be because, although all the investing institutions are interested in both the gilts and the equities markets, each institution is trying to achieve a somewhat different investment objective.

Summary

This chapter has investigated the impact of the long-term investing institutions on stock market investment. The four main types – pension funds, insurance companies, investment trusts and unit trusts – are major holders of equities, gilts and corporate fixed interest securities as well as being interested in the options market, financial futures and international investment. Their investments, both in terms of their investment portfolios and the turnover of securities they generate, dominate the stock market. The majority of investors now invest indirectly in the stock market via these investing institutions.

The chapter has examined each of the four main types of investing institution separately, concentrating on how they have evolved and discussing how their particular characteristics affect their investment objectives and policy. Factors such as their tax positions and the need to hedge against inflation have influenced the investments they hold.

The chapter concluded with a discussion of the main ways that investing institutions have affected the stock market, both in terms of the impact on the securities they invest in and on other participants in the stock market.

Appendix: alternatives to funded pension schemes

Although the UK and US governments have legislated for funded pension schemes, which are legally separate from the companies concerned, other countries have chosen different systems.

---

[29] See the Second Stage Evidence of the Stock Exchange to the Wilson Committee, para. 103.

For example, in Germany, pensions are provided for internally, in the sense that companies make provisions for pension payments in their balance sheets but still have the use of the money for investment purposes. With this system, in the event of a company going into liquidation, the company's assets would be used in paying all the creditors and the present and future pensioners could lose all or most of their benefits. So, pension schemes in Germany are insured against such an eventuality. The same system was commonly used in the UK in the 1930s and 1940s but not necessarily with the protection of insurance. The legal separation from the company of the funded schemes now largely in operation in the UK means that, in the event of a liquidation, the creditors of the company cannot reach the assets of the pension fund. However, the assets of a legally separate pension fund, although reserved for the pension liabilities of the company, may still not be sufficient to fund all the pension liabilities incurred before liquidation; in other words, the pension fund may have 'unfunded liabilities'.

In France, companies usually prefer the 'Pay As You Go' method of providing for pensions. Under this system, no provision is made, either in the company's balance sheet or in a separate fund. Pension payments are made as they fall due out of current income and only then appear in the accounts. This system obviates the need for intermediaries and avoids the problem of having to quantify future uncertainties in order to decide the necessary level of contributions.

However, the Pay As You Go system suffers from the same disadvantage as the German schemes. If a company goes into liquidation, there will be no assets, whether notional or real, set aside for the provision of pensions. Again, Pay As You Go only works if there are insurance schemes in existence to protect the pensioners. In France, these are provided by state guarantees and funds. Thus, non-funded schemes usually require more government intervention than funded schemes. They also allow each company to use the funds set aside as pension provisions for investment as they wish. Funded schemes, on the other hand, channel a substantial proportion of corporate sector savings via the pension funds, and it is up to the managers and trustees of the pension funds to decide how best to invest these resources.

One potential advantage of a funded pension scheme is that it should lead to the employer concerned being aware of the cost of his pension scheme. It is tempting under Pay As You Go to promise generous pension entitlements which may cause problems when there is a declining workforce. In the UK, only the government operates Pay As You Go schemes with respect to state pensions and the pensions of civil service employees. Both local authorities and nationalised industries operate funded pension schemes.

Problems

1. (i) What are the main differences between a unit trust and an investment trust? Do any of these differences explain the decline in popularity of the investment trust relative to the unit trust since the early 1970s?

(ii) Suggest reasons why a large proportion of the shares of investment trusts are held by pension funds, and why there was a spate of takeovers of investment trusts by pension funds in the late 1970s/early 1980s.

2. Insurance companies, pension funds, investment trusts and unit trusts are the major investors in the UK stock market. Which type of securities do each of these investing institutions prefer and why?

3. (i) In the light of the Wilson Report on the functioning of financial institutions, what has been the impact on the Stock Exchange of the growth of the financial institutions as the major investors in the stock market?
   (ii) What recommendations would you have made concerning the problems which have arisen as a result of this switch from private to institutional investors had you chaired the Committee?

4. You have been asked to design the Report and Accounts of a pension fund to be sent to all present and future pensioners of the fund. Describe the main items you think should be included.

5. (i) Describe all the costs incurred by investors in unit trusts and investment trusts, in particular the management charges.
   (ii) The investment trust *Year Book* gives ratios of management expenses/assets managed and management expenses/total gross revenue. Are high ratios good or bad for the investor?
   (iii) Suppose a unit trust manages its portfolio as an index fund. How should management be remunerated in this case?

PART IV

CONCLUSION

CHAPTER 12

Investment objectives, investment policy and performance measurement

Introduction

In the first eleven chapters of this book we looked at different types of Stock Exchange securities, how to value them and how to compare them through the medium of expected holding period return and risk. We also considered the advantages of portfolio investment, both domestic and international, and the different requirements of the institutional (as opposed to the individual) investor. In this final chapter, we examine the investor's overall strategy, from the factors he should take into consideration when quantifying his objectives to the measurement of the performance he actually achieves.

Before the investor can make any investment decisions at all, he must decide on the objectives he is trying to achieve. Although all investors will have an implicit investment policy, this is all too often not stated explicitly. Again, the growth of investment intermediaries has emphasised the need for clearly stated objectives. The objectives of these intermediaries have to be known before their performance can be meaningfully measured and compared. There is no point in comparing the performance of an investment trust with the FT All Share Index when its objective was to be 50% invested in the US and 50% in Japan.

Objectives can only be set once certain characteristics of the beneficiaries or investors are known. These characteristics will include their required risk and return, details of their existing wealth, their tax positions, liquidity requirements, future liabilities and a host of other factors. Until recently, the approach of investment advisers has been to concentrate more on the characteristics of the securities or market they are investing in rather than on the characteristics of their clients. As understanding of the efficient markets hypothesis and the capital asset pricing model has spread, more emphasis has been placed on the construction of optimal portfolios, optimal in the sense of being the best portfolio given the investor's risk and return requirements, rather than in the sense of optimal securities (those offering the highest expected excess returns) to put into the portfolio.

Once the objectives of the investor or fund have been established, the investment policy to be pursued must be decided upon. This hinges very much on the beliefs of the investor or fund manager concerned. Two major investment strategies can be identified – passive and active. A passive investment policy corresponds to the 'fair return for risk' approach discussed in Chapter 9 and will be adopted by investors who believe that markets are efficient with respect to information; in other words, that there are no undue monetary rewards to be gained from studying market trends or trying to pick winners. Such investors believe that their selection skills are not sufficient to warrant an active search for excess returns, after transaction costs. All that they expect is, on average, a fair return for the risk they choose to bear. Active investors, on the other hand, follow a 'picking winners' approach and try, by searching for mispriced securities or by attempting to time investments correctly, to beat the market.

Investment policy does not just involve a once and for all portfolio decision. Both active and passive strategies require that the portfolio, however constructed, be amended from time to time. The frequency and extent of the portfolio revisions are also investment policy decisions, taking into account the objectives of the portfolio and the transaction costs involved.

Finally, investors will be interested in measuring the performance of their investment portfolios, for many different reasons. For example, they will wish to check (particularly if they have used an intermediary) that the investment objectives laid down have been followed. Also, they may wish to compare the performance of alternative investment funds. Performance measurement will in addition identify particular investment skills, such as the ability to pick winners, and allows comparison between active and passive investment strategies.

Despite an obvious need for performance measurement, techniques could only be developed in the wake of portfolio theory and the capital asset pricing model since these were the first models which explicitly quantified risk and return. Once risk could be measured, comparisons could be made between portfolios of different risk. Similarly, once a passive investment strategy based on the CAPM had been identified, comparisons could be made between active and passive investment policies. Performance measurement is now commonplace in the US, where portfolio theory and the CAPM were developed, and is becoming more usual in the UK, in preference to the traditional cursory comparison with an often non-comparable share index.

This chapter begins with a discussion of possible investment objectives and considers the factors which must be taken into consideration when deciding on objectives, for example inflation and tax. The second section compares alternative investment policies, that is, active and passive approaches to investment management. The third and final section describes the alternative, risk-adjusted performance measures which can be used, together with a discussion on their relevance, in different situations.

Investment objectives

These will of course vary widely according to the type of investor. For instance, an individual investor may wish to maximise his return over a ten-year period, taking on a reasonably high level of risk since he already has a substantial earned income. A pensioner would be more likely to require a constant level of income in real terms, to be achieved with minimum risk. A pension fund manager might have the objective of meeting a specified set of future liabilities at minimum overall cost.

Rather than specifying in detail particular sets of objectives, we shall concentrate instead on those factors which must be considered before any investment objectives can be set. We group these factors under five headings – consumption preferences, required risk and return, tax, inflation and asset mix.

Consumption preferences

Each investor will be aware of his own consumption preferences. These will include preferred currency of consumption, so that an investor who spends half the year in New York may require a portfolio denominated in both sterling and dollars. Also, part of the portfolio may need to be in liquid assets, to meet unforeseen liabilities and to allow the investor to pursue an 'active' investment policy. The preference for income or capital gain will be determined partly by the tax position of the investor but also by the need for a regular income as opposed to long-term capital growth. However, this does not always follow; for example, as we saw in Chapter 11, pension funds, despite the fact that they do not currently need income, still prefer regular dividends.

The time horizon of concern to the investor will vary from a few days or weeks for the speculator who believes he has inside information to several decades for the pension fund manager. The time horizon will thus be a function of the future consumption needs of the investor and of the type of investment policy he prefers. The time horizon will also affect the investor's attitude to transaction costs. For example, if the investor wishes to invest in property in the near future, he will wish to minimise the risk and transaction costs of his short-term Stock Exchange investments. On the other hand, a salaried investor with ten years to go before retirement may be willing to invest in a unit-linked life assurance scheme, where the long-term capital growth and tax advantages outweigh the relatively high transaction costs.

Attitude to risk and return

As we have seen throughout the book, the investor's attitude to risk and return is the most important factor needed to be able to quantify his investment objectives. Whether he wishes to pursue a 'picking winners'. or a 'fair return for risk' investment policy, the investor needs to state how much risk he is willing to bear and how much return he requires on average in order to choose between alternative efficient portfolios. The investor can either concentrate on maximising return subject to a maximum risk level, for example an investor merely supplementing his earned income, or on minimising risk subject to a minimum return, such as the pensioner living off his investments. Risk can be expressed in terms of the standard deviation of returns, if the investor is considering his entire wealth and the possibility of its loss, or in terms of beta if the investment considered represents only part of his total wealth.

Since the quantifying of risk is a relatively new concept, it may be difficult for investors to be able to state the maximum standard deviation of returns that they will accept or the minimum return they require. One way round this problem would be to face the investor with all the alternative portfolios which lie on his efficient frontier,[1] each of which will have different risk–return characteristics, and to ask the investor to choose the one he prefers.

Tax

This is also an extremely important factor in real life, as we saw in Chapter 11, although tax was excluded from the portfolio theory and capital asset pricing models. Tax can render certain investments unattractive to the investor, as was the case with gilts for unit and investment trusts before the 1980 Finance Act. Similarly, tax can make certain investments more attractive than they would otherwise be, such as savings schemes which offer the tax advantages attached to life assurance but which may, in fact, earn lower gross returns than equivalent investments without the same tax advantages.

Tax can also affect preferences for income or capital gains, high- or low-coupon stocks, direct versus indirect investment. The tax position of the investor must therefore be taken into account when determining the investment objectives of his portfolio and the portfolios considered must be compared net of tax.

Inflation

A relatively recent phenomenon in investment has been the impact of inflation on the value of investments. Investments and liabilities can no longer be viewed purely in nominal terms. For example, in Chapter 2, Mr Stone wished to buy a house in five years' time. Even if he bought gilts which had fixed redemption values and which matured exactly at the right moment, he could not be sure that house prices would remain fixed in nominal terms over the five years. Similarly, pension funds' liabilities are related to salaries which are certainly not constant in nominal terms. Because of this inflation risk, investment objectives

---

[1] As we saw in Chapter 7, the efficient frontier represents those portfolios which offer the best returns given their risk. The investor will choose amongst these according to his utility function.

must take account of inflation in assessing the investor's requirements, that is, whether the need is to keep up with inflation or merely to cover a nominal liability, such as the repayment of a fixed loan.

Most investors, whether individuals or institutions, need to maintain the value of their investments in real terms. This leads us to consider the different types of investment available in the light of how good a hedge they are against inflation.

We have already noted in Chapter 11 that investment intermediaries, in particular insurance companies, pension funds and investment trusts, all experienced losses from their fixed interest investments in the 1960s and 1970s as interest rates and inflation rates rose. There was a general movement away from fixed interest investments towards equities and property, both of which were believed to represent better hedges against inflation. According to classical economic theory, ordinary shares were supposed to maintain their value in real terms. As interest rates and the required rate of return on equities went up, so would the income of the companies as revenues and costs went up correspondingly. The overall impact on share prices would represent no change in real terms.

Let us first consider a world with no inflation. The value of a share, P_0, can be written, according to the dividend valuation model discussed in Chapter 5, as

$$P_0 = \sum_{n=1}^{\infty} \frac{D_n}{(1 + R)^n} \tag{12.1}$$

where D_n is the dividend to be paid in year n and R is the required rate of return on the share. How will inflation affect equation (12.1)? If the revenues as well as the outgoings of the firm increase in line with inflation, thus allowing dividends also to keep up with inflation, the numerator of equation (12.1) will become, simply, $D_n (1 + i)^n$ where i is the annual inflation rate expected to prevail for the foreseeable future. Similarly, the required rate of return will also adjust for expected inflation, so that the denominator $(1 + R)$ will become instead $(1 + R) (1 + i)$.

Substituting into equation (12.1) gives

$$P_0 = \sum_{n=1}^{\infty} \frac{D_n (1 + i)^n}{(1 + R)^n (1 + i)^n} \tag{12.2}$$

The term $(1 + i)^n$ cancels out and equation (12.2) reduces to

$$P_0 = \sum_{n=1}^{\infty} \frac{D_n}{(1 + R)^n} \tag{12.3}$$

which is exactly the same as equation (12.1).

From equation (12.3), we can see how the classical theory works. If, in an inflationary environment, the dividends of the company are maintained in real terms (as a result of revenues and costs going up exactly in line with inflation) and if the required rate of return also adjusts exactly for expected inflation, the current value of the share, P_0, will remain unchanged, thus representing a complete hedge against inflation.

In real life, there are many reasons why the classical theory may not hold. For example, the company's cash flows may not maintain their value in real terms as a result of, for example, prices not keeping up with costs; the tax system penalising nominal, as opposed to real, increases in profits (as did corporation tax until a rough-and-ready adjustment in the form of stock relief was introduced in 1974);[2] or simply lags between changes in costs and changes in revenues. Also, the required rate of return, R, only takes *expected* inflation into account. No allowance is made in equation (12.2) for unexpected inflation.

This leads us to the conclusion that equities might not be such a good hedge against actual inflation as is predicted in classical economics. The empirical evidence confirms this. Table 12.1 shows the results of work carried out by Cooper and Hodges on the UK stock market for the period 1923–78. They looked at the correlation coefficients of returns on gilts and equities with inflation.

Returns on both equities and long-term gilts (in the form of undated Consols) are correlated in Table 12.1 with the returns on Treasury Bills and with the actual inflation rate. In this way, an attempt is made to separate out the value of equities and gilts as hedges against both expected and unexpected inflation. Returns on equities and gilts are correlated with returns on Treasury Bills to see how good they are as hedges against *expected* inflation. Investment in Treasury Bills, because of their short life, minimises the risk that inflation will be different from

Table 12.1   Impact of inflation on equities and gilts

	Correlation coefficients		
	1923–51	*1952–78*	*1923–78*
Equities/Treasury Bills	0.00	0.12	0.16
Equities/inflation	−0.18	0.26	0.18
Consols/Treasury Bills	0.07	0.43	0.25
Consols/inflation	−0.32	0.27	0.03

Source: Cooper and Hodges (1980).

---

[2] The original stock relief introduced in the November 1974 Budget reduced taxable profit by the increase in the value of stocks over the year (less 10% of taxable profit to allow for some real increase in stocks.)

expected. Returns on Treasury Bills are therefore good indicators of the expected inflation rate.[3] In the case of both equities and gilts, the correlation coefficients with Treasury Bill returns in Table 12.1 are positive, indicating that they are reasonable hedges against expected inflation. When they are correlated against the *actual* inflation rate, which of course reflects both expected and unexpected inflation, the relationship is less clear. If gilts and equities were good hedges of unexpected as well as expected inflation, their correlation coefficients with inflation would be higher than those with Treasury Bill returns. This is only barely true for equities and not at all for gilts. It must also be noted that the period studied affects the results very considerably and that this is one of the reasons why there is still no clear understanding of how good either gilts or equities are at hedging actual inflation.

An alternative approach to hedging against inflation is to acquire those shares which have exhibited the best inflation-proofing in the past. The empirical evidence suggests that those shares which have shown resistance to inflation in the past will do so in the future.[4] However, this will involve a reduction in diversification since it is likely that those shares which exhibit the same resistance to inflation are in the same sector (such as property) and are related in other ways. Specific risk will therefore not be diversified away by acquiring a portfolio consisting only of these shares.

In the case of gilts, as we saw in Chapter 3, the introduction of index-linked gilts in 1981 appeared to offer a true hedge against inflation. (Index-linked gilts were not considered in Table 12.1.) However, even with index-linked gilts, the problem of inflation is not completely solved. First of all, the current supply of index-linked gilts, of around £5b., is by no means sufficient to hedge all the pension funds' inflation risk let alone that of other investors. Secondly, the gilts are indexed to the retail prices index which is meant to reflect the cost of living of the 'average' consumer. It may be that the investor wishes to hedge against a particular price change, such as Mr Stone with his prospective house purchase, and this can be greater than or less than the change in the retail prices index. Thirdly, the required *real* rate of return on gilts may vary and this will affect the price of index-linked gilts. The investor cannot therefore be sure of a certain real rate of return unless he holds the index-linked gilts to maturity.

An alternative way of coping with risk, as we saw in Chapter 2, is by pooling or diversification. One method, discussed in Chapter 10, is to diversify internationally. This will reduce the dependence of the inves-

---

[3] We saw in Chapter 2 that Miss Silver might be better off investing in the most short-term government securities (e.g. Treasury Bills) in times of uncertainty about future inflation.
[4] See Dimson (1979).

tor's portfolio on domestic inflation. Another is to diversify across types of security which may have different reactions to inflation.

Asset mix

The capital asset pricing model leads the investor to a portfolio which consists of the risk-free asset and the 'market' portfolio. This market portfolio, although strictly speaking consisting of all risky marketable securities, is generally restricted to equities. If a wider range of assets were included, each of which had a different relationship with inflation, this would obviously reduce the inflation risk of the portfolio. For example, short and long gilts, represented by Treasury Bills and Consols, have different correlation coefficients with inflation. Similarly, equities, both domestic and international, property and works of art[5] will react differently to inflation. Unfortunately, the extent to which this diversification will reduce inflation and other risks is limited by the relatively high correlation coefficients between returns on the above-mentioned types of asset. For example, the average correlation co-efficient of the returns on equities with the returns on Consols over the period 1923–78 exceeded 0.5,[6] reducing the benefits of diversification across these types of asset. Nevertheless, the advantages of a wide asset mix are still evident. Efficient portfolios in the risk–return sense will therefore include gilts, equities and other marketable assets.

When considering the asset mix and the objectives of his investment portfolio, the investor should also bear in mind the characteristics of his existing wealth. For example, if the investor works in the chemical industry, it might be sensible to include an objective to hold a smaller proportion of his portfolio than might otherwise be the case in the chemical sector. This is because the level of the investor's future earnings will be to some extent linked to the fortunes of the chemical industry. The investor would therefore reduce his risk by having an investment portfolio whose returns were poorly correlated with the chemical industry and hence his other main source of income.

Investment policy

It is common practice in the management of investment funds to specify investment policy in the following manner. Firstly, the percentage of the

---

[5] The British Rail pension fund has included investments in all these types of asset.
[6] In fact, Cooper and Hodges (1980) found it to be 0.54 over the period.

portfolio to be invested in equities is fixed. This is to establish a risk level. Secondly, the maximum proportion of the portfolio which can be invested in any one security, company or industry may be limited. We saw, in Chapter 11, that this is the case for unit trusts and investment trusts as a means of ensuring a reasonable amount of diversification. Thirdly, the equities which can be acquired are restricted to those on a 'buy' list, provided by the analysts.

Active investment policy

This type of investment policy is obviously an 'active' one in the sense that the emphasis is on picking winners (the shares on the buy list), subject to a minimum amount of diversification and a limit on risk. Chapter 9 discussed two principal techniques for picking winners. One method is to use fundamental analysis to identify mispriced securities which assumes *in*efficient markets, has even been extended to incorporate the CAPM, which assumes perfect, and hence, efficient markets.

To determine betas, the excess returns of a security over the risk-free rate, $R_i - R_F$ can be regressed against the market premium, $R_m - R_F$. This will give a regression line of the form shown in equation (12.4):

$$R_i - R_F = \alpha_i + \beta_i (R_m - R_F) \tag{12.4}$$

The CAPM postulates that the expected value of α_i will be zero. In other words, the excess return on security i when the market *premium* is zero will also be zero. In practice, of course, the α term or alpha will not be zero and can be viewed as the excess return obtained on security i. In the London Business School *Risk Measurement Service*, the alpha term is given under the heading 'abnormal return'. (See Table 8.1.) Now, if the CAPM holds, one would expect that over several months or years the alphas will add up to around zero. There is no reason to expect, exactly as for share returns,[7] that a positive alpha will be followed by another positive alpha in the next period. And yet, this is precisely what the new form of fundamental analysis assumes. The CAPM has simply become another weapon in their armoury of investment techniques.

The second method of picking winners is to attempt correct timing of investments, through the use of technical analysis. This can be done either at the individual security level, say with point and figure charts, or

---

[7] In other words, alphas can be said to follow a random walk.

at the market level. The latter method would usually involve altering the asset mix of the portfolio, moving out of equities into gold or fixed interest securities before an expected market fall, and moving into equities before an expected market rise. This technique might be constrained by a prespecified asset mix, as in the case of the pension fund manager who has to conform to an investment policy laid down by the pension fund trustees.

A way round this constraint of a prespecified proportion of equities in the portfolio is again provided by the CAPM. High beta shares will be acquired when a bull market is expected and low beta shares (say, gold shares) when a bear market is predicted. Without altering the proportion of the portfolio invested in equities, the fund manager can alter the risk of that proportion through altering the average beta of the shares. It is obvious from this that the specification of the asset mix does not, as intended, impose risk restrictions on the portfolio. For this reason, it is becoming more common to impose risk limitations on the portfolio in the form of prespecified volatility (standard deviation) or beta levels.

Passive investment policy

The alternative investment policy is a passive approach, based on the results of portfolio theory and the CAPM. All that is expected by the investor is a fair return for the risk involved. Thus, once the risk level has been set and an optimal portfolio (allowing for consumption preferences, time horizons, tax and inflation) has been determined, all that the investor needs to do is to maintain the portfolio at its required diversification and risk levels. Turnover and transaction costs of the portfolio will be lower than that of an actively managed portfolio, as should management fees, since there will be less need for the advice of either technical or fundamental analysts.

Whether an active or passive investment policy is pursued, it must be consistent. An active policy will involve high turnover, high transaction costs and relatively poor diversification (since specific risk must be borne for excess returns to be possible). A passive policy will involve low turnover, low transaction costs and high diversification. Both, however, will require some element of portfolio revision. Active investors will need to re-examine opportunities and estimates of future share price and market movements fairly frequently in their search for 'winners'. Passive investors will only need to revise their portfolios when the factors affecting their objectives change or when their estimates of market risk and return change.

A compromise between the two types of investment policy is now being adopted by many of the larger investing institutions. Most of the portfolio under management will be managed passively, for example it might be run as an index fund with a proportion in fixed interest securities to reduce the risk. The remainder will be actively managed, using whichever analysis techniques the institution favours. Instead of holding all shares in proportion to their market values, as is recommended by the passive, CAPM approach, the portfolio will contain favoured shares in greater amounts and poorly viewed shares in lesser amounts than the amounts prescribed by the CAPM. In other words, the portfolio will approximate the market portfolio and then be adjusted according to the requirements of the active investment policy. This compromise approach therefore differs from a true active policy where only favoured shares are held.[8]

Performance measurement

The final section in this chapter is devoted to performance measurement. The many possible uses of performance measures are obvious. For instance, once the investment objectives of their portfolios have been set, investors will wish to know whether these objectives have been achieved. They may also wish to compare their portfolios' performance with the performance of portfolios which had similar objectives. For example, if an investor has placed his savings in a unit trust promising high income, he may wish to compare its performance with other high-income unit trusts. When investment is via intermediaries, performance measures also serve other functions. They help to check that the fund managers are neither fraudulent nor incompetent and that they are keeping to their stated objectives.

Performance measures can also be used to evaluate investment policy. We saw above that there are two main investment strategies – an active investment strategy which we have called 'picking winners' and a passive strategy referred to as 'fair return for risk' based on the capital asset pricing model.

Given this, any actively managed investment portfolio can be evaluated not only relative to portfolios with similar objectives but also relative to an equivalent passive portfolio.

If we consider the quantity of performance measurement carried out in industry, such as measuring achievement against profit targets or

---

[8] For further details of this mixture of active and passive investment policies, see Sharpe (1981).

examining variances[9] between actual and budgeted performance, it is surprising to note how little is done in the field of investment. Two factors have probably influenced this lack of performance measurement. Firstly, until portfolio theory and the CAPM quantified risk, there was no way that two portfolios of different risk could be fairly compared. Secondly, the relative paucity of disclosure concerning the investment portfolios and policies of the investment intermediaries, especially when compared with the level of disclosure required of companies, has not allowed detailed assessments of performance. As increased competition or regulation encourage more disclosure by intermediaries, so will the use of performance measurement become more prevalent.

Finally, as in industry, performance measures can be used by the investing institutions as a form of monitoring and as a means of identifying the particular investment skills (or lack of them) of their investment managers.

Now, in order to determine a measure of performance for any portfolio, two figures must be known, the return the portfolio achieved and the level of risk it assumed. There are four main aspects which must be considered when measuring performance, the first in calculating the return, the second in coping with risk and the third in breaking the measure down to analyse performance in greater depth. The fourth aspect relates to the general applicability of the performance measures derived.

Calculating return

Let us consider the calculation of the return of a portfolio run by an investing institution. As we saw in Chapter 11, investing intermediaries experience in varying degrees cash flows over the amount of which their fund managers may have no control. For example, pension funds will have cash inflows and outflows at regular intervals representing employer and employee pension contributions and pension payments, whereas unit trusts will experience irregular cash inflows and outflows reflecting demand for the units. So, when comparing the performance of two funds, the timing of their cash flows must be taken into account. If one unit trust experiences a large inflow of funds to be invested just before a bull market whereas another experiences a cash outflow at that time, the first unit trust may well appear on a superficial look to have

---

[9] A budget variance is the difference between the amount forecast for a cost or revenue item and the amount actually incurred.

done better although it may actually have achieved lower returns overall.

Suppose units trusts *A* and *B* have identical equity portfolios and investment policies but they experience different timing of cash flows over years 1, 2 and 3, as outlined in Table 12.2. Unit trust *B* appears to have done better, with a higher terminal value of £226, because, although both trusts received cash inflows of £100 during the period, unit trust *B* received its cash flow before a general market rise in year 2 and unit trust *A* only before a market fall in year 3.

In order to allow for different timing of cash flows, the time-weighted rate of return (*TWROR*) can be used to compare the performance of unit trusts *A* and *B*, instead of simply comparing the terminal values of their portfolios. To do this, we calculate the average of the rates of return achieved in each period between cash flows. From Table 12.2, we can see that, despite the difference in timing of cash flows, unit trusts *A* and *B* are in all other respects identical, including their annual rates of return, which leads to identical *TWROR* of 6%.

To determine the *TWROR*, the date on which each cash flow occurs and the value of the portfolio on each such date must be known. Whereas this may be practicable for unit trusts (which have to calculate

Table 12.2   Impact of timing of cash flows on performance

		End of		
	Now	Year 1	Year 2	Year 3
Unit trust A				
Value of fund (£)	100	110	131	**209**
Cash inflow (at end of year 2)			+100	
Annual rate of return (%)		+10	+19	−9.5
Average R of R^{10}	6%			
Unit trust B				
Value of fund (£)	100	110	250	**226**
Cash inflow (at end of year 1)		+100		
Annual rate of return (%)		+10	+19	−9.5
Average R of R^{10}	6%			

---

[10] The average calculated is the geometric mean

$$GM = \sqrt[n]{(1 + r_1)(1 + r_2) \dots (1 + r_n)} - 1$$

The geometric mean is used rather than the arithmetic mean when averaging percentage increases over time.

the market value of their portfolios on a daily basis[11]), it may be costly for small funds which experience frequent cash inflows and outflows. In these cases it may be necessary to *estimate* the value of the portfolio at the time the cash flow occurred.

For example, suppose that Pigmy Trust plc achieves a return on its portfolio of 10% over a period of six months, as shown in Figure 12.1, with the portfolio increasing in value from £1,000 at the beginning of the period to £1,100 at the end of the six months. Suppose also that Pigmy experienced a cash outflow of £50 half way through the six-month period. Because of this, Pigmy's *TWROR* must in fact be greater than 10% but it cannot be determined since the value of the fund at the date of the cash outflow is unknown.

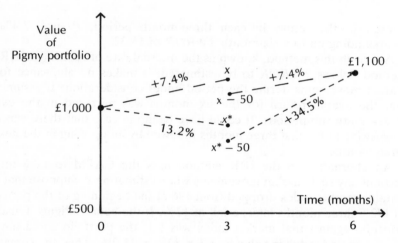

Figure 12.1   Calculating TWROR *when value of portfolio unknown*

x = Value of portfolio estimated using IRR method = £1,074.
x^* = Value of portfolio estimated using CAPM method = £868.

However, the *TWROR* can be estimated if it is assumed that the rate of return achieved in the first three months, say R, was the same as that achieved in the second three months. We can then write, if x is the unknown value of the portfolio at the half-way point, that the returns in each three-month period must be equal. Thus,

$$R = \frac{x - 1,000}{1,000} = \frac{1,100 - (x - 50)}{x - 50} \qquad (12.5)$$

---

[11] Because the bid and offer prices for units are based on the market value of the portfolio.

Cross-multiplying to solve for x in equation (12.5) gives

$$(x - 1,000)\,(x - 50) = (1,100 - (x - 50)\,)\,(1,000)$$

$$x(x - 50) - 1,000\,(x - 50) = 1,100,000 - 1,000\,(x - 50)$$

$$x(x - 50) = 1,100,000$$

$$x^2 - 50x + 1,100,000 = 0$$

Using the quadratic equation formula[12] to find x we get

$$x = £1,074$$

Therefore, the return in each three-month period, P, was 7.4%, compounding up to a six-month *TWROR* of 15.3%.

Although this method, known as the internal rate of return (or IRR) method, allows *TWROR* to be estimated, it makes no allowance for market movements during the period under consideration. It assumes that the overall return for the six months was mirrored in the two three-month sub-periods. It could have been the case that there was a downswing in the first three months followed by an upswing in the next three months.

An alternative to the IRR method uses the CAPM to take into account any such market movements when estimating x. Suppose that a suitable market index dropped from 196 at the beginning of the period to 172.5 three months later, a fall of 12%. If the beta of Pigmy Trust's portfolio against that market index was 1.1, the portfolio could have been expected to fall in value by $1.1 \times 12\% = 13.2\%$. Thus an estimate of x, allowing for market movements, would be £868, 13.2% below the original £1,000. (Note that this assumes Pigmy Trust's portfolio to be well diversified.) This CAPM method leads to two different sub-period returns,

$$\frac{868 - 1,000}{1,000} = -13.2\%$$

in the first three months and

$$\frac{1,100 - 818}{818} = 34.5\%$$

---

[12] The formula used to solve for x when $ax^2 + bx + c = 0$ is

$$x = (-b \pm \sqrt{b^2 - 4ac})/2a$$

in the second three months, giving a total *TWROR* of 16.7%.[13]

Adjusting for risk

Having dealt with the measurement of return for use in performance measurement, we now turn to how to adjust for risk. As a first step, we are aware, from Chapter 11, that the investor can use either the standard deviation or the beta or the portfolio as a measure of risk, according to whether the portfolio under consideration includes all his assets or represents only part of his well-diversified portfolio.

There are two main types of performance measures which can be derived (for either measure of risk) according to whether the risk of the particular portfolio whose performance is being measured is prespecified or not. For example, unit trusts and investment trusts choose their own levels of risk and investors in these trusts can adjust the level of risk if they so wish, by borrowing or lending. In these cases, the individual investor may wish to know which trusts offer the highest return allowing for their risk. Only by doing this will he be able to compare trusts which have different levels of risk, however that risk is measured. On the other hand, a pension fund manager may be operating under a prespecified level of risk, which has been imposed on him by the trustees of the fund. The question to be asked in this case is, given the level of risk imposed, did the pension fund manager do well or badly?

Risk measures have been developed to cater for either of these circumstances and to deal with either measure of risk. This gives rise to a matrix of performance measures, reproduced in Figure 12.2.

The two measures in the reward per unit of risk column give a reward–risk ratio which can be used to rank funds or portfolios. Both the Sharpe measure, which uses the standard deviation as a measure of risk, and the Treynor measure, which uses beta as a measure of risk, are based on the capital asset pricing model. (As has already been said, no risk-adjusted measures can be derived unless some model which quantifies risk is used.) Investors can then, using whichever of the Sharpe and Treynor measures is most appropriate to their personal circumstances, choose to invest in the highest ranking portfolios. They can adjust to their required risk levels by borrowing or lending. For example, suppose three unit trusts have performed as in Table 12.3 in the last year.

Mr Adonis, wishing to place the majority of his funds in one of the above unit trusts, might choose *B*, which has the highest Sharpe measure. Mr Zeus, however, wishes to place only a small part of his

---

[13] The *TWROR* figures of 15.3% and 16.7% are for a six-month holding period.

	Reward per unit of risk	Differential return
Standard deviation	$\dfrac{R_p - R_F}{S_p}$ 'Sharpe' measure	$R_p - R_{benchmark}$ where $R_{benchmark} = R_B$ and $R_B = R_F + \dfrac{(R_m - R_F)}{S_m} S_p$
Beta	$\dfrac{R_p - R_F}{\beta_p}$ 'Treynor' measure	$R_p - R_{benchmark}$ where $R_{benchmark} = R_B$ and $R_B = R_F + (R_m - R_F)\beta_p$ 'Jensen' measure

(left margin label: **Risk**)

Figure 12.2   Risk-adjusted performance measures

total portfolio in one of these unit trusts and so might prefer C, which has the highest Treynor measure of performance. Both Mr Adonis and Mr Zeus can then adjust for risk separately. If Mr Adonis wishes to bear a total risk of 20% (measured by standard deviation), he should invest all his funds in unit trust B and borrow a further 100% and invest that in unit trust B as well. In practice, Mr Adonis may not be able to borrow 100% of his investment at the risk-free rate. In this case, he might settle for a unit trust with a slightly lower Sharpe measure, such as trust C. He

Table 12.3   Reward per unit of risk performance ranking

Unit trust	Return (%)	Risk: Standard deviation (%)	Beta	Sharpe measure	Treynor measure
A	12	25	1.3	0.16	0.031
B	10	10	1.1	0.20	0.018
C	13	30	1.4	0.17	0.036
Risk-free rate	8				

could then achieve his total required risk level by investing ⅔ of his funds in C and ⅓ risk-free.[14]

Of course, for both Mr Adonis and Mr Zeus, basing investment decisions on rankings derived from past returns and risk will not necessarily provide optimal returns in the future.

The two measures denoting differential return in Figure 12.2 can be used in cases where the risk is prespecified, which usually occurs in cases where the portfolio is managed by a fund manager. What is required in these instances is a benchmark portfolio with the same risk as the fund in question. This benchmark portfolio should represent a realistic investment alternative which was open to the fund manager. Again, the capital asset pricing model provides a suitable benchmark portfolio. For example, if we are considering beta as a suitable measure of risk, the CAPM tells us that the optimal investment policy is to hold the market portfolio (or as near as is feasible) and to adjust for risk by borrowing or lending. A comparison of the actual fund's performance with such a benchmark portfolio, which has the same beta, is effectively a test for abnormal returns or alphas, and a comparison of an active investment policy with a passive one. If the Jensen measure yields a positive differential (or abnormal) return, the fund manager may be 'beating the market' because he is good at picking winners. Of course, a positive Jensen measure may also be due to luck, and the fund's performance over a number of periods would have to be examined to gauge whether the positive measure is more likely due to luck or to skill.

For instance, suppose that a company has allocated 10% of its pension fund to be managed by QED investment managers. Since QED only has 10% of the total funds of the company's pension fund, we can say that beta is the appropriate measure of risk in this case. Now, suppose that the beta required by the trustees of the pension fund is 0.9. If the yield on gilts was 10% last year and the return on the FT All Share Index was 17%, the benchmark portfolio would have yielded

$$R_B = R_F + (R_m - R_F)\, \beta_p$$

$$= 0.10 + (0.17 - 0.10)\, 0.9$$

$$= \mathbf{16.3\%}$$

---

[14] His total risk would be

$$S^2 = x^2 S_C^2 + (1 - x)^2\, S_{RF}^2 + 2x(1 - x) S_C S_{RF} CORR_{CRF}$$

where x is the proportion invested in fund C and $(1 - x)$ the proportion invested at the risk-free rate, R_F. Since $S_{RF} = 0$ (it is risk-*free*) we get

$$S = x S_C$$

The required $S = 20\%$ and $S_C = 30\%$, so $x = \dfrac{2}{3}$.

If the fund managed by QED actually achieved a return of 18% with a beta of 0.9, the differential return was $18 - 16.3\% = 1.7\%$. It would remain to be seen whether this level of performance could be maintained in the future, but from the conclusions of Chapter 9 this would appear to be unlikely.

The other differential return measure of performance, which uses standard deviation as a measure of risk instead of beta, will be used in those cases where the portfolio under consideration represents the total wealth of the investor. Interestingly, if the portfolio is fully diversified, this measure will give the same differential return as the Jensen measure since, for a fully diversified portfolio, there is no specific risk and the total risk of the portfolio is simply its beta risk. We can see this in equation (12.6), previously given in Chapter 8 as equation (8.10) on p. 237.

For each security i, we can write

$$V_i = \beta_i^2 \, S_m^2 + S^2 \, (e_i) \qquad (8.10)$$

So, for a portfolio, we have

$$\text{Variance}_p = V_p = \beta_p^2 S_m^2 + \sum_{i=1}^{i=n} S^2 \, (e_i) \qquad (12.6)$$

(Total risk = beta risk + specific risk)

where β_p is the weighted average of the individual β_i and the w_i are the weights attached to each security.

Since, in a fully diversified portfolio, specific risk is zero, the standard deviation of the portfolio will simply be equal to its beta times the standard deviation of the market:

Standard deviation $S_p = \beta_p \, S_m$

or

$$\beta_p = \frac{S_p}{S_m} \qquad (12.7)$$

If we look at the two differential return measures in the matrix of Figure 12.2, we can see that if the equality in equation (12.7) holds, the two differential return measures are identical.

Analysing performance measures

Once a measure of performance has been derived, the next obvious question to ask is how was that performance achieved? The differential return measures discussed in the last section give some indication since, by comparing the performance of the portfolio with that of a passively managed portfolio, we know that the differential abnormal return achieved must be due to some form of active portfolio management.

How can we find out which type of active investment policy was pursued? Unfortunately, the state of the art of performance measurement is still not far advanced and, as we shall see in the next section on the relevance of performance measures, there are problems in placing too much emphasis on the results obtained. However, some attempt can be made to identify the success of selectivity or timing policies, the two basic ways of 'picking winners'.

(i) Selectivity

We start by looking at the Jensen measure of performance. This differential return figure shows whether active portfolio management has achieved positive or negative abnormal returns. What it does not take into account, however, is that in order to achieve those abnormal returns, diversifiable or specific risk is likely to have been borne which would not have been the case if a fully diversified, CAPM portfolio strategy had been adopted.

Fama (1972) graphically analysed the Jensen measure of performance as in Figure 12.3.

In Figure 12.3, the Jensen measure will be the difference between the return on the portfolio under consideration, A, and the return on that combination of the market portfolio and risk-free borrowing or lending which has the same beta as A. In Figure 12.3, this CAPM portfolio is represented by portfolio B. So, the Jensen measure is given by $R_A - R_B$.

Since portfolio B is fully diversified, it will only have beta risk whereas A will have both beta risk and diversifiable risk. The total risk of portfolio A, measured by the standard deviation of its returns, will thus be greater than the total risk of portfolio B. Because of this, it would be fairer to compare the performance of portfolio A with that of a CAPM portfolio which had the same *total* risk, portfolio C in Figure 12.3. C can be found by equating the standard deviation of portfolio A with the market risk of a CAPM portfolio, as in equation (12.8):

$$S_A = \beta_C S_m \tag{12.8}$$

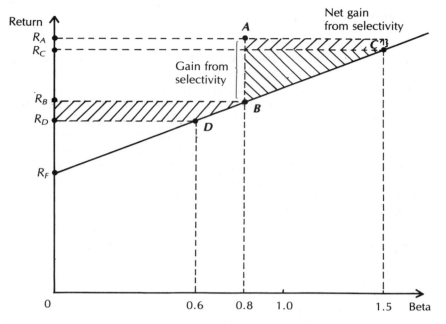

Figure 12.3   Analysis of Jensen performance measure
Source: Fama (1972). By permission of the *Journal of Finance*.

So,

$$\beta_C = \frac{S_A}{S_m}$$

Once we know the total risk of portfolio A we can use equation (12.8) to find the beta of a CAPM portfolio with the same total risk.

For example, suppose that the risk of portfolio A is made up as follows:

$$\beta_A = 0.8$$

$$\text{Specific risk}_A = 25\%$$

and that the market standard deviation of returns, S_m, is 20%.
Substituting these values into equation (12.6) gives:

$$S^2{}_A = (0.8)^2 (0.20)^2 + (0.25)^2$$

$$S_A = 0.3$$

To find portfolio C, we simply substitute the necessary figures into equation (12.8) to get

$$0.3 = 0.2 \, \beta_C$$

Thus,

$$\beta_c = \mathbf{1.5}$$

Note that portfolio C has a higher beta than portfolio A in order to achieve a higher level of risk simply from market risk.

We can now see that the *true* abnormal return earned by A, given its total risk, is not $R_A - R_B$ but the smaller $R_A - R_C$. Fama denoted the first measure the 'gain from selectivity' and the second measure the '*net gain from selectivity*'.

Figure 12.3 can also be used to monitor how closely the portfolio manager has kept to his objectives, provided that these were expressed either in terms of return or of beta. For instance, if the manager had been told to keep to a target beta of 0.6, compared to the actual beta of 0.8, he obviously added to the investors' risk, presumably in the belief that a bull market was on the way. The difference between portfolio D (which has a beta of 0.6) and portfolio B is therefore the return earned by the portfolio manager for correct timing using betas. Note, however, that this analysis will only use the beta at the beginning or end of the period or the average beta and thus will not allow for any changes in the beta of the portfolio which may have occurred during the period under consideration.

The Fama breakdown of the Jensen performance measure gives us a way of identifying more closely the true gains or losses from a 'picking winners' strategy based on selectivity. It shows us that we must take into account the extra risk the manager takes on to try to 'beat the market'. A simple measure which assesses how much diversifiable risk has been taken on is provided in the London Business School *Risk Measurement Service* and is called R^2. This measures the extent to which the portfolio's returns are explained by market returns. In other words, it shows how much of the portfolio's total risk is explained by its beta. The higher the R^2, the more the portfolio's returns are explained by market risk and the lower the amount of diversifiable risk. Table 12.4 shows an excerpt for all the major sectors of the market. If we look at the investment trust sector, since investment trusts are all diversified portfolios, one would expect them to have relatively high R^2. And yet the average R^2 is 74%. This is because we are talking about *UK* market risk. Investment trusts, as already mentioned in Chapter 11, have an important element of *overseas* investment in their portfolios which will not be highly correlated with UK market returns and which will reduce the overall R^2 of investment trusts.

Table 12.4   Non-market risk of investment trusts

F.T. Actuaries Indices

F.T.A. Index Name and Corresponding Stock Exchange Industry Numbers	No of Companies	Aver Capit'n	Market %	Beta	Vari-ability	Specific Risk	Std Error	R-Sq'rd	Qly Ab Return	Ann Ab Return	Ann Act Return	Gross Yield	P/E Ratio	Index 30:6:82
CAPITAL GOODS 11-34,41-43	(209)	109	23.9	1.11	22	8	.05	88	6	8	14	4.3	13.1	387
BUILDING MATERIALS 12-17	(23)	130	3.1	1.24	26	10	.07	84	1	7	13	5.6	10.2	324
CONTRACTING,CONSTRUCTION 18	(28)	58	1.7	1.21	26	13	.08	77	-2	3	9	5.3	7.8	578
ELECTRICALS 19,31	(31)	331	10.7	1.12	24	11	.07	78	16	27	33	2.0	19.0	1491
ENG.CONTRACTORS 25,29-30	(11)	59	.7	.94	23	14	.09	63	-2	-3	3	6.3	9.0	478
ENG.MECHANICAL 20,22-4,26-8	(67)	54	3.8	1.06	23	11	.08	76	2	-9	-2	6.0	10.4	197
METALS,METAL FORMING 21,32-34	(11)	82	.9	1.07	25	14	.09	67	-5	-1	5	8.1	10.2	150
MOTORS 41-43	(20)	29	.6	.95	22	12	.08	69	-8	-16	-9	8.1		86
OTHER INDUSTRIAL MATERIALS 11	(18)	122	2.3	1.13	29	14	.14	76	-4	-7	-1	6.1	.1	351
CONSUMER GROUP 36-40,45-65,67	(202)	148	31.2	1.00	20	5	.04	93	1	6	13	5.8	9.3	302
BREWERS & DISTILLERS 45-46	(22)	221	5.1	.90	21	12	.08	68	5	0	6	6.4	8.4	321
FOOD MANUFACTURING 49-50	(22)	196	4.5	.92	20	9	.06	80	-4	0	6	7.2	6.5	261
FOOD RETAILING 51	(14)	172	2.5	.96	22	13	.08	67	1	11	18	3.7	13.2	611
HEALTH & HOUSEHOLD PRODUCTS 67	(9)	428	4.0	1.06	25	16	.11	62	16	34	41	3.7	15.8	457
LEISURE 36,47-48	(23)	102	2.5	1.07	22	8	.06	86	-7	-6	0	5.6	11.8	413
NEWSPAPERS,PUBLISHING 52-53	(13)	25	.3	.96	22	12	.08	70	-2	0	6	6.2	9.3	506
PACKAGING AND PAPERS 54	(14)	73	1.1	1.14	25	12	.08	76	-2	-3	2	7.8	7.0	140
STORES 55-58	(45)	157	7.4	1.20	25	11	.07	82	-1	5	11	5.1	12.4	272
TEXTILES 37,59-62	(23)	42	1.0	.93	22	13	.09	65	-5	0	7	6.6	8.7	164
TOBACCO 63	(3)	837	2.6	.77	20	14	.09	51	7	29	37	8.3	5.1	332
OTHER CONSUMERS 38-40,64,65	(14)	14	.2	1.06	28	15	.15	70	-9	-13	-6	5.9	30.9	265
OTHER GROUPS 66,68,69,71-76	(76)	103	8.2	.97	20	7	.05	87	-1	10	17	6.7	8.7	250
CHEMICALS 66,68	(15)	209	3.3	.90	21	13	.09	63	0	18	26	7.2	8.4	333
OFFICE EQUIPMENT 69	(4)	115	.5	1.19	27	15	.10	71	-16	-10	-4	8.5	7.8	103
SHIPPING & TRANSPORT 71-72	(13)	72	1.0	.83	21	14	.09	56	-5	0	8	7.5	6.2	546
MISCELLANEOUS 73-76	(44)	76	3.5	1.03	21	7	.05	88	0	8	14	5.8	10.4	325
INDUSTRIAL GROUP 11-69,71-76	(487)	124	63.3	1.04	20	5	.03	95	2	7	14	5.3	10.4	324
OILS 70	(13)	845	11.5	.85	27	21	.13	36	2	-2	5	8.5	4.9	686
500 SHARE INDEX 11-76	(500)	143	74.7	1.00	19	3	.02	98	2	6	12	5.8	8.9	354
FINANCIAL GROUP 77-83,85-87	(117)	135	16.5	1.00	21	9	.06	80	-5	-10	-3	7.0		241
BANKS 77	(6)	650	4.1	.87	23	16	.10	52	-1	-4	2	8.7	2.8	262
DISCOUNT HOUSES 79	(9)	17	.2	.91	28	21	.13	40	-2	-20	-12	10.3		221
INSURANCE (LIFE) 81	(9)	217	2.0	1.13	27	16	.10	65	0	-1	4	7.0		262
INSURANCE (COMPOSITE) 82	(10)	313	3.3	1.13	27	16	.10	65	-5	-11	-5	9.4		150
INSURANCE (BROKERS) 83	(7)	127	.9	.86	23	16	.10	50	4	25	32	5.2	12.1	498
MERCHANT BANKS 85	(12)	61	.8	1.14	26	15	.10	67	-9	-24	-18	6.5		135
PROPERTY 86	(49)	81	4.2	.98	23	13	.09	67	-11	-21	-14	4.0	24.0	403
OTHER FINANCIAL 78,80,87	(15)	72	1.1	.76	18	11	.07	66	-7	-8	0	7.0	6.2	165
INVESTMENT TRUSTS 84	(111)	48	5.5	1.03	23	12	.08	74	-5	-10	-4	5.7		286
MINING FINANCE 92	(4)	440	1.8	1.10	29	20	.12	53	-9	-27	-20	7.8	7.2	181
OVERSEAS TRADERS 89-90,97	(18)	73	1.4	.79	20	14	.09	55	-9	-26	-18	9.4	8.1	340
ALL SHARE INDEX 11-97	(750)	128	100.	1.00	19	0	.00	100	0	0	7	6.1		323

Source: London Business School, *Risk Measurement Service*, July–September 1982. By permission of the publishers.

(ii) TIMING

We saw above that the Fama analysis did not really help us to examine the extent to which fund managers or investors try to earn abnormal returns through correct timing of purchases and sales of particular shares or of a more general market portfolio. This is because, as mentioned earlier, this investment strategy will involve changing the risk of the portfolio over time either through altering the asset mix between, say, gilts and equities or through changing the shares held in the equity portfolio to alter the equity portfolio's beta. So, performance measures which assume constant risk over a period will be of no use in this instance.

One way of examining the impact on a portfolio of changing its beta is to compare graphically the changes in beta with the changes in the market. If the manager got it right, a change to a higher beta should be mirrored by a rise in the market and vice versa. If the manager got it wrong, there should be no clear relationship between the two, as in Figure 12.4.

This rough-and-ready appraisal of performance achieved through correct timing is obviously unsatisfactory. The only consolation that we have is that the evidence supporting the weak form of the efficient markets hypothesis is sufficiently convincing for it to be very unlikely indeed that any abnormal returns can consistently be made from correct timing. We should be looking instead for abnormal losses.

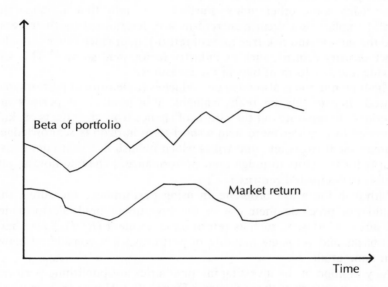

Figure 12.3   Graphical analysis of correct timing of the market

Relevance of the measure

Despite the advantages of performance measures for comparative and monitoring purposes, great care must be taken in their use. For example, we have just seen that the performance measures given in Figure 12.2 are of little use when trying to determine that element of performance which is due to attempts to time investments correctly.

Also, a factor which must be taken into account when using the differential return measures is the possibility that the benchmark portfolio made up of the market portfolio and risk-free borrowing and lending is not a realistic alternative. One reason could be because a high-risk fund could not adopt the benchmark alternative and borrow at the risk-free rate (as was a problem for Mr Adonis). Rankings using the Jensen measure would thus be biased against high-risk funds. Similarly, a particular fund might be precluded from holding certain securities which form part of the market portfolio; it should not, therefore, be compared with a benchmark portfolio which it could not, in practice, hold.

Thought must also be given to the way betas are measured for, say, the Treynor measure. Betas may be measured in different ways against different indices, all of which might be suitable surrogates for the market portfolio. So, rankings using one index could be different from those using some other index. Further, we know that although the CAPM implies that securities' returns are determined by their betas (and the market and risk-free rates of return), in practice other variables affect security returns, such as industry factors and so on.[15] This will provide another form of bias in the measures.

The time horizon is also relevant. Whichever measure of performance is used, it can only be really valuable if a number of periods are examined, to separate out the effects of chance from the effects of skill. The need to consider more than a short-term horizon is acknowledged by investment trusts and unit trusts which publish five-year cumulative returns for investors to judge their performance. (They do not, as yet, publish risk-adjusted returns.)

Although there are problems in using performance measures, this should not preclude their use in the investment field. Performance measures in industry, such as return on investment (*ROI*),[16] also have drawbacks and yet some measure of performance is considered better than none at all.

As yet, none of the investing intermediaries are publishing performance measures such as those shown in Figure 12.2. However, acceptance of the inclusion of risk in measuring performance is imminent. Also, as the CAPM is replaced by more sophisticated models, perhaps by some form of multi-index model, in the future, so the measures of performance available will become more sophisticated.

---

[15] We saw that this was the case when we considered multi-index models at the end of Chapter 8.

[16] *ROI*, return on investment, is usually calculated as profit before tax divided by capital employed. Because of such factors as accounting conventions, *ROI* can be misleading as a measure of performance. For example, the older the machines, the lower their depreciated book value. A lower book value gives a lower capital employed and a higher *ROI*. There may thus be an incentive not to replace old machines which may adversely affect the future profitability of the firm.

Summary

The emphasis of this chapter is somewhat different from that of the rest of the book since it deals with the more subjective aspects of investment, namely objectives, policy and assessment of performance.

The chapter has discussed the setting up of explicit investment objectives, which must be done before a suitable investment policy can be decided on or a portfolio built up. The factors which have to be considered for investment objectives include consumption preferences, attitude to risk and return, tax, inflation and asset mix.

The two basic types of investment policy which can be adopted can be categorised as active or passive. An active policy is based on the desire to beat the market and to make excess returns and involves either 'selectivity' (the search for mispriced securities) or correct 'timing'. A passive investment policy is based on the results of the CAPM which finds that all investors will hold the 'market' portfolio and borrow or lend at the risk-free rate. The investor with a passive policy will therefore hold a well-diversified portfolio or an index fund and not indulge in a high turnover, high transaction cost, management strategy.

Using the results of the CAPM, performance measures can be derived which allow the investor to assess how well he has done, given the risk of his portfolio, both relative to other comparable portfolios (which may have different risk) and relative to the alternative portfolio he could have constructed based on the CAPM with the same risk as his portfolio. However, care must be taken when using the performance measures to ensure that relevant comparisons are being made, bearing in mind the original objectives of the portfolio.

Problems

1. A unit trust manager wishes to set up a new trust for retired persons. A typical investor is seen as one who has just entered retirement at sixty. He has sold his house for, say, £60,000 and bought a small bungalow in a seaside resort for, say, £25,000. He wishes to invest the balance to provide a regular annual income to supplement his pension for himself and his wife who is ten years younger than he is.

   Advise the manager on the type of investments which the trust should hold and state why you think they will fulfill requirements.

2. You are one of the trustees of the Widget Company pension fund, which has £50m. currently invested and a net cash inflow of £5m. per annum. The fund is managed internally. Explain how you would:
   (i) establish objectives for the fund and direct investment accordingly, and

(ii) evaluate the performance of the pension fund investment manager.

3. Mrs Bloggs is a widow of forty with three school-age children. She works as a schoolteacher and earns £7,000 a year but has difficulty making ends meet. Her aunt has recently died and left her a legacy of £20,000.

   Mrs Bloggs has been to see her friend Mrs Smith who is an accountant and who has suggested the following ways of investing the money.

   (i) Building society account. Interest of 9.5% per annum after tax paid six-monthly.
   (ii) Save As You Earn. Monthly investment of any amount over £10 per month for five years and a fixed sum received at the end of it equivalent to a return of 8% per annum.
   (iii) Unit trust, for example those managed by the Target group. These include Target 'Growth', Target 'Extra Income', Target 'Gilt Income' and Target 'Gilt Capital'.
   (iv) Shares of companies such as ICI with a dividend yield (before income tax) of 11.3% per annum, or a property company such as Haslemere Estates with a dividend yield (before income tax) of 2.2% per annum.
   (v) Gilt-edged stock with a redemption yield (i.e. annual return of) 10% before tax until 1986 (Exchequer 3% 1986) or a redemption yield of 14.22% before tax until the year 2000 (Treasury 13% 2000).
   (vi) A life assurance policy.

      (a) Advise Mrs Bloggs on which of the above investments she should make and explain what factors you are taking into consideration.

      (b) Calculate the transaction costs if Mrs Bloggs invested the £20,000
         (i) all in 13% Treasury Stock 2000;
         (ii) all in ICI shares.

4. Suppose you are an investment adviser. What questions would you ask each client before advising on a suitable portfolio?

5. Data on six investments trusts' performances last year are shown below.

Trust	Actual return (%)	Standard deviation (%)	Beta
A	19	6	1.5
B	17	4	0.5
C	21	8	1.0
D	15	6	0.5
E	25	10	2.0

(i) Calculate the reward to variability measure, $(R_p - R_F)/S_p$, known as the Sharpe index, for each trust and rank them accordingly. Suppose $R_F = 9\%$.
(ii) Rank the trusts using the Treynor index, $(R_p - R_F)/\beta_p$.
(iii) What is the essential difference between the Sharpe and Treynor indices of portfolio performance? Which do you think is preferable? Why?
(iv) Calculate the excess return of these trusts (i.e. compared with a portfolio having the same beta) assuming last year's R_m was 13%. This method of judging portfolio performance is known as Jensen's measure. In what way does it differ from the Sharpe and Treynor indices?
(v) Consider investment trust *B*. How would you break down an overall measure of performance, such as the Jensen measure, into different aspects of performance to get a better picture of how well managed the trust was – i.e. which aspects would you like to measure and how would you attempt to measure them?
(vi) Suppose you are considering buying shares in one of the investment trusts listed above. What additional facts would you like concerning the trusts and how would *you* decide between them?

6. What have been the implications of the results of empirical studies on investment trust, unit trust and mutual fund* performance for the efficient markets hypothesis?

* Mutual funds = US investment trusts and unit trusts.

Appendix 1:
transaction costs

Stockbrokers' minimum commissions

A. Securities listed under the following headings in the Official List or the Official List – Irish:
(i) British Funds, etc.
Irish Government Funds
(1) Securities having no final redemption date within ten years
    0.8%   on the first £2,500 consideration
    0.25%   on the next £15,500 consideration
    0.125% on the next £982,000 consideration
    0.1%   on the next £3,000,000 consideration
    0.05%   on the next £6,000,000 consideration
    0.03%   on the excess.
(2) New Issues referred to in Rule 209
    0.8%   on the first £2,500 consideration
    0.125% on the next £15,500 consideration
    0.0625% on the next £982,000 consideration
    0.05%   on the next £9,000,000 consideration
    0.03%   on the excess.
(3) Securities having ten years or less to final redemption
    0.8%   on the first £2,500 consideration
    0.125% on the next £15,500 consideration
    0.0625% on the next £982,000 consideration
    0.05%   on the next £3,000,000 consideration
    0.025% on the next £6,000,000 consideration
    0.015% on the excess.
(4) Securities having five years or less to final redemption and not in default.

    At discretion.
(ii) Sterling issues by Foreign Governments and certain other International Institutions
Corporation and County Stocks – Great Britain and Northern Ireland
Public Boards, etc. – Great Britain and Northern Ireland
Commonwealth Government and Provincial Securities
Commonwealth Corporation Stocks
Irish Land Bonds
Irish Corporation Stocks and Public Boards

(1) Securities having no final redemption date within ten years
    0.8%   on the first £2,500 consideration
    0.25% on the next £15,500 consideration
    0.125% on the excess.
    Bargains subject to Rule 208
    0.1%   on the consideration over £1,000,000 up to £4,000,000
    0.05% on the consideration over £4,000,000 up to £10,000,000
    0.03% on the excess over £10,000,000 consideration
(2) Securities having ten years or less to final redemption
    0.8%   on the first £2,500 consideration
    0.25% on the next £15,500 consideration
    0.125% on the excess.
    Bargains subject to Rule 208
    0.1%   on the consideration over £1,000,000 up to £4,000,000
    0.05% on the consideration over £4,000,000 up to £10,000,000
    0.03% on the excess over £10,000,000 consideration
(3) Securities having five years or less to final redemption and not in default.
    At discretion.

B. Debentures, Bonds, etc.
Debentures and Bonds and any other securities representing loans (Debenture Stocks, Loan Stocks, Notes, Annuities, etc.) other than those included in Section A above.
(1) Registered*
    0.9%   on the first £5,000 consideration
    0.45% on the next £5,000 consideration
    0.35% on the next £40,000 consideration
    0.325% on the next £80,000 consideration
    0.25% on the next £770,000 consideration
    0.175% on the next £1,100,000 consideration
    0.125% on the excess.
    *Including New Issues passing by delivery in scrip form or by letters of renunciation.
(2) Bearer including Foreign Loans listed on The Stock Exchange expressed or optionally payable in a foreign currency
    0.9%   on the first £2,500 consideration
    0.5%   on the next £6,500 consideration
    0.25% on the next £121,000 consideration
    0.2%   on the next £770,000 consideration
    0.175% on the next £1,100,000 consideration
    0.125% on the excess.

C. Stocks and Shares
Stocks and Shares Registered or Bearer (other than those in Sections A, B, D or G) whether partly or fully paid
    1.65% on the first £7,000 consideration
    0.55% on the next £8,000 consideration
    0.5%   on the next £115,000 consideration
    0.4%   on the next £170,000 consideration
    0.3%   on the next £600,000 consideration
    0.2%   on the next £1,100,000 consideration
    0.125% on the excess.
See Rule 204(2)

D. Small Bargains.

	Securities in Section A	*Securities in all other Sections*
The minimum commission to be charged shall be	£7	£10 bought bargains £7 sold bargains

except in the case of
(1) Transactions on which the commission may be — at discretion — at discretion
(2) Transactions amounting to less than £300 in value on which commission may be — at discretion — at discretion

except in the case of	Securities in Section A	Securities in all other Sections
(1) Transactions on which the commission may be	at discretion	at discretion
(2) Transactions amounting to less than £300 in value on which commission may be	at discretion	at discretion

E. London Traded Options

Attention is drawn to the provisions of Rule 210a(1)

Quoted in Sterling

£1.50 per Option Contract (normally of 1,000 shares) plus ad valorem commission of:

2.5% on the first £5,000 Option money
1.5% on the next £5,000 Option money
1.0% on the excess.

The minimum commission to be charged on business in London Traded Options quoted in Sterling shall be:

(a)   On transactions of £20 or less Option money.
        At discretion.
(b)   On transactions of more than £20 Option money.
        £10 overall with a minimum of £5 ad valorem commission or at the Scale laid down whichever is the greater.

Notes

(i) If another agent is used besides the stockbroker, e.g. a bank, a higher scale of commissions is charged which is divisible between the stockbroker and the agent.

(ii) Certain types of transaction attract lower commissions than those above, e.g. securities which are bought and sold within the same Account. For full details, see the Stock Exchange Commission Rules, June 1982.

(iii) These commissions are likely to be altered in the light of the Stock Exchange's declared intention of phasing out minimum commissions by 31 December 1986.

Stamp duty

Ad valorem transfer stamp duty

Consideration	Duty
Not exceeding £50	50p
Exceeding £5 but not exceeding £100	20p for every £10 (or part of £10)
Exceeding £100 but not exceeding £300	40p for every £20 (or part of £20)
Exceeding £300	£1 for every £50 (or part of £50)

Notes

(i) Payable by the *purchaser*. Transfers in certain circumstances are exempt, e.g. a transfer to a beneficiary under a will of a legacy of shares.
(ii) Transfer stamp duty is *not* payable by the purchaser of gilt-edged securities or corporate fixed interest securities.

Contract stamp duty

Consideration	Duty
Exceeding £100 but not exceeding £500	10p
Exceeding £500 but not exceeding £1,500	30p
Exceeding £1500	60p

CSI levy

60p.
Payable on contract notes for transactions in UK securities of more than £5,000 in value.

Appendix 2: annuity and present value tables

Present value of 1 at compound interest: $(1+r)^{-n}$

Years (n)	1	2	3	4	5	6	7	8	9	10	11	12	13	14	15
1	0.9901	0.9804	0.9709	0.9615	0.9524	0.9434	0.9346	0.9259	0.9174	0.9091	0.9009	0.8929	0.8850	0.8772	0.8696
2	0.9803	0.9612	0.9426	0.9246	0.9070	0.8900	0.8734	0.8573	0.8417	0.8264	0.8116	0.7972	0.7831	0.7695	0.7561
3	0.9706	0.9423	0.9151	0.8890	0.8638	0.8396	0.8163	0.7938	0.7722	0.7513	0.7312	0.7118	0.6931	0.6750	0.6575
4	0.9610	0.9238	0.8885	0.8548	0.8227	0.7921	0.7629	0.7350	0.7084	0.6830	0.6587	0.6355	0.6133	0.5921	0.5718
5	0.9515	0.9057	0.8626	0.8219	0.7835	0.7473	0.7130	0.6806	0.6499	0.6209	0.5935	0.5674	0.5428	0.5194	0.4972
6	0.9420	0.8880	0.8375	0.7903	0.7462	0.7050	0.6663	0.6302	0.5963	0.5645	0.5346	0.5066	0.4803	0.4556	0.4323
7	0.9327	0.8706	0.8131	0.7599	0.7107	0.6651	0.6227	0.5835	0.5470	0.5132	0.4817	0.4523	0.4251	0.3996	0.3759
8	0.9235	0.8535	0.7894	0.7307	0.6768	0.6274	0.5820	0.5403	0.5019	0.4665	0.4339	0.4039	0.3762	0.3506	0.3269
9	0.9143	0.8368	0.7664	0.7026	0.6446	0.5919	0.5439	0.5002	0.4604	0.4241	0.3909	0.3606	0.3329	0.3075	0.2843
10	0.9053	0.8203	0.7441	0.6756	0.6139	0.5584	0.5083	0.4632	0.4224	0.3855	0.3522	0.3220	0.2946	0.2697	0.2472
11	0.8963	0.8043	0.7224	0.6496	0.5847	0.5268	0.4751	0.4289	0.3875	0.3505	0.3173	0.2875	0.2607	0.2366	0.2149
12	0.8874	0.7885	0.7014	0.6246	0.5568	0.4970	0.4440	0.3971	0.3555	0.3186	0.2858	0.2567	0.2307	0.2076	0.1869
13	0.8787	0.7730	0.6810	0.6006	0.5303	0.4688	0.4150	0.3677	0.3262	0.2897	0.2575	0.2292	0.2042	0.1821	0.1625
14	0.8700	0.7579	0.6611	0.5775	0.5051	0.4423	0.3878	0.3405	0.2992	0.2633	0.2320	0.2046	0.1807	0.1597	0.1413
15	0.8613	0.7430	0.6419	0.5553	0.4810	0.4173	0.3624	0.3152	0.2745	0.2394	0.2090	0.1827	0.1599	0.1401	0.1229
16	0.8528	0.7284	0.6232	0.5339	0.4581	0.3936	0.3387	0.2919	0.2519	0.2176	0.1883	0.1631	0.1415	0.1229	0.1069
17	0.8444	0.7142	0.6050	0.5134	0.4363	0.3714	0.3166	0.2703	0.2311	0.1978	0.1696	0.1456	0.1252	0.1078	0.0929
18	0.8360	0.7002	0.5874	0.4936	0.4155	0.3503	0.2959	0.2502	0.2120	0.1799	0.1528	0.1300	0.1108	0.0946	0.0808
19	0.8277	0.6864	0.5703	0.4746	0.3957	0.3305	0.2765	0.2317	0.1945	0.1635	0.1377	0.1161	0.0981	0.0829	0.0703
20	0.8195	0.6730	0.5537	0.4564	0.3769	0.3118	0.2584	0.2145	0.1784	0.1486	0.1240	0.1037	0.0868	0.0728	0.0611
25	0.7795	0.6095	0.4776	0.3751	0.2953	0.2330	0.1842	0.1460	0.1160	0.0923	0.0736	0.0588	0.0471	0.0378	0.0304
30	0.7419	0.5521	0.4120	0.3083	0.2314	0.1741	0.1314	0.0994	0.0754	0.0573	0.0437	0.0334	0.0256	0.0196	0.0151
35	0.7059	0.5000	0.3554	0.2534	0.1813	0.1301	0.0937	0.0676	0.0490	0.0356	0.0259	0.0189	0.0139	0.0102	0.0075
40	0.6717	0.4529	0.3066	0.2083	0.1420	0.0972	0.0668	0.0460	0.0318	0.0221	0.0154	0.0107	0.0075	0.0053	0.0037
45	0.6391	0.4102	0.2644	0.1712	0.1113	0.0727	0.0476	0.0313	0.0207	0.0137	0.0091	0.0061	0.0041	0.0027	0.0019
50	0.6080	0.3715	0.2281	0.1407	0.0872	0.0543	0.0339	0.0213	0.0134	0.0085	0.0054	0.0035	0.0022	0.0014	0.0009

Years (n)	16	17	18	19	20	21	22	23	24	25	26	27	28	29	30
1	0.8621	0.8547	0.8475	0.8403	0.8333	0.8264	0.8197	0.8130	0.8065	0.8000	0.7937	0.7874	0.7812	0.7752	0.7692
2	0.7432	0.7305	0.7182	0.7062	0.6944	0.6830	0.6719	0.6610	0.6504	0.6400	0.6299	0.6200	0.6104	0.6009	0.5917
3	0.6407	0.6244	0.6086	0.5934	0.5787	0.5645	0.5507	0.5374	0.5245	0.5120	0.4999	0.4882	0.4768	0.4658	0.4552
4	0.5523	0.5337	0.5158	0.4987	0.4823	0.4665	0.4514	0.4369	0.4230	0.4096	0.3968	0.3844	0.3725	0.3611	0.3501
5	0.4761	0.4561	0.4371	0.4190	0.4019	0.3855	0.3700	0.3552	0.3411	0.3277	0.3149	0.3027	0.2910	0.2799	0.2693
6	0.4104	0.3898	0.3704	0.3521	0.3349	0.3186	0.3033	0.2888	0.2751	0.2621	0.2499	0.2383	0.2274	0.2170	0.2072
7	0.3538	0.3332	0.3139	0.2959	0.2791	0.2633	0.2486	0.2348	0.2218	0.2097	0.1983	0.1877	0.1776	0.1682	0.1594
8	0.3050	0.2848	0.2660	0.2487	0.2326	0.2176	0.2038	0.1909	0.1789	0.1678	0.1574	0.1478	0.1388	0.1304	0.1226
9	0.2630	0.2434	0.2255	0.2090	0.1938	0.1799	0.1670	0.1552	0.1443	0.1342	0.1249	0.1164	0.1084	0.1011	0.0943
10	0.2267	0.2080	0.1911	0.1756	0.1615	0.1486	0.1369	0.1262	0.1164	0.1074	0.0992	0.0916	0.0847	0.0784	0.0725
11	0.1954	0.1778	0.1619	0.1476	0.1346	0.1228	0.1122	0.1026	0.0938	0.0859	0.0787	0.0721	0.0662	0.0607	0.0558
12	0.1685	0.1520	0.1372	0.1240	0.1122	0.1015	0.0920	0.0834	0.0757	0.0687	0.0625	0.0568	0.0517	0.0471	0.0429
13	0.1452	0.1299	0.1163	0.1042	0.0935	0.0839	0.0754	0.0678	0.0610	0.0550	0.0496	0.0447	0.0404	0.0365	0.0330
14	0.1252	0.1110	0.0985	0.0876	0.0779	0.0693	0.0618	0.0551	0.0492	0.0440	0.0393	0.0352	0.0316	0.0283	0.0254
15	0.1079	0.0949	0.0835	0.0736	0.0649	0.0573	0.0507	0.0448	0.0397	0.0352	0.0312	0.0277	0.0247	0.0219	0.0195
16	0.0930	0.0811	0.0708	0.0618	0.0541	0.0474	0.0415	0.0364	0.0320	0.0281	0.0248	0.0218	0.0193	0.0170	0.0150
17	0.0802	0.0693	0.0600	0.0520	0.0451	0.0391	0.0340	0.0296	0.0258	0.0225	0.0197	0.0172	0.0150	0.0132	0.0116
18	0.0691	0.0592	0.0508	0.0437	0.0376	0.0323	0.0279	0.0241	0.0208	0.0180	0.0156	0.0135	0.0118	0.0102	0.0089
19	0.0596	0.0506	0.0431	0.0367	0.0313	0.0267	0.0229	0.0196	0.0168	0.0144	0.0124	0.0107	0.0092	0.0079	0.0068
20	0.0514	0.0433	0.0365	0.0308	0.0261	0.0221	0.0187	0.0159	0.0135	0.0115	0.0098	0.0084	0.0072	0.0061	0.0053
25	0.0245	0.0197	0.0160	0.0129	0.0105	0.0086	0.0069	0.0057	0.0046	0.0038	0.0031	0.0025	0.0021	0.0017	0.0014
30	0.0116	0.0090	0.0070	0.0054	0.0042	0.0033	0.0026	0.0020	0.0016	0.0012	0.0010	0.0008	0.0006	0.0005	0.0004
35	0.0055	0.0041	0.0030	0.0023	0.0017	0.0013	0.0009	0.0007	0.0005	0.0004	0.0003	0.0002	0.0002	0.0001	0.0001
40	0.0026	0.0019	0.0013	0.0010	0.0007	0.0005	0.0004	0.0003	0.0002	0.0001	0.0001	0.0001	0.0001	0.0000	0.0000
45	0.0013	0.0009	0.0006	0.0004	0.0003	0.0002	0.0001	0.0001	0.0001	0.0000	0.0000	0.0000	0.0000	0.0000	0.0000
50	0.0006	0.0004	0.0003	0.0002	0.0001	0.0001	0.0000	0.0000	0.0000	0.0000	0.0000	0.0000	0.0000	0.0000	0.0000

Source: Samuels and Wilkes, *Management of Company Finance*, 3rd edn, Van Nostrand Reinhold, 1980. By permission of the publishers.

Present value of an annuity of 1: $\dfrac{1-(1+r)^{-n}}{r}$

Years (n)	r=1	2	3	4	5	6	7	8	9	10	11	12	13	14	15
1	0.9901	0.9804	0.9709	0.9615	0.9524	0.9434	0.9346	0.9259	0.9174	0.9091	0.9009	0.8929	0.8850	0.8772	0.8696
2	1.9704	1.9416	1.9135	1.8861	1.8594	1.8334	1.8080	1.7833	1.7591	1.7355	1.7125	1.6901	1.6681	1.6467	1.6257
3	2.9410	2.8839	2.8286	2.7751	2.7232	2.6730	2.6243	2.5771	2.5313	2.4869	2.4437	2.4018	2.3612	2.3216	2.2832
4	3.9020	3.8077	3.7171	3.6299	3.5460	3.4651	3.3872	3.3121	3.2397	3.1699	3.1024	3.0373	2.9745	2.9137	2.8550
5	4.8534	4.7135	4.5797	4.4518	4.3295	4.2124	4.1002	3.9927	3.8897	3.7908	3.6959	3.6048	3.5172	3.4331	3.3522
6	5.7955	5.6014	5.4172	5.2421	5.0757	4.9173	4.7665	4.6229	4.4859	4.3553	4.2305	4.1114	3.9975	3.8887	3.7845
7	6.7282	6.4720	6.2303	6.0021	5.7864	5.5824	5.3893	5.2064	5.0330	4.8684	4.7122	4.5638	4.4226	4.2883	4.1604
8	7.6517	7.3255	7.0197	6.7327	6.4632	6.2098	5.9713	5.7466	5.5348	5.3349	5.1461	4.9676	4.7988	4.6389	4.4873
9	8.5660	8.1622	7.7861	7.4353	7.1078	6.8017	6.5152	6.2469	5.9952	5.7590	5.5370	5.3282	5.1317	4.9464	4.7716
10	9.4713	8.9826	8.5302	8.1109	7.7217	7.3601	7.0236	6.7101	6.4177	6.1446	5.8892	5.6502	5.4262	5.2161	5.0188
11	10.3676	9.7868	9.2526	8.7605	8.3064	7.8869	7.4987	7.1390	6.8052	6.4951	6.2065	5.9377	5.6869	5.4527	5.2337
12	11.2551	10.5753	9.9540	9.3851	8.8633	8.3838	7.9427	7.5361	7.1607	6.8137	6.4924	6.1944	5.9176	5.6603	5.4206
13	12.1337	11.3484	10.6350	9.9856	9.3936	8.8527	8.3577	7.9038	7.4869	7.1034	6.7499	6.4235	6.1218	5.8424	5.5831
14	13.0037	12.1062	11.2961	10.5631	9.8986	9.2950	8.7455	8.2442	7.7862	7.3667	6.9819	6.6282	6.3025	6.0021	5.7245
15	13.8651	12.8493	11.9379	11.1184	10.3797	9.7122	9.1079	8.5595	8.0607	7.6061	7.1909	6.8109	6.4624	6.1422	5.8474
16	14.7179	13.5777	12.5611	11.6523	10.8378	10.1059	9.4466	8.8514	8.3126	7.8237	7.3792	6.9740	6.6039	6.2651	5.9542
17	15.5623	14.2919	13.1661	12.1657	11.2741	10.4773	9.7632	9.1216	8.5436	8.0216	7.5488	7.1196	6.7291	6.3729	6.0472
18	16.3983	14.9920	13.7535	12.6593	11.6896	10.8276	10.0591	9.3719	8.7556	8.2014	7.7016	7.2497	6.8399	6.4674	6.1280
19	17.2260	15.6785	14.3238	13.1339	12.0853	11.1581	10.3356	9.6036	8.9501	8.3649	7.8393	7.3658	6.9380	6.5504	6.1982
20	18.0456	16.3514	14.8775	13.5903	12.4622	11.4699	10.5940	9.8181	9.1285	8.5136	7.9633	7.4694	7.0248	6.6231	6.2593
25	22.0232	19.5235	17.4131	15.6221	14.0939	12.7834	11.6536	10.6748	9.8226	9.0770	8.4217	7.8431	7.3300	6.8729	6.4641
30	25.8077	22.3965	19.6004	17.2920	15.3725	13.7648	12.4090	11.2578	10.2737	9.4269	8.6938	8.0552	7.4957	7.0027	6.5660
35	29.4086	24.9986	21.4872	18.6646	16.3742	14.4982	12.9477	11.6546	10.5668	9.6442	8.8552	8.1755	7.5856	7.0700	6.6166
40	32.8347	27.3555	23.1148	19.7928	17.1591	15.0463	13.3317	11.9246	10.7574	9.7791	8.9511	8.2438	7.6344	7.1050	6.6418
45	36.0945	29.4902	24.5187	20.7200	17.7741	15.4558	13.6055	12.1084	10.8812	9.8628	9.0079	8.2825	7.6609	7.1232	6.6543
50	39.1961	31.4236	25.7298	21.4822	18.2559	15.7619	13.8007	12.2335	10.9617	9.9148	9.0417	8.3045	7.6752	7.1327	6.6605

Years (n)	r=16	17	18	19	20	21	22	23	24	25	26	27	28	29	30
1	0.8621	0.8547	0.8475	0.8403	0.8333	0.8264	0.8197	0.8130	0.8065	0.8000	0.7937	0.7874	0.7812	0.7752	0.7692
2	1.6052	1.5852	1.5656	1.5465	1.5278	1.5095	1.4915	1.4740	1.4568	1.4400	1.4235	1.4074	1.3916	1.3761	1.3609
3	2.2459	2.2096	2.1743	2.1399	2.1065	2.0739	2.0422	2.0114	1.9813	1.9520	1.9234	1.8956	1.8684	1.8420	1.8161
4	2.7982	2.7432	2.6901	2.6386	2.5887	2.5404	2.4936	2.4483	2.4043	2.3616	2.3202	2.2800	2.2410	2.2031	2.1662
5	3.2743	3.1993	3.1272	3.0576	2.9906	2.9260	2.8636	2.8035	2.7454	2.6893	2.6351	2.5827	2.5320	2.4830	2.4356
6	3.6847	3.5892	3.4976	3.4098	3.3255	3.2446	3.1669	3.0923	3.0205	2.9514	2.8850	2.8210	2.7594	2.7000	2.6427
7	4.0386	3.9224	3.8115	3.7057	3.6046	3.5079	3.4155	3.3270	3.2423	3.1611	3.0833	3.0087	2.9370	2.8682	2.8021
8	4.3436	4.2072	4.0776	3.9544	3.8372	3.7256	3.6193	3.5179	3.4212	3.3289	3.2407	3.1564	3.0758	2.9986	2.9247
9	4.6065	4.4506	4.3030	4.1633	4.0310	3.9054	3.7863	3.6731	3.5655	3.4631	3.3657	3.2728	3.1842	3.0997	3.0190
10	4.8332	4.6586	4.4941	4.3389	4.1925	4.0541	3.9232	3.7993	3.6819	3.5705	3.4648	3.3644	3.2689	3.1781	3.0915
11	5.0286	4.8364	4.6560	4.4865	4.3271	4.1769	4.0354	3.9018	3.7757	3.6564	3.5435	3.4365	3.3351	3.2388	3.1473
12	5.1971	4.9884	4.7932	4.6105	4.4392	4.2784	4.1274	3.9852	3.8514	3.7251	3.6059	3.4933	3.3868	3.2859	3.1903
13	5.3423	5.1183	4.9095	4.7147	4.5327	4.3624	4.2028	4.0530	3.9124	3.7801	3.6555	3.5381	3.4272	3.3224	3.2233
14	5.4675	5.2293	5.0081	4.8023	4.6106	4.4317	4.2646	4.1082	3.9616	3.8241	3.6949	3.5733	3.4587	3.3507	3.2487
15	5.5755	5.3242	5.0916	4.8759	4.6755	4.4890	4.3152	4.1530	4.0013	3.8593	3.7261	3.6010	3.4834	3.3726	3.2682
16	5.6685	5.4053	5.1624	4.9377	4.7296	4.5364	4.3567	4.1894	4.0333	3.8874	3.7509	3.6228	3.5026	3.3896	3.2832
17	5.7487	5.4746	5.2223	4.9897	4.7746	4.5755	4.3908	4.2190	4.0591	3.9099	3.7705	3.6400	3.5177	3.4028	3.2948
18	5.8178	5.5339	5.2732	5.0333	4.8122	4.6079	4.4187	4.2431	4.0799	3.9279	3.7861	3.6536	3.5294	3.4130	3.3037
19	5.8775	5.5845	5.3162	5.0700	4.8435	4.6346	4.4415	4.2627	4.0967	3.9424	3.7985	3.6642	3.5386	3.4210	3.3105
20	5.9288	5.6278	5.3527	5.1009	4.8696	4.6567	4.4603	4.2786	4.1103	3.9539	3.8083	3.6726	3.5458	3.4271	3.3158
25	6.0971	5.7662	5.4669	5.1951	4.9476	4.7213	4.5139	4.3232	4.1474	3.9849	3.8342	3.6943	3.5640	3.4423	3.3286
30	6.1772	5.8294	5.5168	5.2347	4.9789	4.7463	4.5338	4.3391	4.1601	3.9950	3.8424	3.7009	3.5693	3.4466	3.3321
35	6.2153	5.8582	5.5386	5.2512	4.9915	4.7559	4.5411	4.3447	4.1644	3.9984	3.8450	3.7028	3.5708	3.4478	3.3330
40	6.2335	5.8713	5.5482	5.2582	4.9966	4.7596	4.5439	4.3467	4.1659	3.9995	3.8458	3.7034	3.5712	3.4481	3.3332
45	6.2421	5.8773	5.5523	5.2611	4.9986	4.7610	4.5449	4.3474	4.1664	3.9998	3.8460	3.7036	3.5714	3.4482	3.3332
50	6.2463	5.8801	5.5541	5.2623	4.9995	4.7616	4.5452	4.3477	4.1666	3.9999	3.8461	3.7037	3.5714	3.4483	3.3333

Source: Samuels and Wilkes, Management of Company Finance, 3rd edn, Van Nostrand Reinhold, 1980. By permission of the publishers.

Appendix 3: sources of information

The following list details the main sources of information on UK companies and UK quoted securities. It is by no means comprehensive.

Company report and accounts

Available free of charge from the company secretary.

Extel cards

Summaries of published information, one card for each company.

McCarthys

Press comment on companies.

Stockbrokers' reports

These can be on specific companies, industries or countries.

Financial Times (and other main daily and Sunday newspapers)

The results of UK companies are published in the *Financial Times* and there will usually also be comment for the major companies.

Industry surveys

Many market research companies produce industry reports. These will not usually be available to the general public free of charge.

Datastream

Provides analyses of all UK and many foreign securities interactively on computer terminals. All the major city institutions are subscribers.

Weekly financial press

Note
The main library in London at which most of the above information is available is the City Business Library. This library is open to the general public and is situated at 55 Basinghall Street, London, EC2.

Appendix 4: summary of formulae used

Chapter 2

Holding period return

$$HPR = \frac{D_1 + (P_1 - P_0)}{P_0}$$

Fisher's relation

$$(1 + R) = (1 + r)(1 + E(\mathit{infl}))$$

where R is the nominal interest rate and r the real interest rate

Expected return

$$E(R) = \sum_{i=1}^{i=n} p_i R_i$$

Variance

$$V = \sum_{i=1}^{i=n} p_i(R_i - E(R))^2$$

Standard deviation

$$S = \sqrt{V}$$

Expected utility of wealth

$$E(U(W)) = \sum_{i=1}^{i=n} p_i U(W_i)$$

Interest yield

On a fixed interest security

$$\text{Interest yield} = \frac{D}{P_0} (\times 100)$$

Multiplying by 100 simply expresses the result in percentage rather than decimal form.

Dividend valuation model

$$P_0 = \frac{D_1}{(1 + R)} + \frac{D_2}{(1 + R)^2} + \ldots + \frac{D_n + P_n}{(1 + R)^n}$$

Chapter 3

Redemption yield

The redemption yield is the R in the equation

$$P_0 = \frac{D}{(1 + R)} + \frac{D}{(1 + R)^2} + \dots + \frac{D}{(1 + R)^n} + \frac{100}{(1 + R)^n}$$

Linear interpolation formula

$$r = r_1 + (r_2 + r_1)\frac{PV_1}{(PV_1 + PV_2)}$$

Duration

$$D = \frac{1. \, PV_1}{P_0} + \frac{2. \, PV_2}{P_0} + \dots + \frac{N.PV_N}{P_0}$$

Chapter 4

Spot rates

These are interest rates r_i in the expression

$$P_0 = \frac{D}{(1 + r_1)} + \frac{D}{(1 + r_2)^2} + \dots + \frac{D}{(1 + r_n)^n} + \frac{100}{(1 + r_n)^n}$$

Forward rates

These are implicit in the spot rates. For example,

$$(1 + r_1)(1 + {}_1f_2) = (1 + r_2)^2$$

Chapter 5

Gross dividend yield

$$GDY = \frac{D_0}{P_0} \times \frac{100}{(100 - A)}$$

where D_0 is the net dividend paid and A the ACT rate in %.

Net dividend yield

$$NDY = \frac{D_0}{P_0}$$

Dividend cover

$$\text{Dividend cover} = \frac{eps_0}{dps_0}$$

PE ratio

$$PE = \frac{P_0}{eps_0}$$

Gordon's growth model

$$P_0 = \frac{D_1}{R - g} \qquad R = \frac{D_1}{P_0} + g$$

Payout ratio

$$K_i = \frac{dps_i}{eps_i}$$

Chapter 6

Minimum value of call option

$$C \geqslant S - PV(X)$$

Relationship between put and call option on expiry

$$S + P = C + X$$

Black–Scholes formula

$$C = S\, N(d_1) - Xe^{-R_f t}\, N(d_2)$$

(See Appendix to Chapter 6.)

Value of CULS

$CULS$ = value of equivalent ULS + value of option to convert into ordinary shares

Chapter 7

Expected return and risk of portfolio of two securities

$$E(R_p) = W_1\, E\,(R_A) + W_2\, E\,(R_B)$$

$$V_p = W_1^2\, S_A^2 + W_2^2\, S_B^2 + 2\, W_1 W_2 S_A S_B CORR_{AB}$$

Expected return and risk of portfolio of n securities

$$E(R_p) = \sum_{i=1}^{i=n} W_i E(R_i)$$

where W_i is the proportion held of security i

$$V_p = \sum_{i=1}^{i=n} W_i^2 S_i^2 + \sum_{i=1}^{i=n} \sum_{\substack{j=1 \\ i \neq j}}^{j=n} W_i W_j COV_{ij}$$

Covariance

$$COV_{AB} = \sum_{i=1}^{i=n} (R_{A_i} - E(R_A)) (R_{B_i} - E(R_B)) \, p \, (R_i)$$

Correlation coefficient

$$CORR_{AB} = \frac{COV_{AB}}{S_A \, S_B}$$

Chapter 8

Sharpe's market model

$$R_i = a_i + b_i \, R_m + e_i$$

Capital market line

$$E(R_p) = R_F + (E(R_m) - R_F) \frac{S_p}{S_m}$$

Securities market line

$$E(R_i) = R_F + (E(R_m) - R_F) \frac{COV_{im}}{S_m^2}$$

or

$$E(R_i) = R_F + \beta_i (E(R_m) - R_F)$$

Security risk

$$V_i = \beta_i^2 S_m^2 + S^2(e_i)$$

(Total risk = market risk + specific risk)

Arbitrage pricing model

$$E(R_i) = a_i + b_{i_1}\beta_1 + b_{i_2} \beta_2 + \dots$$

Chapter 9

Excess return

$$\epsilon_{j,t+1} = (R_{j,t+1} - (E(R_{j,t+1})/\phi_t))$$

Fair game

$$\sum_{i=1}^{i=n} \epsilon_{j,t+1} = 0$$

Chapter 10

Forward exchange rate

$$X_f = X_0 \quad \begin{array}{l} + \textit{discount} \text{ quoted in } \textit{Financial Times} \\ - \textit{premium} \text{ quoted in } \textit{Financial Times} \end{array}$$

Interest rate parity

$$\frac{X_f}{X_0} = \frac{1 + R_\$}{1 + R_£}$$

where $R_£$ and $R_\$$ represent the interest rates available in each currency.

Purchasing power parity

$$\frac{X_1}{X_0} = \frac{P_{f_1}/P_{f_0}}{P_{d_1}/P_{d_0}} = \frac{1 + E(\text{infl}_f)}{1 + E(\text{infl}_d)}$$

International Fisher

$$\frac{1 + R_{\pounds}}{1 + E(infl_{\pounds})} = \frac{1 + R_{\$}}{1 + E(infl_{\$})}$$

Chapter 12

Measures of portfolio performance

$$\textit{Sharpe} \text{ measure} = \frac{R_p - R_F}{S_p}$$

$$\textit{Treynor} \text{ measure} = \frac{R_p - R_F}{\beta_p}$$

$$\textit{Jensen} \text{ measure} = R_p - R_B \text{ where } R_B = R_F + \beta_p (R_m - R_F)$$

Geometric mean

$$GM = r = \left(\sqrt[n]{(1 + r_1)(1 + r_2) \dots (1 + r_n)}\right) - 1$$

Solution to quadratic equation

If $ax^2 + bx + c = 0$,

$$x = \frac{(-b \pm \sqrt{b^2 - 4ac})}{2a}$$

Bibliography

R. Z. Aliber (1974) 'Attributes of national monies and the interdependence of national monetary policies', in *National Monetary Policies and the International Financial System*, ed. R. Z. Aliber, University of Chicago Press.

K. Alamouti (1979) 'An empirical analysis of the relationship between inflation rates, security rates and exchange rates', proposal for Ph.D. dissertation, London Business School.

L. Bachelier (1900) *Théorie de la speculation*, Gauthier-Villars.

W. H. Beaver (1981) *Financial Reporting: An Accounting Revolution*, Prentice-Hall.

J. F. O. Bilson (1976) 'A monetary approach to the exchange rate', unpublished Ph.D. dissertation, University of Chicago.

J. F. O. Bilson and R. M. Levich (1977) 'A test of the forecasting efficiency of the forward exchange rate', New York University Working Paper, no. 77–61, June.

F. Black (1972) 'Capital market equilibrium with restricted borrowing', *Journal of Business*, July, pp. 444–55.

F. Black (1973) 'Yes, Virginia, there is hope: tests of the Value Line ranking system', *Financial Analysts' Journal*, vol. 29, no. 5, September–October, pp. 10–14.

M. Blume (1975) 'Betas and their regression tendencies', *Journal of Finance*, vol. 10, no. 3, June, pp. 785–95.

R. A. Brealey (1983) *An Introduction to Risk and Return*, 2nd ed, Basil Blackwell.

I. A. Cooper and S. D. Hodges (1980) 'Returns on UK assets and assets allocation', London Business School Working Paper.

Corporation Tax (1982), Green Paper, Cmnd 8456, HMSO, January.

Council for the Securities Industry (1982) *Rules Governing Substantial Acquisitions of Shares*, revised edn.

G. Cummings (1981) *Investors' Guide to the Stock Market*, 2nd edn, Financial Times.

E. Dimson (1978) 'Measuring investment performance', *Investment Analyst*, vol. 50, September, pp. 15–22.

E. Dimson (1979) 'Investment and inflation', London Business School Working Paper.

E. Dimson, S. D. Hodges and P. R. Marsh (1980) 'International diversification', London Business School Working Paper.

G. Dufey and I. Giddy (1978) *The International Money Market*, Prentice-Hall.

E. J. Elton and M. J. Gruber (1981) *Modern Portfolio Theory and Investment Analysis*, Wiley.

E. F. Fama (1970) 'Efficient capital markets: a review of theory and empirical work', *Journal of Finance*, vol. 25, no. 2, May, pp. 383–417.

407

E. F. Fama (1972) 'Components of investment performance', *Journal of Finance*, vol. 27, no. 3, June, pp. 551–67.

E. F. Fama, L. Fisher, M. C. Jensen and R. Roll (1969) 'The adjustment of stock prices to new information', *International Economic Review*, vol. 10, no. 2, February, pp. 1–21.

M. Firth (1977) *The Valuation of Shares and the Efficient-Markets Theory*, Macmillan.

I. Fisher (1930) *The Theory of Interest*, Macmillan.

Fisons (1979) *Fisons Fourth Stockholder Survey*.

H. R. Fogler and S. Ganapathy (1982) *Financial Econometrics for Researchers in Finance and Accounting*, Prentice-Hall.

J. C. Francis and S. H. Archer (1979) *Portfolio Analysis*, 2nd edn, Prentice-Hall.

G. Gemmill (1981) 'The choice between options and futures contracts', *Investment Analyst*, no. 61, July, pp. 12–19.

I. Giddy and G. Dufey (1975) 'The random behaviour of flexible exchange rates: implications for forecasting', *Journal of International Business Studies*, vol. 6, no. 1, Spring, pp. 1–32.

T. G. Goff (1980) *Theory and Practice of Investment*, 3rd edn, Heinemann.

L. C. B. Gower (1982) *Review of Investor Protection: A Discussion Document*, HMSO, January.

R. L. Hagin (1979) *The Dow Jones–Irwin Guide to Modern Portfolio Theory*, Dow Jones–Irwin.

P. Hastings (1977) 'The case of the Royal Mail', in *Studies of Accounting Theory*, 3rd edn, ed. W. T. Baxter and S. Davidson, Institute of Chartered Accountants in England and Wales, pp. 339–46.

R. G. Ibbotson and R. A. Sinquefield (1979) *Stocks, Bonds, Bills and Inflation: Historical Returns (1926–1978)*, Financial Analysts Research Foundation.

B. Jacquillat and B. H. Solnik (1978) 'Multinationals are poor tools for diversification', *Journal of Portfolio Management*, Winter, pp. 8–12.

R. M. Levich (1977) 'The international money market: tests of forecasting models and market efficiency', unpublished Ph.D. dissertation, University of Chicago.

R. M. Levich and C. G. Wihlborg (1980) *Exchange Risk and Exposure*, Lexington Books.

London Business School, *Risk Measurement Service*, quarterly.

S. Lumby (1981) *Investment Appraisal*, Nelson.

J. H. Lorie and M. T. Hamilton (1973) *The Stock Market: Theories and Evidence*, Irwin.

H. M. Markowitz (1959) *Portfolio Selection: Efficient Diversification of Investment*, Cowles Foundation Monograph No. 16, Yale University Press.

Midland Bank Series New Issue Statistics, February issues, *Midland Bank Review*.

A. B. Moore (1962) 'A statistical analysis of common stock prices', unpublished Ph.D. dissertation, University of Chicago.

V. Niederhoffer and P. Regan (1972) 'Earnings changes, analysts' forecasts, and stock prices', *Financial Analysts' Journal*, vol. 28, no. 3, May–June, pp. 65–71.

Phillips & Drew (1980) *World Capital Markets*, December.

H. V. Roberts (1959) 'Stock market "patterns" and financial analysis', *Journal of Finance*, vol. 14, no. 1, March, pp. 1–10.

S. A. Ross (1976) 'The arbitrage theory of capital asset pricing', *Journal of Economic Theory*, vol. 13, December, pp. 341–60.

W. F. Sharpe (1963) 'A simplified model for portfolio analysis', *Management Science*, January, pp. 277–93.

W. F. Sharpe (1981) *Investments*, 2nd edn, Prentice-Hall.

B. H. Solnik (1974) 'Why not diversify internationally rather than domestically?', *Financial Analysts' Journal*, vol. 30, no. 4, July–August, pp. 48–54.

Stock Exchange (1978) Second Stage Evidence to the Wilson Committee, August.

A. C. Stockman (1978) 'Risk, information, and forward exchange rates', in *The Economics of Exchange Rates*, ed. J. A. Frenkel and H. G. Johnson, Addison-Wesley.

J. C. Van Horne (1978) *Financial Market Rates and Flows*, Prentice-Hall.

Wilson Report (1980) *Report of the Committee to Review the Functioning of Financial Institutions,* Cmnd 7937, HMSO, June.

Index